David Lane

is Professor of Sociology and a member of the Centre for Russian and East European Studies at the University of Birmingham. He is a former Fellow of Emmanuel College, Cambridge.

David Lane has written widely on socialism, the USSR, and East Europe. His previous publications include: *State and Politics in the USSR* (1986), *Soviet Economy and Society* (1986) and *Soviet Labour and the Ethic of Communism* (1987).

Elites and Political Power
in the USSR

Elites and Political Power in the USSR

Edited by

David Lane
Professor of Sociology
University of Birmingham

EDWARD ELGAR

Published by
Edward Elgar Publishing Limited
Gower House
Croft Road
Aldershot
Hants GU11 3HR
England

and distributed in the United States by

Gower Publishing Company
Old Post Road
Brookfield
Vermont 05036
USA

British Library Cataloguing in Publication Data

Elites and political power in the USSR.
  1. Soviet Union. Political elites
  I. Lane, David
  322.4′3′0947

Library of Congress Cataloging-in-Publication Data

Elites and political power in the USSR
edited by David Lane.
    p. cm.
    Bibliography: p.
    Includes index.
    ISBN 1–85278–044–4: (U.S.)
    1. Elite (Social sciences)—Soviet Union.   2. Soviet Union—Politics and
    government—1982–   I. Lane, David Stuart.
HN530.Z9E43   1988
305.5′2′0947—DC1988–3856 CIP

ISBN 1–85278–044–4

Printed in Great Britain at the University Press, Cambridge

Contents

Contents

Contributors

OTTORINO CAPPELLI received his Ph.D in Italy and is currently completing his doctoral dissertation at the Centre for Russian and East European Studies, Birmingham. He has published a book on the experience of city government in Naples (1978) and several articles in Italian journals on the Soviet political system. His current research topic is local politics and government in the USSR.

JULIAN COOPER is Lecturer in Soviet Technology and Industry, Centre for Russian and East European Studies, University of Birmingham. His publications include *The Technological Level of Soviet Industry* (1977), edited with R. Amann and R. W. Davies; *Industrial Innovation in the Soviet Union* (1982) and *Technical Progress and Soviet Economic Development* (1986), both edited jointly with R. Amann; and articles on Soviet industry, science and technology, and economic history.

DAVID DYKER was educated at the University of Glasgow, and the Institute of National Economy, Tashkent, USSR. Since 1968 he has been lecturer in economics, School of European Studies, University of Sussex; between 1976 and 1978 he was seconded to the Economic Commission for Europe, United Nations, Geneva. His main publications are *The Soviet Economy* (1976), *The Process of Investment in the Soviet Union* (1983), *The Future of the Soviet Economic Planning System* (1985); (Editor), *The Soviet Union under Gorbachev: Prospects for Reform* (1987).

THANE GUSTAFSON is Associate Professor of Government at Georgetown University, Washington, D.C. He has previously served on the staff of the Rand Corporation, Santa Monica, California, and on the faculty of Harvard University. He is the author of *Reform in Soviet Politics* (1981) and *Crisis amid Plenty* (in press).

RONALD J. HILL is Associate Professor of Political Science and Fellow of Trinity College, Dublin. He is the author or co-author of four books on modern Soviet politics, the lastest being *The Soviet Union: Politics, Economics and Society, from Lenin to Gorbachev* (1985); he is also a frequent contributor of articles and reviews to scholarly journals, and a regular commentator on Soviet affairs.

EUGENE HUSKEY was educated at Vanderbilt, Essex, and the London School of Economics and Political Science, where he received a Ph.D. in 1983. In 1979–80 he was an exchange scholar in the Law Faculty at Moscow State University. He has written numerous articles and a book, *Russian Lawyers and the Soviet State*, on the politics of the Soviet legal system. He is currently an Assistant Professor in the Department of Government at Bowdoin College in Brunswick, Maine.

DAVID LANE is Professor of Sociology at the University of Birmingham. He studied at Birmingham and Oxford Universities and has taught at the Universities of Essex and Cambridge. He is the author of many books on the Soviet Union, Eastern Europe, and Socialism, including *State and Politics in the USSR* (1985), *Soviet Economy and Society* (1985), and *Soviet Labour and the Ethic of Communism* (1987).

NEIL MALCOLM is a graduate of Oxford and of Birmingham University (Centre for Russian and East European Studies). He is the author of *Soviet Political Scientists and American Politics*, and articles on Soviet foreign policy and policy making and is currently carrying out research on Soviet attitudes towards Western Europe. His present position is that of Principal Lecturer in Russian and Soviet Studies at Wolverhampton Polytechnic.

DAWN MANN is a Fellow, Soviet Program, Center For Strategic and International Studies, Washington, DC. A Phi Beta Kappa graduate of California State University at San Diego, with an MA in Russian Area Studies from Georgetown University, she is in charge of SOVSET, the computer network linking over 200 Soviet and East European scholars. Currently completing a Doctoral program in Government at Georgetown University, she has contributed articles to *Problems of Communism* and *Studies in Comparative Communism* amongst others.

CATHERINE MERRIDALE, is a Research Fellow of King's College, Cambridge. She is currently completing a book on the Communist Party in Moscow in the period 1925–32.

ALEXANDER RAHR, is a Researcher-Analyst, Radio Liberty, Munich. He is involved in various research projects for the Bundesinstitut für Ostwissenschaftliche und Internationale Studien (Cologne). He has been a consultant for Rand Corporation (Los Angeles). His publications include, *A Biographic Directory of 100 Leading Soviet Officials*, Radio Liberty Research, Munich in 3 editions 1986; *Gorbatschow. Der neue Mann,* München. (2nd edition, 1987).

WILLIAM REISINGER is an Assistant Professor in the Department of Political Science at the University of Iowa. He is the author of articles on Soviet-East European relations and on positive political theory. He has recently completed a book manuscript on the role of energy in Soviet-East European bargaining.

MICHAEL URBAN is Associate Professor of Political Science at Auburn University, Alabama. His research has focussed on questions of politics and administration in the USSR and on Soviet political language. He has authored *The Ideology of Administration: American and Soviet Cases*, a number of articles on Soviet affairs for scholarly journals and is currently completing a book on the circulation of political elites in the Belorussian Republic.

STEPHEN WHITE is Reader in Politics and Member of the Institute of Soviet and East European Studies, University of Glasgow. A graduate of Dublin, Glasgow and Oxford universities, Dr White is the author of numerous books and articles on Soviet politics and political history including, *The Origins of Detente* (1986), *Communist Politics: A Reader* (co-editor, 1986) and *The Bolshevik Poster* (forthcoming). He is joint editor of *Coexistence* and a member of the editorial boards of *Soviet Studies*, the *Journal of Communist Studies* and the *Nordic Journal of Soviet and East European Studies*, and is presently working on a study of political change under Gorbachev.

JOHN P. WILLERTON Jr is an Assistant Professor of Soviet politics in the James Madison College of Michigan State University. His publications include articles in *Soviet Studies, Studies in Comparative Communism*, and the *Jerusalem Journal of International Relations*. He is currently revising a book manuscript on patronage and policy in the USSR.

Preface

The changes in leadership, personnel and the roles of elites which have accompanied the rise to power of Gorbachev will be examined in this book. The chapters that follow will consider not only the leading personnel but the networks of key organizations and interests in the structure of power which stand to gain or lose from new policies and which promote or restrict the leadership.

In the first chapter is outlined the ideological and theoretical framework in which the discussion of political power in the USSR has taken place. This involves a critical appraisal of the relevance of the notions of ruling class and political elite to the Soviet system. The chapters that follow explicitly or implicity adopt an elite approach to Soviet politics. They consider the people, structures and processes underlying the Soviet political system. The book does not claim to exhaust the study of the power structure of Soviet society. It represents current trends in research which are largely 'positional' rather than 'decisional'. It concentrates on the backgrounds and connections of people and their institutional affiliations. Case studies of elite decision making and opposition to their implementation are difficult to pursue even in open democracies.[1] Here various political networks are delineated. These are concerned with the organizations and people who, on the one side, wish to introduce new policies and those on the other side who seek to defend existing structures.

Part I is concerned with the top political leadership. Gustafson and Mann focus on the ways that General Secretary Gorbachev has recruited personnel to sustain his values and policies. The chapters by Hill and Rahr consider the crucial personnel of the Party Secretariat and the Apparat. These chapters bring out the importance of people as agents of change and supporters of stability. In Part II, Willerton, Reisinger and Urban analyse the circulation of personnel in the Party at different levels of the power structure, and Huskey considers the legal profession. These chapters consider not only the technical problems involved in the definition and measurement of mobility through political hierarchies but also they attempt to generalize about the way that mobility occurs and the implications of recruitment policies for political control. The papers by Malcolm, Dyker and Cooper constitute Part III and consider expert advisers and interests located in crucial institutions around the legitimate political leadership.

They analyse the organizational autonomy of various institutions and groups (advisors on foreign policy, the 'defence–industrial complex') and their influence on the political leadership. Cooper describes the network of positions involving the political elite and the defence industry and concludes that the latter is not part of a 'power elite'. Rather than a relational perspective, Dyker adopts an organizational one – industrial ministries are primarily work organizations producing commodities in conditions of shortage and supply uncertainty rather than political or 'bureaucratic' interests. The chapters by Merridale and Cappelli in Part IV consider the spatial relationships between centre and periphery and the resistance between various parts of the system. These chapters not only examine positions but relations between the top leadership and the localities. Finally, Stephen White generalizes on the limits of power in the USSR. He adopts a 'positional' perspective utilizing speeches to infer political positions on the part of actors.

The book emanates from a conference held at the University of Birmingham in July 1987 at which in addition to the present authors, the following participated in the panels: Nick Lampert, John Barber, Bogdan Szajkowski, C. M. Davis, R. W. Davies, Karl Ryavec, Paul Bellis, Christel Lane, Neville Brown, David Armstrong and Chris Ward. I would like to thank other members of the University of Birmingham who joined in the discussion, Jackie Johnson and Di Davies who helped check the papers. The conference would not have been possible without grants from the Nuffield and Ford Foundations whom we would like to thank for their support.

David Lane
Birmingham, November 1987

REFERENCE

1   R. Dahl, *Who Governs? Democracy and Power in an American City*, New Haven, Yale University Press, 1961.

Introduction

1. Ruling Class and Political Elites: Paradigms of Socialist Societies

David Lane

Adopting the notion of a ruling and exploited class is one way of expressing the political contours of society in social and economic terms. It is concerned with the wider sociological significance of political leadership, elite structure and political process, with the dynamics of social change and with the underlying legitimacy (or lack of it) of the rulers. A ruling class as conceived of here refers not to the 'decision makers', or to those individuals or groups occupying authority roles, but to those who dominate and exploit others. The notion of ruling class refers to a definable social group which shares a common position in relation to the means of production, to the state and has a common interest with regard to other classes: it has a relational dimension (one of dominance/subordination) and a distributional one (the ruling class apportions systematically society's resources). Classes are social entities which have an awareness (or consciousness) of their distinctive interests *vis à vis* other classes; they are oppositional rather than hierarchical; they are exploitative and privileged rather than stratified and unequal; they are dominant and illegitimate rather than authoritative.

Approaches which have sought to analyse Soviet-type societies in ruling class terms may be grouped into two major paradigms. One stemming from Marxist theory relating the dominant and exploiting class to the ownership and control of the means of production which places its base in the economy. The other considers the ruling class's power to be rooted in control of the state bureaucracy; the source of its power is political rather than economic. The traditional Marxist argument views Soviet-type societies through the prism of Marx's and Engels's analysis of nineteenth century capitalism. The crucial components of this paradigm are the forces of production, the relations of production and the expropriation of surplus value by a dominant ruling class.

A wide range of writers, for quite different reasons, rejects a Marxist-type ruling class analysis of the USSR. Non-Marxists consider the application of economic class related concepts as misconceived. Political power is not a zero-sum equation: it is regarded as being 'interest driven' and has to be related to the group structure of industrial societies. Rather than dichotomous oppositional groups, the study of elites focuses on the configuration of powerful people located in the major institutions of society. An elite is a group of people with authoritative power over some resource (e.g. a business enterprise, a local authority) or social constituency (a political party or a trade union). Elites may be clustered in many ways. *Pluralistic* elites share authoritative power along different dimensions: no single group of people is dominant, power is dispersed and often the elite is responsible and responsive to members of its constituency. Typically then one may think of influential people in the economy, political parties, central and local government, the military, the law, education, the arts, the media and the Church. From the pluralistic elites' point of view no one group of people may form a ruling elite: power is dispersed, and the relationship between elite and non-elite is not exploitative, it is based on trust and reciprocity.

A less benign approach to political power is entailed by the *power elite* approach, associated with the writings of C. W. Mills. Rather than being pluralistic, diverse and autonomous, the power elite model assumes that the dominant institutions of society are integrated and managed by interlocking groups of people. This ruling group illegitimately apportions power and privilege to its own social formation; it is an exploitative stratum and rules through a combination of coercion and manipulation. Hence one thinks of dominent elites located in industry, political party, government, law and the armed forces forming a united power elite. A major difference between the ruling class and power elite approaches is that the former has its origin in the economic sphere or in bureaucratic control of the economy; it is based on political domination derived from economic exploitation. A power elite rests on mutual self interest, ideological identity and privilege. It is a much more amorphous category and is in practice more difficult to pin down and define; its boundaries may change by absorbing within its ranks new social formations (such as trade unions) or influential professions (e.g. media experts).

This chapter will outline recent writing on socialist societies with respect to these two paradigms. It will be argued that as far as the contemporary USSR is concerned, 'ruling class' theories are less useful than the elitist approach.

RULING CLASS

The traditional Western 'critical Marxist' explanation of there being a ruling class in the USSR was located in the notion of 'state capitalism' and 'transitional society'. Both regard the economy as being determinant. From a comparative viewpoint, the theory of state capitalism posits a form of single convergence of 'Bolshevist' societies to the model of capitalism described by Marx. A number of different sets of arguments have been advanced by such thinkers. First, it is contended that the level of productive forces (i.e. the levels of capital investment and productivity) have been far too low to justify a qualitative leap even to the preliminary stage of a communist mode of production which can only proceed from the highest stage of capitalism. Second, the working class is not in fact hegemonic in 'Soviet type' societies, it is divorced from true control of the means of production. The relations of production do not ensure socialism, rather East European or 'Soviet type' societies are a state owned and controlled form of capitalism. A distinguishing feature is that the officials or bureaucracy controlling the means of production fulfil the traditional functions of the capitalist class: they channel surplus product extracted from the direct producers into capital. Concurrently, their social position in the political order turns their administrative privilege into class rights. With the consolidation of the bureaucratic structure a dual conflictual class system with a ruling and exploited class arises akin to capitalist states.

It is important to note, however, that such writers retain the concept of property as an element of the class structure. Milovan Djilas has made this clear.

> Ownership is nothing other than the right of profit and control. If one defines class benefits by this right, the communist states have seen in the final analysis, the origin of a new form of ownership or of a new ruling and exploiting class ... The new class may be said to be made up of those who have special privileges and economic preferences because of the administrative monopoly they hold ... In practice the ownership privilege of the new class manifests itself as an exclusive right ... The so-called social ownership is a disguise for real ownership by the political bureaucracy.[1]

By the mid-1980s, criticisms of the 'state capitalism' thesis associated with the views of Djilas, Schachtman and Cliff, and the *economic* basis of exploitation and domination were sufficiently well grounded to lead to its replacement by the second form of class domination defined above – a politically rooted ruling class. Significant changes have taken place in the critical Marxist framework and these will be considered here. Contemporary writers have emphasized the factor of organization (Wright)[2] and bureaucratic political control (Feher, Szelenyi).[3]

THE BUREAUCRATIC STATE

E. O. Wright's originality lies in his hypothesis that in Soviet-type societies the asset 'alienated' by the ruling class is 'organization'. He is concerned to define the relationship to the means of production which gives rise to exploitation and domination under 'state bureaucratic socialism'. He turns to classical economics where he locates four factors of production or 'productive assets': land, labour, capital, and organization. Capitalism is characterized by the capitalist class owning the principal asset – 'the means of production'; the mechanism of exploitation is market exchanges of labour power and commodities; and the major class actors are capitalists and workers.[4] The mechanism of exploitation is the 'planned appropriation and distribution of surplus based on hierarchy' and the antagonistic classes are managers/bureaucrats and non-management.

Wright endorses the fact that 'anticapitalist revolutions' eliminate the 'distinctively capitalist form of exploitation', that based on private ownership of the means of production. However, such revolutions 'do not eliminate, and indeed may considerably strengthen and deepen inequalities of effective control over organisational assets.' 'Exploitative transfers of surplus' in state bureaucratic socialism involve 'the centrally planned bureaucratic appropriation and distribution of the surplus along hierarchical principles.'[5] The dominant class is made up of people ('managers and bureaucrats') who control organizational assets.

I would query, however, whether this is analogous to the ownership of the other assets associated with feudalism (labour power) and capitalism (means of production). Firstly, 'organization' surely exists in all modes of production. In capitalist societies, officials who run the universities, hospitals, and nationalized industries as well as executives of privately owned corporations provide 'organization', but it is hardly Marxist orthodoxy to call them a separate class. 'Organization' was necessary for production under the capitalism known to Marx, but he does not consider it to be a factor source of income. Marx does not refer to it in *Capital* in his discussion of the labour process. While it is true that the scope of the government in state socialist societies is wider than under capitalism, that the political and economic are subject to fusion, and that groups of 'bureaucrats' and managers have effective control of the means of production, this is not sufficient to identify a Marxist-type ruling class. To sustain a Marxist class analysis of state socialism it is incumbent on one to discover a relationship over property which systematically legitimates the right of a group of persons to a surplus produced by the direct producers.

Secondly, a mechanism must be described by which such surplus is extracted. Critical theorists are agreed that it may only take an administrative form. In other social formations, surplus is a residue left after the direct producers (peasants, wage labourers) have received their dues. It is an economic rent which is not a cost of production. A difficulty arises here in distinguishing between the components of income which are earned and unearned. A feature of state socialism is that surplus must be received as wage income or by transfer payments which are often linked to wage levels. Wages are the payment for services which are provided by members of the administrative and executive strata. In practice it is impossible to distinguish what is payment for socially necessary labour and what represents surplus value.

It is true that in Soviet-type societies the direct producer does not receive in income the total return from his or her labour. Surplus is extracted by the State (as under feudalism, or capitalism); Marx, however, acknowledged that in all types of society 'surplus-labour in general must remain'.[6] It is necessary for the expansion of the process of production, for the renewal of capital as well as for the maintenance of non-productive labour, such as children and other dependants. The distinctive factor about a ruling class is that it does not exchange income for labour but is a parasitic stratum. State socialist societies have channelled surplus into capital formation and renewal, indeed this has been a characteristic of such societies. One can agree with Roemer that 'the historical task of the socialist revolution is to eliminate that form of exploitation due to differentiated ownership of alienable assets'.[7] Capitalist exploitation, in the sense of returns from private ownership of property, has been abolished, as have the class relations that go with it.

In attempting to grapple with the nature of domination and exploitation in Soviet-type societies, elements of the critical Marxist ruling class type of theory mentioned above have been grafted onto the paradigm of totalitarianism. These ideas have been developed by Feher, Heller, Markus (1983), Szelenyi (1982) and Lefort (1986).[8]

For Feher et al. 'Soviet-type societies' are not capitalist in the traditional sense but neither are they socialist; the antinomy between market and plan, between the production of use value and exchange value is rejected. The nationalization of the means of production is not socialist because it does not, in the state socialist societies, lead to the 'effective transformation of economic relations, establishing a collective-social property in the sense of the real power of immediate producers to decide and dispose collectively over the conditions and products of their labour ...'[9] Under capitalism, valorization takes place through a market in which the core of the contradictions of capitalism is located. In state socialist societies, however, the state appropriates the surplus of labour as use-values '... (T)hese are economies that directly produce use values and not values at all'.[10] There is a lack of correspondence between much of what is produced or planned and what satisfies a social want and a contradiction between administratively determined use-value and real social utilities. Soviet-type societies produce waste and poor quality goods which meet no social needs; there is production for the sake of production.[11]

Such societies are not transitional because their logic does not require a movement through contradiction to socialism. East European societies are 'integral social system[s]' in the sense that they possess 'a reasonable ability to reproduce themselves with all the strains and contradictions that implies'.[12] Hence the explanation of inadequacies or imperfections in such societies being due to 'backwardness' or to phenomena which are left-overs from previous social formations, is not acceptable. Soviet-type societies are self-sustaining and reproducing.

Ivan Szelenyi has developed this line of approach by pointing to the structured ways that privilege is reproduced. Taking housing as an example, he argues that in Hungary, Poland and Czechoslovakia the 'redistributive' mechanism consistently favours the higher status groups.[13] He points out that the consumption of the most highly subsidized consumer goods (food products) and payments in kind (medical and educational services) benefit the higher social strata more than the lower. In the state socialist societies, he argues, a 'new system of inequalities is emerging ... [T]hey are products of the basic economic institution which guarantee the expropriation of surplus from the immediate producer in state socialism, namely redistribution, they are inherent inequalities of state socialism.' The surplus extracted from the direct producers is allocated through political power. This is legitimated by the principle that the 'better qualified "deserves" higher income, ... "deserves" also better housing, better medical services and better chances for ... children to get a good education.'[14] The extent of the inequalities is not the main issue for Szelenyi, rather he is concerned to specify that structured relational inequalities are products of the mechanism of state socialism.

This new social formation has the character of a modern form of oppression and political domination. The bureaucracy is dominant:

> not only the technical organisation of the process of production, but also all the socio-economic decisions concerning what to produce and how to employ the gross product socially are established and made by a distinct and separate social group (the bureaucracy) whose corpus is continuously replenished through mechanisms of a selective co-optation ...[15]

There are no centres of institutional autonomy, there is one centre; Eastern European countries are 'mono-organizational societies'. The party 'penetrates all these structures of the administration control' and the Party elite 'exercises command' over the bureaucratic hierarchy which in turn secures 'the perfect atomisation of the individual'. This school of thought echoes Raymond Aron when it conceives of the 'classless' society[16] – in the sense of a pulverized and fragmented social structure.

The dependency of the working class and the population on this dominant group is complete. The working class has 'no effective and direct power of bargaining either individually or collectively'. Its share of the gross national product is settled by the administrative decisions of

the same bureaucratic apparatus, all the more effectively because it is not only the principal employer, but also shapes (through educational policy, legislation, etc.) and to a large extent determines the macrostructure of the supply of labour-power, and simultaneously establishes the market prices for consumer goods as well.[17]

Where Feher et al. part company with the totalitarian theorists such as Friedrich and Brzezinski is over the source of power. Whereas the latter see power stemming from the political elite's political control, the former see power in terms of effective ownership of the means of production by the bureaucracy.[18] This is not in a legal sense but in its capacity to dispose of economic surplus. The top group, like the bourgeoisie, 'retains identity and perpetuity'. 'The nationalised means of production are to all practical purposes the property of a politically constituted group, that of the top Party leadership.'[19] The essence of this new ruling class lies not so much in its distributional privilege but in its institutionalized power. The bureaucratic apparatus as a whole 'actually exercises all the functions of disposition and control over the nationalised means of production ... (Through) this power to dispose over the resources and the surplus produced, this group actually realises its common interests ...'[20] Its relationship to the population of the country is one of 'mutual opposition of interests centering around the disposition and appropriation of surplus product ...'[21] Rather than the division of labour, with a graded hierarchical social structure, these writers visualize antagonism which culminates 'at specific historical moments' into 'overt antagonism' between the members of the apparatus as a corporate ruling group and the whole working population.[22]

Unlike capitalist society in which politics and social stratification are (in the last instance) outgrowths of economic based class relationships, Soviet-type societies ensure the 'primacy of the political state over the whole of societal life; society is an annexe to the omnipotent political state rather than a relatively independent entity'. Individual and group demands are not articulated and 'command ... irredeemably comprises the elements of arbitrariness and the deliberate disregard of needs ...'[23]

While Feher et al. in places concede that the powers of the political Party elite are limited, it is clear that social outcomes are largely shaped by politics; the reproduction of the system is at the behest of the political bureaucratic ruling class. Societal forces play at best a marginal role. This approach is a contemporary version of the state capitalist thesis, save that it locates the source of class power in political control of the means of production and violence.

Whatever insights Feher, Szelenyi and Wright may have brought to the analysis of Soviet-type societies, they do not fulfil the criteria I have defined as necessary to qualify as a type with a ruling class (see p. 3 above). There may be elements of exploitation and domination on the part of those who rule the USSR. But there is no consciousness which promotes class awareness *vis à vis* the masses. Alex Nove demarcates the boundaries of the 'ruling class' as being coterminous with the *nomenklatura* (i.e. a list of crucial positions controlled by the Party). This is an acceptable rule of thumb identification of those with political positions, those who 'do the ruling.'[24] But this does not necessarily imply exploitation or domination. Nove likens class division to the 'qualitative distinction between . . . officers and other ranks, between "we" and "they", between rulers and ruled, which not only exists in reality but also impregnates people's consciousness in the Soviet Union itself.'[25] But this hardly amounts to class antagonism envisaged by Marxists. There is no clear mechanism for the (economic) exploitation of the masses. While there are asymmetric power relations, giving rise to political elites with privilege, there is little evidence to support a notion of *class* domination.

State socialist society may be better characterized by the activity of elites and a hierarchical system of social and political stratification. This involves political inequality, and privileged access to goods and services – including education and placement in the occupational structure. It entails conflict engendered through interests.

THE ISSUE OF PRIVILEGE

There can be no doubt that privilege and inequality persist in the USSR. Feher and Szelenyi have argued that the 'dictatorship over needs' leads to a similar 'structure' or 'system' of inequality as under market systems, albeit through administrative allocation.[26] This kind of convergence cannot be accepted at face value. If one is concerned with comparisons between state socialist and capitalist systems as a whole, one must distinguish between different sub-sets of capitalist and state socialist countries. Distributive arrangements in capitalist 'welfare states' such as Denmark and Sweden overlap in many ways with Czechoslovakia and the German Democratic Republic. One might concede that there are cases where inequalities are greater in some socialist societies than in some capitalist ones.[27]

To argue, however, that there is a 'dictatorship over needs' which is inherent in state socialist societies is unwarranted. Such an argument ignores and distorts a number of salient features of the development of socialist systems. The levels of backwardness at the time of socialist development would have left needs unfulfilled whatever kind of regime was in power. A comparision might here be made with developing capitalist societies of the Third World where there are enormous political and social inequalities quite unparallelled in Eastern European states. State socialism has ensured the widespread availability of rudimentary social services, mass literacy and elementary education. In addition to the confiscation of property, other measures have contributed to the social equalisation of need fulfilment; land reforms, for instance, met the needs of the peasant population. In the USSR a great geographical narrowing of welfare between centre and periphery has taken place, though urban–rural inequalities remain.

This does not imply, of course, that 'needs' are equally fulfilled or that inequalities in need fulfilment are distributed according to 'socialist principles'. Even in the richest Western welfare states, distribution 'according to need' has yet to be achieved. The point may be taken, moreover, that some wealth is squandered and unjustly distributed in state socialist societies. (The contemporary discussion of injustice and waste in the USSR is an indication of this.) There will *always* be differentials and inequalities as long as there are chronic shortages of commodities and services. No market or administrative system can meet the objective need for a thousand square metres of housing space when there are only eight hundred in existence. It is shortage rather than 'planning' that is at the root of inequalities under socialism. The question which has to be addressed is not whether 'socialist measures' may create inequalities[28] but whether such inequalities are unjust – in the sense of being unnecessarily large.

The principle of reward 'according to one's work' has undoubtedly led to the growth of inequalities in the distribution of services. But the absolute and relative levels of income of the administrative and executive strata are in no way comparable to exploiting classes under other modes of production, even when payments in kind are taken into account. The argument sometimes advanced that like early ascetic entrepreneurial capitalists they consume little of the surplus is fallacious: early capitalists postponed self-gratification – their wealth accumulated to them and their heirs. The inequalities created by ownership of capital cannot be ignored or regarded as unimportant. In the USA, as Lenski has reminded us, '94% of all people with adjusted incomes (for tax purposes) of one million dollars or more received the largest share of their income either from capital gains (despite the fact that half of capital gains are not even recorded as income) or from dividends.'[29] In the USSR the distribution of money income has moved over time to the advantage of manual workers – according to many contemporary commentors, too much so. For example, the ratio of workers' income in industry to the average of all employed rose from 96.9 per cent in 1940 to 110.28 per cent in 1970 and 111.36 per cent in 1985; the figures for skilled non-manuals (ITRs) fell from 210.2 per cent in 1940 to 145.9 per cent and 122.67 per cent in 1970 and 1985 respectively, and for unskilled non-manuals (*sluzhashchie*) the comparable data are 108.7 per cent and 86.58 per cent.[30]

A major cause of greater equality under developed socialism compared to capitalist states is the full employment economy with its consequent high labour utilization rates (particularly for women). The only source of income under state socialism is from labour and this ensures a fairly even distribution of resources even if some are unjustly distributed in kind: whereas under capitalism, poverty is associated with unemployment. It is in this context that the 'appropriation of surplus' occurs under state socialism. Privilege accrues to executive and administrative position. Roemer has suggested that this be termed 'status exploitation' meaning that excess payments are made for services provided by bureaucrats, and that this status is inherited through education.[31] Processes of both the educational system and the family reproduce the existing social structure. A form of 'social closure' occurs. As Ferge has put it: 'the best-off groups are making greater efforts to close their ranks. (They are trying, for instance, to strengthen their educational and occupational monopolies, by reviving meritocratic or genetic arguments.)'[32] Such inequalities are unjust in that they are not legitimated by increasing the welfare of the least well off. Rather than confuse this type of 'exploitation' with that defined above, I would define it as unjustifiable privilege.

The inequalities of power in a relational and distributional sense existing under state socialism may be analysed quite independently from a Marxist class conflict paradigm. Inequalities are not epiphenomena under state socialism. They are contradictions built into the system: they originate from underdevelopment, bureaucratic structures and from processes which are relatively autonomous in the family and educational sphere. It is beyond the scope of this chapter to examine the nature of contradictions in state socialist societies – some are dealt with in the chapters that follow. The essence of the position adopted by Marxists in state socialist societies is that within a non-antagonistic class structure the social division of labour becomes the major basis on which rest political advantage, social conflict, hierarchy, privilege and inequality. This emphasis marks a shift in the traditional Marxist paradigm to a more Weberian one: from class opposition in pre-socialist society to a hierarchically ordered system of social stratification; from antagonistic contradictions to non-antagonistic ones. Furthermore, the resolution of non-antagonistic contradictions leads to a growing social homogeneity which accompanies the tradition to full socialism.[33] Contemporary writers, such as Zaslavskaya, point up interests and emphasize the nature of contradiction which nevertheless are to be located within this framework.[34]

The arguments advanced earlier in this chapter endorse the view that state socialist societies are not characterized in a Marxist sense by classes or class conflict. The economic relations to the means of production are not determinant of social relations. Stratification, in the sense of a perceived hierarchical differentiation of groups of individuals, is a more powerful analytical concept in socialist states than class; and social structure, in the sense of recurring positions and the conditions that shape them, is more useful than 'ownership' of assets. The social structure gives an institutional setting for groups of individuals to have differential positions with respect to power, authority, status and income. Furthermore, these positions engender in their incumbents a world view, a political and social consciousness, which sets them off from other groups. This kind of approach draws attention not only to institutional positions, but also to levels of social consciousness and political interest. It entails a series of elites, of social and political interests, rather than Marxist-type class groups as defined by 'ruling class' theorists.

CONSTRAINTS ON THE STATE

State socialist societies are distinguished from capitalist ones not only by fundamental differences in the pattern of ownership but also by the dominant goals of the state. Marxism–Leninism in the early days of these regimes was primarily a developmental value-system. The appeal of the model of the Soviet Union has been to societies at relatively low levels of economic development lacking a strong indigenous bourgeois class. The new Communist political elites have been able not only to exploit natural and human resources but to concentrate them into industrial development.

However, the role of politics as an institution of collective will to change society is not omnicompetent, but it is limited by the relative autonomy of value systems, traditional patterns of social integration and stratification, forms of management and administration and by the level and relations of production. Moreover, with the economic development of these societies and with the achievement of the initial economic and political goals, the infrastructure of society changes: the educational level of the population rises, differentiation of work activity occurs and is accompanied by the mushrooming of work organizations – the numbers of specialized committees and ministries rise – professional and work-linked groups grow. Rather than patterns of political and social inequalities being the expression of the political leadership's preferences and policies, they are the result of adaptations by the leadership to relatively independent social forces and interests.

Furthermore, the political leadership itself is in many ways a reflection of these forces and as they change so does the pattern of leadership, the social composition of the elites and their institutional origins. These are detailed below, particularly in the chapters by Gustafson and Mann, Hill and Rahr, Reisinger and Willerton, Urban, and Huskey. Rather than there being a unitary and solidary elite and the Communist Party maintaining 'a system of closely knit integration' and a state which 'transcends the division between the "economic" and the "political" characteristic of class society',[35] with the development of these societies comes much greater diversity and relative autonomy between apparatuses and more plurality within them. This is the cause of the resistance to leadership, discussed by Cappelli in Chapter 11. Not only are there different individual and institutional interests, but also ideological, generational, ethnic and regional ones.

This approach legitimates an analysis of the social formation of state socialism in sociological and political science terms rather than in a political class conflict one; it is premised on a political sociology of state socialism. Table 1.1 illustrates four types of society: developed socialism (the current position of the USSR), Western pluralist, developmental (the Soviet Union under Stalin) and traditional society (pre-capitalist). Developed socialism, with its low integration of elites is dependent on a differentiated social structure and wide activity of the state – performed by many different institutions.

Table 1.1: Typology of the state

		Activity of the State			
		Wide	Limited		
	Differentiated	DEVELOPED SOCIALISM (3)	WESTERN PLURALIST (4)	Low	
Social Stratification					*Integration of Ruling Elites*
	Undifferentiated	DEVELOPMENTAL (2)	TRADITIONAL (1)	High	

During the early period of communist rule, the political elite tends to be 'closed' and limited to party activists and particularly to those who have played a role in the political revolution.[36] Such leaders tend to stress ideal distributive relationships and advocate equality in income and education, and common identity in style of life. Initially, the party is dominant among the various groups making up the ruling elite (administrative, industrial, police). The new incumbents of power are confronted with problems of running the economy and asserting state power. They have inevitably turned to their own political inheritance and adapted features of the pre-revolutionary structures. In Soviet Russia there was a symbiosis between the 'command' type political regimes of the Tsars and the forms of public planning and ownership legitimated by the revolution. During this modernization period a 'power elite' may have characterized the political leadership. A *power elite* occurs when recruitment is closed (incumbents originate from a governing stratum) and when positions overlap in the major institutions of society, particularly government ministries, state committees and Party organizations (integration is high).

Generally, with the advancement of industrialization and the maturation of state socialist societies, recruitment to elite positions becomes more 'open' and the 'revolutionary' element comes to be excluded. This may be done either by a change in the composition of the governing political elite or by greater reliance on expert advice and decision. Industrial interests, police and military become more important and begin to influence policy in different ways. The younger, post-revolutionary managerial cadres advocate more rational (and unequal) forms of distribution to promote industrial efficiency. Difficulties in co-ordinating activities, in optimizing interests lead to greater reliance on market-type exchanges i.e. reliance on individuals and groups to articulate their own interests within the state structure, or even to resolve them through a market. (Examples of the former are greater freedoms afforded to writers and professionals and of the latter, the growth of commodity production for sale, and greater opportunity for labour to bargain a wage.) Such topics are taken up below by Reisinger and Willerton, Cooper and Dyker. The ruling elite may be characterized as a group of people who control the dominant institutions but with increasingly low levels of integration, i.e. it is composed of people having different interests and outlooks, with different sets of people being concerned with various activities. The ruling elite (typically) 'takes decisions' but increasingly 'makes' fewer decisions.

The composition of the ruling elite depends on the unique political factors affecting a society at given periods of time: the age profile and political socialization of party leaders, the importance of various groups (army, intellectuals, industrialists) to the reproduction and growth of the society. The degree of integration of elites tends to be symmetrical with the pattern of recruitment, high integration being associated with closed recruitment and low integration with open recruitment. Individuals from different constituencies (military, industrial, police, judiciary, Party, science) find a place on such bodies as the Politburo and the Central Committee of the Party. Fleron has argued that the modern Soviet pattern of recruitment to the Central Committee consists largely of co-opting officials who have 'established very close professional-vocational ties outside the political elite.'[37] Gehlen and McBride[38] have also documented a change towards a more technically competent and managerially orientated elite. Rigby has shown that similar changes occurred in the CPSU politbureau.[39]

Developments under Gorbachev are less a radical departure from this
pattern but more an 'acceleration' of processes already under way.[40]
Huskey (Chapter 6) poses the question as to whether the greater
professionalization of the procuracy may impede the functions of political
patronage networks which in turn may brake a recruitment system
intending to mould a new political generation committed to reform.
Reisinger and Willerton (Chapter 4) also consider patronage ties in the
context of the expanded representation of interests and the growing
importance of education, training and technical competence. Malcolm
(Chapter 9) notes the long-term developmental imperatives of better
technical advice. Finally, the greater emphasis put on *glasnost'* by the
political leadership may reduce bureaucratic inflexibility and enhance
organizational autonomy. Such a process conforms to Almond and
Powell's maxim that system autonomy leads to better problem solving.[41]
The totalitarian form of leadership and control has been superceded by an
interest driven form of political process in which, as White (Chapter 12)
notes, there are many constraints on leadership.

Patterns of recruitment to the political elite and the integration (or lack
of it) of various interests have important effects on the process and style of
politics. Elite recruitment and process may not parallel social developments and 'lagging' may occur. This particularly seems to have been the
case in the latter period of Brezhnev's ascendancy. Study of the composition of the political elites is important not so much because it gives us an
understanding of the personal psychology of the leaders, but because the
empirical study of the elites helps demarcate the interest formation which is
in the ascendancy and to which the elites show allegiance and responsibility. The changing background of the political elites is adumbrated below
by Mann and Gustafson, Hill and Rahr and Reisinger and Willerton.
Political participation increases with the shift from developmental to
developed socialism. Government activity is diffused and subject to more,
not less, participation and control. By the same token change in policy is
more difficult to achieve and resistance grows, this is illustrated below by
Cappelli – which may be compared with the earlier period described by
Merridale. As part of the general process of differentiation, there is a
tendency towards a greater separation of politics from other institutional
interests. Regional factors also become more important, as noted in the
following chapters by Reisinger and Willerton, Urban, and Cappelli.
Soviet politics may be characterized as being interest driven, the configuration of top leadership, as described by Mann, Gustafson, Cooper, Hill and
Rahr, is an indication of the personal agents rather than determinants of
change.

NOTES AND REFERENCES

1   M. Djilas, *The New Class*, Allen and Unwin, London, 1957.
2   E. O. Wright, 'A General Framework for the Analysis of Class Structure', *Politics and Society*, 1984, vol. 13, no. 4, pp. 383–424.
3   F. Feher, A. Heller and G. Markus, *Dictatorship over Needs*, St Martins, New York, 1983.
4   E. O. Wright (1984) pp. 394–6.
5   E. O. Wright (1984) p. 396
6   K. Marx, *Capital*, vols 1–3. Lawrence and Wishart, London, 1959, Chapter XLIX p. 799.
7   John Roemer, *A General Theory of Exploitation and Class*, Harvard University Press, Cambridge, 1982, p. 238.
8   F. Feher et al. (1983); I. Szelenyi, 'Inequalities and Social Policy under State Socialism', *International Journal of Urban and Regional Research*, 1982, vol. 6; Claude Lefort, *The Political Forms of Modern Society: Bureaucracy, Democracy and Totalitarianism*, Polity Press, Cambridge, 1986.
9   Feher et al., see pp. 18–19.
10 Feher et al., p. 31.
11 Feher et al., p. 32.
12 Feher et al., p. 40.
13 I. Szelenyi, 'Inequalities and Social Policy' p. 66.
14 I. Szelenyi, 'Inequalities and Social Policy' pp. 71, 76.
15 Feher et al., p. 45.
16 Feher et al., pp. 247–8, 250.
17 Feher et al., p. 45.
18 Feher et al., p. 47.
19 Feher et al., pp. 56, 57.
20 Feher et al., p. 60.
21 Feher et al., p. 118.
22 Feher et al., p. 22.
23 Feher et al., pp. 253–4.
24 A. Nove, 'Is there a Ruling Class in the USSR?', *Soviet Studies*, 1975, vol. 27, no. 4, pp. 626–7; and 'The Class Nature of the Soviet Union Revisited', *Soviet Studies*, 1983, vol 35, no. 3, p. 307.
25 A. Nove, 'Is there a Ruling Class in the USSR?' p. 624.
26 I. Szelenyi, 'Inequalities and Social Policy under State Socialism', *International Journal of Urban and Regional Research*, 1982, vol. 6, p. 124.
27 Christian Morrison, for example, has grouped together on the basis of income distribution Denmark, the UK and Sweden; and Bulgaria, Rumania, GDR and Czechoslovakia. Poland and the USSR have more unequal distributions but the USA is greatest of all. 'Income Distribution in East European and Western Countries', *Journal of Comparative Economics*, 1984, vol. 8, no. 2, June, p. 127.
28 I. Szelenyi, *Urban Inequalities under State Socialism*, Oxford University Press, Oxford, 1983, pp. 4–5.
29 G. Lenski, 'Marxist Experiments in Destratification: An appraisal', *Social Forces*, 1978, vol. 57, no. 2, December, p. 370.
30 *Narodnoe khozyaistvo SSSR v 1985g.* (Moscow 1986) p. 397. Abram Bergson in an exhaustive survey of Western estimates of wage inequality also concludes that wage inequality is less in the USSR than in western capitalist countries.

See Abram Bergson, 'Income Inequality under Soviet Socialism', *Journal of Economic Literature*, Sept. 1984 see particularly table 6, p. 1070.

31   Roemer on differentials, p. 240– , especially pp. 243–7.

32   Z. Ferge, 'The dynamics of the reproduction of social relations' in R. Andorka and T. Kolosi (eds), *Stratification and Inequality*, Hungarian Sociological Studies, vol 1, Budapest, Institute of Social Sciences, 1984, p. 221.

33   See, for example, M. N. Rutkevitch, 'Social structure of socialist society in the USSR and its development towards social homogeneity', in M. N. Rutkevitch et al., *Transformations of Social Structure in the USSR and Poland*, Academy of Sciences of USSR and Polish Academy of Sciences, Moscow, Warsaw, 1974. W. Wesolowksi and M. Anasz, in the same volume, come to similar, but more muted, conclusions, see: 'Changes in social structure of people's Poland', esp. pp. 79–81).

34   For a review of the literature see Ernst Kux, 'Contradictions in Soviet Socialism', *Problems of Communism*, 1984, vol. 33, no. 6, Nov–Dec, pp. 1–27. T. I. Zaslavskaya, 'Sociologist on Identifying Interest Groups', *The Current Digest of the Soviet Press*, 1987, vol. 39, no. 16. (Translation of interview reported in *Izvestiya* 21 April 1987.) See (in Russian) discussion in *Voprosy ekonomiki* no. 1 (1986) particularly article by Abalkin and especially writings of Butenko in EKO and *Voprosy filosofii* 1987.

35   A. Giddens, *The Class Structure of the Advanced Societies*, Hutchinson, London, 1973, pp. 243, 136.

36   Carl Beck, 'Leadership Attributes in Eastern Europe: The Effect of Country and Time', in C. Beck et al. (eds), *Comparative Communist Political Leadership*, David McKay, New York, 1973.

37   F. J. Fleron (ed.) *Communist Studies and the Social Sciences*, Rand McNally, Chicago, 1969, p. 123.

38   M. P. Gehlen and M. McBride 'The Central Committee in an Elite Analysis', in R. E. Kanet (ed.), *The Behavioural Revolution and Communist Studies*, Free Press, New York, 1971.

39   T. H. Rigby, 'The Soviet Politbureau: A Comparative Profile 1951–1971', *Soviet Studies*, 1972, vol. 24, no. 1. See also 'The CPSU elite: Turnover and Rejuvenation from Lenin to Khrushchev', *Australian Journal of Politics and History*, 1971, vol. 16, no. 1.

40   See T. Gustafson and D. Mann, 'Gorbachev's First Year: Building Power and Authority', *Problems of Communism*, 1986, vol. 35, no. 3.

41   G. A. Almond and G. Powell, *Comparative Politics: A Developmental Approach*, Little Brown, Boston, 1966.

PART I:
The Political Leadership

2. Gorbachev and the 'Circular Flow of Power'

Thane Gustafson and Dawn Mann

INTRODUCTION

In the year and a half since the 27th Congress of the Communist Party of the Soviet Union (CPSU), General Secretary Gorbachev has pursued an unprecedented strategy to consolidate his personal power. If he succeeds we will need to re-examine some of our basic assumptions about the rules of the game in Soviet politics.

Previous general secretaries began by building their personal power gradually. Typically, they used policy issues as tactical pawns to build a centrist consensus within the elite, while simultaneously wielding the 'personnel weapon' (the power of appointment) to build a loyal following, principally among the provincial chiefs of the party. The leader then parlayed this backing into support first at party congresses and ultimately at the top of the political structure: in the Central Committee (CC), the Secretariat, and the Politburo. Only after this game was won and the new general secretary had enough power to silence or displace his rivals did he formulate a full policy programme of his own.[1] This circular build-up of patronage-based loyalties, while never the sole source of the general secretary's power in the past, has always been one of its most essential ingredients.[2]

But Gorbachev has reversed the usual order. Although the policy proposals of his first year were restrained enough,[3] since the 27th CPSU Congress he has advanced a policy programme that has grown more radical by the day – before he has fully consolidated his power at the top and middle levels of the system! Despite unprecedented personnel turnover during his first year (see Chapter 3 below, by Hill and Rahr), by the spring of 1986 Gorbachev had not achieved a clear majority of 'new' men in the Council of Ministers or in the provincial party apparatus. Indeed, the further down the ranks and away from Moscow one looked, the fewer new men there appeared to be.[4]

The slimness of his following is not fully reflected in the numbers. The

21

Central Committee elected at the 27th CPSU Congress in March 1986 contained 30.6 per cent 'new' full members (i.e., individuals who had not been elected a full or candidate Central Committee member or a member of the Central Auditing Commission in 1981 or earlier) – a better score than any previous general secretary had achieved in his 'first' Central Committee. Despite this, Gorbachev appeared very far from having a majority even nominally committed to his side. Moreover, according to established practice, he could not anticipate making any major changes in CC composition until 1991, when the next party congress would elect a new Central Committee.

That Gorbachev fell short of a solid majority in the Central Committee after only one year is not surprising; no Soviet leader has ever consolidated his power that quickly. But the result is a unique 'power inversion': after two-and-a-half years as general secretary, Gorbachev appears to enjoy more solid support (in the demonstrable sense of being able to impose his way or to appoint his people) in the Politburo and the Secretariat than in the Central Committee or in the rest of the elite. His ability to name four new members to the Politburo at a single sitting, as he did in June 1987, was his most impressive display of strength to date.[5] It is revealing that of the Politburo's 14 voting members, six are senior secretaries, a departure from carefully balanced regional and institutional representation in the body observed under Brezhnev; this suggests that Gorbachev's greatest strength currently resides in the Secretariat of the Central Committee.

The Central Committee itself is another matter. Since the party congress, Gorbachev has complained repeatedly about resistance to his programme among leading cadres, and he has said plainly that this resistance can even be found in the Central Committee, although he has been careful to distinguish between resistance and opposition. 'There are concrete carriers of resistance (*tormozhenie*)', he complained to the Komsomol last April, 'in the Central Committee and the government'.[6]

The events surrounding the January 1987 CC Plenum provide the most evidence of resistance to date. The meeting, which had initially been scheduled for the autumn of 1986, was postponed three times because, as Gorbachev put it, 'We could not go into the plenum without clarity on basic questions.'[7] According to Politburo member Lev Zaikov, when the Central committee finally met, Gorbachev's opening speech was received with 'a tense silence', and some of the speeches that followed disagreed with the General Secretary.[8] One can sense the intensity of the exchange that took place from Gorbachev's words to an audience in Riga the following month: 'I have posed the issue in many places, even in the Central committee, "If there is any alternative to perestroika and acceleration, then propose it."'[9]

The Central Committee has not proposed any alternatives, but it is clearly ambivalent about Gorbachev's programme. The final resolution adopted by the Central Committee in January 1987 fell short of Gorbachev's proposals in several places. In particular, his ideas on reforming voting procedures in party elections were diluted to a noncommittal phrase.[10]

The spring of 1987 saw more skirmishing, this time over the date of the next Central Committee plenum, which was expected to consider the leadership's proposals on economic reform. If this meeting, convened in June 1987, proved more successful, it may be because the Politburo postponed submitting the full texts of the draft decrees to the Central Committee and sought only its general endorsement for a programme whose details would come later.[11] Less than six weeks after that, the full texts were officially promulgated by decree and published in an edition of 500,000 copies.[12] Gorbachev may have chosen to use his control of the agenda to avoid a debate over the details of the reform package in the Central Committee. This suggests that his ability to push policy measures through is not an accurate measure of his real support in the Central Committee.

How serious a threat does such resistance pose to Gorbachev? Could it lead to a show-down between the General Secretary and the Central Committee? Such questions raise one of the central puzzles about power and the unwritten rules of the game in Soviet politics. Formally speaking, according to the party statutes, it is the Central Committee, not the Politburo, that elects the General Secretary.[13] But only once in the last half-century has the Central Committee come to a real vote and exercised real power in supporting or opposing a general secretary – and what happened in that one instance is still being debated by Western scholars. Consequently, the Central Committee's potential power is untested in this generation, and Gorbachev's real vulnerability to a Central Committee revolt against him is impossible to assess.

The issue is further complicated by the fact that as part of his campaign for democratization, Gorbachev promised at the January 1987 Plenum to give elective bodies – first and foremost the Central Committee – greater authority over executive ones. In short, Gorbachev has seemingly promised to give greater power, or at least a greater voice, to a Central Committee that he does not yet securely control.

If Gorbachev faces at least a remote threat of an adverse vote in the Central Committee, can one infer that he tailors his strategy accordingly? Does he count votes? Most important, does he consciously guard against creating too many 'dead souls' in the Central Committee (i.e., full members who have lost the state or party posts that gave them Central Committee status in the first place)?[14] But do 'dead souls' really vote? If they do, they could presumably constrain Gorbachev's entire personnel policy. However, we do not know whether they do, or even whether they continue to attend Central Committee meetings. In short, we are missing some of the most important pieces of the puzzle.

Even if resistance to Gorbachev in the Central Committee never comes to an overt challenge, it is clear enough that the elites represented in it can present obstacles to his programme by watering down his measures and impeding their implementation. In addition, the knowledge that a large number of Central Committee members have misgivings about the General Secretary's policies almost certainly affects the calculations and behaviour of the Politburo, which itself is far from fully united. Thus, even in the absence of an open test of strength, the behaviour of the General Secretary will be subtly constrained.

Therefore, whether directly or indirectly, the present 'power inversion' theatens Gorbachev's programme and ultimately his position. There are indications that Gorbachev shares this assessment. Gorbachev has served notice that precedents exist for using party conferences to make changes in the party rules and in personnel at both the local level and in the Central Committee itself. At the June 1987 Plenum, harking back to the early years of the regime, Gorbachev said:

> As you know, party-wide conferences were frequently convened in our Party between congresses. There was a period before 1941 when this was a regular practice. Many conferences held at important turning-points of our history resolved issues that went far beyond the bounds of the tactical. In a number of cases, tasks of a strategic character were raised at them; changes were made in the party rules and in the composition of the central party organs.[15]

That is clearly throwing down the gauntlet: Gorbachev is serving notice that he will use the party conference to weed out opponents in the top ranks of the party. The process (he hopes) will work this way: the months leading up to June 1988 are to be devoted to an intense reports-and-elections campaign throughout the party apparatus that will provide him with an opportunity to bring in active supporters of *perestroika*. In discussing the process, Gorbachev stated:

> It is very important ... that the most active supporters of social transformation join the leadership (*prishli k rukovodstvu*) of the party organizations ... people of princple, who understand the demands of the times, real '*proraby*' [engineers] of *perestroika*.[16]

These supporters would control the election of the delegates to the party conference. Gorbachev has already pursuaded the Central Committee to agree that the delegates are to be selected by secret ballot (although there has been no mention so far of multiple candidacies, an idea that Gorbachev broached at the January plenum but has soft-pedalled since).[17]

At the party conference, Gorbachev will undoubtedly try to secure a majority in the Central Committee, and he may press ahead with new proposals, such as instituting secret ballots and multiple candidacies in all party elections, and establishing fixed terms of office for party officials. If he is successful, the circular flow of power could become a rush, sweeping the opponents of *perestroika* from the party apparatus and replacing them with a loyal Gorbachev following.

The question is, will Gorbachev be able to do it? That depends, first, on what the powers of the June 1988 Party Conference turn out to be. The current party rules provide only that party conferences may 'discuss pressing matters of party policy.'[18] To find authority for party conferences to make changes in Central Committee membership, one must go back to the 1939 version of the party rules, which state that up to one-fifth of the full membership may be renewed at a party conference, with the new members to be selected from the ranks of the candidate members, and new candidate members to be elected to replace them.[19] Thus, with the current rules silent and the last precedent nearly a half-century old, it seems likely that the authority of the party conference will itself be a major political issue. Indeed, the only thing the party rules do say on this subject could pose a problem for Gorbachev: it is the Central Committee that determines the powers of a party conference, and the Central Committee could meet twice before June 1988.

The second crucial question is whether Gorbachev can find the people he is looking for. After all, he has been wielding the broom right along, ever since the 27th Congress. By the time of the June 1987 Plenum, 67 per cent of all USSR ministers and heads of state committees and 55 per cent of the provincial first secretaries had been appointed under Gorbachev. If he has not succeeded in appointing the right people thus far, why not, and why should he be able to do so now?

Third, and more fundamental, is it possible for Gorbachev's confrontational strategy to work in this way, in the open, against high-level resistance? If so, it would be a unique achievement, the first time that a general secretary ever built his power by so frontal an assault on the elite and its vested interests, and the first time that a general secretary's consolidation of power at middle and lower levels followed (and stemmed from) his achievement of pre-eminence in the Politburo and his control of the Secretariat. If Gorbachev pulls it off, we will be required to take a new look at what we mean by 'the circular flow of power', Not to mention the 'law of diminishing general secretaries'.

If this head-on challenge is to succeed, Gorbachev must have complete control of the personnel weapon. Any restraint that he may have shown so far must be traceable to calculation or forbearance, and possibly the lack of enough proven 'new' men, but not political weakness or to discord within the Politburo. Is this, in fact, the case? Gorbachev told the June 1987 Plenum:

> When we demanded of the leading cadres of the party, the soviets, and the economy to start straightening out their work and making it more efficient, we often heard the answer: 'We understand the new tasks, but give us time to appraise the situation, to learn the new methods and ways of acting, and to apply them in practice.' The politburo reacted to this with understanding. We said then that everyone will be given time and opportunity for *perestroika*. But matters will no longer wait ... The workers correctly write to us that whoever wanted to restructure himself has already done so and has gotten down to work. And those who haven't yet reached an understanding of the new tasks are still clinging to the past and through their lack of action are in actual fact sabotaging *perestroika*.[20]

Has Gorbachev, up to now, been showing forbearance, caution, or weakness? The prospects for the success of his strategy over the next year depends on the answer to this question. In the rest of this chapter, we shall attempt to shed light on it by reviewing the patterns of personnel turnover in high-level party and government organs since Gorbachev became general secretary. To avoid unnecessary overlap with the chapter that follows by Hill and Rahr on the Central Party Secretariat and the Apparat, its character is only briefly noted here.

THE SECRETARIAT

With the departure of Mikhail Zimyanin from the Central Committee's Secretariat in January 1987, the turnover of party secretaries is almost complete; only two remain from the time of Brezhnev's death in November 1982: Gorbachev himself and Vladimir Dolgikh. Most of the new secretaries, including at least three of the senior ones, are beholden to Gorbachev for their positions and have closely associated themselves with his policies;[21] Anatolii Luk'yanov and Georgii Razumovskii, have close ties to the General Secretary and only Egor Ligachev has increasingly taken public positions that differ in tone from those of Gorbachev.

Turnover among the Central Committee department chiefs has been equally spectacular. Only one, Nikolai Savinkin, Chief of the Administrative Organs Department, remains from before 1982: 4 of the current incumbents were appointed by Andropov; and the remaining 11 are Gorbachev-era appointees.

Since the 27th Party Congress, the newly-named department chiefs have constituted a more varied group, with representatives from Moscow central institutions less prominent than they were among the officials selected in Gorbachev's first year. Several department chief positions lay vacant for long periods, suggesting possible conflict over who was to be chosen. There were similar delays in filling vacancies in some of the corresponding state organizations (a five-month delay in naming a successor to Yurii Marchuk as chairman of the State Committee on Science and Technology, and a two-month delay before Vasilii Zakharov replaced Petr Demichev as minister of culture). The most intriguing question about Gorbachev's control over personnel policy is the mixture of change and continuity in the Central Committee departments in charge of such matters. The most important of these is the Organizational Party Work (OPW) Department, which handles the placement of leading party cadres throughout the country. All but one of the five current deputy chiefs are new since Gorbachev's accession.

In addition, the role of the OPW Department has been expanded to include the preparation of cadres working within the department itself for further advancement, most notably to positions as party first secretaries of oblasts in the Russian republic (RSFSR). Two positions in particular – deputy chief and inspector – have become virtual revolving doors, as potential candidates for promotion acquire experience and leave to assume new responsibilities.

Links to the past are also visible in the other two departments that manage personnel. The Department for Cadres Abroad has been headed by Stepan Chervonenko since 1983; his first deputy, Georgii Tsukanov, formerly one of Brezhnev's aides, has been his first deputy for only a slightly shorter period of time. An even more striking case of continuity is found in the Administrative Organs Department, which is in charge of overseeing personnel appointments in the military and the police. Its chief, the 74-year-old Nikolai Savinkin, has held high positions in the department since the 1950s and has headed it since 1968.

Not only are these departments still staffed by men with ties to the Brezhnev era, but the 'soft landings and promotions' patterns of personnel turnover within these departments, as well as within the OPW Department, shows the same caution that Gorbachev has exercised in most areas (with the prominent exception of Central Asia), as we shall see below.

USSR COUNCIL OF MINISTERS

Turnover has been high in the USSR Council of Ministers (CM) both before and after the 1986 party congress. Twenty-six new ministers and chairmen of state committees were appointed between March 1986 and June 1987, compared with 30 in Gorbachev's first year. In addition, the more recent period has seen the appointment of four new members to the Presidium of the CM, versus seven appointees in the earlier period. As a result, 68 of the 106 current members of the Council are new since March

1985. In the Presidium, there has been nearly a clean sweep in the years
since 1985, when Ryzhkov was appointed premier.

Appointments to the USSR CM since the party congress are, however,
noticeably different from those made in Gorbachev's first year. In an earlier
article, we observed that the new ministers and heads of state committees
appointed prior to the 27th Congress averaged a surprisingly high 57 years
of age, and that nearly half had had conventional 'Brezhnevian' careers,
rising straight up the ladder of their ministries or near-equivalent
organizations.[22] In other words, the pattern of promotions was still rather
conventional. By contrast, the post-congress appointees are younger (the
new ministers and Presidium members, in particular, average four years
younger at appointment) and their careers have been less conventional.
Several appointees in technical fields spent a few years in the all-Union or
republican party secretariats, mostly after Brezhnev's death, instead of
rising straight up the ladder of their ministries. Even those appointed from
a position of first deputy or its equivalent frequently have turned out to
have unusual twists to their career histories. (see Table 2.1).

Another striking feature of the post-congress group of Council of
Minister appointees is the high percentage of provincials. Half had spent
two years or less in Moscow jobs; many were promoted directly from
enterprise director or oblast party committee first secretary to minister.
They, like Gorbachev himself before 1978, have spent most of their
working lives in only one province.

The post-congress pattern of appointments conveys a strong impression
of purpose, tied more to economic policy than to vote-counting in the
Central Committee. The absence of conventional career backgrounds and
the strong presence of provincials fits with the stated determination of the
new leaders (many of whom are provincials themselves) to challenge the big
Moscow bureaucracies. There is a noticeable absence of clear 'patronage
tails' associated with specific leaders. Only one appointment is patently a
career-end gift from Ligachev: Fedor Loshchenkov, named to a minor
state committee after 25 years in Yaroslavl, has ties to Ligachev going back
45 years. Three appointees have connections to Stavropol: Aleksandr
Budyka, Marat Gramov, and Sergei Manyakin (although only Budyka has
a clear and direct tie to Gorbachev himself). Yet each of these administers a
relatively minor agency – the Ministry of Grain Products, the State
Committee for Physical Culture and Sports, and the People's Control
Committee respectively – and collectively they hardly amount to a
Gorbachev network. A handful of other appointees may have other high-
level patrons. In contrast to Gorbachev's first year, there is less of an
observable 'Uralo–Siberian connection' in recent appointments, and only a
faint 'Leningrad connection'. In sum, personal and geographic connections
do not appear to be very significant. What is much more striking is that

Table 2.1: Recent Career Patterns of New USSR Ministers and State Committee Chairmen (N = 26)

Technical specialists promoted from the number two position of same or related ministry (or close equivalent)

Evgenii Chazov	deputy minister
Nikolai Panichev	first deputy minister
Lev Ryabev	first deputy minister
Aleksandr Volkov	deputy commander, Air Force
Kondrat Terekh	deputy chair, Belorussian Council of ministers (for trade)
Boris Belousov	first deputy minister
Nikolai Gorshkov	deputy minister
Valentin Pavlov	career in Gosplan and the Ministry of Finance
Dmitrii Yazov	deputy minister
Leonid Bibin	Deputy chair, State Construction Committee

Technical specialists with service in apparatus of all-Union or republic Central Committee

Oleg Anfimov	Latvian party and Central Committee
Yurii Bespalov	CC Chemical Industry Department
Vladimir Durasov	CC Heavy Industry Department
Aleksandr Budyka	CC Agriculture Department
Nikolai Ol'shanskii	Ukrainian CC Chemical Industry Department

Political specialists with long service in apparatus of all-Union CC Secretariat

Marat Gramov	16 years in CC apparatus
Aleksandr Kamshalov	16 years in CC apparatus

Direct rise from a position in the field (or the equivalent)

Yurii Vol'mer	Far East shipping
Nikolai Kotlyar	Far East fishing
Nikolai Lukonin	nuclear power plant director
Nikolai Pugin	GAZ auto plant
Vadim Malyshev	nuclear power plant director

Move up from an oblast party committee first or second secretaryship

Fedor Loshchenkov	25 years in Yaroslavl'
Sergei Manyakin	26 years in Omsk
Leonid Smagin	21 years Party work in Tatariya
Vasilii Zakharov	10 years Party work in Leningrad

---

several of the post-congress appointees owe their promotion to their ties to major policies of the last decade, which is presumably what brought them to the attention of the top leadership.

In short, there is no suggestion of blockage, paralysis, log-rolling, or decision-by-committee in appointments to the Council of Ministers. The current situation suggests one person's will, or at least a strong consensus, rather than disunity and a scramble to build lines of patronage. Gradually, Gorbachev appears to be finding the unconventional executives he could not quite locate in the first year. If it is too early to call them alumni of *perestroika*, they have at least distinguished themselves in the five years since Brezhnev's death.

As has generally been the case throughout the party and state apparatus, very few of the post-1982 appointees to the Council of Ministers have been challenged. Almost all of the officials replaced since the party congress, just as in Gorbachev's first year, were holdovers from the Brezhnev era, and only 15 of those now remain. In contrast, only four post-Brezhnev appointees have been replaced, even though some have now been in their current jobs for nearly five years.

Gorbachev has been notably unadventurous in making changes in the military–industrial sector. Here the overall rate of turnover has been slower than elsewhere, and the successors fit the conventional pattern of advancement without exception: in the military–industrial ministries, three ministers remain from the Brezhnev period, and all six of those appointed since November 1982, were previously first deputies of their ministries or close equivalents – the classic 'Brezhnevian' promotion pattern. Does this reflect caution or high opinion? The large numbers of former military–industrial executives who were appointed to high positions since Brezhnev's death suggests the latter.[23]

THE PROVINCIAL ELITE

In this section we shall explore developments within the exceptionally important Russian republic, examine general developments in other republics, and then attempt to unravel what is going on in the Ukraine – the last a subject of considerable speculation and controversy.

Provinces of the RSFSR

The first secretaries of the Russian republic have traditionally comprised the core of the CPSU Central Committee membership and the single most important source of future leaders. All 72 of the RSFSR oblast, territory, and autonomous republic party committees in office at the time of the 27th Congress were elected full members of the Central Committee at that gathering. At that time, one-third of these officials had been appointed in Gorbachev's first year and were considered new members of the CC.

In the following 16 months, turnover in this key group slowed sharply (16 left their first secretaryship compared with 25 in Gorbachev's first year).[24] The pattern of change in both periods is significant. First, in each period, the departing secretaries were almost entirely holdovers from the Brezhnev or even the Khrushchev years; in other words, the first secretaries appointed since November 1982, with few exceptions, have been left in place, presumably both to provide stability and also to allow them to prove themselves further.

Secondly, only one of the changes in regional first secretaries since the party congress was an outright dismissal; many, indeed, consisted of promotions, although not such glittering ones as in Gorbachev's first years (rather more typical is Loshchenkov's previously mentioned transfer to the Council of Ministers). This pattern suggests the same general policy as in the first year: to promote the best (or the best-connected) of the holdovers and to treat most of the rest with care (see Table 2.2).

One clear aim has been to retire the oldest of the group. Of the secretaries born in 1922 and before, only three remain out of the group of 26 that

Table 2.2: Current position of Regional Party Committee First Secretaries replaced between March 1986 and August 1987:

	Name	Position held
Transferred	Nikolai Mal'kov	First secretary, Chita oblast
	Gennadii Vedernikov	Deputy chairman, USSR Council of Ministers
	Fedor Loshchenkov	Chairman, USSR State Committee for Material Reserves
	Dmitrii Kachin	Ambassador to Vietnam
	Sergei Manyakin	Chairman, People's Control Committee
	Gennadii Kolbin	First secretary, Kazakh CP
	Vadim Bakatin	First secretary Kemerovo
	Vadim Ignatov	Deputy chairman, USSR Agroindustrial Committee
Retired	Mikhail Matafonov	For health reasons, age 58
	Nikolai Antonov	Pensioned, age 65
	Ivan Klimenko	Pensioned, age 66
	Aleksei Rybakov	Pensioned, age 62
Fired	Midkhat Shakirov	
Deceased	Ivan Morozov	
	Pavel Smol'skii	
	Nikolai Ermakov	

existed at the time of Brezhnev's death. Not surprisingly, the rate of retirements is now slowing sharply: in Gorbachev's first year, 13 out of 25 departures were retirements; on the second period, only four. In short, Gorbachev is running out of easy targets.

The three biggest promotions from among RSFSR regional party leaders deserve special mention, because none had originally been a Brezhnev appointee and each has been on a fast track since 1983. Gennadii Vedernikov moved from Chelyabinsk to become Deputy Chairman of the USSR Council of Ministers; Gennadii Kolbin was named from Ulyanovsk to replace Dinmukhamed Kunayev as first Secretary of the Kazakhstan Communist Party; and Vadim Bakatin returned from Kirov to become First Secretary in his home oblast of Kemerovo. None of the three has obvious ties with either Gorbachev or Ligachev, but all three had been favourably featured in the media before their promotion.

Little information is available about the RSFSR regional party committee first secretaries appointed since the 27th Congress other than their most recent position.[25] Yet even this single piece of information shows a decline in the application of the innovative practice – seen in the Andropov years as well as Gorbachev's first year – of sending potential regional first secretaries for a brief spell to the central apparatus in Moscow. Of the 25 new secretaries appointed during Gorbachev's first year, 19 had served in some capacity in Moscow (16 in the Central Committee apparatus alone) immediately prior to their appointment as regional first secretary. But of the 16 new appointees promoted between March 1986 and August 1987, only five show a similar rotation, whereas seven were promoted from within their own region (see Table 2.3). Thus, we seem to be witnessing a return to the Brezhnev pattern of promotion from within a region.

The treatment of the RSFSR regional party committee first secretaries is one of the most important features of Moscow's personnel policy to watch. Their treatment under Gorbachev so far suggests caution and a concern for stability. Whatever the intention, the effect has been to minimize the number of 'dead souls' in the Central Committee from this particularly important group. Of the eight transfers since the Party Congress, only three now stand to lose their status as full members at the June 1988 Party Conference, and if one includes the four retirees and one dismissal, the total number of 'dead souls' from the ranks of the RSFSR regional first secretaries is at most eight.

The non-Russian republics

Movement of cadres generally remains high in the non-Russian republics, but extreme variations exist from republic to republic. Central Asia (especially Kazakhstan) has led the way in every major category of

Table 2.3: Previous Position of Regional First Secretaries Appointed between March 1986 and August 1987:

Promoted from within same region	
Aleksandr Bogdanov	Second secretary
Stanislav Osminin	Second secretary
Petr Reznikov	Second secretary
Yurii Samsonov	Second secretary
Igor Tolstoukhov	Second secretary
Evgeniy Pokhitailo	Chairman, oblast executive committee
Vladimir Mel'nikov	Chairman, ASSR Council of Ministers
Transferred from another region	
Nikolai Mal'kov	First secretary
Vadim Bakatin[a]	First secretary
Transferred from Moscow	
N. D. Shvyrev	Inspector, CC CPSU
Ivan Nikulin[b]	Inspector, CC CPSU
Gennadii Kabasin	Deputy Chief, OPW Department, CC CPSU
Yurii Pogorelov	Sector head, OPW Department, CC CPSU
Anatolii Vlasenko	Sector head, CC CPSU Agriculture Department
Leonid Khitrun	Council of Ministers
R. Khabibullin	Council of Ministers

[a] Bakatin was the second secretary in Kemerovo before serving as first secretary in Kirov.
[b] Shvyrev was second secretary in the same oblast before moving to the CC. Nikulin was a secretary in a different oblast.

turnover both before the 27th CPSU Congress and since, suggesting a continuing high priority attached by Moscow to fighting corruption and reasserting central control there. The Ukraine, to date, represents the other extreme, with the fewest changes in nearly every category.

In all the republics, there is the same evidence of continuity of policy that we have noted for the central apparatus and the RSFSR: on the whole, officials appointed under Andropov and Chernenko have not been replaced (except to be promoted). Thus, turnover since the congress, as in Gorbachev's first year, continues to occur largely at the expense of Brezhnev-era appointees.

Six of the 14 republican party first secretaries have been replaced by Gorbachev, but their fates have varied quite widely. Four Central Asians have been dismissed, and one of these (Kunaev) was subsequently expelled from the Central Committee; two non-Central Asians (Shevardnadze of Georgia and Slyun'kov of Belorussia) have been promoted. If one leaves the Central Asians aside, the remaining pattern (i.e. two promotions, eight unchanged) suggests a cautious policy similar to that being practised toward the RSFSR regional first secretaries. In this light, the otherwise surprising survival of both Semen Grossu of Moldavia and Vladimir Shcherbitskii of the Ukraine is part of a larger puzzle.

The republican party second secretaries are a different story. Only one second secretary from the Brezhnev era (Aleksei Tytarenko of the Ukraine) is still in place today. Indeed, the policy applied to second secretaries under Gorbachev is virtually the opposite of that applied to first secretaries: wherever the first secretary has not been replaced, the second secretary generally has – the only exceptions to this policy, in addition to the Ukraine, are Azerbaidzhan and Moldavia, where the second secretaries were appointed under Andropov and Chernenko respectively (see Table 2.4).

The traditional Stalinist practice of sending Russians from Moscow to serve as second secretaries in the non-Russian republics evidently remains as strong under Gorbachev as in the past.[26] Nearly all of the Gorbachev appointees are Russians or have Russian-sounding names; and nearly all had previously served in the Central Committee in Moscow (see Table 2.4). Only Belorussia and the Ukraine are definitely known to have both first and second secretaries who belong to the dominant nationality of their respective republic.

Turnover among regional party first secretaries in republics other than the RSFSR has remained high since the congress, 21 in all compared to 23 in the period March 1985–March 1986.[27] The highest rate of turnover is, once again, found in Central Asia. As in the RSFSR, the retirees (a total of 17, ten of whom retired in Gorbachev's first year) are, without exception, Brezhnev appointees. There have been a surprising 18 lateral transfers among the non-RSFSR first secretaries: (10 in year one, 8 since); even more surprising is the fact that 12 came from Central Asian republics. The transfers were almost evenly divided between Brezhnev and post-Brezhnev appointees (10 and 8 respectively). In contrast, only seven have been dismissed (2 in Gorbachev's first year and 5 since).

The most striking feature of the non-RSFSR regional party first secretaries appointed since March 1985 is that the vast majority of them come directly from their home republic. The pattern of promotion, however, is not exactly 'Brezhnevian', in that few of the appointees come from previous positions in their home regions (see Table 2.5). Only a handful come from the apparatus of the Central Committee in Moscow, in sharp contrast to the case with republic party second secretaries.

This does not resemble the policy of 'inter-regional exchange of cadres' that Ligachev recommended at the 27th Party Congress and others have since endorsed. Apparently, Moscow has opted to continue the tradition of

Table 2.4: Backgrounds of Republic Party Second Secretaries appointed since Brezhnev

Previous positions of second secretaries appointed under Andropov and Chernenko

Aleksei Tytarenko	Republic CC secretary (same republic)
Vasilii Konovolov	CC CSPU OPW Department sector chief
Gennadii Bartoshevich	First secretary, city party committee (Minsk)
Viktor Smirnov	CC CSPU OPW Department sector chief
Boris Nikol'skii	City party committee secretary (Moscow)

Nationality of appointees listed above

To Ukraine	Tytarenko	Ukrainian
To Azerbaidzhan	Konovalov	Russian
To Belorussia	Bartoshevich	Belorussian
To Georgia	Nikol'skii	Russian
To Moldavia	Smirnov	Unknown

Previous positions of second secretaries appointed under Gorbachev

Petr Luchinskii	CC CPSU Department deputy chief
Nikolai Mitkin	CC CPSU OPW Department sector chief
Vitalii Sobol'ev	CC CPSU OPW Department sector chief
Gennadii Kiselev	CC CPSU inspector
Yurii Kochetkov	CC CPSU inspector
Sergei Nesterenko[a]	CC CSPU deputy instructor
Georgii Aleshin	City party committee secretary (RSFSR)
Vladimir Anischev[b]	Secretary republic CC (same republic)
Sagidullah Kubashev	Oblast party first secretary (same republic)

Nationality of appointees listed above

(New from March 1985 to March 1986)

To Armenia	Kolchetkov	Russian
To Estonia	Aleshin	Russian
To Kirgizia	Kiselev	Unknown
To Tadzhikistan	Luchinskii	Moldavian
To Uzbekistan	Anishchev	Russian

(New after March 1986)

To Kazakhstan	Kubashev	Kazakh
To Latvia	Sobol'ev	Russian
To Lithuania	Mitkin	Russian
To Turkmenistan	Nesterenko	Unknown

[a] Second previous position – second secretary Tashkent city party committee.
[b] Second previous position – CC CPSU inspector.

expressing its wishes through the second secretary rather than instituting the direct rotation of regional first secretaries.[28]

Table 2.5: Previous Position of Non-RSFSR Regional Party First Secretaries Appointed under Gorbachev:

	When appointed	Same region[a]	Same republic	outside
Central Asia	3/85–3/86	5	15	1
	3/86–6/87	4	11	1
Ukraine	3/85–3/86	1	2	1
	3/86–6/87	1	7	0
Belorussia	3/85–3/86	1	2	1
	3/86–6/87	1	1	0

[a] Included in the total for 'Same republic'.

The Ukrainian case

The figures for personnel turnover in the Ukraine since Gorbachev became general secretary have been among the lowest of any republic. Only one full member of the Ukrainian Politburo has been replaced; three candidate members have been dropped and four added. Turnover among secretaries and Central Committee department heads has been somewhat higher (57 and 39 per cent respectively), but the Ukrainian Council of Ministers has been among the most stable (a new chairman was recently elected to replace the ailing 75-year-old Aleksandr Lyashko); only Lithuania, Estonia, and the RSFSR have had more continuity in their councils. Ten regional party first secretaries out of a total of 25 have changed hands under Gorbachev as of 1 August 1987; of these changes three were retirements, three were transfers and four were dismissals.

In the replacements that have occurred, Moscow's hand has been not nearly as visible in Ukraine as in the other non-Russian republics. Only one regional first secretary comes directly from a previous job in the Central Committee in Moscow. The only other major 'emissary' from Moscow (albeit an important one) is the new first secretary of the Kiev city committee, Konstantin Masyk, appointed in April 1987.

By comparison, Ukraine has fared rather better in 'exporting' cadres to the central government in Moscow, suggesting that the Ukrainians' overall performance is not viewed badly in the Soviet capital. The list of prominent Ukrainians appointed to leading positions in Moscow includes Georgii Kyuchkov (appointed Deputy Chief of the OPW Department after many years as chief of the corresponding department in Kiev); Vladimir Reshetilov (appointed USSR Minister of Construction in 1986, after serving as deputy and first deputy ministry of heavy industrial construction in the Ukraine from 1980 to 1983); and Arkadii Shchepetil'nikov (promoted to USSR Minister of Industrial construction after heading counterpart ministry in the Ukraine). The list also includes USSR ministers Vladimir Luk'yanenko and Nikolai Ol'shanskii, who were promoted directly from Sumy; Ivan Skiba, First Deputy Chief of the CC CPSU Agriculture and Food Industry Department; Viktor Myronenko, First Secretary of the Komsomol, and Aleksandr Kapto, the current ambassador to Cuba.

The abrupt dismissals in the spring of 1987 of the first secretaries of Voroshilovgrad, Dnepropetrovsk, and Lvov regional party committees in the Ukraine amid charges of gross misconduct have been taken as evidence that Moscow has been 'closing in' on Shcherbitskii by eroding his support in his own apparatus.[29] It is true that two of the ousted officials, Viktor Boiko of Dnepropetrovsk and Viktor Dobryk of Lvov, come from Shcherbitskii's base in the Dnepropetrovsk party organization,[30] and the dismissals do appear to represent a break in the pattern of the previous two years, in which criticism from Moscow did not lead to dismissal of the officals involved. Upon close examination, however, it is not clear that these three cases can be interpreted as part of an effort to weaken Schcherbitskii. Dnepropetrovsk and Lvov had long been criticised on numerous grounds; and Boris Goncharenko's departure in Voroshilovgrad appears to be connected to the 'Berkhin affair', in which local KGB officials illegally arrested Viktor Berkhin, a local investigative reporter.[31] In all instances, although the investigations were launched by Moscow, the dismissals were announed by Shcherbitskii himself, and perhaps most significant, in every case the replacements came from high up in the Ukrainian party, suggesting that they are Shcherbitskii's own choices, not Moscow's.

The most recent dismissals occurred in Volyn oblast, where Zinovii Koval'chuk, the party first secretary, and V. Zhibrov, the second secretary, were both fired for misconduct. Their dismissal is apparently related to a housing scandal in the city of Lutsk, where the local prosecutor successfully brought charges against the former chairman of the city executive committee (among others) but subsequently found the charges reversed by the oblast party committee.[32] The Ukrainian CP Central Committee investigated the matter, it upheld the decision of the prosecutor and relieved Zhibrov of his duties on the spot. At that time, Koval'chuk received a reprimand, which – it now appears – was considered insufficient punishment.

Is there a struggle going on, then, for control of the Ukraine, consisting of rising pressure from Moscow and a stubborn rear-guard action by Shcherbitskii? This question has become especially interesting in light of the removals of Viktor Grishin and Kunaev relieved from their party posts in Moscow and Kazakhstan respectively. Both were clearly weakened by a vigorous campaign to undermine their base; there were high rates of personnel change in Moscow and in Kazakhstan long before the two leaders were toppled. So far the story in the Ukraine has been quite different. Is it plausible to conclude that Shcherbitskii has succeeded where Grishin and Kunaev failed? Is the Gorbachev who can name four new members of the Politburo at a sitting unable to remove this one? Or is there perhaps something more complicated going on? At this point we do not know.

CONCLUSIONS

Are there any patterns to post-congress turnover?

The patterns of personnel movement in the Soviet elite since the 27th CPSU Congress show some significant changes compared to those of Gorbachev's first year. Appointments to the Council of Ministers and to the top posts in Central Committee departments have become distinctly more innovative. In addition (although we have not analysed it here), turnover has accelerated at the top levels in three major state institutions that had previously been relatively unaffected: the KGB, the military, and the diplomatic service.

But far more striking are the elements of continuity. First, in both periods, sharp distinctions can be observed in every category between officials appointed under Brezhnev and of those named since. The Brezhnev holdovers, especially the older ones, are still the principal targets for removal; officials appointed since 1982 have mostly not been challenged.

Second, a careful, even respectful, treatment of certain categories of officials has prevailed. These include RSFSR regional party committee first secretaries (except for the oldest Brezhnev appointees), non-Russian party leaders outside Central Asia, and to a lesser extent, senior officials in charge of cadres within the Central Committee apparatus.

Third, a 'Brezhnevian' pattern of promotion – i.e., promotion up the ladder of a single organization or region – has continued (or returned) among some important groups. These include the leaders of military–industrial ministries and regional party committee first secretaries (despite a declared policy of 'inter-regional circulation of cadres').

On the whole, then, Gorbachev has continued to exploit the easiest and least controversial targets, the Brezhnev holdovers. But there are few of them left – indeed, the largest single group of remaining 'Brezhnevians' consists of the six republic party first secretaries who have remained in office since 1982. Gorbachev's failure to challenge them, as well as the post-1982 appointees at all levels, has left them largely free to build (or rebuild) their own followings below them.[33] This is true even in Central Asia, where few 'Varangians' have been parachuted from the centre, except in the traditional spot of republic second secretary. Sooner or later, Gorbachev will have to confront these groups, including some of his own appointees; this carries the certain danger of disrupting the tacit contract that the easy distinction between 'Brezhnevian' and 'post-Brezhnevian' cadres has made possible until now.

Does Gorbachev control the personnel weapon?

The evidence suggests that until the 27th CPSU Congress, Gorbachev shared the levers of personnel appointment, but that since then he has gained essentially undivided control of them. The promotions of Luk'yanov and Razumovskii to the Secretariat, and the apparent distancing of Ligachev from a direct role in cadres appointments, have given the General Secretary a freer hand. More recently, the emergence of Razumovskii, rather than Ligachev, as the man in charge of preparations for the June 1988 Party Conference points in the same direction.[34]

How then can one explain Gorbachev's continued caution in using the personnel weapon? Our guess (and it is hardly more than that) is that it has been due to a combination of self-restraint and constraint by circumstances, rather than restraint by others. There have been enough easy and obvious targets to work on without disrupting the Andropov/Gorbachev continuity; and it has presumably not been easy to find new people one could be sure of. Several of Gorbachev's patterns of behaviour reinforce this impression: first, his habit of promoting lower-ranking officials on the basis of short personal acquaintance (Yazov and Yakovlev); second, his decisiveness in taking advantage of unexpected opportunities to clean house, such as Chernobyl and the Rust affair. As more officials emerge who have shown themselves able to perform successfully under *perestroika*, that particular source of constraint will fade.

This line of reasoning suggests that Gorbachev is increasingly in a position to adopt a more aggressive cadres policy if he chooses. An indirect indication of his growing control (or willingness to assert control) over personnel since the party congress is that although there have been few signs of a 'Stavropol mafia' rising to power, there have been no major 'patronage tails' associated with any other top leader either. In particular, the dramatic rise of the Uralo-Siberians in 1985, perhaps associated with Ligachev's protection, has faded since the congress. And while some recent appointments show connections to Ryzhkov, the dominant pattern of appointments in the Council of Ministers suggests a strong hand coming from the party side.

Gorbachev's political strategy can be summed up this way: unlike his predecessors, he is attempting to build support for a radical policy programme *before* fully consolidating his power within the elite by conventional means, and he is looking for this support primarily at the local level. He is gambling that through the secret ballot, local party elections, and the party conference, this support can be converted quickly into solid power at all levels of the system, thus enabling him to overcome resistance and implement *perestroika*. Other general secretaries, notably Khrushchev, have played with populist approaches in the past, attempting to mobilize the masses against resistance to the party leader's policies at middle levels, but Gorbachev's strategy is true 'party populism', something that has not been tried by any Soviet politician since Lenin.

His strategy is a gamble in two senses. The first is that Gorbachev, for the first time since he became General Secretary, is openly defying the conservatives to do their worst. The second sense is more fundamental; Gorbachev is ultimately gambling that the election of delegates by secret ballot will confirm that the party rank and file are overwhelmingly in favour of *perestroika*. Thus, he is staking the future of his reforms, and possibly his own political future as well, on the balance of friends and foes of change within the entire party membership. If he wins, Gorbachev's gamble could write very new rules to the game of Soviet politics. But is his silent majority really there?

POSTSCRIPT

Since the summer of 1987, when this chapter was first presented,[35] the mood among the reformers in Moscow (and, correspondingly, among observers in the West) has swung hard towards pessimism about Gorbachev's power and the prospects for his reforms. Several key events in autumn 1987 certainly appeared to support this view, notably Gorbachev's unaccountably long seven-week 'vacation' from August to October, his carefully measured speech on the 70th Anniversary of the October Revolution, and above all, the still-baffling Eltsin Affair.

How does this perception accord with the analysis contained in the present chapter? Our starting observations were that Gorbachev's unprecedented approach to rule, the anomalous 'power inversion' that first became apparent in 1986–87, and the challenge this poses to Gorbachev's policies, have created a highly unstable political situation. The central questions we raised were: Why does Gorbachev not yet 'have his own men'? Is the explanation forebearance and caution, or weakness? Has he already fought and lost, or do the main battles still lie ahead?

Many observers would now say the answer is weakness, and that Gorbachev has already suffered some important losses. But our review of personnel changes since March 1985 suggests opportunism, patience, and cautious advance, constrained as much by the lack of proven candidates as by political forces. This picture implies a wilier, more patient, and more resourceful Gorbachev than the naive reformer the pessimists describe. On this reading, the General Secretary has not yet endured any major defeats and the main battles for control of the apparatus still lie ahead. Nevertheless, the evidence is highly ambiguous and the central puzzle remains: How strong is Gorbachev, and how do we know?

What, in particular, do recent events add to our knowledge? There are several key issues. The first and obvious one is the role of Ligachev himself. Michel Tatu is most likely on solid ground in arguing that Ligachev's career owes nothing to Gorbachev,[36] and there can be little doubt that Ligachev's policy positions differ from Gorbachev's along several important dimensions: *glasnost'* and the treatment of the past, or Party privileges, of agricultural cooperatives, and of 'non-formal' associations, just to mention a few.

How broad is Ligachev's jurisdiction? Tatu agrees with our view that Gorbachev tried to contain Ligachev by adding agriculture to his portfolio while transferring primary responsibility for some of his other major accounts to new men of his own, notably personnel to Razumovskii and ideology to Yakovlev.[37] But Tatu believes the effort failed, and that it is Yakovlev who has been limited, mainly to the domain of international propaganda,[38] while Razumovskii's allegiance is not yet clear. The record of Ligachev's public appearances from autumn 1987 through to spring 1988 confirms that he remains broadly responsible for media, cultural, scientific, and educational affairs. Meanwhile, in an interview with *Le Monde* in December Ligachev revealed that he chairs weekly meetings of the Secretariat;[39] and the Eltsin Affair indirectly suggested that Ligachev continues to influence personnel appointments, at least in Moscow. In short, there is some evidence to support Peter Reddaway's observation that Ligachev now has the 'confidence to flex his muscles discretely in public.'[40]

Yet it remains uncertain how far Ligachev's writ runs. Chairing the meetings of the Secretariat appears to be a routine administrative duty, which second secretaries have commonly performed in the past. Meanwhile, Ligachev's oversight of agriculture accounts for more than half of his recent public appearances, which makes one question how thorough his control of other areas can be. Moreover, in the agricultural sphere he is seconded by Murakhovskii, a clear Gorbachev ally, and by Nikonov, whose public pronouncements on agriculture differ substantially from Ligachev's (notably on the subject of cooperatives and family contracts). Finally, Razumovskii's recent elevation to candidate status in the Politburo would seem to remove Ligachev even further from direct control over cadres. In short, Ligachev's own powers are ambiguous.

The second major issue, related to the first, is the state of relations among the leaders within the Politburo and the Secretariat. The battle, Tatu argues, is between a small handful of Gorbachev appointees and a much larger group of 'Andropovians.'[41] But the key issue is how much divides them. While agreeing that there are obvious differences of view within the Politburo, one could equally plausibly argue that there is plenty over which 'Gorbachevians' and 'Andropovians' can still collaborate, and more important, that the members will line up in different ways on different issues, giving Gorbachev room for manoeuvre if he can hold the centre.

Furthermore, dividing the Politburo into Gorbachevians and Andropovians captures only one dimension of the diversity of tendencies among Brezhnev's successors. An equally prominent cleavage runs between what one might call the 'Moscow/Novosibirsk' and the 'Leningrad/Sverdlovsk' styles of *perestroika*. Moscow is the capital of *glasnost'*; while Novosibirsk has brought us Gorbachev's decentralizing economic advisors. The Leningrad/Sverdlovsk approach stresses technology, machinery, and industrial discipline – very much the programme pursued by Romanov in Leningrad since the beginning of the 1970s, and the only one, incidentally, to show real results to date.[42]

Other cleavage lines can be drawn as well: thus Ligachev leaves little doubt that he puts social programmes first, which probably puts him at odds with machine-builders like Ryzhkov, Zaykov, and Maslyukov. The machine-builders, for their part, are presumably keen on harnessing defence industry in the cause of economic modernization, and thus may line up with Gorbachev and Shevardnadze on arms control against relative foreign-policy conservatives such as Gromyko. Gromyko, however, will stress the centrality of US–Soviet relations, while Yakovlev may argue for more focus on West Europe and East Asia. The issue of legal reform may find Ligachev and Yakovlev on the same side against Chebrikov. Finally, on issues such as corruption in Uzbekistan, alcoholism, nationalist riots in Latvia and Armenia, faked production figures in Moldavia, incompetence in the nuclear-power industry, and indiscipline and absenteeism in the workplace generally, the entire Politburo probably sees eye to eye.

On the most divisive issues of reform, moreover, it is by no means clear that Gorbachev is always a liberal, or that recent conservatism in policy is a sign that the Gorbachevians have been getting the worst of it. For example, basic food prices will not be raised any time soon and severe restrictions have been placed on the managers' power to release workers – but these could well be the result of common caution in the face of popular anxiety and the genuine complexity of the issues rather than a conservative swing in the Politburo. It is, after all, Gorbachev's own insistence on combining central control with local autonomy, accelerated growth with modernization, and improved efficiency with continued safety and predictability –

not the opposition of conservatives – that accounts for much of the compromise appearance of the economic reform to date.[43]

Not all of these cleavages need lead to conflict, but one issue over which liberals and conservatives are most likely to square off is that of democratization of the Party and reform of its functions, together with the related issues of patronage and privilege. It is here that Gorbachev has had the most visible difficulty with the Central Committee elected at the 27th Party Congress. In December 1987 and January 1988 the elected committees of every level of the Party except the very top 'rendered accounts' to their 'electors' (that is, to the corresponding party committees and bureaux). To judge from the many brief but frequently lively reports in the press, these meetings varied widely: some 'recalled' unsatisfactory secretaries; others drew up radical-sounding suggestions for the upcoming Party Conference; some were held a second time because their first performance was deemed unsatisfactory. On the whole, turnover of personnel was low,[44] but one has the impression of a vast pulling and hauling throughout the Party apparatus as the Party Conference approaches, with the outcome not yet decided – but in any case no decisive victories by the conservatives thus far.

The most powerful single argument in the pessimists' case is the Eltsin affair. Unfortunately, we are still lacking the most basic facts: Was the 21 October Central Committee plenum really 'sudden and unplanned', and Eltsin's outburst truly spontaneous? Or was it, as Reddaway and Tatu suggest, a set-up by Ligachev and the moderates against Eltsin?[45] Just whom did Eltsin attack? And most important, did Gorbachev defend him to the bitter end, as Tatu suggests?[46]

We do not know the answers to these questions, yet a few comments are in order. It is far from clear that Gorbachev still considered Eltsin an asset by late 1987. The General Secretary consistently had warmer praise for reform in Leningrad than for Moscow (and so it is not impossible that the appointment of the Leningrader Zaykov to succeed Eltsin is an improvement as far as Gorbachev is concerned). Eltsin served his purpose – that of purging Grishin's Moscow apparatus, from which over 9000 officials were removed in two years – but by summer 1987 he may have been overdoing things.[47] Tatu mentions a joint letter from several raikom secretaries denouncing Eltsin's rough-and-ready methods;[48] and we have it from Gorbachev himself that Eltsin had been planning a new round of dismissals, which the Politburo had to head off.[49] In short, Gorbachev's many subsequent sharp references to Eltsin's 'adventurism' may be heartfelt.

In the Soviet political system, control of the personnel weapon is still the 'necessary if not sufficient condition' for power, and therefore one's appraisal of Gorbachev's strength must depend on whether he is able to appoint his people and block his opponents' choices. The changes of recent months have not been unfavourable to Gorbachev: Aliev's retirement, Razumovskii's promotion, and Talyzin's removal from the key Gosplan position all seem to reinforce Gorbachev's hand. By and large the recent changes continue the patterns observed in our chapter. The waltz of the defence-industry officials continues (Talyzin to the Social Bureau, Masliukov to Gosplan, Baklanov to the Secretariat, Belousov to the VPK), together with further ministry mergers. At the republic level, having lost the battle against corruption, Usmankhodzhaev was replaced by Rafik Nishanov as first secretary of the Uzbek Communist Party, while the slow-down in Party obkom turnover is more evident than ever, with Brezhnev-era appointees and/or corrupt officials as the targets (two in the RSFSR, four in the non-Russian republics). None of these appointments suggests a weak General Secretary, however, nor do they suggest that the personnel weapon is being wielded by any rival.

In the final analysis, assessments of Gorbachev's strength depend largely upon judgements concerning Gorbachev's own political skill and character. There is plenty of evidence to indicate that the process of *perestroika* has not been stopped: resolutions on education, unemployment, and the environment have been passed recently, while *glasnost'* continues apace with the rehabilitation of Bukharin and the publication of previously banned works (e.g., the novels of Rybakov and Grossman). Most important, none of the changes enacted thus far has been reversed, nor have any alternative programmes been proposed. Compromise on policy need not indicate weakness on Gorbachev's part but instead may be a recognition of the reality of brokerage politics.

Gorbachev is facing a tough political agenda in 1988, but one with possibilities for great successes. According to Tatu, Gorbachev must pass two tests to be considered fully in control: he must succeed in replacing twenty per cent of the full membership of the Central Committee at the Party Conference and he must dislodge Ligachev from the number two spot.[50] The first test is quickly approaching, but the second may be farther off. Neither Khrushchev nor Brezhnev defeated their chief rivals until well into their tenure as general secretary, and Gorbachev has not yet given any indication that he is attempting to remove Ligachev.

Will Gorbachev's strategy succeed? It is still too early to know for certain, but the last six months, while perhaps not Gorbachev's best, certainly do not signal his defeat.

ACKNOWLEDGEMENTS

The authors would like to thank Timothy Colton, Werner Hahn, Michel

Tatu, and Elizabeth Teague for their advice and criticism. Information herein, where not explicitly sourced is based on the authors' reading of the central Soviet press, Foreign Broadcast Information Service translations of Soviet radio broadcasts, the files of Radio Liberty (Munich), and the on-line computer services of SOVSET' and SOVT. Additional biographical information of Soviet officials was drawn from *Deputaty Verkhovnogo Soveta SSSR, odinnadtsatyi sozyv* (Deputies of USSR Supreme Soviet, 11th Convocation), Moscow, Izvestiya, 1984.

NOTES AND REFERENCES

1   For commentary on past strategies, see e.g., T. H. Rigby. 'Khrushchev and the Rules of the Game' in Robert F. Miller and Ferenc Feher (eds), *Khrushchev and the Communist World*, Croom Helm, London, 1984, pp. 39–81. George Breslauer's portrait of the initial political strategies of Nikita Khrushchev and Leonid Brezhnev in *Khrushchev and Brezhnev as Leaders: Building Authority in Soviet Politics*, Allen & Unwin, London, 1982, is cast in similar terms. Stalin's strategy is described in many sources, but see particularly Jerry F. Hough and Merle Fainsod, *How the Soviet Union is Governed*, Harvard University Press, Cambridge, MA, 1979, pp. 143–6. A valuable account of the origins of the strategy is T. H. Rigby 'Early Provincial Cliques and the Rise of Stalin', in *Soviet Studies*, 1981, vol. 33, no. 1, January, pp. 3–28.
2   The term 'circular flow of power' originated with Robert V. Daniels. See his 'Soviet Politics since Khrushchev', in John W. Strong (ed.), *The Soviet union under Brezhnev and Kosygin*, Van Nostrand-Reinhold, New York, 1971, pp. 22–3. Jerry Hough comments on the applicability of the theory in the various successions in *How the Soviet Union is Governed*, pp. 145, 200, 213, 454, and 455.
3   See Thane Gustafson and Dawn Mann, 'Gorbachev's First Year: Building Power and Authority'. *Problems of Communism* (Washington, DC), 1986, vol. XXXVI, no. 4, May–June, p. 16, and S. Bialer and J. Afferica, 'The Genesis of Gorbachev's World', *Foreign Affairs* (New York), 1985, vol. 64, no. 3, p. 620.
4   See Gustafson and Mann, loc. cit.; also Elizabeth Teague, 'Turnover in the Soviet Elite under Gorbachev; Implications for Soviet Politics', *Radio Liberty Research Bulletin* (Munich), 1986, Supplement 1/86, 8 July.
5   Yakovlev and Yazov are clearly Gorbachev choices, since their rise is unambiguously tied to Gorbachev's patronage. Slyun'kov's career, on the other hand, is closely associated with that of Nikolai Ryzhkov. Slyun'kov's official pronouncements on economic reform, however, line up closely with Gorbachev's positions. Nikonov's promotion is the most ambiguous of the four, but he presumably gained Gorbachev's good opinion when he was Deputy Minister of Agriculture, from 1979 to 1983; Nikonov has no apparent ties to any other patron (unless one considers Ligachev, who appears to have added agriculture to his portfolio at the beginning of 1987 – see E. Ligachev, 'The Human Factor, Economic Accountability, and *Perestroika* in the Agroindustrial Complex', *Kommunist* (Moscow), 1987, no. 4, March, pp. 28–42).

6   M. S. Gorbachev, 'Youth – The Creative Force of Revolutionary Renewal', *Pravda* (Moscow), 17 April 1987.

7   Gorbachev's speech to the 8th Trade Union Congress. '*Perestroika* – A Vital Concern of the Nation', *Pravda*, 26 February 1987.

8   Zaikov was speaking to an audience in Czechoslovakia. See *Pravda* (Bratislava), 5 March 1987, trans. in Foreign Broadcast Information Service, *Daily Report: Soviet Union* (Washington, DC) 11 March 1987, p. F/3. In particular, it is known that there were disagreements over *glasnost'*, Gorbachev's policy of openness. See, e.g., V. V. Karpov, 'Act! Act in a Creative Manner!', *Literaturnaya Gazeta* (Moscow), 4 February 1987.

9   *Pravda*, 20 February 1987.

10 See 'Resolution of the CC CPSU Plenum On Restructuring and the Cadre Policy of the Party', *Pravda*, 29 January 1987.

11 Gorbachev's statement at a preparatory meeting on economic reform held at Central Committee headquarters on 8 and 9 June 1987. See the TASS account as published in *Pravda*, 13 June 1987 under the title of 'The Fundamental Question of *Perestroika*'.

12 *O korrenoi perestroike upravleniya ekonomiki: sbornik dokumentov (On a Fundamental Restructuring of the Management of the Economy: A Collection of Documents)*, Politizdat, Moscow, 1987.

13 See *Ustav Kommunisticheskoi Partii Sovetskogo Soyuza* (Rules of Communist Party of the Soviet Union – hereafter *Party Rules*), adopted 1 March 1986, Section 4, Par. 38, in *Pravda*, 7 March 1986.

14 For elaboration on the principle that Central Committee status is awarded to holders of certain job slots, rather than the reverse, see Robert V. Daniels, 'Office Holding and Elite Status: The Central Committee of the CPSU', in Paul Cocks, Robert V. Daniels, and Nancy Whittier Heer (eds), *The Dynamics of Soviet Politics*, 1977, Harvard University Press, Cambridge, MA, pp. 77–9.

15 Gorbachev's speech to the June CC CPSU Plenum, *Pravda*, 26 June 1987.

16 Ibid.

17 See V. Malyaev and T. Popov, 'The All-Union Party Conference', *Partiinaya Zhizn'* (Moscow), 1987, no. 14, July, pp. 30–32.

18 *Party Rules*, op. cit., Sect. 4, par. 40.

19 The 1939 party rules were adopted by the 18th CPSU Congress and remained theoretically in force until new rules were adopted at the 19th CPSU Congress in 1952. The latter did not provide for party conferences at all, and it was not until the 23rd CPSU Congress in 1966 that the provisions for holding party conferences returned to the party statues. In the 1939 rules, Central Committee members not selected as delegates to party conferences could attend, but with a consultative vote only. See Malyaev and Popov, loc. cit.

20 Speech to June Plenum, Loc. cit.

21 This is true of Lev Zaikov, one of several highly placed Leningraders who switched their allegiance from Grigorii Romanov and joined Gorbachev's bandwagon in 1985. Aleksandr Yakovlev has had clear ties to Gorbachev since the two men met in Canada in 1983. Nikolai Slyun'kov is a less clear case.

22 Gustafson and Mann, op. cit., p. 8.

23 See Paul Cocks, 'Soviet Science and Technology Strategy; Borrowing from the Defense Sector', paper presented at the Annual Meeting of the American Association for the Advancement of Slavic Studies, New Orleans, November 1986.

24 This count includes all changes through 1 August 1987.

25 The 1986 yearbook of the *Great Soviet Encyclopaedia* covers 1985 and thus did not include biographical information on new members of the Central Committee (and hence on the new regional party first secretaries). Presumably this information will appear in the 1987 edition.

26 As John H. Miller observes, this administrative device has actually gained in use throughout the post-Stalin period with the brief exception of a few years under Khrushchev, and it represented a major exception to Brezhnev's avowed policy of local recruitment of cadres. See Miller, 'Cadres Policy in Nationality Areas: Recruitment of CPSU First and Second Secretaries in non-Russian Republics of the USSR', *Soviet Studies*, 1977, January, pp. 3–36.

27 As of 1 August, 1987.

28 At the same time, it might be noted that several scholars have argued that the real power of the second secretary over local cadres appointments may actually be fairly weak. See, e.g., Miller, loc. cit., and Selnik, 'The Ethnic and Political Determinants of Elite Recruitment in the Soviet National Republics: The Uzbek Soviet Elite, 1952–1987', unpublished PhD dissertation, Columbia University, NY, 1984.

29 See, e.g., Philip Taubman, 'Gorbachev Pushes to Win Control in Ukraine', *The New York Times*, 22 March 1987.

30 See Roman Solchanyk, 'A Gorbachev-Inspired Purge in Ukraine?' RFE–RL, *Radio Liberty Research*, RL 164/87, 2 April 1987.

31 Shcherbitskii, KGB Chairman Viktor Chebrikov, and USSR Minister of Internal Affairs Aleksandr Vlasov all responded to *Pravda* articles concerning the 'Berkhin affair'. See *Pravda*, 8 and 30 January, 1987.

32 See *Pravda Ukrainy* (Kiev), 12 June 1987.

33 A. Salutskii, 'One's Own and Strangers', *Pravda* 14 January 1987; and Yu. Makhrin, 'Renewal', *Pravda*, 14 January 1987.

34 On Razumovskii's role, see Martin Walker, 'New Struggle in Run-Up to Soviet Party Conference', *The Guardian*, 5 August 1987. On developments in Bashkiriya, see *Pravda*, 11 and 24 June 1987.

35 An earlier and slightly longer version of this chapter was published as 'Gorbachev's Next Gamble,' *Problems of Communism*, 1987, vol. 36, no. 4, pp. 1–21.

36 Michel Tatu, *Gorbatchev: l'URSS Va-t-elle Changer?*, 1987, Editions du Centurion/Le Monde, Paris, p. 229. Tatu's assumption is that a newly-minted General Secretary could not have had the power to make his own appointments within a month of his election, and therefore the promotions of Ryzhkov, Ligachev, and Chebrikov in April 1985 must have been part of the same 'package deal' that gave Gorbachev his job. In contrast, Jerry Hough argues that Gorbachev won his own election from his Politburo colleagues through his strength in the Central Committee, and that the April promotions were the result of Gorbachev's alliance with the 'Kirilenko machine'. The two interpretations are not entirely incompatible, but on balance we find Tatu's more plausible. (See Jerry Hough, 'Gorbachev Consolidating Power', *Problems of Communism*, 1987, vol. 26, no. 4, July–August, p. 28.)

37 Tatu, p. 239.

38 Tatu, p. 241–3.

39 Michel Tatu and Daniel Vernet, 'Un entretien avec le numero deux sovietique', *Le Monde*, 4 December 1987.

40 Peter Reddaway, 'The Battle for Moscow', *The New Republic*, 1 February 1988, p. 34.

41   Tatu, pp. 225–7.
42   On the modernization of Leningrad and the impact of the Romanov years, see Blair Ruble, *Leningrad:Shaping the Face of a Soviet City* (forthcoming).
43   On this point, see Ed A. Hewett, *Reforming the Soviet Economy:Equality vs. Efficiency* 1988, The Brookings Institution, Washington, D.C., Chapter 7. Also, we must not forget that some of Gorbachev's economic advisors are more liberal than their boss, who is still a very recent and visibly ambivalent convert to the notion of market and shows little real understanding of the nature and proper functions of price.
44   After about half of the meetings had taken place, Party secretary and candidate Politburo member Razumovskii gave an interim report: at the PPO level, more than 57000 members of bureaux and party commmittees had been replaced and over 13000 secretaries recalled. At higher levels, 200 members of raikom and gorkom bureaux were removed. See, G.P. Razumovskii, 'Partiinyi komitet i perestroika', *Pravda*, 24 December 1987. At the PPO level, this amounts to about one person for every eight PPOs; at the gorkom and raikom levels, one official for every 22 gorkom/raikom committees.
45   Reddaway, p. 36, Tatu, pp. 246–7.
46   Tatu, p. 248, suggests that as late as 3 November an effort was being made to keep Eltsin at the head of the gorkom, and that his fate was not decided until 10 November, at a full meeting of the Politburo. Clearly, if Gorbachev fought hard for his man and lost, that would make the implied loss to himself far more damaging than if he had turned decisively against Eltsin on 21 October.
47   See Timothy Colton, 'The Moscow Party Organization and Soviet Politics', *Problems of Communism*, March/April 1988.
48   Tatu, p. 244.
49   *Pravda*, 13 November 1987.
50   Tatu, p. 219.

3. The General Secretary, the Central Party Secretariat and the Apparat

Ronald J. Hill and Alexander Rahr

It is commonplace to observe that the primary need of a newly-elected Soviet leader is to re-fashion the 'team' (of which he is himself a part) inherited from his predecessor. The Central Committee, Politburo and party Secretariat he inherits are, by definition, not of his own choosing.[1] Among these, the Politburo is usually paid the greatest attention, and not without reason. It comprises the men who collectively rule the Soviet Union. They perform the functions of a Cabinet, ordering priorities and deciding policy, and involving themselves directly in foreign affairs. The Politburo is therefore a crucially important body whose influence cannot be denied. As pointed out by Gustafson and Mann, on attaining office, any General Secretary has to win the backing of a majority of its members. However, concentration on the Politburo as the source of the General Secretary's power may prompt a misleading interpretation of the political summit in the Soviet Union. Other central institutions – notably the Secretariat and the *apparat* (administrative apparatus), which function alongside the Politburo in the process of policy making and implementation – are of the utmost significance.

THE SIGNIFICANCE OF THE CENTRAL PARTY APPARATUS

The Central Committee consists of two 'pillars', as it were. On the one hand, there are the *elected* leadership organs: the Central Committee and the Central Auditing Commission. On the other hand, there are the *appointed* party officials: the party's 'civil servants' in the various Central Committee departments. The members and candidate members of the Central Committee elected at the party congress – constituting the first 'pillar' – are summoned to the Kremlin only once or twice a year and are not involved in day-to-day decision making. The second 'pillar', therefore, is all-important, and is the focus of this chapter: the elected and appointed officials who work – in some cases for a lifetime – in the branches of the huge central party apparatus. Their role in the Soviet system is easily underestimated.

The Central Committee departments are first of all filters through which information passes from the ministries and the lower party bodies to the Politburo. They have a permanent staff estimated at over a thousand *apparatchiki*. Every department has a department head or chief, with one or two first deputy and several deputy heads under him, their number reflecting the size and importance of the department. The deputy heads are in charge of sub-departments or sectors (*podotdely* or *sektory*), which consist of instructors (*instruktory*), inspectors (*inspektory*), lectors, consultants, research assistants (*referenty*) and senior officials (*otvetstvennye rabotniki*).[2]

It is said that Georgii Oganov, head of the Central Committee press sector, once asserted that the Soviet Union would never have a better General Secretary than Leonid Brezhnev. Asked to elaborate on this statement, Oganov explained that, throughout his leadership, Brezhnev never returned a single document to the Central Committee apparatus, but signed everything passed to him by these officials.[3] Thus it was that, under Brezhnev, a lowly instructor of the Central Committee often enjoyed more power than a Soviet minister.

It is in the Secretariat, however, that the power to control the levers of the party apparatus is located. Through the various departments of the *apparat*, the Secretariat controls the execution of directives issued by the Politburo at all levels and has complete authority in running the country's affairs: selecting cadres and controlling ministries, state committees and provincial party organs.[4]

In Stalin's day, indeed, it was the real centre of power.[5] The Politburo was treated with contempt, and scarcely permitted to function as a ruling body. In recent decades, with the restoration of more businesslike functioning to the Politburo, and its assumption of the role of collective decision maker, the Secretariat has been paid rather less attention. After all, its members enjoy less public prominence than do the members of the Politburo, and, in any case, it is the Politburo that ultimately decides policy.

In a general way, the Secretariat's importance has correctly been related to the position of the General Secretary. As Armstrong notes, it was the acquisition of the position of head of the Secretariat that permitted both Stalin and Khrushchev to acquire 'commanding positions' in the Soviet political system.[6] Moreover, on the deaths of Brezhnev, Andropov and Chernenko, observers stressed the significance of dual membership of Politburo and Secretariat as the one crucial qualification for potential successors.[7] Furthermore, its functioning appears to have become more regular: since Brezhnev's day, party congresses have been given reports of the frequency of the Secretariat's meetings – it meets regularly on Wednesdays, in advance of the Thursday meetings of the Politburo. The Secretariat's real significance relates to its role in supervising the *nomenklatura* system of staffing the apparatus of both party and state, and in assisting with the formulation of policy and supervising its implementation.

There is a further consideration that affects political relationships among those at the pinnacle of the system. In order to rise in the hierarchy, each Secretary tries to gain influence by bringing as many departments as possible under his own jurisdiction. The party's so-called Second Secretary – at present Egor Ligachev – supervises the day-to-day work of the entire central party apparatus with its twenty-one departments. In fact, the position of 'Second Secretary' in the party apparatus is so powerful that it may even rival that of the General Secretary. Gorbachev, for example, upon becoming 'Second Secretary' under Chernenko, assumed responsibility for ideology, cadres, the party apparatus, economics and agriculture, and supervised the work of twenty departments (out of a total of twenty-four in 1984).

The higher a Secretary's position in the hierarchy, the broader and more important is his sphere of responsibility in the central party apparatus. A Secretary who is simultaneously a Politburo member has a number of 'junior' Secretaries subordinate to him. 'Junior' Secretaries are in turn in charge of specific Central Committee departments, or themselves head a department if the given department is of particular importance.[8] Such 'major' departments are the Economic Department, the Party-Organizational Work Department, the International Department, and the Department for Liaison with Communist and Workers' Parties of the Socialist Countries (i.e. ruling parties).

In this chapter, we consider changes in the composition of the Secretariat since the political demise of Khrushchev, and examine the scope of Gorbachev's re-staffing exercise.[9]

THE SECRETARIAT UNDER BREZHNEV

In the Brezhnev period certain distinct phases can be identified in the General Secretary's[10] initial team-building and subsequent adjustment. First, he prepared the ground in the period until his first congress (the 23rd, in 1966), at which what can be thought of as 'Brezhnev's team' was placed in office. In the second phase, piecemeal changes strengthened his position prior to a lengthy stable period lasting from 1968 until the 25th Congress in 1976. After that, in the third phase, cronyism set in, and the ageing

Brezhnev brought in old associates, and the whole managerial 'team' – Politburo, Secretariat and *apparat* – grew steadily older and more infirm as the years passed. The one bright spot in this period was the promotion from Stavropol to Moscow of Mikhail Gorbachev in November 1978.

The practice of engaging in a major reshuffle among the occupants of positions in the central apparatus following the emergence of a new party leader is an established feature of the Soviet political process, as experience under Brezhnev demonstrates. Immediately after succeeding Khrushchev in 1964, he set about ousting Khrushchev's men and placing his own supporters in key positions within the *apparat*: by the end of the following year it was firmly in the hands of his or Suslov's men. The changes included, most prominently, the release in November 1964 of Khrushchev's putative successor, Frol Kozlov, from both the Politburo and the Secretariat for reasons of health (he died in January 1965 after a serious illness); the same plenum removed Vasilii Polyakov from the Secretariat; Leonid Il'ichev left the Secretariat on 26 March 1965, and was replaced by Dmitrii Ustinov; a further Secretary from the Khrushchev era, Vitalii Titov, lost his position in September 1965, following his transfer to party work in Kazakhstan; and Polyakov's replacement as head of the Agriculture department, Fedor Kulakov, became a Secretary; just over two months later, on 6 December, came the appointment of Ivan Kapitonov, in charge of party cadres – a significant appointment on the eve of the twenty-third congress, since it allowed a Brezhnev ally to supervise the appointment of officials throughout the CPSU structure and the selection of congress delegates in the party election campaign that preceded the 23rd Congress. Just three days later, Nikolai Podgorny lost his secretaryship on election as State President (Chairman of the USSR Supreme Soviet Presidium), the post vacated by Anastas Mikoyan. Other significant appointments included those of Konstantin Chernenko (to head the General Department), Georgii Pavlov (business manager), Sergei Trapeznikov (science and educational institutions), Vasilii Shauro (culture), Yakov Kabkov (trade and consumer services), Vladimir Stepakov (propaganda), Pavel Sizov (light and food industries), and Viktor Bushuev (chemical industry).

The 23rd CPSU Congress convened on 29 March 1966, and the Central Committee's leading bodies were elected on 8 March (see Table 3.1). The Secretariat elected along with the new Politburo comprised 11 men, some of whom had, of course, served under Khrushchev, but several of whom had been brought in under the leadership of Brezhnev: Ustinov, Kapitonov, Kulakov, and Andrei Kirilenko, newly elected at the Congress. The longest-serving member of the Secretariat, seen by some as the *eminence grise* behind the power of Brezhnev and Kosygin,[11] was Mikhail Suslov, who had already served 19 years as a Secretary, and was to remain until his death in January 1982, acquiring a degree of influence that belied his

Table 3.1: Secretariat elected at the twenty-third Congress, March 1966

Name	Date of Birth	Age	Nationality	Politburo status*	Responsibility	Social origin	Joined CPSU	Joined Secretariat
Brezhnev, L. I.	1906	60	Russian	F	Gen. Secretary	Peasant	1931	1952
Andropov, Yu. V.	1914	52	Russian	N	Int. Dept.	White collar	1939	1962
Demichev, P. N.	1918	48	Russian	C	Ideology	Worker	1939	1956
Kapitonov, I. V.	1915	51	Russian	N	Cadres	Peasant	1939	1965
Kirilenko, A. P.	1906	60	Russian	F	Cadres; Economy	Worker	1931	1966
Kulakov, F. D.	1918	48	Russian	N	Agric. Dept.	Peasant	1940	1965
Ponomarev, B. N.	1905	61	Russian	N	Int. Dept.	White collar	1919	1961
Rudakov, A. P.	1910	56	Russian	N	Ind. & Const.	?	1931	1962
Suslov, M. A.	1902	64	Russian	F	Ideology	Peasant	1921	1947
Ustinov, D. F.	1908	58	Russian	C	Def. Ind.	Worker	1927	1965
Shelepin, A. N.	1918	48	Russian	F	?	Worker	1940	1961

*F = Full   C = Candidate   N = Not a member

apparent modesty and asceticism. All were of Russian nationality – a feature of the Secretariat that marks it off from practically all other institutions, including the Politburo: subsequent decades have brought in only two non-Russians – both of them Belorussian – and then not simultaneously.

In 1966, the members' ages ranged from 48 to 64, with an average of 55. Their social origins were principally peasant (four known cases) or worker (four cases), with two white collar (information on the social origins of Rudakov is unavailable). All had acquired tertiary education, with a preponderance of engineering or technical training: exceptions were Kulakov (agriculture), Suslov (economics), Ponomarev (history) and Shelepin (humanities). Their party membership ranged from 26 years (in the cases of Kulakov and Shelepin, who joined the party in 1940) to 47 years (Ponomarev, who claimed to have become a communist in 1919, at the age of 14); three members (Brezhnev, Kirilenko and Rudakov) had joined in 1931 (a 'vintage' year that also brought Konstantin Chernenko, Andrei Gromyko, Nikolai Shchelokov, Sergei Trapeznikov and other prominent figures of the 1970s: it was also coincidentally the year of Gorbachev's birth); a further three (Andropov, Petr Demichev and Kapitonov) had entered the party's ranks in 1939, a year of rapid recruitment following the purges, producing a whole crop of 'successes' of the Brezhnev era, including Nikolai Baibakov, Viktor Grishin, Ivan Kapitonov, Dinmukhamed Kunaev, Dmitrii Polyanskii, and Sharaf Rashidov.

They had accumulated substantial service in central party institutions. Their experience as members of the Secretariat varied from Suslov's 19 years to the newly elected Kirilenko; Brezhnev, the General Secretary had enjoyed intermittent membership from 1952 (prior to his posting to Moldavia as First Secretary), and Demichev since 1956. Four – Andropov, Ponomarev, Rudakov and Shelepin – were Khrushchev appointees of 1961 and 1962; the remainder (Kapitonov, Kulakov, and Ustinov – together with Kirilenko) were all first appointed to a Central Committee secretaryship under Brezhnev. Their membership of the Central Committee likewise went back some years: Suslov, again the man of greatest experience, had served since 1941 – already a quarter of a century. Five members had joined the Committee at Stalin's last party congress (the 19th, in 1952), and two at the historic twentieth (1956), when the anti-Stalin campaign was launched; the remaining three had reached this status at the 22nd Congress of 1961 (including the future General Secretary, Yuri Andropov). Following the 23rd Congress, six Secretaries were simultaneously members of the Politburo, four as members and two as candidates.

When Secretaries' previous careers are analysed, we find signs of the origins of what was to become known as Brezhnev's 'Dnepropetrovsk mafia': Kirilenko, brought into the Secretariat at the twenty-third congress, had served as Dnepropetrovsk *obkom* first secretary a decade after Brezhnev had done so. Two members (Andropov and Shelepin) had established their political careers in the Komsomol; two (Demichev and Kapitonov) had served in the post of Moscow *gorkom* first secretary, in the days before that position acquired its virtually *ex officio* association with full or candidate membership of the Politburo; two others (Suslov and Kulakov) had served – albeit with a significant gap between their tenures – as first secretary of the Stavropol *kraikom* (a position from which Gorbachev was later to rise to national prominence); Shelepin had been chairman of the KGB, the post to which Andropov was shortly to be transferred. Ustinov, Secretary in charge of co-ordinating defence-related industries, was unique among the Secretaries in never having held a significant party post: his rise had been entirely through the armaments and defence-related branch of the state administration (and he was eventually transferred from the Secretariat to become USSR Minister of Defence).

During the phase following the 23rd Congress, piecemeal changes affected the composition of the Secretariat, as deaths and the assignment of members to new duties created opportunities for further adjustment. The Secretary responsible for heavy industry, A. P. Rudakov, died on 10 July 1966 after a protracted illness, and was replaced on 13 December by M. S. Solomentsev, until then first secretary of the Rostov-on-Don *obkom*. Half a year later, in June 1967, the Secretary in charge of relations with socialist countries, Andropov, left the Secretariat, a month after becoming chairman of the KGB. These changes were a prelude to what was to come over the summer, when in a complex series of moves Viktor Grishin became first secretary of Moscow *gorkom*, and his position as chairman of the trade union council was taken by Shelepin, who lost his place on the Secretariat on 26 September. In political terms this was a victory for the 'moderate' Brezhnev against the much tougher group surrounding Shelepin, and the process of undermining Shelepin's power was completed nearly eight years later, on 16 April 1975: then, he was removed from the Politburo 'at his own request', following a visit to Britain in which he encountered hostile demonstrations and generated much bad publicity; in May 1975 he lost his trade union post.

By the end of September 1967, therefore, barely a year and a half after the party congress, the Secretariat had lost Rudakov, Andropov and Shelepin, and gained Solomentsev. It now consisted of nine members, all Russians, with an average age of 56; three Secretaries were voting members of the Politburo, and two were candidate members. The Socialist Countries department needed a head, following Andropov's departure, and there was scope for Brezhnev to bring in a protégé in place of the hostile Shelepin. On 10 April 1968, at a plenum that discussed problems of the solidarity of the world communist movement, a new Secretary was appointed to head the department: Konstantin Katushev, first secretary of the Gorky *obkom*, aged 41 – nearly a decade younger than the next youngest members of the Secretariat. Katushev's appointment symbolized the start of an extended transition to a new generation of party leaders. A teenager during the Second World War, he joined the party in 1952 near the end of Stalin's rule. His training in mechanical engineering linked him with his older colleagues – but his practical experiences as an automobile designer already identified him with modern rather than traditional forms of engineering. His formative political experiences, moreover, were those of a different generation: his party career was launched in 1957 when the anti-Stalin campaign was under way. He rose to prominence in December 1965, when, following a successful engineering and party career in Gorky city, he was elected *obkom* first secretary, in the presence of Brezhnev himself, at the age of only 38;[12] at the 23rd Congress he joined the Central Committee as a full member. The common interpretation of these events identifies Katushev as a client of Brezhnev; he has also, however, been seen as a protégé of Suslov.[13] This was, by Soviet standards, a meteoric rise, which culminated in his translation to Moscow and the Central Committee Secretariat after only 18 months in the *obkom* post.

Although he may still have had rivals and even opponents among his Politburo colleagues, Brezhnev now clearly had a Secretariat with which he could comfortably work, for its composition remained unchanged through the 24th Congress in April and beyond. Indeed, until the 25th Congress, in 1976, changes were few. In the autumn of 1971, Solomentsev was appointed Prime Minister of the RSFSR in succession to Gennadii Voronov (later ousted from the Politburo), and simultaneously entered the Politburo as a candidate member. In May 1972, Ponomarev, Secretary in charge of the International Department, became a non-voting Politburo member. At the end of that year, the Siberian, Vladimir Dolgikh, was brought in from the Krasnoyarsk *kraikom* to take over Solomentsev's former position as head of the Heavy Industry Department, at the age of 48 the central leadership's second youngest member. At the plenum of 26–27 April 1973, in the major reconstruction that brought the KGB chairman (Andropov), the Foreign Minister (Gromyko) and the Defence Minister (Grechko) into the Politburo as full members, and the Leningrad *obkom* first secretary, Grigorii Romanov, as a candidate member, no changes were made to the Secretariat. Finally, on 16 December 1974, Demichev, after serving on the Secretariat since 1956 and continuously since 1961, with responsibility for internal ideological questions, was relieved of that position following his appointment as USSR Minister of Culture a month earlier.

The mid-1970s saw the onset of the cronyism that characterized Leonid Brezhnev's last years in office. At the plenum that concluded the 25th Congress, on 5 March 1976, significant changes were made to both the membership of the Secretariat and its presentation. This inaugurated a lengthy period of change after several years of relative stability in this central party institution.

Two new members were brought in. The first was Mikhail Zimyanin, a Belorussian, previously editor-in-chief of *Pravda*, although he had enjoyed a widely varied career since joining the party in the 'classic' year of 1939. He was given responsibilities in the area of propaganda, thereby effectively becoming a delayed replacement for Demichev, and perhaps also serving as a Brezhnevite counterweight to Suslov, the acknowledged 'chief ideologist' (however, other analysts assert a close relationship between the two: Suslov too had served as editor of the party newspaper).[14] The second appointment, Konstantin Chernenko, a party member of the 1931 vintage, was an old Brezhnev associate, having worked alongside him in the apparatus in Moldavia in the early 1950s; in 1956, when Brezhnev became a Central Committee Secretary after his period in Kazakhstan, Chernenko was brought to Moscow to head the central *agitprop* department; and when Brezhnev took the post of Supreme Soviet Presidium chairman, in 1960, Chernenko crossed to a position in that body; finally, following Brezhnev's election to the supreme party post, Chernenko was placed in charge of the Central Committee General department, which kept him exceptionally close to the General Secretary and gave him access to a vast amount of material that went before the Politburo. As Central Committee Secretary from March 1976, he continued to head that department, serving his patron loyally; he was rewarded with candidate membership of the Politburo in October 1977 and full membership some fourteen months later, and was a strong contender for Brezhnev's mantle in November 1982.

The addition of these two Secretaries, both well turned sixty (Zimyanin was 62, Chernenko 65 in 1976), was a symptom of the ageing of the central leadership that became chronic thereafter. At the conclusion of the 25th Congress, the average age of the Secretariat had risen to 63 years, with eight of the eleven members already over 60, and some already in their seventies – a trend that paralleled the ageing of the Politburo. Compared with a decade earlier, the Secretariat was on average eight years older.

A further interesting feature appeared at the congress of 1976: for the first time the members of the Secretariat were listed in order of rank, with Brezhnev at the top, followed by Suslov and Kirilenko, and the new Secretaries, Zimyanin and Chernenko, at the foot of the list. This feature, repeated on subsequent occasions, permitted observers to note changes in individuals' relative positions. In 1976 Zimyanin ranked above Chernenko: however, Chernenko's rapid advancement as Brezhnev's right-hand man placed him in contention for the leadership in November 1982.

The latter years of Brezhnev's rule brought further changes. Marshal Grechko, the Defence Minister, died on 26 April 1976, and was replaced by the Secretary in charge of armaments, Ustinov, who shortly thereafter joined the Politburo; he was never formally released from the Secretariat,[15] but was replaced by Yakov Ryabov, a protégé or client of Kirilenko, under whom he had served in the Sverdlovsk *oblast* party organization.

Further change came on 24 May 1977, when following a challenge to Brezhnev supposedly over his proposal to become president, Podgorny was dropped from the Politburo. Simultaneously, changes were made in the composition of the Secretariat. Katushev, the 'blue-eyed boy' of a decade earlier, was relieved following transfer to a less prestigious post in Comecon: he was later sent to Havana as ambassador, but returned in 1985 to the modest position of chairman of the state committee for foreign economic relations. Also, one of Brezhnev's personal aides, Konstantin Rusakov, joined the Secretariat at the age of 57, after a richly varied career, and now took over as head of the Department for Liaison with ruling communist parties. The pattern of Brezhnev steadily re-building the strength of his own supporters in the Secretariat is clear, and it continued at the next plenum, on 3 October, when Chernenko was elected a Politburo candidate member, improving his rank above Kapitonov and probably Ponomarev, both of whom had been Secretaries since the 1960s.

The death, possibly by suicide,[16] of Kulakov, Secretary in charge of the Agriculture Department, on 17 July 1978, led later in the year to an appointment of great significance. In a major shake-out at the plenum of 27 November, First Deputy Prime Minister Nikolai Tikhonov and the Georgian First Secretary Eduard Shevardnadze became Politburo candidate members, while First Deputy Prime Minister Kirill Mazurov was dropped from the Politburo, and Chernenko was raised to full membership, placing him now clearly ahead of Ponomarev. Finally, the 47-year-old First Secretary of the Stavropol *kraikom*, Mikhail Gorbachev, was brought into the Secretariat and placed in charge of agriculture (he did not, however, head the Agriculture Department). Gorbachev was a protégé of Kulakov, first secretary of the Stavropol *kraikom* in the early 1960s, when Gorbachev headed the Komsomol in the territory, switching to work in the party apparatus during Kulakov's tenure; Gorbachev was also, apparently, well known to Andropov and Suslov, both frequent visitors to the spas of Stavropol territory. The newcomer attracted attention initially because of his youth: he was younger than Dolgikh had been on his appointment in 1972 (although several years older than Katushev in 1978), and the contrast with other leaders was now more striking; he had, moreover, joined the party, like Katushev, in 1952, and his political experience was essentially in the post-Stalin era. He also stood out because of his unusual training: the son of peasants, he had studied law at Moscow State University and followed this with a degree in agriculture; this appointment was thus a further modest step in the erosion of the technically trained leadership. The arrival of a man in his forties had no perceptible impact on the average age of the Secretariat, however, which remained at 63: Ryabov, in charge of defence industries, was now 50, and four of the Secretaries were aged over 70 in 1978. Ryabov, in any case, did not remain much longer in the Secretariat: he was shortly appointed First Deputy Chairman of Gosplan and was relieved of his secretaryship on 17 April 1979. Towards the end of the year, Gorbachev was elected a candidate member of the Politburo, and eleven months later, on 27 October 1980, raised to full membership.

At the end of the 26th Congress, no changes were made to the composition of the Secretariat, which now contained 10 members, all but one (Zimyanin) of whom were Russians. Gorbachev was still the youngest, at 49, seven years younger than Dolgikh; four members were in their sixties and four in their seventies, including the patently sick Brezhnev, and Suslov, the eldest of the central leaders; the average age was now 66. Chernenko ranked fourth, after Brezhnev, Suslov and Kirilenko, followed by Gorbachev as the fifth Secretary who was a Politburo full member. The rapid promotion of the energetic Gorbachev was the only clear sign of dynamism in a party leadership that was visibly crumbling. The death of Suslov on 25 January 1982 took away the potential 'king-maker' in the event of Brezhnev's death, and the size of the Secretariat declined to nine. On 24 May, Dolgikh was made a candidate member of the Politburo, elevating him above Kapitonov, and, most significantly, Yuri Andropov relinquished the post of chairman of the KGB, held since 1967, and returned to the Secretariat, where, as a voting member of the Politburo, he now ranked fourth. This was a rather transparent attempt by Andropov to place himself within striking distance of the General Secretaryship by occupying positions on both the Politburo and the Secretariat, while at the same time relieving himself of the supposed handicap of his fifteen years' close association with the security police.[17] This body of ten men supervised the party until Brezhnev's death half a year later. The period since then, into 1987, has witnessed a rapid turnover among the members of the Secretariat, and of the senior officials in the *apparat*, associated with the swift succession of General Secretaries and, more especially, Gorbachev's consolidation of his political position since March 1985.

TWO INTERREGNUMS

After Brezhnev's death in 1982, the apparatus underwent a much-needed thorough overhaul, as Andropov put through his own personnel policy in the central apparatus, replacing seven department heads (out of a total of twenty-three in 1983). In the Secretariat, too, significant changes came swiftly. Within days of Brezhnev's death, Kirilenko was gently forced into retirement. Once the Kremlin's second-in-command, and a man with a substantial string of political clients, his position had waned substantially during 1982, and his retirement was inevitable. He was the same age as Brezhnev had been, with the same length of party membership and only four years' less membership of the Central Committee; his departure left only Chernenko among the Secretaries who had joined the party in 1931, and eroded the position of Brezhnev's former associates in his pre-war days in Ukraine. Andropov clearly had no need for a third, elderly colleague who was in any case fading politically.

The new leader had to move swiftly to consolidate his own position and attempt to shake up the country after the drift and inertia of the late years of Brezhnev's rule: Andropov was already 68 years old, and believed to be in indifferent health – although there was no immediate indication that he might suffer a massive renal failure within three months. He also had to make some provision for the inevitable succession to a new generation, preparations for which could not be delayed indefinitely. While a Politburo of elderly politicians might direct policy formulation (as the recent experience of China had shown), the Secretariat, more concerned with everyday administration, ought to be staffed by energetic individuals, some of whom, at any rate, would inevitably be called on to take over responsibility for the country in the shorter rather than the longer term. With the retirement of Kirilenko, a new Secretary was appointed the Secretariat: Nikolai Ryzhkov, an impressive industrial manager from the Urals city of Sverdlovsk, who had more recently served as a deputy chairman of Gosplan. These two changes heralded some rejuvenation: the average age of the Secretariat fell two years to 64. Nevertheless, of the nine current members, only three were under 60 years of age, with Ponomarev and Chernenko over 70, and Andropov and Zimyanin 68 (Zimyanin's sixty-eighth birthday was on the previous day).

Andropov's rapid decline in physical health and stamina must have retarded the pace of his intended political and personnel changes. At the plenum of 14 June 1983, the size of the Secretariat was restored to ten, when Romanov, a full member of the Politburo since 1976, with an independent political base in the Leningrad region, was made a Secretary and given responsibility for party administration and industry. He was 60 years old, four years younger than the average for the Secretariat, and now ranked fourth after Andropov, Chernenko and Gorbachev: at least one Western commentator now marked him as a serious contender for the succession if Andropov were to die.[18] Gorbachev's range of responsibilities, too, was widened to include more general questions of the economy in addition to agriculture. At the end of the year, another new Secretary was appointed: Egor Ligachev, the First Secretary of the Tomsk *obkom*; he was now placed in charge of party-organizational work, taking over the management of the party's personnel policy from Kapitonov, who switched to light industry. Under Andropov, therefore, the Secretariat had its depleted numbers restored and its complexion somewhat rejuvenated by bringing in three new members (two of them already turned 60, however). It also underwent a reallocation of responsibilities. In addition to the changes already noted, Dolgikh added energy questions to his portfolio, while Chernenko spoke on ideology and propaganda-related themes – a potentially important function given the 'leader's' need to establish a measure of control over the development of the ideology as a means of setting the political agenda and securing his political position.[19]

Had Andropov enjoyed full vigour, he might have moved to relieve the central Secretariat (and Politburo) of more of the elderly, faded talent of the Brezhnev era: Ponomarev, for example, born in 1905, the long-standing head of the International Department; probably Chernenko, a Brezhnev crony who had plainly been Brezhnev's favoured successor; perhaps also Zimyanin, the 69-year-old propaganda chief, whose inflexible approach seemed inappropriate in a regime that wished to change its stance in a number of areas, including how it interpreted itself and projected itself to the world. The death of Andropov on 9 February 1984, and the attendant unwillingness of the senior politicians in the Kremlin (notably the veteran Foreign Minister, Andrei Gromyko, and the Defence Minister and former Secretary, Dmitrii Ustinov) to hand over the reins of power to a physically or politically younger generation, led to a Brezhnevite restoration, with the selection of Konstantin Chernenko as General Secretary – one of the 'class of 1931' in which Gromyko, Brezhnev, Kirilenko and so many others had graduated. Physically ailing from the moment he took office, unable or unwilling to make changes to the leading team, Chernenko presided over a tired, elderly leadership while Gorbachev, it later emerged, exercised a number of the regular functions of the General Secretary, including chairing Politburo meetings. There was little surprise, and a substantial measure of relief, when Gorbachev – along with Romanov the only individual to sit both on the Secretariat and among the voting members of the Politburo – secured election on 11 March 1985.

GORBACHEV'S NEW BROOM

In the mood of urgency to get the country – particularly the economy – moving again, Gorbachev wasted little time in adjusting the membership of the Politburo, the Secretariat and the staffing of the *apparat*; moreover, within a year of his election he enjoyed the prospect of a party congress at which turnover of personnel could be regularly and legitimately engineered.

Gorbachev took over a Secretariat of nine members, including himself, whose average age was approaching 66; only Gorbachev himself and Ryzhkov were under 60, while Ponomarev had turned 80, and Kapitonov and Zimyanin were past 70. There was obviously a great need for rejuvenation, and scope for restoring the ranks to the normal ten or eleven members. Moreover, from the political point of view, Gorbachev obviously needed to demote or remove rivals and opponents and to advance allies: Romanov, in particular, his defeated rival, had to be got rid of. Gorbachev moved swiftly and deftly to effect changes in the party's top leadership, involving members of both the Politburo and the Secretariat.[20] At the first business plenum after Gorbachev reached office, on 23 April 1985, the Russian republic's minister of agriculture, Viktor Nikonov, possessing a sound agricultural background plus experience of party administration, was appointed to the Secretariat as head of the Central Committee Agriculture Department; and Ligachev was elected to full membership of the Politburo, making him second-in-command, if it is assumed that there was no effective working relationship between Gorbachev and Romanov.

This supposition was confirmed on 1 July, when Romanov left both the Politburo and the Secretariat. Several other changes were made among Gorbachev's close colleagues, including the appointment of two new Secretaries from his own political, if not chronological, generation: Boris Eltsin and Lev Zaikov. Eltsin was born, like Gorbachev, in 1931, and joined the party in 1961, long after the Stalin era had ended. He was associated with the group around Ryzhkov, who had past connections with the engineering city of Sverdlovsk, and who in September took over as Prime Minister following Tikhonov's retirement; at the plenum of October

1985, Ryzhkov was relieved of his responsibilities in the Secretariat. Gorbachev kept up the momentum of change, making significant adjustments to his team only weeks before the party congress. In December 1985, the veteran leader of the Moscow *gorkom*, the former Brezhnev ally Viktor Grishin, was replaced by Eltsin, a rising star whose performance at the party congress in February 1986 placed him firmly on the party's radical reformist wing. At a pre-congress plenum on 18 February, Eltsin was promoted to Politburo candidate membership and released as party Secretary, and Brezhnev's former personal aide, Rusakov, retired owing to genuine deteriorating health. At the end-of-congress plenum, two more stalwarts of the Brezhnev era were honourably moved aside from everyday responsibilities in the top leadership. The first was Ponomarev, who remained on the Central Committee and apparently maintained some link with the Academy of Sciences; he was joined in honourable retirement by Kapitonov, who took Gennadii Sizov's place as chairman of the Party Control Commission, of which he became a member.

Within a year of attaining office, therefore, five members of the inherited Secretariat had been removed or re-deployed; two positions had already been filled; but some positions had remained vacant for some time, giving an opportunity to adopt a radical approach. Gorbachev took that opportunity, displaying both boldness and imagination. Moreover, in announcing the names of the new Central Committee Secretaries, he reverted to the egalitarian practice of reading names (apart from his own!) in alphabetical order (see Table 3.2).[21] Further change came in January 1987, when Zimyanin retired on pension: the last septuagenarian in the Secretariat to depart, the last of the Secretaries to have joined the party in 1939, perhaps also the last clear client of Suslov, the last Secretary to have been born before the revolution, the last to have served on a Central Committee elected under Stalin, and the individual who for over a decade had been the only non-Russian in the Secretariat. His departure may thus be seen as symbolic of a change in political era.

Table 3.2: Secretariat elected at the twenty-seventh Congress, March 1986

Name	Date of Birth	Age	Nationality	Politburo status*	Responsibility	Social origin	Joined CPSU	Joined Secretariat
Gorbachev, M. I.	1931	54	Russian	F	Gen. Secretary	Peasant	1952	1978
Biryukova, A. P.	1929	56	Russian	N	Social policy	Peasant	1956	1986
Dobrynin, A. F.	1919	66	Russian	N	Foreign Relations	Worker	1945	1986
Dolgikh, V. I.	1924	61	Russian	C	Heavy Ind.	White collar	1942	1972
Zaikov, L. N.	1923	62	Russian	N	Defence Ind.	?	1957	1985
Zimyanin, M. V.	1914	71	Belorussian	N	Propaganda	Worker	1939	1976
Ligachev, E. K.	1920	65	Russian	F	Ideology	?	1944	1983
Medvedev, V. A.	1929	56	Russian	N	Educ. & Science	?	1952	1986
Nikonov, V. P.	1929	56	Russian	N	Agric.	Peasant	1954	1985
Razumovskii, G. P.	1936	49	Russian	N	Cadres	?	1961	1986
Yakovlev, A. N.	1923	62	Russian	N	Propaganda	?	1944	1986

* F = Full   C = Candidate   N = Not a member

Zimyanin was replaced by another Belorussian, Nikolai Slyun'kov, first secretary in Belorussia since January 1983, having previously served almost a decade as deputy chairman of Gosplan, for part of that time working under Ryzhkov as first deputy chairman. Another new member of the Secretariat (bringing its size to twelve members, for the first time since late 1976, when there was some doubt about the formal status of Ustinov) was Anatolii Luk'yanov, who had been running the General department of the Central Committee since 1985 after a distinguished career as an academic lawyer: indeed, his student years at Moscow University's law faculty overlapped with Gorbachev's, so conceivably their acquaintanceship goes back to then.

Change continued at the plenum of 25–26 June, which ended with three personnel changes affecting members of the Secretariat, when Yakovlev, Slyun'kov and Nikonov were elevated to voting membership of the Politburo: Slyun'kov had been a candidate member since the 27th Congress, while Yakovlev had attained that status in January 1987, and Nikonov – of the three, the longest-serving member of both the Central Committee and the Secretariat – came straight in as a full member. This means that six of the twelve Secretaries were now voting members of the Politburo, and one (Dolgikh) a candidate member – clearly overtaken by Gorbachev's nominees.

The strategy of reconstructing the leadership team by making adjustments to the Secretariat was further demonstrated by this move, which left in position on the Politburo even the discredited Shcherbitskii and the Brezhnevite Aliev. Of the fourteen voting members of the Politburo – the largest within recent memory – six were also members of the Secretariat, and a seventh Secretary was a Politburo candidate member.

The Secretariat in October 1987 therefore consists of twelve individuals, the vast majority of whom are new to the job: nine of the twelve current members were introduced under Gorbachev; indeed, five were not on the Central Committee even as candidate members until the 27th Congress in 1986. All but Dolgikh (who has headed the Heavy Industry Department since 1972) came into the Secretariat after Gorbachev himself. In another respect, too, Dolgikh is an odd-man-out, since alone among the present members of the Secretariat, he apparently owed some of his earlier advancement to Chernenko. Clearly, his promotion has been unspectacular, and he may be a candidate for early retirement.

The average age is now 60 – half a decade younger than for much of the Brezhnev period – with seven members in their fifties and the remaining five in their sixties: Gorbachev is still the second youngest member (born in 1931). Six members joined the party in the Stalin period, the remainder during Khrushchev's time (including the youngest – Razumovskii – as late as 1961). Clearly, a significant number gained their earliest political experience as citizens in the Stalin era; however, it is apposite to note that only Ligachev and Yakovlev – the one concerned with ideology, the other with propaganda – occupied political posts before 1953.[22] The remainder either began their effective careers after Stalin's death, or were launched on a career in industry or similar economy-related management before switching to the political sector. Dobrynin, as a career diplomat from the late 1940s, who served as ambassador to the United States from 1962 until 1986, followed an unusual route into the Secretariat, and his appointment displays the imaginativeness with which Gorbachev has approached the task of fashioning a team. Similarly, the recruitment of Luk'yanov and Aleksandra Biryukova reveals a refreshing boldness in seeking responsible officers outside the ranks of the career party apparatchiki. Not only are the individuals concerned suitably qualified by their experience in fields relevant to Gorbachev's reformist aspirations, but their lack of base of support acquired in the provincial party *apparat* appears to confirm their dependence on the General Secretary, and hence their support for him and his policies. It may also reflect Gorbachev's undogmatic approach to ideological matters: what is important is that the task of restructuring should be successfully carried through: that demands professional competence above all.

In Biryukova, the Secretariat today contains the first woman for a generation, recruited following a distinguished career in the Soviet trade union organization, which brought candidate membership of the Central Committee in 1971 and full membership five years later. The appointment of a woman was, of course, itself a significant event, given the expressed intention to involve women rather more in the country's public life; her appointment also drew attention to the areas for which she was given responsibility: social policy and light industry. Similarly, Luk'yanov, a prolific writer on questions of the law and soviets (councils), gave hope at least to the scholars who had for many years been urging various kinds of political reforms, about which Gorbachev was now speaking in tones of ever greater urgency.

What can be said, therefore, is that what the Gorbachev Secretariat lacks in experience of work in the central party organs it makes up for in relevant experience and expertise, and also, in view of its age structure, in energy and vigour. There may be scope for further change, but since the death of Brezhnev there has been a massive transformation in the composition of those charged with running the party's affairs.

RESTRUCTURING THE *APPARAT*

Gorbachev's changes have gone way beyond the Politburo and Secretariat, however, striking hard at the leading (but little-known) figures in the *apparat*. By the late summer of 1987, he had appointed nineteen new department heads (the chiefs of the Construction, Economic and General Departments have been changed twice), and replaced more than half of the first deputy heads; only five of the heads nominated before he came to power remained in their posts. These are Nikolai Savinkin, since 1968 head of the Administrative Organs Department, to which senior military personnel, the KGB and the Ministry of Internal Affairs (MVD) are all to some extent subordinated; the Business Manager (*upravlyayushchii delami*), Nikolai Kruchina; and the heads of the departments for Cadres Abroad (Stepan Chervonenko), the Chemical Industry (Venyamin Afonin), and Heavy Industry and Power Engineering (Ivan Yastrebov). Of these five, Afonin and Kruchina had already become Gorbachev's key men in the apparatus under Andropov: Afonin was brought to Moscow from Gorbachev's home region of Stavropol, and Kruchina had worked as first deputy head of the Agriculture Department when Gorbachev occupied the post of Secretary for agriculture, during 1978–1983.

Who are the *apparatchiki* of *perestroika*? what is their background? What criteria were used in their recruitment?

Of the heads of the Central Committee departments appointed under Gorbachev, only three – Arkadii Vol'skii (Department for Machine-Building), Valerii Boldin (General Department) and Oleg Belyakov (Defence Industry Department) – had worked in the central apparatus before 1983. Of nineteen department heads nominated under Gorbachev, eleven (almost three-fifths) transferred to the central apparatus only in the last two years.

Like his mentor Andropov, Gorbachev has conducted a number of reorganizations of the central party apparatus. The Letters Department (headed by Boris Yakovlev), the Agriculture Machine-Building Department (Ivan Sakhnyuk), and the International Information Department (Leonid Zamyatin) – all three created in the late period of Brezhnev's rule – were abolished before the 27th Congress.[23] The duties of the International Information Department are now being performed jointly by the International and the Propaganda Departments, while the Letters Department has been merged into the General Department.

The appointment of a former Gorbachev aide, the 52-year-old agronomist Valerii Boldin, to head the General Department emphasized yet again the General Secretary's intention of gaining firm control over the party apparatus. That department is the central chancellery of the *apparat*, controlling party security and communications, and registering and checking all the Central Committee's incoming and outgoing confidential documents. During Stalin's time it was known as the 'Special Sector' and was the key to Stalin's control of the party. Under the management of

Chernenko (1965–82), Klavdii Bogolyubov (1982–85) and Anatolii Luk'yanov (1985–87), the department has continued to play a key role as part of the General Secretary's 'inner cabinet'.[24] Following Luk'yanov's promotion to the Secretariat, Gorbachev chose a personal adviser, who had worked closely with him on agricultural questions since 1981, to take care of his chancellery.

Another of Gorbachev's key aides is Georgii Razumovskii, the Secretary who heads the Department of Party-Organizational Work. That department, long headed by Kapitonov (1964–83) and then by Ligachev (1983–85), exercises control over regional affairs, especially personnel appointments at the local level. In recent years a new trend in personnel selection for the provinces has been apparent: before reassignment to regional party committees as first secretaries, local party secretaries are summoned for approximately one year to the central *apparat*; there, serving as inspectors or even as deputy heads of the Party-Organizational Work Department, they strengthen their allegiance to the centre and acquire the necessary authority to conduct the new policy line in the provinces.[25]

On 29 March 1987, the provincial newspaper *Gor'kovskaya pravda* published an article by a lecturer at the local party school, who complained that 'There are some people who claim to be ready and able to direct the social and ideological process who have not studied so much as a single work by Marx or Lenin'. This criticism seems to have been directed against certain 'ideologists' of the pre-Gorbachev era. Since the 27th Congress, members of the 'Suslovite' old guard have been leaving the ideological apparatus of the Central Committee. Men such as Ponomarev, Rusakov, Zimyanin and Shauro have been removed to make way for a new generation of better educated and less dogmatic officials. To implement what he calls 'new thinking', Gorbachev requires a well-functioning propaganda team within the central apparatus, where responsibilities for world communist affairs, culture and internal and external propaganda have been assumed by specialists such as Dobrynin, Yakovlev, Vadim Medvedev, Yurii Voronov, Yurii Sklyarov and Valentin Grigor'ev.

One year after he came to power, Gorbachev enhanced the status of the International Department, at the expense of the Foreign Ministry. Under its new head, Dobrynin, the department has been granted more powers to influence Soviet foreign policy and to oversee appointments within the diplomatic corps. Thus, Dobrynin also gained control over the Department for Cadres Abroad, which oversees the training of Soviet diplomats. The higher status of Dobrynin's department was emphasized by the transfer of Georgii Kornienko, a first deputy foreign minister, to the post of First Deputy Head of the International Department. In previous years, the department had only one First Deputy, Vadim Zagladin, whose functions remain unchanged: he continues to supervise Soviet party relations with capitalist and developing countries. His new colleague, Kornienko, has been given responsibilities in the field of arms control – one of Gorbachev's high foreign policy priorities. Under Dobrynin, therefore, the department's scope has been extended from relations with non-ruling communist parties, socialist parties and national liberation movements to embrace superpower relations in general as well. This was further emphasized by the transfer of a professional soldier, Lieutenant-General Viktor Starodubov, from the Standing Consultative Commission for US–Soviet arms control discussions to the International Department, presumably as head of a sector dealing with arms control matters.[26]

While Dobrynin was reorganizing that department, Yakovlev, who headed the Propaganda department during 1985–86, was widening the range of Soviet propaganda activities. Yakovlev had previously held the post of first deputy head of this department (1965–72), and working under him as deputy heads were the present heads of the Department for Liaison with Ruling Communist Parties (Medvedev), and the Department of Propaganda (Sklyarov). Brezhnev seems to have excluded all three from active ideological duties during the second half of the 1970s, and only after his death were they permitted to return to the central apparatus. Now all three are playing key roles in Gorbachev's team: Yakovlev and Medvedev as Secretaries, and Sklyarov as Yakovlev's replacement at the head of the Propaganda Department, after Yakovlev assumed additional functions as overseer of the new cultural thaw and of Soviet scientific institutions.

To correct a perceived weakness in the presentation of propaganda to explain Gorbachev's foreign policy abroad,[27] Yakovlev divided the Propaganda Department into two units, concentrating on either domestic or foreign affairs. Sklyarov, the new head, acquired two first deputies. The first, Al'bert Vlasov, former deputy head of the International Information Department, was placed in charge of foreign propaganda (he subsequently accompanied Gorbachev to the Reykjavik summit conference); his colleague, Petr Slezko, former *obkom* secretary for ideology in Ligachev's power base, Tomsk, assumed responsibility for domestic propaganda.

Yakovlev's subordinates, in addition to Sklyarov, are Voronov (head of the Department of Culture) and Grigor'ev (in charge of the Department of Science and Educational Institutions). The appointment of Voronov, former editor-in-chief of the youth newspaper *Komsomol'skaya pravda* during the short period of liberalization under Khrushchev, is noteworthy. In disgrace since 1965, he has now been entrusted with the formulation of party policy towards the arts. Grigor'ev, hitherto a relatively unknown scientist, now has the task of supervising the country's scientific and scholarly institutes, including the Academy of Sciences. Unlike his predecessors, Trapeznikov and Medvedev, Grigor'ev is not a party official, and came to the central apparatus direct from the Academy of Sciences.[28] This may indicate that the political leadership is willing to relax ideological control over the Academy and that Soviet scientists will be given more rights in the future.

As noted above, at the 27th Congress, Yakovlev's former reform-oriented subordinate in the Propaganda Department, Medvedev, was appointed a Central Committee Secretary and entrusted with the Department for Liaison with Ruling Communist Parties, including those of Eastern Europe, China, Vietnam and Cuba. The department has gained in importance under Gorbachev, and in accordance with Gorbachev's new diplomacy, Medvedev's task is to direct a creative comparison of attitudes towards reform among the various socialist countries, and he has stated on several occasions that the CPSU has been drawing on the experience accumulated by fraternal parties. An indication of a change in the role of this department was the promotion of Georgii Shakhnazarov to the rank of First Deputy Head. As President of the Soviet Political Sciences Association and Vice-President of the International Political Science Association, he has attracted attention over the years as an advocate of reform and an exponent of some of the most interesting ideas to be found in the Soviet press. In particular, he has long advocated a more open information policy and called for the democratization of Soviet society.[29] He replaced the hard-liner Oleg Rakhmanin, who had a reputation for being very critical of reform developments in Eastern Europe and China.

Before the Kremlin leadership introduced changes in ideology and foreign policy, certain arrangements were made in restructuring those organs of the party apparatus that dealt primarily with economic affairs. The Planning and Finance Organs Department was eliminated, and in its place there appeared the new Economic Department under Ryzhkov, which was directed to co-ordinate the work of the other industrial departments, and to develop new, more effective methods of management in industry. The Economic Department was a first step towards setting up a new system of interaction between the different branches of industry and Gosplan, and under Gorbachev it has become one of the brain centres of *perestroika*. After Ryzhkov's appointment as Prime Minister, the post as head of the department went to the Central Committee Secretary Lev Zaikov, who was elected a full member of the Politburo at the 27th Congress, thus becoming the Kremlin's chief overseer of the economy in the central party apparatus. Apart from running the Economic Department, Zaikov's functions also encompass military industry and heavy industry.[30] The post of First Deputy Head of the Department has been given to Vladimir Mozhin, a former chairman of the Council for the Study of Productive Forces, at Gosplan. In May 1982 (during Brezhnev's last year), he published an article in *Komsomol'skaya pravda*, in which he touched on the subject of economic reforms and referred to the necessity of launching a campaign against alcohol abuse.[31]

Mozhin is not the only reform-minded official recently recruited to the central *apparat* from Gosplan: as noted above, Ryzhkov and Slyun'kov both served in the Planning committee in the 1970s and early 1980s. Slyun'kov subsequently took over the Economic department from Zaikov, who concentrated on the military sector. The heads of the departments for the Defence Industries (Oleg Belyakov), Machine-Building (Arkadii Vol'skii), Heavy Industry and Power Engineering (Ivan Yastrebov), and Transport and Communications (Viktor Pasternak) are more or less subordinated to Zaikov. As 'senior' Secretary with responsibility for military matters, he also supervises the work of the Main Political Directorate of the Army and Navy, headed by army General Aleksei Lizichev, which is responsible for the political instruction of Soviet armed forces personnel, and which also has the status of a Central Committee department.

In 1983, under Andropov, responsibility for food processing was removed from the Department for Light and Food Industries, which became the Light Industry and Consumer Goods Department (headed since 1986 by Leonid Bobykin, former Second Secretary of the Sverdlovsk *obkom*), and transferred to the Agricultural Department, renamed Department for Agriculture and the Food Industry (now headed by Ivan Skiba). These changes were apparently connected with the desire of the post-Brezhnev leadership to step up the production of consumer goods and to ensure better food supplies to the population. These tasks are also carried out in one way or another by three other departments: Trade and Consumer Services (headed by the former Belorussian minister of trade, Nikolai Stashenkov); Chemical Industry (headed by Gorbachev's man from Stavropol, Afonin); and Construction (headed by Ligachev's protégé, the former party chief of Tomsk, Aleksandr Mel'nikov).

CHANGING POLICIES

Gorbachev has shown himself quite as adept as his predecessors at manipulating the party apparatus to strengthen his own position. In the knowledge that the fate of every General Secretary has depended on getting his own people into the Central Committee organization, thereby also to ensure that his policies are administered by individuals who support both the man and his policies, Gorbachev has undertaken various reorganizations and instituted personnel changes in almost all the departments. A large number of Brezhnev's and Andropov's former protégés and clients have relinquished their posts and been replaced by party officials from

Stavropol, Tomsk or Sverdlovsk – from outside the central apparatus, in other words. By placing these 'outsiders' in leading positions within the central apparatus, Gorbachev has dismantled the old order established under his predecessors and imposed his own stamp on the party apparatus, reasserting control over Soviet ideological, economic and foreign policy. Gorbachev, Ligachev, Ryzhkov and others have established new patronage networks, comprising trustworthy officials whom they have known for many years. That has been the main thrust of the turnover in the party apparatus, which now appears complete, subject of course to adjustment.

The long-awaited generational change also portends changes in the way Soviet policy will be planned or managed in the future. Although the new party *apparatchiki*, who are ten – sometimes twenty – years younger, come from much the same background as the party technocrats they have replaced, some of them are better educated, advocate different policies and have different views of the world. Gorbachev needs their professionalism and experience to implement the policy of 'new thinking' in foreign affairs or ideology. Examples are the new head of the International Department, and the man responsible for world communist affairs (Dobrynin), who spent half of his career as ambassador to Washington, and the 'senior' Secretary Yakovlev, who served ten years as ambassador to Canada. There is no one in the Kremlin leadership whose detailed knowledge of the psychology and methods of dealing with or influencing Western politicians can match that of Dobrynin and Yakovlev.

A new type of party *apparatchik* has also emerged in the sphere of ideology and culture. Whereas leading positions in the ideological apparatus were formerly occupied by officials who had spent most of their careers in the provinces and who projected a rather dull and bureaucratic image, Gorbachev has promoted better travelled, better educated and more sophisticated types of leader, who are probably seen as better suited than their predecessors for the continuing *perestroika* of Soviet life and the continuation of the campaign for *glasnost'*.

In selecting new cadres and new colleagues, Gorbachev has employed an effective psychological technique: he has advanced officials who might have expected promotion earlier, but whose careers were apparently retarded by Brezhnev's predilection for giving preference to members of his so-called 'Dnepropetrovsk mafia'. Officials such as Yakovlev, Medvedev, Voronov or Sklyarov began their careers with hopes of positive changes, which seemed possible under Khrushchev, but they then became victims of their 'liberal' and 'progressive' views, and they fell into disgrace in the 1970s. Now they have gained the opportunity to conduct the reforms that they advocated long ago. Like the General Secretary who has given them this opportunity, it appears that their time has come.

Gorbachev, in addition to his high public profile in presenting innovative domestic policies and new initiatives in foreign policy, has worked effectively behind the scenes to ensure the existence of an invigorated *apparat* as a means of guaranteeing the implementation of his ideals. While Politburo and Secretariat colleagues, particularly Ligachev, clearly possess power and influence that might be deployed to frustrate Gorbachev's zealous reformism, so far that has not happened. True, Ligachev has expressed cautious conservatism in his endorsement of *glasnost*'; but he has presented no practical alternative, and his is but one voice – although a powerful one – in a team that appears to consist mainly of enthusiasts for reformist change. Within the Secretariat and the central *apparat*, the majority are beholden to Gorbachev for their positions, and may therefore be presumed to be loyal supporters. That support could be more significant for the success of Gorbachev's policies than any opposition and resistance among his colleagues on the Politburo.

NOTES AND REFERENCES

1 Archie Brown, 'Leadership Succession and Policy Innovation', in Archie Brown and Michael Kaser (eds), *Soviet Policy for the 1980s*, Macmillan, London, 1982, pp. 232–5. (p. 228).
2 Jerry F. Hough and Merle Fainsod, *How the Soviet Union is Governed*, Harvard University Press, Cambridge, Mass., 1979, p. 422; and Elizabeth Teague, 'The Foreign Departments of the Central Committee of the CPSU', *Radio Liberty Research Bulletin*, 27 October 1980. The International Department, for example, is now staffed by a department head, two first deputies and seven deputy heads.
3 Friedrich Neznansky, writing in *Posev*, June 1980, p. 31.
4 For general information on the Central Committee, see, for example, Ronald J. Hill and Peter Frank, *The Soviet Communist Party* 3rd ed., Allen & Unwin, Boston and London, 1986, pp. 64–70; Hough and Fainsod, *How the Soviet Union is Governed*, pp. 409–48, 455–66; Werner Hahn, *Postwar Soviet Politics*, Cornell University Press, London, 1982.
5 Leonard Shapiro, *The Communist Party of the Soviet Union* 2nd ed., Methuen, London, 1970, pp. 319, 451.
6 John A. Armstrong, *Ideology, Politics, and Government in the Soviet Union: An Introduction* 3rd Ed., Nelson, London, 1973, p. 91.
7 The point was repeatedly made by, for example, Archie Brown: see, for example, his 'Andropov: Discipline *and* Reform', *Problems of Communism*, 1983, Jan–Feb. p. 18; also his 'Gorbachev: New Man in the Kremlin', *Problems of Communism*, 1985, May–June, p. 1; for a fuller elaboration, see his 'Leadership Succession and Policy Innovation' *loc. cit.*
8 Michael Voslensky, *Nomenklatura: Anatomy of the Soviet Ruling Class*, Bodley Head, London, 1984, p. 375; also Radio Liberty RL 439/84, 'The Central Committee Secretariat', 16 November 1984.
9 In compiling personal data on members of the Secretariat, the standard available sources were relied on. Particular use was made of Alexander G. Rahr (compiler), *A Biographic Directory of 100 Leading Soviet Officials* 2nd

ed., Central Research, Radio Liberty, RFE/RL, Munich, 1984, and 3rd ed., 1986; Borys Lyvytsky, compiler, *The Soviet Political Elite*, Xeroxed manuscript distributed by the Hoover Institution, Stanford, Calif., 1970; and various editions of the official handbook, *Deputaty Verkhovnogo Soveta SSSR*, Izvestiya, Moscow, various years; also invaluable was the wealth of biographical detail unearthed by Jerry Hough and included in Jerry F. Hough and Merle Fainsod, *How the Soviet Union is Governed*. Further details came from the work of other scholars, whose contribution we acknowledge even if no specific reference is given.

10 'First Secretary' until the 23rd Congress in 1966.

11 A. Avtorkhanov, *Sila i bessilie Brezhneva*, Posev, Frankfurt-am-Main, 1979, p. 169.

12 John Dornberg, *Brezhnev: The Masks of Power*, Deutsch, London, 1974, p. 280.

13 Avtorkhanov, *Sila i bessilie*, p. 169.

14 The view of Zimyanin as a counterweight to Suslov comes from Avtorkhanov, *Sila i bessilie*, p. 169; the reference to the close relationship between Suslov and Zimyanin comes from Alexander G. Rahr, *Biographic Directory, 1984*, p. 244.

15 Hough and Fainsod, *How the Soviet Union is Governed*, p. 411, Table 29, note.

16 Mark Frankland, *The Sixth Continent*, Hamish Hamilton, London, 1987, p. 159; the circumstances were odd, and are summarized in Avtorkhanov, *Sila i bessilie*, pp. 24–5.

17 Brown, 'Andropov: Discipline *and* Reform?', p. 18.

18 Vadim Medish, 'A Romanov in the Kremlin?', *Problems of Communism*, 1983, vol. 32, no. 6, November–December, pp. 65–6.

19 Graeme Gill, 'Personal Dominance and the Collective Principle: Individual Legitimacy in Marxist–Leninst Systems', in T. H. Rigby and Ferenc Fehér (eds), *Political Legitimation in Communist States*, Macmillan, London, 1982, pp. 94–110.

20 For a summary of Gorbachev's restructuring of these bodies during his first year in office, see Ronald J. Hill and Peter Frank, 'Gorbachev's Cabinet Building', *Journal of Communist Studies*, 1986, vol. 2, no. 2, pp. 168–81.

21 *XXVII s˝ezd Kommunisticheskoi partii Sovetskogo Soyuza*, Politizdat, Moscow, 1986, vol 2, p. 296; names appear in *Russian* alphabetical order.

22 The significance of this is unclear, however: see below.

23 See Boris Eltsin's interview in *Die Zeit*, 7 May 1986.

24 Avtorkhanov, *Sila i bessilie Brezhneva*, p. 180.

25 Radio Liberty, RL 385/86, 'New Trends in Party Personnel Policy', 9 October 1986.

26 Wallace Spaulding, 'Shifts in CPSU ID', *Problems of Communism*, 1986, vol. 35, no. 4, July–August, pp. 80–6.

27 Both Andropov and Gorbachev were highly critical of the performance of the International Information department under Zamyatin, and the department was abolished in 1986.

28 The biographies of the new department heads are published in *Sovetskii entsiklopedicheskii slovar'* (Moscow, 1986).

29 For some examples, see Ronald J. Hill, *Soviet Politics, Political Science and reform* Martin Robertson, Oxford; M. E. Sharpe, White Plains, NY, 1980, esp. pp. 108–11.

30 The areas of work assigned to a given Secretary may be determined from (1) the context and content of his published articles; (2) the meetings that he attends;

(3) the nature of foreign delegations that he meets; and (4) the obituaries that he signs.

31   *Komsomol'skaya pravda*, 27 May 1982.

Appendix:
Biographies of the Soviet Party Elite

Alexander Rahr

POLITBURO CPSU MEMBERS FEBRUARY 1988
FULL MEMBERS

GORBACHEV Mikhail Sergeevich Present Positions: General Secretary, CC CPSU; Chairman, USSR Council of Defense; Full Member, Politburo, CC CPSU; Member, Presidium, USSR Supreme Soviet. **Date of Birth:** 2 March 1931. **Place of Birth:** Privolnoe, Krasnogvardeiskii Raion, Stavropol Krai, RSFSR. **Nationality:** Russian. **Family Background:** Peasant. **Higher Education:** Graduated from law faculty, Moscow State University, 1955; completed correspondence course at Stavropol Agricultural Institute, 1967. **Career:** 1946–50 Workhand at Machine-Tractor Station (MTS), Stavropol Krai; 1952– Party member; 1952–54 All-Union Komsomol organizer, Law Faculty, Moscow State University; 1955–56 Komsomol and Party work, Stavropol Krai; 1956–58 First Secretary, Stavropol Gorkom, All-Union Komsomol; 1958 Deputy Chief, Department of Propaganda and Agitation, Stavropol Kraikom, All-Union Komsomol; 1958–62 Second Secretary, then First Secretary, Stavropol Kraikom, All-Union Komsomol; 1962–63 CPSU organizer of territorial production administration of collective and state farms, Stavropol Kraikom, CPSU; 1963–66 Chief, Department of Party Organs, Stavropol Kraikom, CPSU; 1966–68 First Secretary, Stavropol Gorkom, CPSU; 1968–70 Second Secretary, Stavropol Kraikom, CPSU; 1970–78 First Secretary, Stavropol Kraikom, CPSU; Member, Military Council, North Caucasian Military District; 1970– Deputy (and Member, Commission on Conservation, 1970–74; Chairman, Commission on Youth Affairs, 1974–79; Chairman, Commission on Legislative Proposals, 1979–84; Chairman, Commission on Foreign Affairs, 1984–85), Council of the Union, USSR Supreme Soviet (since 8th convocation); 1971– Full Member, CC CPSU; 1978–83 Secretary, CC CPSU (responsible for agriculture); 1979–80 Candidate Member, Politburo, CC CPSU; 1980– Full Member, Politburo, CC CPSU; 1980– Deputy, RSFSR Supreme Soviet (since 10th convocation); 1983–84 Secretary, CC CPSU (responsible for economy, cadres affairs, agriculture); 1984–85 Secretary, CC CPSU (responsible for ideology, culture, world communism affairs, economy, agriculture and cadres); 1985– General Secretary, CC CPSU; Chairman, USSR Council of Defense; Member, Presidium USSR Supreme Soviet

CHEBRIKOV Viktor Mikhailovich Present Positions: Chairman, USSR Committee for State Security (KGB); Full Member, Politburo, CC CPSU; Army General. **Date of Birth:** 27 April 1923. **Nationality:** Russian. **Family Background:** Blue-collar. **Higher Education:** Attended Metallurgical Institute (Dnepropetrovsk), 1946–50, and graduated in 1950 with engineering degree. **Career:** 1941–46 Soldier; platoon commander; commander of company; chief of staff of a battalion; deputy commander, commander of a battalion; 1944– Party member; 1950–51 Engineer at Petrovskii Metallurgical Plant in Dnepropetrovsk; 1951–55 Department chief, Secretary, First Secretary, Lenin Raikom, Ukrainian CP, Dnepropetrovsk City; 1955–58 Secretary, Party Committee; Party organizer, Metallurgical Plant, Dnepropetrovsk; 1956–61 Member of Auditing Commission, Ukrainian CP; 1958–59 Second Secretary, Dnepropetrovsk Gorkom, Ukrainian CP; 1959–61 Party work in Dnepropetrovsk; Secretary, Lenin Raikom, Dnepropetrovsk City, Ukrainian CP; 1961–63 First Secretary, Dnepropetrovsk Gorkom, Ukrainian CP; 1961–71 Candidate Member, CC Ukrainian CP; 1963 Second Secretary, Dnepropetrovsk Obkom (for Industry), Ukrainian CP; 1963–64 Secretary, Dnepropetrovsk Obkom (for Industry), Ukrainian CP; 1963–67 Deputy, Ukrainian SSR Supreme Soviet (6th convocation); 1964–65 Secretary, Dnepropetrovsk Obkom, Ukrainian CP; 1965–67 Second Secretary, Dnepropetrovsk Obkom, Ukrainian CP; 1967–68 Chief, Administration of Cadres, USSR Committee for State Security (KGB); 1968–82 Deputy Chairman, USSR KGB (identified in 1968 with rank of Major General and in 1974 with rank of Lieutenant General; held rank of Colonel General from 1978 to 1983); 1971–81 Candidate Member, CC CPSU; 1974– Deputy (and Member, 1979–83, Commission on Foreign Affairs), Council of Nationalities, USSR Supreme Soviet (9th–11th convocations); 1981– Full Member, CC CPSU; 1982 First Deputy Chairman, USSR KGB; 1982– Chairman, USSR KGB; 1983– Army General; 1983–85 Candidate Member, Politburo, CC CPSU; 1985– Full Member, Politburo, CC CPSU

GROMYKO Andrei Andreevich Present Positions: Chairman, Presidium, USSR Supreme Soviet; Full Member, Politburo, CC CPSU. **Date of Birth:** 18 July 1909. **Place of Birth:** Starye Gromyki (now in Vetka Raion, Gomel Oblast, Belorussian SSR). **Nationality:** Russian. **Family Background:** Peasant. **Higher Education:** Attended a technical school in Gomel from 1926 to 1929; graduated as economist from Economics Institute, Borisov

Agricultural Technicum, 1932; graduated as agronomist from Lenin Agricultural Institute, Minsk, 1934; graduated as Candidate of Economics (major subjects: political science, economics) from Lenin All-Union Scientific Research Institute for Agronomy, Moscow, 1936; Doctor of Economics, 1956. **Career:** Before beginning his studies, Gromyko was employed in the archive of the local Gomel newspaper, *Gomel'skaya pravda*; 1931–   Party member; 1936–39 Senior Associate (Professor), Institute of Economics, USSR Academy of Sciences; 1939–43 Deputy Chief, then Chief, United States of America Department, USSR People's Commissariat of Foreign Affairs; counselor, Soviet Embassy in Washington; 1943–46 USSR Ambassador to US; also USSR Minister to Cuba; 1946–48 USSR Permanent Representative to UN; USSR Deputy Minister of Foreign Affairs; 1946–50 Deputy, Council of the Union, USSR Supreme Soviet (2nd convocation); 1948–49 Deputy USSR Minister of Foreign Affairs; 1949–52 First Deputy USSR Minister of Foreign Affairs; 1952–53 USSR Ambassador to Great Britain; 1952–56 Candidate Member, CC CPSU; 1953–57 First Deputy USSR Minister of Foreign Affairs; 1956– Full Member, CC CPSU; 1957–85 USSR Minister of Foreign Affairs; 1958–   Deputy, Council of the Union, USSR Supreme Soviet (since 5th convocation); 1973–   Full Member, Politburo, CC CPSU; 1983–85 First Deputy Chairman, USSR Council of Ministers; 1985–   Chairman, Presidium, USSR Supreme Soviet

LIGACHEV Egor Kuz'mich Present Positions: Secretary, CC CPSU; Full Member, Politburo, CC CPSU. **Date of Birth:** 29 November 1920. **Place of Birth:** Dubinkina. **Nationality:** Russian. **Higher Education:** Studied from 1938(?) to 1943 at Ordzhonikidze Institute for Aircraft Construction in Moscow and graduated with technical engineering degree; studied by correspondence at Higher Party School (Moscow) in 1951. **Career:** 1943–44 Chief engineer in production group, technology department, V. I. Chkalov Plant (Novosibirsk); 1944–   Party member; 1944–46 Secretary of a raikom in Novosibirsk Oblast, All-Union Komsomol; 1946–49 Secretary, then First Secretary, Novosibirsk Obkom, All-Union Komsomol; 1949–51 Lecturer, Novosibirsk Gorkom, CPSU; 1951–52 Chief, Department of Culture, Novosibirsk Gorkom, CPSU; 1952–53 Chief, Department of Culture, Novosibirsk Obkom, CPSU; 1953–55 Worked in Novosibirsk Oblast Administration for Culture; 1955–58 Deputy Chairman, Executive Committee, Novosibirsk Oblast Workers' Soviet; 1958–59 First Secretary of Sovetskii Raikom, Novosibirsk Oblast, CPSU; 1959–61 Secretary, Novosibirsk Obkom, CPSU; 1961–63 Deputy Chief, Department of Propaganda and Agitation, CC CPSU Buro for RSFSR; 1963–65 Deputy Chief, Department for Party Organs, CC CPSU Buro for RSFSR; 1965–83 First Secretary, Tomsk Obkom, CPSU; Member, Military

Council, Siberian Military District; 1966–76 Candidate Member, CC CPSU; 1966– Deputy (and Member, 1966–68, Commission on Industry, Transport, and Communications; Chairman, 1968–74, Commission for Youth Affairs; Member, 1974–79, Commission on Planning and Budget; Deputy Chairman, 1979–84, Commission on Science and Technology; Chairman, 1984–85, Commission on Legislative Proposals, since 1985 Chairman, Commission on Foreign Affairs), Council of the Union, USSR Supreme Soviet (7th–11th convocations); 1976– Full Member, CC CPSU; 1983–85 Chief, Department for Party Organizational Work, CC CPSU; 1983– Secretary, CC CPSU (responsible for cadres, 1983–85; responsible for ideology, cadres and Party administration, 1985–); 1985– Full Member, Politburo, CC CPSU

RYZHKOV Nikolai Ivanovich Present Positions: Chairman, USSR Council of Ministers; Full Member, Politburo, CC CPSU. **Date of Birth:** 28 September 1929. **Place of Birth:** Donetsk Oblast (Ukraine). **Nationality:** Russian (some sources state Ukrainian). **Education:** Attended Technicum for Machine-Building, Kramatorsk, until 1950; graduated in 1959 with engineering degree from Ural Polytechnical Institute imeni Kirova (Sverdlovsk). **Career:** 1950–59 Mining foreman; head of a railroad section; shop superintendent; 1956– Party member; 1959–65 Smelting foreman; deputy director, S. Ordzhonikidze Heavy Machine-Building Plant (Uralmashzavod), Sverdlovsk; 1965–70 Chief engineer, Uralmashzavod, Sverdlovsk; 1970–71 Director of Uralmashzavod; 1971–75 General Director, Uralmash Production Association; 1974–79 Deputy (and Secretary, Commission on Planning and Budget), Council of the Union, USSR Supreme Soviet; 1979–84 Deputy (and Member, Commission on Industry), Council of Nationalities, USSR Supreme Soviet (10th convocation); 1975–79 USSR First Deputy Minister of Heavy and Transport Machine-Building; 1979–82 First Deputy Chairman, USSR State Planning Committee (Gosplan) (responsible for heavy and military industry); 1981– Full Member, CC CPSU; 1982–85 Secretary, CC CPSU (responsible for economic questions); Chief, Economic Department, CC CPSU; 1984– Deputy (and Chairman, Commission on Legislative Proposals, 1985), Council of the Union, USSR Supreme Soviet (11th convocation); 1985– Deputy, RSFSR Supreme Soviet; 1985– Full Member, Politburo, CC CPSU; 1985– Chairman, USSR Council of Ministers

SHCHERBITSKII Vladimir Vasil'evich Present Positions: First Secretary, CC Ukrainian CP; Full Member, Politburo, CC CPSU. **Date of Birth:** 17 February 1918. **Place of Birth:** Verkhnedneprovsk (now in Dnepropetrovsk Oblast). **Nationality:** Ukrainian. **Family Background:** Blue-collar. **Higher Education:** Graduated from Dnepropetrovsk Chemical Technological Institute in 1941; also attended a military academy in 1941. **Career:** 1934–35 Instructor, Verkhnedneprovsk Komsomol Raikom; 1941 Mechanical engineer and deputy chief engineer at an experimental factory in Dnepropetrovsk; 1941– Party member; 1941–45 Officer in Red Army on North Caucasian Front; 1945–46 Technical engineer in Dneprodzerzhinsk; Chief, Scheduled Preventive Repair Bureau, Ordzhonikidze Coke-Chemical Industry Plant; 1948 Chief, Department of Organization and Instruction, Dnepropetrovsk Gorkom, Ukrainian CP; 1948–51 Second Secretary, Dneprodzerzhinsk Gorkom, Ukrainian CP; 1951–52 Party organizer for CC All-Union CP(b) at F.E. Dzerzhinskii Metallurgical Plant, Dnepropetrovsk; 1952–54 Member, Central Auditing Commission, Ukrainian CP; 1952–54 First Secretary, Dneprodzerzhinsk Gorkom, Ukrainian CP; 1954–55 Second Secretary, Dneprodzerzhinsk Obkom, Ukrainian CP; 1954–56 Candidate Member, CC Ukrainian CP; 1955–57 First Secretary, Dnepropetrovsk Obkom, Ukrainian CP; 1955– Deputy, Ukrainian SSR Supreme Soviet (since 4th convocation); 1956–61 Member, Central Auditing Commission, CPSU; 1956– Full Member, CC Ukrainian CP; 1957–61 Secretary, CC Ukrainian CP; 1957– Full Member, Presidium (after 1966: Politburo), CC Ukrainian CP; 1958– Deputy, Council of the Union, USSR Supreme Soviet (since 5th convocation); 1961–63 Candidate Member, Presidium, CC CPSU; 1961–63 Chairman, Ukrainian SSR Council of Ministers; 1961– Full Member, CC CPSU; 1963–65 First Secretary, Dnepropetrovsk Obkom, Ukrainian CP for industry; 1965–71 Candidate Member, Presidium (after 1966: Politburo), CC CPSU; 1965–72 Chairman, Ukrainian SSR Council of Ministers; 1971– Full Member, Politburo, CC CPSU; 1972– Member, Presidium, USSR Supreme Soviet; 1972– First Secretary, CC Ukrainian CP; Member, Presidium, Ukrainian SSR Supreme Soviet; member, Military Council, Kiev Military District

SHEVARDNADZE Eduard Amvrosievich Present Positions: USSR Minister of Foreign Affairs; Full Member, Politburo, CC CPSU. **Date of Birth:** 25 January 1928. **Place of Birth:** Mamati, Lanchkhuti Raion, Georgian SSR. **Nationality:** Georgian. **Family Background:** Son of a teacher. **Higher Education:** Graduated in 1951 from Party School, CC Georgian CP (Tbilisi); graduated in 1960 from history faculty, Kutaisi Pedagogical Institute. **Career:** 1946– Instructor; department chief of a raikom, Georgian Komsomol; instructor, CC Georgian Komsomol; 1948– Party member; 1952–53 Secretary, Second Secretary, Kutaisi Obkom, Georgian Komsomol; 1953 Instructor, Kutaisi Gorkom, Georgian CP; 1953–56 First Secretary, Kutaisi Gorkom, Georgian Komsomol; 1956–57 Second Secretary, CC Georgian Komsomol; 1957–61 First Secretary, CC Georgian Komsomol; Member, Buro, CC Georgian Komsomol; 1958–62

Member, CC All-Union Komsomol; 1958–64 Full Member, CC Georgian CP 1958 Member, Presidium, Soviet Committee for Solidarity with Asian and African Countries; 1959–60 Candidate Member, Buro, CC All-Union Komsomol; 1959–85 Deputy (and Chairman, Mandate Commission, 1963–67), Georgian SSR Supreme Soviet (since 5th convocation); 1960–61 Candidate member, Buro, CC Georgian CP; 1961 Full Member, Buro, CC All-Union Komsomol; 1961–63 First Secretary, Mtskheta Raikom, Georgian CP; 1963–64 First Secretary, Pervomaiskii Raikom in Tbilisi city, Georgian CP; 1964–65 Georgian First Deputy Minister for Maintenance of Public Order; 1965–72 Georgian Minister for Maintenance of Public Order (after 1968: Minister of Internal Affairs); MVD General 3rd rank; 1966–86 Full Member, CC Georgian CP; 1968–85 Member, Military Council, Transcaucasian Military District; 1972 First Secretary, Tbilisi Gorkom, Georgian CP; 1972–85 First Secretary, CC Georgian CP; Full Member, Buro, CC Georgian CP; 1972–85 Member, Presidium, Georgian Supreme Soviet; 1974– Deputy (and Chairman of Mandate Commission, 1974–79), Council of Nationalities, USSR Supreme Soviet (since 9th convocation); 1976– Full Member, CC CPSU; 1978–85 Candidate Member, Politburo, CC CPSU; 1985– Full Member, Politburo, CC CPSU; 1985– USSR Minister of Foreign Affairs; Member, USSR Council of Ministers

SLYUN'KOV Nikolai Nikitovich Present Positions: Secretary, CC CPSU; Full Member, Politburo, CC CPSU; Chief, Economics Department, CC CPSU. **Date of Birth:** 26 April 1929. **Place of Birth:** Gorodets (Rogachev Raion, Gomel Oblast, BSSR). **Nationality:** Belorussian. **Family Background:** Peasant. **Higher Education:** Attended Technicum for automechanics in Minsk until 1950; graduated from Institute for Agricultural Mechanization in Minsk in 1962. **Career:** 1950–60 Assistant to foreman; foreman; senior foreman; deputy shop supervisor; shop supervisor; deputy chairman; chairman, trade union committee, Lenin Tractor Plant, Minsk; 1954– Party member; 1960–65 Director of Spare Parts Plant, Minsk; 1965–71 Director of Lenin Tractor Plant, Minsk; 1971–72 General Director, Production Association for Tractor Construction, Minsk; 1966–76 Full Member, CC Belorussian CP 1966–70 Deputy (and Member, Commission on Industry, Transport and Communications), Council of Nationalities, USSR Supreme Soviet; 1971–75 Deputy, BSSR Supreme Soviet; 1972–74 First Secretary, Minsk Gorkom, Belorussian CP; 1974–83 Deputy Chairman, USSR Gosplan (responsible for machine-building); 1983–87 First Secretary, CC Belorussian CP; Member, Presidium, BSSR Supreme Soviet; 1983–87 Member, Presidium, USSR Supreme Soviet; 1983– Deputy, Council of the Union, USSR Supreme Soviet (elected mid-term, since 10th convocation); 1985– Deputy, Belorussian Supreme

Soviet; 1986–   Full Member, CC Belorussian CP; 1986–   Full Member, CC CPSU; 1986–87 Candidate Member, Politburo, CC CPSU; 1987– Secretary, CC CPSU (responsible for economic administration, Comecon); 1987–   Chief, Economics Department, CC CPSU; 1987– Full Member, Politburo, CC CPSU

SOLOMENTSEV Mikhail Sergeevich Present Positions: Chairman, Party Control Committee, CC CPSU; Full Member, Politburo, CC CPSU. **Date of Birth:** 7 November 1913. **Place of Birth:** Erilovka (now in Elets Raion, Lipetsk Oblast). **Nationality:** Russian. **Family Background:** Peasant. **Higher Education:** Graduated from Leningrad Polytechnical Institute in 1940. **Career:** 1930–40 Collective farm worker; 1940–49 Factory worker in Lipetsk; craftsman, deputy shop foreman, shop foreman, chief engineer of a heavy industry plant in Chelyabinsk, where he was also CP(b) organizer; 1940–   Party member; 1949–54 Director of a heavy industry plant in Chelyabinsk; 1954–57 Secretary, then Second Secretary, Chelyabinsk Obkom, CPSU; 1957–59 Chairman, Chelyabinsk Sovnarkhoz; 1958– Deputy (and Chairman, Commission on Legislative Proposals, 1966–71), Council of the Union, USSR Supreme Soviet (since 5th convocation); 1959–62 First Secretary, Karaganda Obkom, Kazakh CP; 1960–64 Full Member, CC Kazakh CP; 1961–   Full Member, CC CPSU; 1962–64 Second Secretary, CC Kazakh CP; Full Member, Presidium, CC Kazakh CP; 1963–66 Member, Presidium, Kazakh SSR Supreme Soviet; 1963–67 Deputy, Kazakh SSR Supreme Soviet; 1964–66 First Secretary, Rostov Obkom, CPSU; 1966–71 Secretary, CC CPSU; Chief, Heavy Industry Department, CC CPSU; 1967–   Deputy, RSFSR Supreme Soviet (since 7th convocation); 1971–83 Chairman, RSFSR Council of Ministers; 1971–83 Candidate Member, Politburo, CC CPSU; 1983–   Chairman, Committee for Party Control, CC CPSU; 1983–   Full Member, Politburo, CC CPSU.

VOROTNIKOV Vitalii Ivanovich Present Positions: Chairman, RSFSR Council of Ministers; Full Member, Politburo, CC CPSU. **Date of Birth:** 20 January 1926. **Place of Birth:** Voronezh. **Nationality:** Russian. **Higher Education:** Graduated from Voronezh Technicum in 1947; graduated from S. P. Korolev Aviation Institute in Kuibyshev. **Career:** 1942–44 Apprentice fitter in a locomotive repair works in Voronezh; 1947–   Party member; 1947–55 Foreman, technician, shop supervisor, chief supervisor in a machine-building plant in Kuibyshev; 1955–60 Secretary of Party committee of machine-building plant in Kuibyshev; 1960–61 Chief, Industry Department, Kuibyshev Obkom, CPSU; 1961–63 Secretary, Kuibyshev Obkom, CPSU (responsible for industry); 1963–64 Second Secretary, Kuibyshev Obkom, CPSU for industry; 1963–71 Deputy (and Member,

Commission for Industry and Construction), RSFSR Supreme Soviet; 1965–67 Second Secretary, Kuibyshev Obkom, CPSU; 1967–71 Chairman, Executive Committee, Kuibyshev Oblast Workers' Soviet; 1970– Deputy (and Member, Commission on Health and Social Security, 1970–74; Member, Commission on Legislative Proposals, 1974–79), Council of the Union, USSR Supreme Soviet (since 8th convocation); 1971–75 First Secretary, Voronezh Obkom, CPSU; 1971– Full Member, CC CPSU; 1975–79 First Deputy Chairman, RSFSR Council of Ministers; 1979–82 USSR Ambassador to Cuba; 1982–83 First Secretary, Krasnodar Kraikom, CPSU; 1983– Chairman, RSFSR Council of Minister; 1983 Candidate Member, Politburo, CC CPSU; 1983– Full Member, Politburo, CC CPSU; 1983– Deputy, RSFSR Supreme Soviet

NIKONOV Viktor Petrovich Present Positions: Secretary, CC CPSU; Full Member, Politburo, CC CPSU. **Date of Birth:** 28 February 1929. **Place of Birth:** Unknown. **Nationality:** Russian. **Family Background:** Peasant. **Higher Education:** Studied at Azov-Black Sea Agricultural Institute (Rostov); graduated as agronomist in 1950. **Career:** 1950–52 Chief Agronomist, Machine and Tractor Station (MTS), Uzhur, Krasnoyarsk Krai; 1952–55 Deputy Director, Agronomist School in Uyar, Krasnoyarsk Krai; 1954– Party member; 1955–58 Director, Machine and Tractor Station (MTS), Rybinskii Raion, Krasnoyarsk Krai; 1958–61 Deputy Chief; Chief, Department of Agriculture, Krasnoyarsk Kraikom, CPSU; 1961 Instructor, Department of Agriculture, CC CPSU; 1961–67 Second Secretary, Tatar Obkom, CPSU; 1962– Deputy (and Member, Commission on Agriculture, 1966–70), Council of Nationalities, USSR Supreme Soviet (6th–7th convocations); Deputy (and Member, 1970–74, Deputy Chairman, Commission on Agriculture, 1974–84) Council of the Union, USSR Supreme Soviet (8th–10th convocations); Deputy (and Deputy Chairman, Commission on Agroindustrial Complex), Council of Nationalities, USSR Supreme Soviet (11th convocation); 1967–79 First Secretary, Mari Obkom, CPSU; Member, Military Council, Volga Military District; 1971–76 Candidate Member, CC CPSU; 1976– Full Member, CC CPSU; 1979–83 Chairman of *Soyuzsel'khozkhimiya* association; USSR Deputy Minister of Agriculture; 1983–85 RSFSR Minister of Agriculture; Chairman, All-Russian Council of Collective Farms; Member, Russian Council of Social Welfare for Peasants; Member, Commission on Agroindustrial Complex, Presidium, RSFSR Council of Ministers; 1985– Secretary, CC CPSU (responsible for agriculture); 1987– Full Member, Politburo, CC CPSU

ZAIKOV Lev Nikolaevich Present Positions: First Secretary, Moscow Gorkom, CPSU; Secretary, CC CPSU; Full Member, Politburo, CC

CPSU. **Date of Birth:** 3 April 1923. **Nationality:** Russian. **Higher Education:** Graduated in 1963 from engineering-economics institute in Leningrad with degree in engineering. **Career:** 1940–44 Apprenticeship, then work as fitter in Leningrad; 1944–61 Shop foreman, deputy plant foreman, foreman, then production chief at a scientific-production association in Saratov, Moscow and Leningrad; 1957– Party member; 1961–76 Director (1961–71), director general of production-technical association (1971–74), then director general of scientific-production association in Leningrad; 1976–83 Chairman, Executive Committee, Leningrad City Workers' Soviet; 1975–80 Deputy, RSFSR Supreme Soviet (9th convocation); 1979– Deputy (and Member, 1979–84, Commission on Foreign Affairs), Council of the Union, USSR Supreme Soviet (since 10th convocation); 1979–84 Member, Committee, USSR Parliamentary Group, USSR Supreme Soviet; 1981– Full Member, CC CPSU; 1983–85 First Secretary, Leningrad Obkom, CPSU; Member, Military Council, Leningrad Military District; 1984–86 Member, Presidium, USSR Supreme Soviet; 1985– Secretary, CC CPSU (responsible for military-industrial complex); 1986– Full Member, Politburo, CC CPSU; 1987– First Secretary, Moscow Gorkom, CPSU.

YAKOVLEV Aleksandr Nikolaevich Present Positions: Secretary, CC CPSU; Full Member, Politburo, CC CPSU. **Date of Birth:** 2 December 1923. **Nationality:** Russian. **Higher Education:** Attended rifle-machine gun training school during the war; graduated from K. D. Ushinskii Pedagogical Institute in Yaroslavl (1946) as teacher; attended Academy of Social Sciences, CC CPSU (1956–60); Doctor of Historical Sciences; Professor; studied at Columbia University as exchange student in 1959. **Career:** 1941–43 Served in the Red Army: first as a cadet at infantry school, then as a platoon and company commander; 1944– Party member; 1946–48 in apparat of Yaroslavl Obkom, CPSU; 1948–50 Chief of a department, Yaroslavl Oblast paper *Severnyi rabochii*; chief lecturer at Party School, Yaroslavl Oblast; 1950–53 Deputy chief, then chief of a department, Yaroslavl Obkom, CPSU; 1953–56 Deputy Chief, Department of Science and Culture, CC CPSU; 1960–62 In apparat of CC CPSU; 1962–64 Instructor, Department of Propaganda and Agitation, CC CPSU; 1964–65 Chief, Radio and TV Broadcasting Section, Propaganda Department, CC CPSU; 1966–73 Member, editorial staff, journal *Kommunist*; 1965–73 First Deputy Chief and Acting Chief, Propaganda Department, CC CPSU; 1971–76 Member, Central Auditing Commission, CPSU; 1973–83 USSR Ambassador to Canada; 1983–85 Director, Institute of World Economics and International Relations (IMEMO), USSR Academy of Sciences; 1984– Deputy (and Member, Commission on Foreign Affairs), Council of Nationalities, USSR Supreme Soviet (11th Convocation); Member,

Committee, USSR Parliamentary Group; 1984– Corresponding Member, USSR Academy of Sciences (Economics Department); 1985–86 Chief, Propaganda Department, CC CPSU; 1986– Full Member, CC CPSU; 1986– Secretary, CC CPSU (responsible for propaganda, culture); 1987 Candidate Member, Politburo, CC CPSU; 1987– Full Member, Politburo, CC CPSU

CANDIDATE MEMBERS

DEMICHEV Petr Nilovich Present Positions: First Deputy Chairman, Presidium, USSR Supreme Soviet; Candidate Member, Politburo, CC CPSU. **Date of Birth:** 3 January 1918. **Place of Birth:** Pesochnaya (now: Kirov, Kaluga Oblast). **Nationality:** Russian. **Family Background:** Blue-collar. **Higher Education:** Graduated as engineer from Mechanical Engineering Technicum in Lyudinovo, Orel Oblast (now Kaluga Oblast); graduated with chemical technology degree from D. I. Mendeleev Institute of Chemical Technology (Moscow), 1944; graduated in 1953 from Higher Party School, CC CPSU, (correspondence course). **Career:** 1937 Secretary of a Komsomol raikom; 1937–44 Served in Red Army; 1939– Party member; 1944–45 Assistant Professor, D. I. Mendeleev Institute of Chemical Technology, Moscow; 1945–47 Chief, Department of Organization and Instruction, Sovetskii Raikom, Moscow city, All-Union CP(b); 1947–50 Secretary, Sovetskii Raikom, Moscow city, All-Union CP(b); 1950–52 Deputy Chief, Department of Agitation and Propaganda, Moscow Gorkom, All-Union CP; 1952–56 Held posts in CC CPSU; 1956–58 Secretary, CC CPSU; Full Member, Buro, Moscow Obkom, CPSU; 1958–59 Administrator of Affairs, USSR Council of Ministers; 1958–62 Deputy, Council of Nationalities, USSR Supreme Soviet (5th convocation); 1959–60 First Secretary, Moscow Obkom, CPSU; 1959–61 Member, Buro for RSFSR, CPSU; 1960–62 First Secretary, Moscow Gorkom, CC CPSU; 1961–74 Secretary, CC CPSU (responsible for internal ideology); 1961– Full Member, CC CPSU; 1962–65 Chairman, Buro for Chemical and Light Industry, CC CPSU; 1962–66 Member, Presidium, USSR Supreme Soviet; 1962– Deputy, Council of the Union, USSR Supreme Soviet (since 6th convocation); 1964– Candidate Member, Presidium (after 1966: Politburo), CC CPSU; 1965–74 Chairman Commission on Ideology, CC CPSU; 1974–86 USSR Minister of Culture; 1986– First Deputy Chairman, Presidium, USSR Supreme Soviet; 1986 Chairman, Organizational Committee, Soviet Cultural Foundation.

DOLGIKH Vladimir Ivanovich Present Positions: Secretary, CC CPSU; Candidate Member, Politburo, CC CPSU. **Date of Birth:** 5 December 1924. **Place of Birth:** Ilanskoe (now: Ilanskii, Krasnoyarsk Krai). **Nationality:** Russian. **Family Background:** Father believed to have been high official in

USSR Ministry of Internal Affairs. **Higher Education:** Studied at Mining-Metallurgical Institute (Irkutsk), 1943–49; engineering degree and Candidate of Technical Sciences, 1968. **Career:** 1942– Party Member; 1949–58 Shift and shop superintendent, later chief engineer in Krasnoyarsk plants; 1958–62 Chief engineer, A. P. Zavenyagin Mining-Metallurgical Combine, Norilsk; 1962–69 Director, A. P. Zavenyagin Mining-Metallurgical Combine, Norilsk; 1966– Deputy (and Member, Commission on Budget and Planning, 1966–70; Commission on Industry since 1970), Council of the Union, USSR Supreme Soviet (since 7th convocation); 1969–72 First Secretary, Krasnoyarsk Kraikom, CPSU; 1971– Full Member, CC CPSU; 1972– Secretary, CC CPSU (responsible for heavy industry and energy); 1976–83 Chief, Department of Heavy Industry, CC CPSU; 1982– Candidate Member, Politburo, CC CPSU; 1983–84 Chief, Department of Heavy and Power Industry, CC CPSU

RAZUMOVSKII Georgii Petrovich Present Positions: Secretary, CC CPSU, Politburo Candidate Member, CC CPSU; Chief, Department for Party Organizational Work, CC CPSU. **Date of Birth:** 19 January 1936. **Nationality:** Russian. **Higher Education:** Graduated as agronomist from Krasnodar Agricultural Institute in 1958. **Career:** 1958–59 Agronomist on a kolkhoz; 1959–61 First Secretary of a Komsomol raikom, Krasnodar Krai; 1961– Party member; 1961–64 Instructor, then section chief, Krasnodar Kraikom, CPSU; 1964–67 Secretary, CPSU committee of a kolkhoz-sovkhoz production association; First Secretary, Korenovsk Raikom, Krasnodar Krai, CPSU; 1967–71 Chief, Department of Agriculture, Krasnodar Kraikom, CPSU; 1971–73 Deputy chief, then chief of a section of a department, CC CPSU; 1973–81 Chairman, Executive Committee, Krasnodar Krai Workers' Soviet; 1973– Deputy (and Member, 1974–79, Commission on Consumer Goods; Mandate Commission, 1979–84; Chairman, Commission on Agro-Industrial Complex, 1984–85; Chairman, Commission on Legislative Proposals, since 1985), Council of the Union, USSR Supreme Soviet; 1981–83 Chief, Department of Agro-Industrial Complex, Administration of Affairs, USSR Council of Ministers; 1983–85 First Secretary, Krasnodar Kraikom, CPSU; 1985– Chief, Department for Party; Organizational Work, CC CPSU; 1986– Full Member, CC CPSU; 1986– Secretary, CC CPSU (responsible for cadres affairs). **Evident Patron:** Gorbachev

YAZOV Dmitrii Timofeevich Present Positions: USSR Minister of Defence; Candidate Member, Politburo, CC CPSU; Army General. **Date of Birth:** 8 November 1923. **Place of Birth:** Yazovo, Okoneshnikovo Raion, Omsk Oblast, RSFSR. **Nationality:** Russian. **Family Background:** Father, a peasant, died during period of collectivization. **Higher Education:** Military

School for the Artillery (now: Higher Officers' School of RSFSR Supreme Soviet), Moscow, 1941–42; Frunze Military Academy (Moscow) until 1956; Military Academy of General Staff (Moscow), 1965–67. **Career:** 1942–45 Commander of a platoon, deputy commander of a company of 483rd rifle regiment (lieutenant), Volkhovo Front; leader of 9th company of 483rd rifle regiment, Leningrad Front; 1944– Party member; 1945–48 Commander of a company; 1948–58 Commander of a battalion, then of a regiment; 1958–61 Post(s) in staff of Leningrad Military District; Lieutenant Colonel (1959); 1961–63 Commander of a regiment, Leningrad Military District; 1963–65 Post(s) in staff of Leningrad Military District; Colonel (1965); 1967–71 Commander of a division, Transbaikal Military District; General Major (1969); 1971 Chief of staff of an army; 1972–74 Commander of an army in Azerbaijan, Transcaucasian Military District; General Lieutenant (1973); 1974–76 Post in Main Directorate for Cadres, USSR Ministry of Defense; 1976–79 First Deputy Commander, Far East Military District; Colonel General (1976); 1979–80 Commander, Central Group of Forces (Czechoslovakia); 1979– Deputy (and Member, Energy Commission, 1982–87), Council of Nationalities, USSR Supreme Soviet (10th–11th convocations); 1980–84 Commander, Central Asian Military District; Army General (1984); 1981–84 Member, Buro, CC CP Kazakhstan; 1981–87 Candidate Member, CC CPSU; 1981–86 Member, CC CP Kazakhstan; 1984–86 Commander, Far East Military District; 1986–87 USSR Deputy Minister of Defence for personnel; Chief, Main Directorate for Cadres, USSR Ministry of Defence; 1987– USSR Minister of Defence; 1987– Candidate Member, Politburo, CC CPSU; 1987– Member, CC CPSU

SOLOV'EV Yurii Filippovich Present Positions: First Secretary, Leningrad Obkom, CPSU; Candidate Member, Politburo, CC CPSU. **Date of Birth:** 20 August 1925. **Nationality:** Russian. **Higher Education:** Graduated from V. N. Obraztsov Engineering Institute for Rail Transport, Leningrad, in 1951. **Career:** 1943–44 Soldier in Red Army; 1951–61 Shift leader; leader of a construction section; chief engineer on construction of Leningrad subway; 1955– Party member; 1961–67 Chief engineer; 1967–73 Head of Construction Administration, Leningrad subway (*Lenmetrostroi*); 1973–74 Deputy Chairman, Executive Committee, Leningrad City Soviet; 1974–75 Secretary, Leningrad Obkom, CPSU (responsibile for industry); 1975–80 Deputy, RSFSR Supreme Soviet; Member, Presidium, RSFSR Supreme Soviet; 1975–78 Second Secretary, Leningrad Obkom, CPSU; 1976– Full Member, CC CPSU; 1978–84 First Secretary, Leningrad Gorkom, CPSU 1979– Deputy (and Member, Commission on Public Education and Culture, 1979–84), Council of the Union, USSR Supreme Soviet (since 10th convocation); 1984–85 USSR Minister for Industrial

Construction; 1985–   First Secretary, Leningrad Obkom, CPSU; Member, Military Council, Leningrad Military District; 1986–   Candidate Member, Politburo, CC CPSU; 1986–   Member, Presidium, USSR Supreme Soviet

TALYZIN Nikolai Vladimirovich Present Positions: First Deputy Chairman, USSR Council of Ministers; Candidate Member, Politburo, CC CPSU. **Date of Birth:** 28 January 1929. **Place of Birth:** Moscow. **Nationality:** Russian. **Family Background:** Blue-collar. **Higher Education:** Graduated as engineer from Moscow Electrical Engineering Institute of Communications, 1955; Doctor of Technical Sciences, 1970; Professor, 1975. **Career:** 1942–50 Electrical fitter, electrical engineer, designer; 1955–65 Engineer, design supervisor, senior scientific associate, then deputy chief for scientific questions, Scientific Research Institute of Radio Engineering, USSR Ministry of Communications; 1960–   Party member; 1965–71 USSR Deputy Minister of Communications; 1971–75 USSR First Deputy Minister of Communications; 1975–80 USSR Minister of Communications; 1975–82 Member, Organizational Committee, 1980 Summer Olympic Games; 1976–81 Candidate Member, CC CPSU; 1976–   Chairman, Central Board, USSR-Finland Society; 1979–   Deputy, Council of the Union, USSR Supreme Soviet (since 10th convocation); 1980–85 Deputy Chairman, USSR Council of Ministers; 1981–   Full Member, CC CPSU; 1985–   First Deputy Chairman, USSR Council of Ministers; 1985–88 Chairman, USSR State Planning Committee (Gosplan); Candidate Member, Politburo, CC CPSU; 1987–   Chairman, Soviet-Chinese Commission on Economic, Trade and Scientific-Technological Cooperation; 1988–   Chairman, Bureau of the USSR Council of Ministers for Social Development

MASLYUKOV Yurii Dmitrievich Present Positions: First Deputy Chairman, USSR Council of Ministers, Chairman, USSR State Planning Committee (Gosplan), Candidate Member, Politburo, CC CPSU. **Date of Birth:** 30 September 1937. **Place of Birth:** Leninabad (Tajik SSR). **Nationality:** Russian. **Higher Education:** Graduated from Leningrad Institute of Mechanics with an engineering degree in 1962. **Career:** 1962–70 Engineer at a technological-scientific research institute, technological engineer, Deputy Chief of a department, Chief Engineer at technological-scientific research institute; 1966–   Party member; 1970–74 Chief Engineer, branch of Izhevsk Machine-building Plant; 1974–82 Chief of a main administration, USSR Ministry of Defence Industry; 1979–82 USSR Deputy Minister of Defence Industry; 1982–85 First Deputy Chairman, USSR Gosplan (responsible for armaments); 1984–   Deputy (and

Member, Commission on Foreign Affairs, 1984–85), Council of Nationalities, USSR Supreme Soviet; 1985–88 Deputy Chairman, USSR Council of Ministers, Member Presidium, USSR Council of Ministers, Chairman, Military-Industrial Commission, Presidium, USSR Council of Ministers; 1986–   Full Member, CC CPSU; 1988–   First Deputy Chairman, USSR Council of Ministers, Chairman, USSR State Planning Committee (Gosplan); 1988–   Candidate Member, Politburo, CC CPSU

SECRETARIES CC CPSU (not members of Politburo)

BAKLANOV Oleg Dmitrievich Present Positions: Secretary, CC CPSU. **Date of Birth:** 1932. **Nationality:** Ukrainian. **Higher Education:** Graduated from All-Union Power Institute by correspondence (Moscow) in 1950, candidate of technical science. **Career:** 1950–75 Engineer at an instrument plant in Kharkov, Ukraine; 1953–   Party member; 1975–76 General Director, Production Association, USSR Ministry of General Machine Building; 1976–81 USSR Deputy Minister of General Machine Building; 1981–83 USSR First Deputy Minister of General Machine Building; 1983–88 USSR Minister of General Machine Building; 1984–   Deputy, Council of the Union, USSR Supreme Soviet; 1986–   Full Member, CC CPSU; 1988– Secretary, CC CPSU (responsible for military-industrial complex)

BIRYUKOVA Aleksandra Pavlovna Present Positions: Secretary, CC CPSU. **Date of Birth:** 25 February 1929. **Place of Birth:** Moscow Oblast. **Nationality:** Russian. **Family Background:** Peasant. **Higher Education:** Graduated from Moscow Textile Institute in 1952; wrote dissertation at Dolukhaev Soil Institute, Moscow, in 1958. **Career:** 1952–59 Foreman, shop supervisor of 1st Printed Fabric Works, Moscow; 1956–   Party member; 1959–63 Chief specialist, department head, Textile and Knitwear Industry Administration, Moscow City, Sovnarkhoz; 1963–68 Chief engineer, Dzerzhinsky 'Trekhgornaya manufaktura' Cotton Combine, Moscow; 1968–   Member, Central Council of Trade Unions; 1968–85 Secretary, Central Council of Trade Unions; 1968–86 Member, Presidium, Central Council of Trade Unions; 1971–76 Candidate Member, CC CPSU; 1971–   Deputy (and Member, Commission on Industry, 1971–75; Chairman, Commission on Working and Living Conditions of Women, Mother and Child Care, since 1976) RSFSR Supreme Soviet (8th–11th convocations); 1976–   Full Member, CC CPSU; 1985–86 Deputy Chairman, Central Council of Trade Unions; 1986–   Secretary, CC CPSU (responsible for light industry, consumer goods production, domestic trade, labour affairs, and women's issues)

LUK'YANOV Anatolii Ivanovich Present Positions: Secretary, CC CPSU. **Date of Birth:** 7 May 1930. **Nationality:** Russian. **Higher Education:** Graduated from Law Faculty, Moscow State University, 1953; Doctor of Juridical Sciences (1980). **Career:** 1943-? Worker, *Arsenal* munitions factory; 1955– Party member; 1956–61 Senior consultant of Legal commission, USSR Council of Ministers; 1969–76 Deputy Chief, Department of Soviet Activities, Presidium, USSR Supreme Soviet; 1976–77 Consultant in CC CPSU apparat; 1977–83 Chief of Secretariat, Presidium, USSR Supreme Soviet; 1978– Member, editorial staff, *Sovetskoe gosudarstvo i pravo*; 1981–86 Member, Central Auditing Commission, CPSU; 1983–85 First Deputy Chief, General Department, CC CPSU; 1984–86 Member, Buro, Central Auditing Commission, CPSU; 1985– Deputy, RSFSR Supreme Soviet (11th convocation); 1985–87 Chief, General Department, CC CPSU; 1986– Full Member, CC CPSU; 1987– Secretary, CC CPSU (oversight of military, security, intelligence, and legal institutions, Politburo staff work); 1987– Deputy, Council of the Union, USSR Supreme Soviet (elected in mid-term)

DOBRYNIN Anatolii Fedrovich Secretary, CC CPSU; Chief, International Department, CC CPSU. **Date of Birth:** 16 November 1919. **Place of Birth:** Krasnaya Gorka (Uvarovka Raion, Moscow Oblast). **Nationality:** Russian (several US sources: Ukrainian). **Family Background:** Blue-collar. **Higher Education:** Attended S. M. Ordzhonikidze Aviation Institute in Moscow (until 1942); attended Higher Diplomatic School of the USSR Ministry of Foreign Affairs (1944–46); Candidate of Historical Sciences (1947). **Career:** 1942–44 Engineer in a large aircraft construction plant; 1945– Party member; 1947–49 In apparat of USSR Ministry of Foreign Affairs; lecturer on questions related to Soviet-US relationship, Institute of International Relations (Moscow), USSR Ministry of Foreign Affairs; 1949–52 Aide to USSR Deputy Minister of Foreign Affairs (Gromyko); 1952–55 Counsellor, 1954–55 Minister Counsellor in USSR Embassy in USA; 1955–57 Aide to USSR Minister of Foreign Affairs (Molotov, Shepilov); 1957–60 UN Under Secretary General, Department of Political and Security Council Affairs; 1960–62 Chief, United States of America Department, USSR Ministry of Foreign Affairs; 1962–86 USSR Ambassador to the United States of America; 1966–71 Candidate Member, CC CPSU; 1971– Full Member, CC CPSU; 1986– Secretary, CC CPSU (responsible for foreign affairs); 1986– Chief, International Department, CC CPSU

MEDVEDEV Vadim Andreevich Secretary, CC CPSU; Chief, Department for Liaison with Communist and Workers' Parties of Socialist Countries, CC CPSU. **Date of Birth:** 29 March 1929. **Nationality:** Russian. **Higher Education:** Graduated from Leningrad State University in 1951; Doctor of

Economic Sciences; Professor (1968). **Career:** 1951–56 Chief lector, Leningrad State University; 1952– Party member; 1956–61 Assistant Professor, Leningrad Institute of Rail Transport; 1961–68 Held chair at Leningrad Technological Institute; 1968–70 Secretary, Leningrad Gorkom, CPSU (for ideology); 1970–78 Deputy Chief, Department of Propaganda, CC CPSU; 1972– Member, Editorial Collegium, journal *Politicheskoe samoobrazovanie* (Political Self-Education); 1976–86 Member, Central Auditing Commission, CPSU; 1978–83 Rector, Academy of Social Sciences, CC CPSU (Moscow); 1983–86 Chief, Department of Science and Educational Institutions, CC CPSU; 1984– Corresponding Member, USSR Academy of Sciences (Economics Section); 1984– Deputy (and Member, Commission on Science and Technology), Council of the Union, USSR Supreme Soviet; 1986– Full Member, CC CPSU; 1986– Secretary, CC CPSU (responsible for bloc relations); 1986– Chief, Department for Liaison with Communist and Workers' Parties of Socialist Countries, CC CPSU. **Evident Patron:** Yakovlev

CHIEFS OF CENTRAL COMMITTEE DEPARTMENTS

KRUCHINA Nikolai Efimovich Administrator of Affairs, CC CPSU. **Date of Birth:** 14 May 1928. **Place of Birth:** Novaya Pokrovka, Altai Krai. **Nationality:** Russian. **Education:** Graduated in 1953 from Azov-Black Sea Agricultural Institute in Zernograd (Rostov Oblast). **Career:** 1952–54 First Secretary, Novocherkassk Gorkom (Rostov Oblast), All-Union Komsomol; 1954–57 Second Secretary, First Secretary, Kamensk Obkom, All-Union Komsomol; 1957–59 First Secretary, Smolensk Obkom, All-Union Komsomol; 1959–62 Chief, Rural Youth Department, CC All-Union Komsomol; 1962–63 Instructor of a department, CC CPSU; 1963–65 Secretary, Virgin Lands Kraikom, Kazak CP (dissolved in 1965); 1965–78 First Secretary, Tselinograd Obkom, Kazak CP; 1966–71 Member, Central Auditing Commission, CPSU; 1966– Deputy (and Member, 1966–70, Commission on Budget and Planning; Member, since 1970, Commission on Youth Affairs), Council of the Union, USSR Supreme Soviet; 1971–76 Candidate Member, CC CPSU; 1976– Full Member, CC CPSU; 1978–83 First Deputy Chief, Department of Agriculture, CC CPSU; 1983– Administrator of Affairs, CC CPSU. **Evident Patron:** Gorbachev

SAVINKIN Nikolai Ivanovich Chief, Department of Administrative Organs, CC CPSU. **Date of Birth:** 11 December 1913. **Nationality:** Russian. **Higher Education:** Graduated from Kashira Technicum for Mechanization and Electrification of Agriculture in 1932; graduated from V. I. Lenin Military-Political Academy (Moscow) in 1950. **Career:** 1932–34 Deputy director of a post and telegraph facility; 1934–35 Chief of a department of a Komsomol raikom; 1935–50 Held political posts in Red (after 1946: Soviet) Army in Transbaikal region; 1937– Party member; 1941–44 Chief instructor of a Red Army political department; chief of a political department of an army brigade; also deputy chief of a political leadership department at the front; 1950–60 Held high posts in CC All-Union CP(b) (after 1952: CPSU), including that of deputy chief of Department of Administrative Organs, CC CPSU; 1960–68 First Deputy Chief, Department of Administrative Organs, CC CPSU; 1966–71 Member, Central Auditing Commission, CPSU; 1968– Chief, Department of Administrative Organs, CC CPSU; 1970– Deputy (and Member, Commission on Legislative Proposals), Council of Nationalites, USSR Supreme Soviet; 1971–81 Candidate Member, CC CPSU; 1981– Full Member, CC CPSU. **Evident Patron:** Brezhnev

SKIBA Ivan Ivanovich Chief, Department of Agriculture and Food Industry, CC CPSU. **Date of Birth:** 8 March 1937. **Nationality:** Ukrainian. **Higher Education:** Graduated from Odessa Agricultural Institute in 1959. **Career:** 1959– Party member; 1959–62 Assistant Professor, Odessa Agricultural Institute; Instructor, Odessa Obkom, Ukrainian Komsomol; Instructor, then chief of a sector, chief of Department of Agriculture, CC Ukrainian Komsomol; 1962–68 Secretary, CC Ukrainian Komsomol (responsible for agriculture); 1968–70 Second Secretary, CC Ukrainian Komsomol; 1970–72 Inspector, CC Ukrainian CP; 1972–78 Second Secretary, Transcarpatian Obkom, Ukrainian CP; 1978–83 First Secretary, Ivanovo-Frankovsk Obkom, Ukrainian CP; 1979– Deputy (and Member, Commission for Youth Affairs, 1979–84; Member, Commission on Agroindustrial Complex, since 1984), Council of the Union, USSR Supreme Soviet; 1983–87 First Deputy Chief, Department of Agriculture and Food Industry, CC CPSU; 1986– Candidate Member, CC CPSU; 1987– Chief, Department of Agriculture and Food Industry, CC CPSU

CHERVONENKO Stepan Vasil'evich Chief, Department for Cadres Abroad, CC CPSU. **Date of Birth:** 16 September 1915. **Place of Birth:** Okop, Lokhvitsa Raion, Poltava Oblast, Ukrainian SSR. **Nationality:** Ukrainian. **Family Background:** Peasant. **Higher Education:** Graduated in 1936 from Taras Shevchenko State University (Kiev); in 1940 completed advanced courses for instructors of Marxism-Leninism, CC Ukrainian CP; in 1948 and 1949, doctoral studies in Marxism-Leninism, history, and philosophy at Academy of Social Sciences, CC CPSU (Moscow), where he earned degree of Candidate of Philosophical Sciences. **Career:** 1937–40 History teacher and director of a secondary school in Kiev Oblast; 1940– Party member; 1941–44 Political agitator in Red Army; 1944–48 Lecturer on dialectical and historical materialism, then professor of Marxism-Leninism, deputy director, then director, Pedagogical Institute, Cherkassy; 1949–56 Party work in CC apparat, Ukrainian CP; 1949–51 Head of a group of lecturers, CC Ukrainian CP; 1951–56 Chief, Department of Science and Culture, CC Ukrainian CP; 1956–59 Secretary, CC Ukrainian CP (responsible for ideology); 1958–62 Deputy (and Chairman, 1958–60, Mandate Commission), Council of Nationalities, USSR Supreme Soviet; 1958–62 Member, USSR Parliamentary Group, USSR Supreme Soviet; 1959–65 USSR Ambassador to People's Republic of China; 1961–   Full Member, CC CPSU; 1965–73 USSR Ambassador to Czechoslovakia; 1973–83 USSR Ambassador to France; (1973–74 concurrently USSR Ambassador to Madagascar); 1983–   Chief, Department for Cadres Abroad, CC CPSU; 1984–   Deputy (and Member, Commission on Foreign Affairs), Council of Nationalities, USSR Supreme Soviet. **Evident Patron:** Suslov

AFONIN Ven'yamin Georgievich Chief, Department of Chemical Industry, CC CPSU. **Date of Birth:** 1931. **Career:** 1956–68 Worked as an engineer; 1957–   Party member; 1968–   Party work; 1970s First Secretary, Nevinnomyssk Gorkom, CPSU (Stavropol Krai); 1978–80 Chief of a department, Stavropol Kraikom, CPSU; 1980–83 Secretary, Stavropol Kraikom, CPSU; 1983–   Chief, Department of Chemical Industry, CC CPSU; 1986–   Candidate Member, CC CPSU. **Evident Patron:** Gorbachev

MEL'NIKOV Aleksandr Grigor'evich Chief, Department of Construction, CC CPSU. **Date of Birth:** 21 October 1930. **Nationality:** Russian. **Higher Education:** Attended Engineers' Institute for Construction in Moscow and graduated as construction engineer in 1953; attended Higher Party School in Moscow, CC CPSU. **Career:** 1953–55 Engineer in an administration for investment construction; 1955–59 Komsomol work; 1957–   Party member; 1959–70 Chief of a gorkom department, CPSU, Tomsk Oblast; chairman of executive committee, city Soviet, Tomsk Oblast; first secretary of gorkom, CPSU, Tomsk Oblast; 1970–83 Chief of a department; Secretary (for industry); Second Secretary, Tomsk Obkom, CPSU; 1983–86 First Secretary, Tomsk Obkom, CPSU; 1984–   Deputy (and Deputy Chairman, Commission on Construction and Construction Materials Industry), Council of the Union, USSR Supreme Soviet; 1986–   Chief, Department of Construction, CC CPSU; 1986–   Full Member, CC CPSU. **Evident Patron:** Ligachev

VORONOV Yurii Petrovich Chief, Department of Culture, CC CPSU. **Date of Birth:** 17 January 1929. **Place of Birth:** Leningrad. **Nationality:**

Russian. **Higher Education:** Graduated in 1952 from A. A. Zhdanov University in Leningrad (studied journalism at philology faculty). **Career:** 1951– Party member; 1952–55 Secretary, Leningrad Obkom, All-Union Komsomol; Editor, Komsomol journal, *Smena*; 1955–59 Deputy Chief Editor, *Komsomol'skaya Pravda*; 1959–65 Chief Editor, *Komsomol'skaya Pravda*; 1959–65 Member, Buro, All-Union Komsomol; 1966–73 Executive Secretary, Editorial Board, *Pravda*; 1973–82 Chief, *Pravda* newspaper office in GDR and West-Berlin; 1982–85 Secretary of Board, USSR Writers' Union; 1985–86 Chief Editor, *Znamya*; 1986– Chief, Department of Culture, CC CPSU. **Evident Patron:** Yakovlev

BELYAKOV Oleg Sergeevich Chief, Department of Defence Industry, CC CPSU. **Date of Birth:** 1933. **Career:** 1958–64 Worked as an engineer; 1961– Party member; 1964–72 Party work; 1972–82 Post(s) in the CC CPSU *apparat*; presumably in Department of defence Industry, CC CPSU; 1982–85 Deputy Chief, Department of Defence Industry, CC CPSU; 1985– Chief, Department of Defence Industry, CC CPSU; 1986– Full Member, CC CPSU; 1986– Deputy (and Member, Energy Commission, since 1986), USSR Supreme Soviet

SLYUN'KOV Nikolai Nikitovich (see Politburo CPSU Members above)

BOLDIN Valerii Ivanovich Chief, General Department, CC CPSU. **Date of Birth:** 1935. **Nationality:** Russian. **Higher Education:** Graduated from Timiryazev Academy for Agriculture (Moscow) in 1961; graduated as Candidate of Economics from Academy of Social Sciences (Moscow), CC CPSU in 1969. **Career:** 1960– Party member; 1961–69 Journalist, literary critic for *Pravda*, then Party work and studies; 1969–73 Commentator on economy, Deputy Editor of an editorial section of *Pravda*; 1973–81 Member, Editorial Collegium, *Pravda*; Editor of Agricultural section, *Pravda*; 1981–85 In CC CPSU apparat (aide to CPSU CC Secretary Gorbachev); 1985– Deputy (and Member, Commission of Foreign Affairs), Council of the Union, USSR Supreme Soviet; 1985–87 Aide to General Secretary, CC CPSU (on questions of agriculture); 1986– Candidate Member, CC CPSU; 1987– Chief, General Department, CC CPSU. **Evident Patron:** Gorbachev

YASTREBOV Ivan Pavlovich Chief, Department for Heavy Industry and Power, CC CPSU. **Date of Birth:** 20 January 1911. **Nationality:** Russian. **Higher Education:** Graduated from Ural Polytechnical Institute, Sverdlovsk, in 1936. **Career:** 1936–46 Foreman, group leader, chief of a technical department of a metallurgical plant in Lys'va (Perm Oblast); 1941– Party member; 1946–50 in Party apparat; 1950–51 First Secretary, Lys'va Gorkom (Perm Oblast), CPSU; 1951–53 Chief of a department, Perm

Obkom, CPSU; 1953–54 First Secretary, Perm Gorkom, CPSU; 1954–62 Deputy Chief, Department for Heavy Industry, CC CPSU; 1962–84 First Deputy Chief, Department for Heavy Industry (since 1983 Heavy Industry and Power), CC CPSU; 1971–81 Member, Central Auditing Commission, CC CPSU; 1981– Candidate Member, CC CPSU; 1984– Chief, Department for Heavy Industry and Power, CC CPSU

BOBYKIN Leonid Fedorovich Chief, Department for Light Industry and Consumer Goods, CC CPSU. **Date of Birth:** 1930. **Career:** 1955– Engineer; 1956– Party member; 1966–71 First Secretary, Ordzhonikidze Raikom, CPSU, Sverdlovsk City; 1971–76 First Secretary, Sverdlovsk Gorkom, CPSU; 1976–83 Secretary (responsible for industry); Second Secretary, Sverdlovsk Obkom, CPSU; 1983–86 First Deputy Chief, Department for Light Industry and Consumer Goods, CC CPSU; 1986– Chief, Department for Light Industry and Consumer Goods, CC CPSU; 1986– Candidate Member, CC CPSU. **Evident Patron:** Ryzhkov

VOL'SKII Arkadii Ivanovich Chief, Department of Machine-Building, CC CPSU. **Date of Birth:** 15 May 1932. **Career:** 1966–? Secretary, Party Committee, Likhachev Automobile Plant, Moscow; 1972– Member, editorial staff, *Agitator*; 1978–81(?) Deputy Chief, Department of Machine-Building, CC CPSU; 1981(?)–83 First Deputy Chief, Department of Machine-Building, CC CPSU; 1983–85 Aide to General Secretary, CC CPSU (Andropov, then Chernenko); 1984– Deputy (and Member, Commission on Industry, 1985–), Council of Nationalities, USSR Supreme Soviet; 1985–Chief, Department of Machine-Building, CC CPSU; 1986– Full Member, CC CPSU. **Evident Patron:** Andropov

RAZUMOVSKII Georgii Petrovich (See Politburo CPSU Members above)

SKLYAROV Yurii Aleksandrovich Chief, Propaganda Department, CC CPSU. **Date of Birth:** 8 February 1925. **Higher Education:** Graduated as historian from Kharkov State University in 1951; Candidate of Historical Sciences (1955). **Career:** 1943–45 Soldier in Red Army; 1944– Party member; 1955–63 Post(s) in Party apparat of Kharkov Gorkom and Obkom, Ukrainian CP; 1963–64 Lector and Secretary of Party Committee, Kharkov State University; 1964–69 Secretary, Kharkov Obkom, Ukrainian CP (responsible for ideology); 1969–76 Deputy Chief, Propaganda Department, CC CPSU (responsible for Party press); 1976–82 First Deputy Chief Editor, *Pravda*; 1981– Candidate Member, CC CPSU; 1982–86 Chief Editor, *Problemy mira i sotsializma*, (Prague); 1986– Chief, Propaganda Department, CC CPSU. **Evident Patron:** Yakovlev

GRIGOR'EV Valentin Aleksandrovich Chief, Department of Science and Education Institutions, CC CPSU. **Date of Birth:** 1929. **Higher Education:** Doctor of Technical Sciences; Professor. **Career:** 1958– Party member; 1970s–85 Rector, Moscow Institute of Energetics; 1981– Corresponding Member, USSR Academy of Sciences (Physical Technical Problems of Power Engineering Department); 1985 Deputy Chief; 1985–87 First Deputy Chief; 1987– Chief Department of Science and Educational Institutions, CC CPSU. **Evident Patron:** Medvedev

STASHENKOV Nikolai Alekseevich Chief, Department of Trade and Consumer Services, CC CPSU. **Date of Birth:** 15 March 1934. **Place of Birth:** Dryageli (Rudnya Raion, Smolensk Oblast, RSFSR). **Nationality:** Belorussian. **Higher Education:** Graduated in 1957 from Institute of Economics in Minsk; attended USSR Academy of Economics in Moscow 1978–80. **Career:** 1957–71 worked in trade sector, Vitebsk Oblast Soviet, BSSR; 1960– Party member; 1971–78 Chief, Department of Trade and Consumer Services, CC Belorussian CP; 1980–81 Belorussian Minister of Trade; 1981–83 USSR Deputy Minister of Trade; Chairman, Council for Consumer Research, USSR Ministry of Trade; 1983–84 Permanent Representative of Belorussian Council of Ministers at USSR Council of Ministers; 1984–85 Deputy Chief of Department for Trade and Consumer Services, CC CPSU; 1985– Chief, Department of Trade and Consumer Services, CC CPSU; 1986– Candidate Member, CC CPSU. **Evident Patron:** Slyun'kov

PASTERNAK Viktor Stepanovich Chief, Department of Transport and Communications, CC CPSU. **Date of Birth:** 1931. **Nationality:** Russian. **Higher Education:** Graduated from Khabarovsk Institute of Rail Transport Engineering. **Career:** 1953–55 Assistant to an engine operator, Engineer at a locomotive depot of railway station Khabarovsk-2; 1955–63 Fitter, construction engineer, foreman at a crane repair-shop, assistant to head of a department at *Amurstal'* plant; 1959– Party member; 1963–66 Secretary, Second Secretary, Khabarovsk Gorkom, CPSU; 1966–73 Secretary, Khabarovsk (?) Gorkom, CPSU; 1973–76 Second Secretary, Jewish Autonomous Obkom, CPSU; 1976–81 First Deputy Chairman, Executive Committee, Khabarovsk Krai Workers' Soviet; 1981–86 Chairman, Executive Committee, Khabarovsk Krai Workers' Soviet; 1984– Deputy (and Member, Commission on Transport and Communications), Council of Nationalities, USSR Supreme Soviet; 1986– Chief, Department of Transport and Communications, CC CPSU

LIZICHEV Aleksei Dmitrievich Chief, Main Political Administration, Soviet Army and Navy. **Date of Birth:** 22 June 1928. **Place of Birth:**

Vologda Oblast. **Nationality:** Russian. **Family Background:** Blue-collar. **Higher Education:** Attended Military School (1946–49) and Lenin Military-Political Academy in Moscow. **Career:** 1949– Party member; 1949–61 Political officer for Komsomol work in a regiment, then a division; assistant for Komsomol work to Chief of Political Administration, Northern Military District; later Leningrad Military District; 1961–65 Assistant for Komsomol work to Chief of Main Political Administration, Soviet Army and Navy; 1965–71 Chief of Political Administration, Army Corps, Volga Military District; Deputy Chief, First Deputy Chief, Political Administration, Moscow Military District; 1971–75 First Deputy Chief, Political Administration, Group of Soviet Troops in Germany; 1975–80 Chief of Political Administration, Transbaikal Military District; 1980–82 Deputy Chief, Main Political Administration, Soviet Army and Navy (on questions of ideology); 1982–85 Chief of Political Administration, Group of Soviet Troops in Germany; 1984– Deputy (and Member, commission on Foreign Affairs, since 1985), Council of Nationalities, USSR Supreme Soviet; 1985– Chief, Main Political Administration, Soviet Army and Navy; 1986– Army General; 1986– Full Member, CC CPSU

DOBRYNIN Anatolii Fedrovich (See Secretaries CC CPSU above)

MEDVEDEV Vadim Andreevich (See Secretaries CC CPSU above)

PART II
Elite Stratification and Circulation

4. Elite Mobility in the Locales: Towards a Modified Patronage Model

William M. Reisinger and John P. Willerton, Jr.*

What types of politicians build successful careers in regional Party organizations, and what elements underlie their success? To what extent have elite mobility norms varied across different national leaderships since 1950? This chapter provides a systematic examination of the changing practices of regional elite recruitment and mobility during the post-Stalin period. We assess the relative importance of a number of factors, including expertise, performance, and patronage connections, to career success. We posit that a modified patronage model, encompassing these factors, works best in explaining upward political mobility.

Important changes in the Soviet system have necessitated an increasing reliance upon better trained and more skilled politicians. The advanced industrial setting requires decision makers who can effectively direct an ever more complex economy and society. Yet aspiring politicians, even if better qualified to deal with the complexities of the modern industrial society, must continue to be politically reliable. Career connections to prominent national politicians often signify such reliability, especially in securing an important regional-level post. The politician with patronage ties and expertise becomes an optimal choice for a leadership position. The continued concentration of power in the Soviet system assures Moscow's definitive role in the assessment of a politician's political performance. How important is the performance of a regional Party leader, in assuring his region's economic growth and political stability, to his continued tenure and future mobility prospects?

The relative importance of expertise, patronage, and performance to the mobility of regional politicians is evaluated in this study. Recruitment and mobility norms are shown to have varied over the Stalin, Khrushchev, and Brezhnev periods. While describing general tendencies, this study elabo-

* We would like to express our appreciation to our research assistants, Garrison Beik, Lisa Dawson, Donnett Flash, Timothy Kleczynski, and Carol Pruisner, for their contributions to this study and to the broader project.

rates upon the rather different mobility practices that characterize various regions. Our findings justify the Gorbachev regime's interest in the political implications of different mobility strategies; mobility strategies which can be applied by the national leadership to structure the composition and behaviour of the regional decision-making elite.

BACKGROUND AND RATIONALE

The post-Stalin period has entailed important changes not only in the Soviet system, but in the political regimes that have governed it. These changes, transcending the high politics of elite successions, have involved an important shift in the bases of system and regime legitimacy, as increasing reliance has been placed upon system performance. They represent the increased rationalization of Soviet politics if, by rationalization, one means the enhanced focus on economic growth and the improved performance of the political system as overriding goals guiding the polity. The post-mobilization Soviet society experienced the emergence of a bureaucratic system that has required incremental progress toward stated collective goals. The 'building of communism' has assumed a more pragmatic meaning for political elites. In this setting, coercion no longer serves as the exclusive means to assure programmatic success and legitimacy.[1] System support and programmatic success increasingly require economic productivity. As a result, leadership effectiveness, as viewed by the Soviet elite itself, is increasingly evaluated on the basis of the fulfilment of directives. These developments have had important implications for the behaviour of regimes, affecting the norms of elite recruitment and mobility and leading to changes in the processes of coalition building and government formation.[2]

Western theories about the nature and consequences of the Soviet system have reflected changes in the Soviet polity and society. These theories have attempted to account for the Soviet political elites' commitment to both modernization and continued centralized political control. The Harvard Project on the Soviet System[3] concluded as early as 1954 that:

> the technical and managerial personnel, having a stake in the existing system, have developed an interest in maintaining it in predominantly its present form. They are concerned mainly with reducing interference and extreme pressure from the center, and beyond that in improving the system, and making it work more smoothly.

The totalitarian model[4] has given way to several generations of theories which anticipate not only a more complex regime–society relationship, but altered political elite behaviour.

It has been argued that significant changes have occurred in the structure of decision making within the post-Stalinist system[5]. Rules governing the political system have become more explicit and are more formally defined. Clearer distinctions are drawn among various decision-making organs, with greater autonomy possibly resulting for various political bodies both at the centre and in the periphery. One result is increased elite disagreement about policy priorities and the ways to achieve them.[6] Another result is an elite perception of greater security, providing cadres with less severe consequences for upward and downward mobility.[7] Elites at intermediate levels of authority become more assertive and are increasingly tempted to participate in the national policy process.[8]

The economic and political imperatives of the industrialized, post-mobilization society accentuate the need for what Janos[9] terms 'mechanics of social change'; that is, politicians with both the Party background and expertise that permits a deeper familiarity with the industrial economy and polity. The old distinction between Party hack ideologues and trained experts[10] is not relevant to this post-mobilization Soviet reality. A more competent and skilled political and economic elite is necessary in order to respond more readily to changing supply and consumption demands (given the inherent relationship of increased consumption standards of the population to the balanced economic growth that is desired[11]). This elite may include the increased participation of influential subgroups which represent vested societal interests.[12] According to its proponents, such an interest group understanding of post-Stalin elite politics is substantiated by the increased diversity of individuals found in the highest decision-making organs.

Similar arguments are offered in support of the corporatist contention that the post-Stalin recruitment calculus requires a balancing of interests across functional, institutional, and regional distinctions.[13] Corporatism assumes a system of interest representation whereby major political interests are included in the policy process by the top ruling elite. The role of the state is an activist one, but one necessitating the mediation of diverse interests within a routinized policy process.[14] The increased diversity of interests represented within the top elite reflects the regime's commitment to system stability through enhanced system performance. The result is what has been termed a 'welfare state authoritarian' system.[15] Societal behaviour is more effectively regulated by meeting the minimal economic needs of the population, with a more diversified elite better able to accomplish this. Expanded representation of interests is conducive to elite co-operation, consensus, and stability.

While more diverse and representative of a wider range of interests, aspiring elites must continue to be politically reliable. They must have the expertise and experience to (1) function within the established hierarchy of Party and state institutions, and (2) cope with the economic complexities inherent in the modern industrial society. Certain 'troubleshooter' elites will often move up through different bureaucracies, serving in diverse regional and organizational settings (e.g., personnel recruited into republic Party second secretaryships). Other elites will make careers in a narrower range of institutional settings, with more focused policy concerns. However, the competence and political reliability of all such elites will put them in a strong position to trumpet the policy concerns of the governing regime.

These rational–technical and corporatist approaches to political elite recruitment and mobility correctly emphasize the importance of expertise and performance. However, expertise is an increasingly necessary but not sufficient criterion for political mobility. This is partially due to the limitations of the Soviet political opportunity structure.[16] There is a scarcity of political resources, with many aspirants competing for a very limited number of political slots. Mobility opportunities continue to be highly structured and centralized. No diffusion of power has occurred so far as cadres selection is concerned. Promotion continues to depend upon superiors' evaluations, making not only performance but other political factors salient.

In this context, rational–technical criteria may be of importance, yet the decisive factor would involve an aspirant's 'connections' with the selectorate power elite.[17] These connections, or patronage linkages, are often the necessary condition for recruitment because they assure the best prospects for political reliability in a subordinate. In the final analysis, moreover, this is likely to be paramount because, above all else, a politician is concerned to safeguard his position of authority. Elites will be recruited not only for the positive skills and experience they bring to a job, but also for the reliability and predictability that they can offer superiors. Top-level politicians are committed to the society's 'economic mission' only to the extent that they can at least maintain, if not strengthen, their own political position in the process. This is 'rationality' for politicians with ambitions. The skilled subordinate who helps realize the mission while undercutting the superior is no asset.

The modern Soviet system requires politicians with both expertise and connections. Both major models, the rational–technical and patronage models, correctly capture aspects of contemporary Soviet reality. The divergent system goals and consequent preferred elite traits identified by these two models may be summarized as follows:

Model	Rational–Technical	Patronage
System goals	Performance	Control
Preferred traits of politicians	Expertise and experience	Reliability

In observing the 'rules' that facilitate the effective functioning of the Soviet system, elites must balance these different economic performance and political concerns. It may prove critical to promote personnel who possess the appropriate qualities to help realize the incremental goals set by the regime. However, a tension exists among societal, regime, and specific politicians' interests that may not be easily resolved. Norms governing the recruitment of personnel and the formation of governing political teams, not only at the all-union (national) but also at lower levels of authority, reflect this tension.[18] The continued lack of specificity in guidelines governing recruitment and mobility and the differential experience of the various regions and Party organizations only confirms this. Party Second Secretary Egor Ligachev's comments at the 27th CPSU Congress about the need to re-evaluate recruitment norms and practices indicate this matter is of priority to the Gorbachev leadership. Current regime interest in increased interregional exchange of personnel points to the importance of recruitment practices for both performance and political (e.g., anti-corruption) purposes. Such interest is but the latest example of changing national regime strategies of regional elite recruitment.[19] However, change in norms of personnel selection and elevation must be seen as an outcome not only of regime priorities but of long-term system imperatives that are both economic and political.

These concerns about the changing nature of the Soviet system and the composition and behaviour of its elites, as well as the relevance of Western theoretical propositions that address them, cannot be adequately assessed without appropriate, empirically grounded, research. This chapter stems from a broader project we have initiated to examine long-term political and economic trends in the Soviet Union. We are interested in assessing changing patterns of elite recruitment and regime formation, evaluating how regional economic and political performance, patronage, and other factors structure such patterns. Personnel policies which include the recruitment of local politicians and the selective cross-regional and centre–regional movement of officials are examined. We test hypotheses that emerge out of the rival rational–technical and patronage models. We desire to evaluate systematically the relative importance of expertise, performance, connections, and regional prominence in predicting a politician's mobility prospects.

This investigation is directed at the regional level and at the nexus between all-union and regional politics. In this study, regional level is defined as those administrative units, responsible for policy making, which fall immediately under the legal purview of the larger union republics. This includes autonomous republics (ASSRs), territories (krais), and provinces (oblasts). These administrative units, while created on the basis of rather different considerations, are all on a commensurate level of political jurisdiction. We have collected aggregate data for a representative sample of 44 such regional administrative units within the Russian Republic and their elites. These data permit the systematic testing of hypotheses about centre–periphery relations as well as about the differential impact of centrally-determined cadres and mobility norms across regional and organizational settings.

HYPOTHESES

Who are the politicians who come to lead the regional Party organizations? Are there particular background characteristics that are critical to their mobility? Do they have patronage ties to superiors that are conducive to advancement into the critical regional policy-making positions? Are their connections to the political centre, Moscow, strong ones; strong enough to permit them mobility opportunities into top national policy-making bodies? Have the recruitment criteria applied in the selection of such regional politicians changed over the period since the death of Stalin?

Any aspiring politician must successfully operate in an environment structured by hierarchies, institutions and traditions. The career prospects of politicians are significantly affected by the regional and institutional settings in which they operate. Are they building careers in important settings which are conducive to visibility and to the opportunity to cope with important political questions? It has been contended that prominence of regions is important in explaining the advance of particular politicians to national positions of responsibility.[20] Prominent regions are said to offer the heightened national profile, the stronger connections to Moscow elites, and the more multifaceted experience which combine to make such regions better springboards to higher office. Efforts have been made to rank-order regions and their Party organizations so as to identify the more prominent settings from which powerful politicians will come.[21] Our view of this regional prominence factor leads us to posit that:

1. There is a positive correlation between prominence of region (and regional Party organization) and mobility prospects of political elites.

However, we qualify this by noting that the salience of regional prominence is moderated by the impact of other factors. First, it is moderated by the impact of the relative economic performance of that region, where the relative economic performance is measured by, among other things, the degree to which the plan is fulfilled relative to plan fulfilment by other regions. Both prominence and performance influence mobility prospects. However, the regional leader's success in assuring effective performance, which encompasses both economic growth and continued political stability in that leader's bailiwick, is critical.

Those who have studied Soviet politics are aware of the fluctuations in economic (and political) performance that often characterize the locales. While certain regions are stable and predictable in their behaviour, others are not. What are the implications of economic growth fluctuations and political volatility for leadership turnover?

Moscow has a number of options in monitoring and influencing the performances of leaders and their bailiwicks. An important option is personnel selection and the promotion of outsiders to head a region. Is there a relationship between the performance of regions and patterns of leadership recruitment? Are regional Party organizations permitted greater or lesser involvement in the selection of a successor in light of their past track records?

Politicians, either sent from Moscow or transferred from another region, can be relied upon to address political and economic performance problems. To what extent are there 'political troubleshooters' in the Soviet polity; politicians who are brought in from outside a region and who are not linked to the local established elite? We understand that these politicians would be transferred to enhance a region's performance, whether this means bolstering productivity or dealing with political or societal problems. Their presence in the periphery would serve to bridge national concerns and local conditions.

2. There is a positive correlation between a region's good economic and political performance and the promotion of local cadres to top Party positions within that region.
3. Certain politicians function as troubleshooters in order to provide special attention to regions of concern to the political centre. These politicians are recruited from outside a region and will make careers which evince mobility across different regional settings.

Comparing indicators of economic productivity figures would prove helpful in identifying the critical regional organizations and key positions that an ambitious politician will see as providing maximum mobility opportunities. Indeed, we want to manipulate such indicators so as to rank order regions in regard to their relative performance. We can rank order these regions according to their all-union political importance (although we are still in the process of developing appropriate systematic measures for tapping political performance). Combined, these rank orderings would permit us to understand better how forms of performance and prominence affect the types of politicians who successfully compete for top regional slots.

Related to these concerns are patronage considerations. We are interested in contrasting rational–technical and patronage explanations for elite recruitment and mobility. We examine the rational–technical theoretical proposition that there is a random choice in personnel recruitment between

(a) a political client with expertise and (b) a politician with expertise but lacking connections to political superiors. We contend that expertise is a necessary but insufficient criterion for political mobility. The changing needs of a more complex society have necessitated a better educated and more multifaceted political elite. However, the continuing emphasis on political reliability and the need to assure Moscow's control over the periphery ensure that patronage connections will affect recruitment decisions. Patronage connections should be critically important to aspirants' chances of promotion, and especially to the more prominent regional Party leadership positions.

4. Regional Party first secretaries evince increasingly high levels of expertise in the post-Stalin period, regardless of whether or not they have patronage connections to superiors.
5. There is a positive correlation between a politician's patronage connections to all-union politicians and a politician's recruitment to top regional Party organizational positions.

Overall, we anticipate that our analyses will qualify the rational–technical proposition that a politician's efficiency in advancing societal goals of economic development is the primary variable explaining his career success. In qualifying this proposition, however, we intend to provide a multivariate explanation for career success in the Soviet system. Previous research has led us to conclude that a modified patronage model containing patronage ties, economic success, an interactive term between patronage and economic success, and a dummy variable controlling for the period in Soviet history (and different national recruitment strategies), will fit the career data well.

DATA BASE

The population of elites used here includes all Party first secretaries who governed 44 Russian Republic (RSFSR) regions during the period 1950–82 (i.e., through the end of the Brezhnev period). We have selected 44 regional administrative units which constitute a representative sample of the total 72 autonomous republics, krais, and oblasts making up the Russian Republic (see Figure 4.1). At least three regional units were selected from each of the ten different geographic–economic zones that the Soviet government identifies as constituting the RSFSR.[22] These 44 regions vary in size, population, nationality composition and level of development. As a group they reflect the variety of settings found within the largest Soviet republic.

The population of political elites examined here is a diverse one,

Geographic Economic Zones
RSFSR

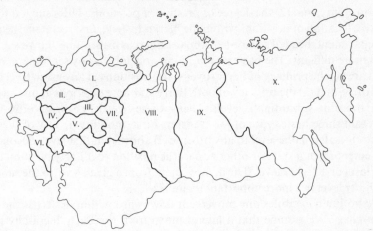

Figure 4.1 Forty-four regional political units within the ten RSFSR geographic economic zones
I. Northwest zone (Karelia, Komi, Novgorod, Pskov); II. Central zone (Kalinin, Kaluga, Orel, Smolensk, Tula, Yaroslavl); III. Volga-Vyatka zone (Chuvash, Gorky, Kirov); IV. Blackearth central zone (Lipetsk, Tambov, Voronezh); V. Volga zone (Astrakhan, Bashkir, Kuibyshev, Saratov, Tatar, Volgograd); VI. North caucasus zone (Checheno-Ingush, Krasnodar, Rostov, Stavropol); VII. Ural zone (Chelyabinsk, Orenburg, Perm, Sverdlovsk); VIII. West siberian zone (Altai, Kemerovo, Novosibirsk, Omsk, Tomsk, Tyumen); IX. East siberian zone (Buryat, Chita, Irkutsk, Krasnoyarsk, Tuva); X. Far eastern zone (Amur, Khabarovsk, Primorye).

representing a range of national and political contexts. It permits the testing of hypotheses about Slavic, Russian, and non-Russian political elites. To the extent that information sources permit, these data encompass the most influential regional-level politicians for over three decades.

Biographical and career information used in this study are drawn primarily from Soviet sources. The most useful sets of sources are the all-union and republic series, *Deputaty Verkhovnogo Soveta*, which provide biographical information on all deputies of a given Supreme Soviet convocation. These biographical precis are expanded upon by consulting yearbooks of the *Great Soviet Encyclopedia*, as well as by using published obituaries. Additional Western sources have also been used (e.g., the journal, *Current Soviet Leaders*).

While our biographical precis for politicians include both demographic and career data, evaluation of the latter is especially critical. We are very interested in measuring the mobility of politicians. Assessing whether positional changes represent promotion, lateral moves, or demotion, can be tricky. The set of decision rules we use to weight different positions differentiates across (1) the degree of policy-relevant influence and responsibility, and (2) the degree of prestige of positions. Titles suggest the relative location of positions within the hierarchy (e.g., first secretary, head of department, head of section). Comparing across institutions, however, is even more difficult. The basic assumptions we apply to any set of decision rules are (1) the primacy of Party (over state) positions at any given level of authority, and (2) the primacy of both Party and state positions at one level over those at subordinate levels. Using these, we define promotion to represent three basic types of job transfer. First, mobility up any of these hierarchies, from one level to any other level above that first level. Second, movement from a state or other apparatus position to a Party position at that level or a higher level. Third, movement from a given level to the same or higher level in a more important region.[23]

Demotion constitutes any movement downward within or across these hierarchies. We assume that a lateral move from the Party hierarchy to another hierarchy also constitutes a demotion, though certain subtleties in norms of transfer are lost in the process. In general, assessing lateral moves is the most difficult aspect of evaluating elite mobility. Many arguments put forward by Stewart et al.[24] have helped us in sorting out such positional shifts as we refine our own set of decision rules. However, we do not define a politician's transfer from heading one region to heading another as a lateral move, as Stewart et al. do (p. 1273). We understand a transfer to a very prominent region as a promotion, with a transfer to a less prominent region as a demotion.

Special attention in this study is given to the role of political patronage to elite mobility. To measure patronage ties, several decision rules are applied. First, two politicians must have been in geographic proximity for a given period of time during their careers. This means determining that two individuals served together within the same region on at least two different, identifiable occasions. There must be a pattern of upward career mobility on the part of both politicians, though the actual levels of authority may vary and the rates of advance may be different. In addition, common experience during the Second World War or within the same educational institution can also serve as an indicator of a patronage tie. Finally, two different career promotions of a subordinate under a patron during the patron's initial five-year period of authority (e.g., as republic Party first secretary) also constitutes evidence of a patronage connection. We have adopted Breslauer's thinking that the first five to seven years of a Party leader's rule is critically important to his power and authority-building efforts. Such a politician, at whatever level of authority, is likely to provide desired promotion opportunities to more trusted subordinates, with two different promotions during that critical first five-year period signifying an especially profound investment in a given subordinate's career.

Although data on elite careers have been employed by Western scholars over the past twenty years, the questions that we seek to answer require that economic data at the regional level be brought to bear on career patterns. Such data are available, moreover. Within the volumes of the Soviet statistical yearbook series, *Narodnoe khozyaistvo RSFSR*, available since the late 1950s, are regional breakdowns of numerous types of useful data. These include gross output of industrial production, growth in industrial productivity, housing construction, and total output of different groups of agricultural products. For most of these data, time series can be obtained for the years 1950–75; the regional breakdowns were discontinued in 1975. Volumes of *Narodnoe khozyaistvo* for particular regions are also available in the West. The regional statistical data have been published in sufficient detail to permit the testing of our propositions.

In order to include a crude estimation of the relative industrial performance of the 44 regions which are in our sample, we employ data on growth in industrial output for each region over twenty-five years. These data, however, are not an illuminating measure of economic performance unless they are transformed. As investments in heavy industry change over time, or other factors cause industrial production to shift nationwide, the standards by which Moscow would judge a region's growth in industrial output are also likely to shift. We therefore divide the regional growth figures by the industrial growth rate of the RSFSR in the corresponding year. This produces a ratio indicating the degree to which a region's output is above or below the republic level.

A further transformation is required before industrial output can be employed in our analysis. In addition to judging a region's output in relation to national output figures, Moscow is likely to take into account the characteristics of the region. How much of its economy is agricultural? How much infrastructure does it have? How urbanized and educated is the populace? This leads us to take the ratios noted above and standardize them for each region over the twenty-five year period. How does a given region's industrial growth during a particular year relate to what is normal for that region over time as well as to what is going on across the rest of the country? Accordingly, our measure of industrial performance is designed to hold temporal and cross-regional variations constant, thereby highlighting actual improvements or declines in performance.

Before employing this industrial performance measure, we can calculate each region's average over the previous two years. This reflects the likelihood that a single year's poor performance will not be as damaging (or a single year's good performance as rewarding) as a pattern of several years. Employing a three-year average produces no significant differences in the results. We rely upon two-year averages, however, because longer time periods will increase the likelihood of measuring the performance of the region for more than a single Party first secretary.

We are aware that this economic performance measure completely ignores an important dimension of the local economy, agriculture. Because our measure of performance only taps the industrial dimension, our findings on the relevance of performance to elite career mobility must be understood as tentative. Developing an indicator of agricultural performance, likely derived from gross production figures, for which adequate cross-regional data are available, will broaden our account of economic growth performance and enhance our confidence in the results presented here.

Finally, this analysis of the factors responsible for regional elite mobility includes a consideration of a region's prominence in the broader Soviet system. Regional prominence can be understood in both political and economic terms, with a region's political standing reflecting, to some extent, its size and the strength of its economy. Information available to us at this stage of the project allows us to apply a measure of the relative political prominence of a region. The number of Communist Party members found in a given region is a useful first measure because it reflects important quantitative and qualitative aspects of a region and its population. While such CPSU membership figures are not available for the regional level, we can approximate them by summing up the number of regional delegates selected to attend the Communist Party Congress. Party rules specify that a designated number of Party members are represented by each delegate to a national congress. While not perfectly linked to relative economic strength, this measure does to some extent reflect population size, degree of urbanization and size of the regional economy. It can be linked systematically with regional elite recruitment patterns in providing a first cut measure of regional prominence.

ANALYTICAL RESULTS

Our explanation of regional elite career success begins with an evaluation of the regional-level factors that structure all aspirants' prospects. Among these factors, the relation of a region's political prominence to regional elite mobility patterns merits initial consideration. When the prominence factor is considered singly, and is correlated with national-level status of regional Party first secretaries, the findings reveal that a region's prominence is only weakly associated with the relative standing of the given office holder. Employing Central Committee membership of regional leaders as a measure of politicians' national standing, we find but a slight positive correlation between prominence of region and their Party leaders' inclusion in the Central Committee. This is not surprising, given that nearly all Russian Republic regional Party first secretaries gain entry into the Central Committee. Becoming a Russian Republic regional first secretary signifies promotion to an influential slot within the CPSU hierarchy. However, the prospects of future upward mobility for politicians who head the more prominent regions are not significantly better than those of other regional leaders. The explanatory power of regional prominence for career mobility proves to be limited. It is only when we include several ascriptive and behavioural elements into the analysis that the level of explanation of upward mobility becomes significant.

Why might regional prominence have relevance to political mobility? It could be contended that prominent regions provide a more secure setting where local politicians can aspire to top political positions. Here it is reasoned that prominent regions tend to recruit their own personnel, being less subject to the intervention of Moscow. An examination of mobility trends in the prominent regional Party organizations leads us to identify different recruitment patterns: promotion of local cadres, promotion of outsiders, and a mixed reliance upon both types of officials. Correlating regional prominence with these recruitment patterns reveals a statistically weak relationship (Table 4.1). There is only a slight tendency for the more prominent (and larger) regions to recruit local politicians to the Party first secretaryship, with a higher proportion of first secretaries in less prominent Party organizations recruited from outside. Some prominent regions, for instance, Altai, Krasnoyarsk, and Kuibyshev, have been guided almost exclusively by local politicians. In these cases outsiders, if they are transferred into the region, assume secondary positions (e.g., the Party second secretary or the regional executive committee chairman). For instance in the Altai Party organization, after the 1961 removal of K. G. Pysin as Altai Party boss, his successor, a local politician, A. V. Georgiev, maintained power until his death in 1976, being succeeded by a political client and local network member, N. F. Aksenov. The few outsiders we can identify as having served in Altai were only at the secondary level.

Table 4.1: Regional prominence and recruitment patterns

		Regional political prominence	
		Below mean	Above mean
Recruitment pattern	Locals	8 = 30.1%	7 = 38.9%
	Mixed	6 = 23.1%	4 = 22.2%
	Outsiders	12 = 46.2%	7 = 38.9%
		26 = 100%	18 = 100%

Chi^2 = 0.339   Sig. = 0.844   N = 44

In other regions, more direct Moscow manipulation of leadership recruitment has occurred, with the promotion of outsiders into the top regional slots. Party first secretaries such as P. I. Morozov (Amur), N. V. Bannikov (Irkutsk), S. I. Manyakin (Omsk), B. E. Shcherbina (Tyumen), and E. K. Ligachev (Tomsk), served previously in Moscow or in other regional Party organizations. Their careers correspond to our understanding of the political troubleshooter; the politician who can function in a variety of organizational and regional settings and who often is called upon to deal with challenging or priority issues. While we do not measure the degree of local autonomy of these regions, the constant transfer of outsiders to head them points to one means by which Moscow can assure itself of more direct influence over their Party organizations.

Finally, there are a number of regions, among them some of the most prominent, which exhibit the promotion of both local cadres and outsiders into the top slots (e.g., Novosibirsk, Rostov, Stavropol', and Volgograd). Several of these regions and their Party organizations (e.g., Rostov and Stavropol') have served as important political stepping stones for politicians with national career aspirations (e.g., N. S. Patolichev, A. I. Kirichenko, M. S. Solomentsev, and, more recently, A. V. Vlasov in Rostov; N. I. Belyaev, F. D. Kulakov, and M. S. Gorbachev in Stavropol'). However, the over time changes in Moscow's proclivity to transfer outsiders to head these regions reveals other calculations and factors are at work.

Considered in isolation, regional prominence is not strongly linked to elite mobility. Regional economic performance, here measured by industrial growth, proves to be a somewhat better predictor of mobility. A brief examination of industrial output growth figures reveals that there are discernable differences in the performance of the regions comprising our population (Table 4.2). Some regions are fairly consistent in their over-time growth performance (e.g., Gorky), while others experience fairly significant fluctuations (e.g., Tuva). Examination of these growth performances against the overall national performance level places these figures in some perspective.

We are in a position to assess the likelihood that a region's leadership will be changed because of strong or weak industrial growth performance, while factoring in the political prominence of that region. Table 4.3 presents the results of a multiple regression analysis designed to examine whether or not a region's first secretary is replaced in a given year. The data for all 44 RSFSR regions from 1952–75 are pooled, producing 930 cases. To explain whether a particular region in a given year experienced leadership change, the model employs five variables. Among these variables are regional prominence and performance. Two dichotomous variables, Stalin and Khrushchev, provide a way of separating the years

Table 4.2: Industrial output of 44 RSFSR regions, calculated on the basis of percentage growth from previous year (varied years by oblast, 1950–77), and political prominence[a]

Region	Mean	Standard Deviation	Minimum	Maximum	# of Years	Political prominence
Altai	109.654	3.452	104	118	26	13
Amur	107.840	2.939	103	115	25	36
Astrakhan'	106.920	3.785	100	114	25	38
Bashkir	111.920	4.261	105	123	25	9
Buryat	108.808	3.837	102	118	26	40
Chechen-Ingush	108.160	4.394	100	115	25	40
Chelyabinsk	108.160	2.511	105	113	25	9
Chita	106.920	2.783	102	112	25	32
Chuvash	112.280	2.685	106	116	25	36
Gorky	108.880	2.223	106	114	25	3
Irkutsk	110.600	3.830	105	121	25	22
Kalinin	108.600	4.223	103	118	25	14
Kaluga	110.960	3.062	107	117	25	28
Karelia	107.542	4.222	102	118	24	43
Kemerovo	108.000	2.872	104	117	25	9
Khabarovsk	109.417	3.335	98	115	24	24
Kirov	108.760	3.586	103	117	25	26
Komi	107.720	3.089	103	114	25	38
Krasnodar	109.040	4.363	102	116	25	2
Krasnoyarsk	110.760	2.891	106	120	25	14
Kuibyshev	112.320	4.793	105	124	25	5
Lipetsk	112.360	4.760	106	128	25	30
Novgorod	110.440	3.150	105	119	25	33
Novosibirsk	110.800	4.301	103	127	25	17
Omsk	110.880	3.574	103	119	25	22
Orel	114.160	4.580	106	122	25	33
Orenburg	110.240	3.632	103	117	25	21
Perm	108.800	2.309	106	114	25	17
Primorye	109.875	3.791	104	120	24	33
Pskov	111.240	3.295	105	117	25	33
Rostov	109.520	3.501	103	118	25	1
Saratov	110.440	3.606	106	120	25	6
Smolensk	110.560	3.754	106	121	25	31
Stavropol	110.200	4.143	105	126	25	16
Sverdlovsk	108.280	2.337	105	113	25	4
Tambov	109.920	3.239	102	115	25	27
Tatar	110.440	4.823	104	127	25	7
Tomsk	109.440	4.093	103	119	25	40
Tula	108.875	3.261	103	117	24	19
Tuva	111.192	6.236	100	127	26	44

Table 4.2 (continued)

Region	Mean	Standard Deviation	Minimum	Maximum	# of Years	Political prominence
Tyumen	113.038	5.056	105	121	26	28
Volgograd	111.320	3.955	105	117	25	8
Voronezh	110.600	5.568	102	124	25	9
Yaroslavl	107.240	2.420	102	112	25	24
RSFSR	109.500	3.127	106	120	26	—
USSR	109.821	3.454	105	123	28	—

[a] The standard deviation provides an indication of how widely the data for a given region vary from the mean. Thus, Voronezh, with a standard deviation of 5.6, showed the greatest variability in its industrial output over the years 1950–77, whereas Gorky, with a standard deviation of 2.2, performed the most steadily during that period. Political prominence rank orderings are based upon the total number of delegates elected to the 25th CPSU Congress. The number of delegates reflects the total number of Party members comprising a region's Party organization at the time of a Congress.

into three periods. From 1965 on, both variables are zero. We can thus determine whether regional mobility patterns vary, given different national regimes. Regional performance is evaluated on the basis of growth in industrial output. This variable is calculated by dividing a region's annual growth rate by the growth rate for the RSFSR as a whole, standardizing these figures across all years, and then taking the average of the previous two years. This allows us to examine whether two years of below-average industrial growth increases the chance of a leadership change.

What Table 4.3 reveals is that the previous two years' industrial record, as well as regional political prominence and Khrushchev's tenure, have effects on the probability of leadership change. The positive coefficients for prominence and Khrushchev indicate that prominent regions are more likely to experience turnover and that turnover is more likely under Khrushchev than under Stalin or Brezhnev. The negative coefficient for industrial growth confirms that a poor record increases the likelihood that a first secretary will be replaced. The low levels of significance for all but one of these factors, however, reveal that only shifting mobility patterns linked with national leaderships are strongly tied to turnover rates. In the aggregate, regional prominence and industrial growth rates do not significantly explain leadership changes.

Table 4.3 also provides the results of the same regression carried out only for those regions which have at least 50 per cent of their population located in urban areas. Since the measure of economic performance is industrial

Table 4.3: Results of multiple regression to explain the probability of leadership turnover, 44 selected RSFSR regions[a]

	All regions			Urban regions only	
	Coefficient	*t*-statistic	Signif.	*t*-statistic	Signif.
Industrial growth, previous 2 years	−.029	−1.984	.048	−2.137	.033
Prominence of the region	.001	2.556	.011	1.946	.052
Is population 50% urban or more?	−.012	−.524	.600	—	—
Was Stalin General Secretary?	−.034	−.678	.498	−.339	.735
Was Khrushchev General Secretary?	.076	3.474	.001	3.718	.000
R^2			.024		.036
			(N = 930)		(N = 633)

[a] Multiple regression is employed to sort out the impact of several explanatory variables on one dependent variable. The R2 statistic indicates the overall performance of the explanatory variables in explaining the variance in the dependent variable. The statistic varies between zero and one, with one indicating perfect fit. Each explanatory variable has a coefficient, which indicates how much (and in what direction) the dependent variable is altered by a change in the explanatory variable by one unit. When the dependent variable is dichotomous, as in this table, the coefficient indicates how much the odds of a correct prediction are increased by knowing the value the explanatory variable takes on. The *t*-statistic judges the likelihood that the results are due to random sampling error. A high *t*-statistic allows one to have greater faith in the conclusion that the positive coefficient reflects a positive impact on the dependent variable by the given explanatory variable. A strong, dependable relationship between a given explanatory variable and the dependent variable will result in a highly positive or highly negative coefficient which has a large *t*-statistic and a low significance level (below .05, generally).

growth, it is perhaps not useful to include predominantly agricultural regions in the sample. The results, however, do not change greatly. Only distinguishing the Khrushchev period from other years provides a strong explanation for regional elite turnover among these factors.

We find that different national regimes, with different recruitment norms, account for changing turnover rates of regional politicians. We also find that national regimes vary in their preferences for suitable regional Party leaders (Table 4.4). The Khrushchev period entailed not only an extensive turnover of cadres, but also a discernable reliance upon outsiders

Table 4.4: Results of multiple regression to explain the probability of recruitment of an outsider as regional first secretary, 44 selected RSFSR regions

	All Regions		
	Coefficient	t-Statistic	Significance
Industrial growth previous 2 years	−.072	−.770	.443
Prominence of the region	.025	.268	.789
Mobility of prior incumbent (upward, lateral, downward)	−.300	−3.141	.002
Was Khrushchev General Secretary?	.358	3.845	.000
R^2		.245	

(N = 94)

to head up regional Party organizations. Since there were minimal regional leadership changes during the 1950–53 period, the data in Table 4.4 essentially reflect recruitment differences between the Khrushchev and Brezhnev periods. The actual figures are shown in Table 4.5. These data reveal that the 'stability of cadres' policy of the Brezhnev regime significantly altered the prior Khrushchev approach of constantly shifting many politicians from one regional Party organization to another or of bringing them in from Moscow. They do raise some doubts about Brezhnev's 1971 assertion that the recruitment of outsiders to regional slots was 'the exception'. His regime tended to rely upon local administrators who knew their locales well. However, nearly 40 per cent of these cases still merited the movement of outsiders into top organizational positions.

One key feature of these cases was the poor record of a regional Party leader. The results of Table 4.4 reveal that the career fates of incumbent regional elites had implications for the types of successors selected. During not only the Khrushchev but also the Brezhnev periods, the demotion of an incumbent tended to result in the selection of an outsider. The actual figures for the selection of local officials or outsiders if the prior incumbent is

Table 4.5: Recruitment differences between Khrushchev and Brezhnev periods

		General Secretary	
		Khrushchev	Brezhnev
Recruitment	Local	28 = 26.4%	35 = 61.4%
pattern	Outsider	78 = 73.6%	22 = 38.6%
		106 = 100%	57 = 100%

Chi^2 = 19.137   Sig. = .000   N = 163

demoted, promoted, or laterally moved are shown in Table 4.6. Quite often, such outsiders brought experience from various institutional and regional settings. Their careers very much conform to our characterization of political troubleshooters. These officials could be relied upon to assume command of regions and Party organizations that Moscow viewed as having been mismanaged by the prior leadership.

Table 4.6: Mobility direction of prior regional first secretary

		Demoted	Lateral	Promoted
Type of	Local	19 = 26%	12 = 42.9%	29 = 64.4%
politician	Outsider	54 = 74%	16 = 57.1%	16 = 35.6%
recruited		73 = 100%	28 = 100%	45 = 100%

Chi^2 = 17.017   Sig. = .000   N = 146

The analysis, to this point, has revealed that regional-level factors, especially performance, and national recruitment policies influence the career prospects of aspiring politicians. However, where do the characteristics of the individual politician, identified by the rational–technical and patronage models, fit in? In particular, how do expertise, past experience, and patronage connections affect mobility prospects? What combination of these factors works best in optimizing the career prospects of an aspiring lower-level official?

When we consider a politician's expertise, we have in mind the possession of the necessary knowledge and experience to cope with work responsibilities. Expertise includes a number of aspects. One is formal education. A second is the politician's professional experience, which can signify either (1) multifaceted experience in a diversity of settings, or (2) considerable experience in a single or limited number of settings. A third aspect of expertise is the overall knowledge gained from both formal and on-the-spot training and experience. The lack of information on the specific activities of politicians limits our opportunity to consider systematically the third aspect. However, biographical data are available to develop measures that partially account for the first two aspects. On the basis of both the rational–technical model and the modified patronage model, we expect increasingly higher levels of expertise on the part of regional elites.

Because we are interested in work-related formal training, we have examined the post-secondary school levels of education for our regional elite population. We have ignored advanced political training (i.e., higher party schools) and considered only completed higher education. Comparing regional first secretaries at four time points (1950, 1960, 1970, and 1980), we find that these elites are increasingly better educated in the course

of the past three decades (Table 4.7). While the published Soviet biographies of elites' academic records are likely to exaggerate actual
achievements, these figures reflect the broad trend of a better-trained
cohort. They support the rational–technical model's proposition of an
increasingly educated group of politicians.

*Table 4.7: Degree of advanced academic training of regional first secretaries, by
patronage connections, 1950–80*

	1950		1960		1970		1980	
	Higher educ.	None	Higher educ.	None	Higher educ.	None	Higher educ.	None
No patronage tie	6	3	23	12	28	3	30	3
Patronage tie	3	1	8	1	13	0	11	0
	N = 13		N = 44		N = 44		N = 44	

In addition to formal training, expertise also encompasses past experience. What can we determine about the past experience which successful
aspirants bring to top regional positions? Greater expertise could reflect
either familiarity with a diversity of settings or focused experience in one or
a limited number of settings. For the regional Party boss, assuming
ultimate responsibility for the functioning of his bailiwick, the necessity for
a more multifaceted set of background is more relevant. Thus, in regard to
expertise as including experience in a diversity of work settings, the
rational–technical model would posit that successful aspirants to top
regional positions would be increasingly diverse in their professional work.
The ever-more-complex Soviet society would require regional leaders to
have familiarity not only with the Party, but with other (e.g., state,
Komsomol, trade union) organizations and settings.

Again comparing four time points (1950, 1960, 1970, and 1980) that span
the Stalin, Khrushchev, and Brezhnev regimes, we find the average regional
Party first secretary exhibiting an increasing range of institutional and
regional experiences which are brought to this top regional leadership
position. A comparison of the average number of institutional and regional
settings in which politicians served, prior to becoming a regional first
secretary, reveals that the post-Stalin regional first secretaries had experience in an increasing number of settings.

	1950	1960	1970	1980
Avg. No. of prior work settings	4.8	5.3	5.9	5.7

The regional first secretary of the Brezhnev period, on average, had served previously in early six different institutional or regional settings.

These results, employing measures which tap formal education and diversity of professional background, are compatible with the expectation of greater expertise on the part of regional leaders. The elites of the post-Stalin era bring higher levels of education and a greater diversity of past experience to their regional leadership positions. How do patronage connections fit into the mobility prospects of regional elites? Is the modified patronage model for the post-Stalin period correct in positing that successful regional politicians bring with them both 'connections' and higher levels of formal training? Is there evidence that they bring with them experience from a greater diversity of regional and institutional settings? Are those with heightened expertise and connections likely to experience greater upward mobility than others?

An application of our measures of expertise does not reveal significant differences in the level of expertise between politicians who have advanced with patronage ties and those who have advanced lacking them. Regional first secretaries with patronage ties to powerful superiors exhibit levels of education only slightly superior to their peers (Table 4.7). A comparison of the figures for number of prior work settings for the two groups reveals an interesting development (Table 4.8).

Table 4.8: Prior work settings of regional first secretaries by patronage connections

	1950	1960	1970	1980
No patronage ties (nonclients)	4.1	5.0	5.9	5.7
Patronage ties (clients)	6.3	6.4	5.8	5.6

In the Stalin and immediate post-Stalin periods, politicians with patronage connections tended to have made their careers in a wider range of settings. However, from the Stalin period through the Brezhnev years, the careers of other politicians exhibit an increased diversification of work settings. The gap between the two groups narrowed to the point that both clients and nonclients bring comparably diverse backgrounds to top regional policy-making positions. More diverse experience, as an important component of regional elite expertise, is expected of all.

If all politicians, regardless of patronage ties, bring heightened expertise to successful career building, then where do patronage relationships fit in? Patronage connections enhance the opportunities for skilled politicians to be recruited to regional first secretaryships. An examination of career mobility patterns of the two, client and nonclient, groups reveals that the clients experience significantly higher levels of upward mobility. A correlation of patronage ties with mobility yields the results shown in

Table 4.9 for our population of elites. In what proves to be a statistically significant relationship, politicians with powerful patrons tend to experience high rates of upward mobility. Others, lacking such connections, experience lower rates of upward mobility but high rates of downward mobility. Over half of all regional first secretaries, with patronage ties to national elites, experience upward mobility from their regional leadership position. Less than 20 per cent of those regional first secretaries lacking such ties experience comparable upward mobility. While less than one-quarter of our total population of regional elites evinced such patronage ties, they were the politicians most likely to succeed to higher Party and state positions.

Table 4.9: A correlation of patronage ties with mobility

	No patronage ties	Patronage ties
Demoted	73 = 61.8%	7 = 15.6%
Lateral	23 = 19.5%	11 = 24.4%
Promoted	22 = 18.6%	27 = 60.0%
	118 = 100%	45 = 100%

$Chi^2 = 33.152$ Signif. $= .000$ N = 163

These results have demonstrated that certain individual-level factors and regional-structural constraints significantly influence political elite mobility. Can we combine the factors into one analysis to identify their relative explanatory power?

Table 4.10 presents the results of a multivariate regression that employs regional performance and prominence, national recruitment policy, and patronage in explaining regional elite mobility. Patronage connections are found to explain upward mobility at a statistically significant level. In fact, such connections are the single strongest factor predicting upward mobility. Regional prominence only slightly enhances mobility prospects. National recruitment policy has some relevance; the negative coefficient for the Khrushchev period reflects the fact that local regional elites fared less well during Khrushchev's tenure. Performance, again understood in terms of over-time industrial growth, is also relevant. The negative coefficient reveals that industrial performance serves less to help than to constrain the upward mobility prospects of aspiring regional politicians.

These findings, combined with our earlier results, indicate the importance of individual-level factors in predicting political elite mobility. Patronage and heightened expertise maximize the prospects of an aspirant. However, the national and regional-level factors, especially changing recruitment policies and performance records, do structure the career channels through which aspiring politicians move.

Table 4.10: Results of multiple regression to explain the mobility of regional first secretaries, 44 selected RSFSR regions

	All regions		
	Standardized coefficient	*t*-Statistic	Significance
Industrial growth, previous 2 years	−.133	−1.436	.154
Prominence of the region	.019	.200	.842
Was Khrushchev General Secretary?	−.025	−.253	.801
Patronage connections	.433	4.259	.000
R^2			.225

(N = 96)

Our analyses for 44 RSFSR regions reveal a complex interaction among the factors that underly Soviet political elite career building. What do our results signify in regard to specific types of regions and situations? Broad generalizations aside, an examination of individual cases reveals a variety of regional experiences. We can cite a number of regions where poor or strong economic performance is related to leadership turnover. However, these are complicated by patronage and other factors. The Altai oblast experienced a number of leadership changes in the period between 1960 and 1980, with the replacement of K. G. Pysin in 1961 following three years of sub-par industrial growth in the province. Using z-scores, which account for the degree of performance fluctuation considered against the figures for all years in the period considered, Pysin's tenure is found to have the weakest performance for the entire 1950–70 time span for which we have economic performance data. Yet, Pysin was a political outsider, having made the sort of career in regional and Moscow positions that reveal him as a system 'troubleshooter'. He had patronage ties to a powerful national politician, Gennadii Voronov, and was indeed promoted in 1961 to be USSR First Deputy Minister of Agriculture. Pysin was succeeded by a local politician, A. V. Georgiev, who headed the region until his death in 1976. Georgiev was succeeded by another local politician, N. F. Aksenov, who had patronage ties to Georgiev. Aksenov had served with Georgiev in a number of different capacities as the two moved up in the Altai Party organization. He guided Altai for the duration of the period considered here. For the years following Pysin's ouster for which we have performance data, fluctuations in industrial growth do not entail a multi-year downward trend. Indeed, a comparison of the industrial performance data for this region and the USSR overall reveals a close fit in changing annual upward and downward growth trends. The region performed well under Georgiev and Aksenov. The political longevity of their local network is not surprising.

Meanwhile, the experience of the Kemerovo oblast elite demonstrates that extended periods of poor industrial performance can result in the ouster of Party leaders. Three sub-par years from 1957 to 1959 preceeded the 1960 ouster of S. P. Pilipets. He had succeeded as first secretary in 1955, with the region's industrial performance figures reflecting poor and declining growth throughout his tenure. The oblast performed initially better under his successor, L. I. Lubennikov, but several sub-par years came prior to his 1963 departure. The poor performance of the Kemerovo oblast resulted in both these leadership changes and in the selection of outsiders to head the region. The experience of other regions (e.g., Omsk and Tomsk) reveals very similar patterns.

Finally, the experience of another relatively prominent region, the Novosibirsk oblast, which underwent five leadership changes between 1955 and the late 1970s, demonstrates the complex interaction of the factors responsible for elite turnover and mobility. We have Novosibirsk industrial growth rate data for the periods 1950–60 and 1970–75, during which three successions occurred. In each case (1955, 1957, and 1959), a change in the first secretaryship followed a period of industrial growth decline. The 1955 removal of I. D. Yakovlev followed four years of stagnant or declining growth rates; the 1957 removal of B. I. Deryugin followed continued stagnation and decline, albeit over a very brief period; and the 1959 departure of B. N. Kobelev came after only two years of no increase in industrial productivity growth figures. In contrast to the experience of these three short-term Party leaders is that of the long-serving Party first secretary, F. S. Goryachev (1959–78). Goryachev was an outsider and troubleshooter, having previously served as first secretary in several regions (Penza, Tyumen and Kalinin). While our performance data only include the 1970–75 portion of his tenure, this six-year period reveals more stable growth rates than are found for his predecessors. It is not surprising that the politically experienced Goryachev would retain his Novosibirsk position and Central Committee membership until his honorable retirement some twenty years later, in 1978. It is also not surprising that after twenty years of stable regional leadership, a political protege of the long-serving first secretary would be selected to replace him.

CONCLUSION

The interaction of individual, regional and national-level factors that influence political elite mobility is complex. Our findings offer support for a modified patronage model of elite mobility; a model bridging the rational-technical emphasis on an increasingly skilled elite and the traditional patronage emphasis on a politically reliable one. Successful regional politicians are increasingly better-educated, with more multi-faceted backgrounds. Yet they continue to rely upon patronage connections to influential national and regional politicians in building their careers.

Our analysis also reveals the importance of regional-level factors. These factors structure the opportunities for career advancement of all aspiring regional elites, both skilled clients and nonclients. Accordingly, the changing recruitment norms of national regimes can favour certain types of elites. A general secretary and group of top elites can promote a policy line that favours particular types of politicians. The Khrushchev period especially illustrates this. The heightened national profile of a regional Party organization can favour certain aspirants, as politicians in more prominent regions enjoy some edge in competing with peers. The performance, both political and economic, of a region can advance (or retard) the mobility prospects of local officials. The previous incumbent's political record and fate influences the type of successor selected. However, the relationship among the individual-level skills and attributes, and these regional-level constraints, is an interactive one. Structural contingencies can serve to either reinforce or dampen the upward mobility prospects of even the most advantaged aspiring politician identified here: the competent political client.

Our findings are compatible with the observations of other students of the Soviet system. One recent study, for instance, has examined the link between the economic performance of Russian regions and the career success of the first secretaries of those regions.[25] That study concludes that poor industrial performance hindered a politician's chances of upward mobility but did not lead to demotion. Indeed, in strategic agricultural regions, poor agricultural performance did not prevent career advancement. This work also reveals that a combination of factors serves to predict the mobility prospects of regional elites. Thus, for example, it is found that first secretaries whose regions experienced average industrial growth are more likely to be promoted than those guiding an above-average region. This difference is more pronounced than the difference in probability of promotion between the above-average and below-average regions. These findings suggest that other factors are also influencing the mobility prospects of elites. We argue that chief among these are patronage connections, which can confound the performance-mobility link, but which can account for a good number of anomalies. Such connections can help one politician whose region is struggling economically, but they can hurt another politician whose region is performing well but whose national-level patron-promoter is in decline.

Medvedev has written that 'the crucial ingredients for the promotion of obkom and kraikom secretaries are economic success in their own areas and the ability to attract national attention by undertaking new initiatives which can be adapted by other areas.'[26] We agree with Medvedev's assessment, to the extent that the Soviet system increasingly values economic growth and effective performance. However, performance must be understood not only in its economic but also its political meaning. It includes continued stability and control.

Changes in the Soviet system since the death of Stalin have not entailed a fundamental redistribution of political power. Power continues to be highly centralized and concentrated in the national political elite. However, the composition and the behaviour of that top elite, which includes powerful regional leaders, have changed in the succeeding thirty-five years. An increasingly complex Soviet society and economy have required a diverse and competent governing elite. The programme and political agenda of the Gorbachev regime is but the most recent, albeit a most unexpected, manifestation of this.

Among the politicians who comprise our population of regional elites are a number of the most prominent members of a regime who later promoted perestroika and glasnost' (e.g., Gorbachev, Ligachev, Vorotnikov, and El'tsin). They were socialized and their careers were built during the post-Stalin transformation of the Soviet polity. This is a better-skilled and more competent cohort, but a self-confident one fully linked to the system. Their technical competence and their patronage connections have taken them to the highest policy positions. Their behaviour demonstrates that the altering of mobility norms and the recruiting of different types of politicians, with different skills, can be conducive to important policy change. Western models and explanations of Soviet elite mobility and behaviour must take these changes into account. We believe that a modified patronage model, incorporating traditional rational–technical and patronage factors, does so effectively.

NOTES AND REFERENCES

1   Seweryn Bialer, *Stalin's Successors*, Cambridge University Press, Cambridge, 1980; Alexander Dallin and George W. Breslauer, *Political Terror in Communist Systems*, Stanford University Press, Stanford, 1970.
2   Zygmunt Bauman, 'Twenty Years After: The Crisis of Soviet-type Systems', *Problems of Communism*, 1971, vol. 20, no. 6, November–December, pp. 45–53; Ronald J. Hill, and Peter Frank, 'Gorbachev's Cabinet-Building', *Journal of Communist Studies*, 1986, vol. 2, no. 2, June, pp. 168–181.
3   Harvard Project on the Soviet Social System, 'Strategic Psychological and Sociological Strengths and Vulnerabilities of the Soviet Social System', October, 1954, p. 52.

4   Hannah Arendt, *The Origins of Totalitarianism*, Harcourt, Brace, New York, 1951; Carl J. Freidrich and Zbigniew Brzezinski, *Totalitarian Dictatorship and Autocracy*, Harvard University Press, Cambridge, 1956.

5   Jerry F. Hough, and Merle Fainsod, *How the Soviet Union is Governed*, Harvard University Press, Cambridge, 1979.

6   Jerry F. Hough, *The Soviet Union and Social Science Theory*, Harvard University Press, Cambridge, 1977; Jerry F. Hough and Merle Fainsod, *How the Soviet Union is Governed*, Harvard University Press, Cambridge, 1979.

7   John P. Willerton, Jr, 'Clientelism in the Soviet Union: An Initial Examination', *Studies in Comparative Communism*, 1979, vol. 12, nos 2 & 3, Summer/Autumn, pp. 159–83.

8   George W. Breslauer, 'Is there a Generation Gap in the Soviet Political Establishment? Demand Articulation by RSFSR Provincial Party First Secretaries', *Soviet Studies*, 1984, vol. 36, no. 1, January, pp. 1–25; Peter Hauslohner, 'Prefects as Senators: Soviet regional Politicians Look to Foreign Policy', *World Politics*, vol. 33, 1 October 1980, pp. 197–233.

9   Andrew C. Janos, (ed.), *Authoritarian Politics in Communist Europe*, University of California, Berkeley, Institute of International Studies, Research Series, no. 28, 1976.

10   Frederic Fleron, 'Representation of Career Types in the Soviet Political Leadership', in R. Barry Farrell, (ed.) *Political Leadership in Eastern Europe and the Soviet Union*, Aldine Publishing Co., Chicago, 1970, pp. 108–39.

11   Marc Rakovski, *Towards an East European Marxism*, St. Martin's Press, New York, 1978.

12   Roman Kolkowicz, 'Interest Groups in Soviet Politics: The Case of the Military', in Dale R. Herspring and Ivan Volgyes (eds), *Civil-Military Relations in Communist Systems*, Westview Press, Boulder, 1978, pp. 9–25; H. Gordon Skilling, and Franklyn Griffith (eds), *Interest Groups in Soviet Politics*, Princeton University Press, Princeton, 1971.

13   Phillippe Schmitter, 'Still the Century of Corporatism', *Review of Politics*, 1974, vol. 36, pp. 85–131.

14   Valerie Bunce and John M. Echols III, 'Soviet Politics in the Brezhnev Era: "Pluralism" or Corporatism?', in Donald R. Kelley (ed.), *Soviet Politics in the Brezhnev Era*, Praeger, New York, 1980, pp. 1–26.

15   George W. Breslauer, *Five Images of the Soviet Future*, University of California, Berkeley, Policy Papers in International Affairs, no. 4, 1978.

16   Joseph A. Schlesinger, *Ambition and Politics*, Rand McNally and Co., Chicago, 1966.

17   John P. Willerton, Jr, *Patronage and Politics in the Soviet Union*, unpublished dissertation, University of Michigan, 1985; John P. Willerton, Jr, 'Patronage Networks and Coalition Building Efforts in the Brezhnev Era', *Soviet Studies*, 1987, vol. 39, no. 2, April, pp. 175–204.

18   Dennis Ross, 'Coalition Maintenance in the Soviet Union', *World Politics*, 1980, vol. 32, no. 2, January, pp. 258–80.

19   Ronald J. Hill and Peter Frank, *The Soviet Communist Party*, Third Edition, Allen and Unwin, Inc., Boston, 1986.

20   Kenneth N. Ciboski, 'The Significance of Party Organisations in the Careers of Top Soviet Leaders', paper presented at the Annual Meeting of the Midwest Political Science Association, April 1986; Joel C. Moses, 'Regionalism in Soviet Politics: Continuity as a Source of Change, 1953–1982', *Soviet Studies*, 1985, vol. 37, no. 2, April, pp. 184–211.

21   Peter Frank, 'Constructing a Classified Ranking of CPSU Provincial Commit-
     tees', *British Journal of Political Science*, 1974, vol. 4, no. 2, April, pp. 217–30;
     Mary McAuley, 'Hunting the Hierarchy', *Soviet Studies*, 1974, vol 26, no. 4,
     October, pp. 473–501.
22   J. P. Cole and F. C. German, *A Geography of the USSR: The Background to a
     Planned Economy*, Rowman and Littlefield, Totowa, N.J., 1971; George Kish,
     Economic Atlas of the Soviet Union Second Edition, Revised, University of
     Michigan Press, Ann Arbor, 1971.
23   Mary McAuley, 'Hunting the Hierarchy', *Soviet Studies*, 1974, vol. 26, no. 4,
     October, pp. 473–501.
24   Philip D. Stewart, Robert L. Arnett, William T. Ebert, Raymond E. McPhail,
     Terrence L. Rich, and Craig E. Schopmeyer, 'Political Mobility and the Soviet
     Political Process', *American Political Science Review*, 1972, vol. 66, no. 4,
     December, pp. 1269–90.
25   Mark R. Beissinger, 'Economic Performance and Career Prospects in the
     CPSU Apparatus', paper delivered at the 19th Annual Convention of the
     American Association for the Advancement of Slavic Studies, New Orleans,
     November 20–23, 1986.
26   Zhores A. Medvedev, *Gorbachev*, Norton, New York, 1986, p. 72.

5. Elite Stratification and Mobility in a Soviet Republic*

Michael Urban

Among the more vexing problems attending the study of Soviet political elites is that of hierarchy. In order to analyse elite mobility and the political issues associated with it – direction-compliance, incentives-performance, control-resistance, policy formulation and implementation, and so forth – some conception of the gradation of office is required. Indeed, the concept of elite, to risk emphasis on the obvious, presupposes some hierarchy which constitutes a given group of office holders as an elite. Yet serious questions remain in the field as to how we might order the array of offices hierarchically, which jobs should be regarded as above or below others, which career moves should be taken as promotions, demotions or lateral transfers.[1]

This elementary question of hierarchy is not present in elite studies outside of the Soviet (or, more broadly, state socialist) context. It may be that there is something unique, and for the analyst uniquely frustrating, about the issue of hierarchy under Soviet circumstances. On the one hand, there is the matter of what may be regarded as multiple hierarchies in the Soviet system – the array of party jobs, state jobs, jobs in mass organizations or soviets – all of which intersect in various committees and bureaus at various levels. Inasmuch as the careers of actors commonly span a number of these, the student of Soviet elites must be something of a juggler, keeping a number of such balls in motion simultaneously in order to chart promotions, demotions and simple transfers. On the other hand, Soviet organizations do not evince the legal-rational gradations of authority associated with bureaucracy in advanced capitalist systems. Jerry Hough's work on the obkom secretaries alerted us to this some twenty years ago,[2] but his insights seem to have counted more for the attention given to obkom first secretaries in subsequent research than for rethinking the basic questions of bureaucratic organization and hierarchy in the Soviet context.

* This study was funded in large part by the National Science foundation and the National Council for Soviet and East European Research.

Previous attempts at mapping out an explicit hierarchy of positions in the Soviet system have in my view given too little attention to this 'unbureaucratic' character of Soviet organization.[3] Tacitly, the assumption seems to have been that there is a hierarchy 'out there' which the analyst can locate.[4] Location, in turn, has been largely nominal; a position's name and the duties, authority, or importance known or thought to be associated with it would place it above, below, or on par with some other position.[5] It appears that the methodological orientation has been to designate the hierarchy in order to study mobility, but the resulting by-product of this orientation, a separation of hierarchy from mobility in the basic conception and approach of the analyst, has passed unnoticed. As a consequence, our efforts have tended to focus on the characteristics of this job or that – its formal rank, whether it is represented on central committees, the size of the organization in which it exists, the 'importance' of the unit in the economy, and so on – and the drawing of comparisons between these characteristics and those of other jobs. This method would likely encounter few if any difficulties were we dealing with hierarchies in advanced capitalist systems. But given those unique features of Soviet organization mentioned above, it produces results that are difficult if not impossible to validate.

A more serious problem bearing on the issue of elites and political power, which is associated with our reliance on formal job titles as an adequate representation of the Soviet personnel system, is that it invites us to think in terms of those bureaucratic hierarchies with which we are most familiar, namely, those in modern capitalist systems. Here we may well be making an unfortunate substitution of what exists in the West for what may not exist, or may exist in quite a different way, in the East. Take, for instance, the central question located by Max Weber in his study of bureaucracy, the mechanism by which orders are given, received and carried out. Weber referred to this mechanism as a relationship of 'domination' which obtained between superiors and subordinates in a bureacracy, a relationship in which the command of the superiors is received by the subordinates as if the latter 'had made the content of the command the maxim of their conduct for its own sake'.[6] Certainly, as Weber knew, formal titles of 'superior' and 'subordinates' would be insufficient to sustain domination. Rather, what is required is the thoroughly rationalized form of life which bureaucracy introduces. For our purposes, the salient aspect of this mode of organization is the gradation of offices *and the rules for advancement* in the hierarchy – namely, by steps taken one at a time on the basis of the decision of superiors who enforce their will on subordinates by granting promotions in exchange for obedience. When the mechanism of advancement functions according to other rules, as it does in the Soviet Union, then we have no reason to assume that formal organizations will behave in a bureaucratic way. Specifically, Weber's concept of 'domination,' the generation and deployment of power in and among administrative units, takes on a fundamentally different character in the USSR.[7] We can shed some light on the distinctions between advanced capitalist (bureaucratic) forms of organization and their Soviet counterparts by addressing the question of the hierarchy of offices in the USSR from the standpoint of the patterns of mobility of the officeholders.

Conjoining the concepts of hierarchy and mobility makes it possible (1) to see each as a function of the other and (2) to reverse their order of determination. If we wish to specify a hierarchy in order to study mobility, might we not study mobility in order to specify a hierarchy? This is the approach adopted here. My objective is to specify a hierarchy of positions in a single republic in the USSR, Belorussia,[8] by isolating first a top stratum of elite jobs. Succeeding strata are then determined on the basis of probabilities that incumbents in other jobs can reach jobs in the stratum above them, such that if there is a certain probability that an incumbent in job X will be promoted to a job in the first stratum, then job X belongs to stratum 2. Accordingly, should an incumbent in job Y have a certain probability of taking a job in stratum 2, then job Y is grouped into stratum 3, and so on. This approach, in short, seeks to resolve the problem of determining the hierarchy by treating the issue as the empirical correlate of mobility.

We might underline in this respect some of the assumptions and implications associated with such a method. First, we are bracketing the notion of an objective hierarchy based on the names of offices. In this approach there is no *a priori* reason to assume that jobs with the same name belong to the same stratum, nor is there reason to designate jobs as above or below one another simply on the basis of their respective appellations. As we shall see in what follows, the assigning of jobs to strata in accordance with their probabilities of transition to higher strata yields results which are often at odds with nominalist assumptions regarding both the equivalence and the gradation of positions.

Second, the hierarchy of job stratification produced by the method employed here is specific to time and place. It cannot claim to be 'the' hierarchy of positions in Belorussia; even less should it be taken as a hierarchy applicable to other republics in the USSR. Its status is restricted to the Belorussian Republic over the period 1966–86. This characteristic of the method follows from the purpose for which the method was devised (i.e., a broad study, in progress, of the Belorussian elite for this time period). Hence, what is generalizable from this study is not the specific results derived from the method (although these may suggest hypotheses which subsequent research in other areas of the USSR might wish to consider) but the method itself. That is, those analysing Soviet elites at any level might use this method for delinating elite stratification in the context of their own data and research interests.

DATA AND METHOD

Personnel data on Belorussian elites for the period 1966–86 have been compiled from a number of sources.[9] A computerized data file was constructed wherein each actor appeared as a 'case', and to each 'case' was appended a code which designated the position held by the actor in specified years. This yielded a matrix of 3,127 rows (officeholders) and 21 columns (each a one year interval over the period 1966–86) into which the 2032 jobs which appeared in the sample were entered. The jobs spanned the following hierarchies: Communist Party of Belorussia, governmental positions in the Belorussian Republic (ministeries, state committees and soviets), Komsomol, trade union, cultural and educational posts. The vertical range extended from republic-level positions in these hierarchies through *oblast* (and, for party and soviet positions, *raion*) level jobs, and to the positions of directors (and in some cases deputy directors) and the secretaries of primary party organizations and trade union presidents in large enterprises. Additionally, 24 jobs at the all-union level known to have been taken by former officeholders in Belorussia were included.

The matrix of officeholders/years (1966–86) with offices as the entries was then transformed into a matrix of offices/years (1966–86) wherein the entries were the officeholders.[10] This matrix of 2032 rows (each representing a job) and 21 columns (each designating a year) is illustrated in Table 5.1. Each actor who held a given position at the end of a particular year occupies the cell in the matrix designated by the intersection of the corresponding row (position) and column (year). Row entries then change with mobility into and out of the positions which designate the row. This is illustrated in row 3 of Table 5.1 by the replacement of D. F. Filimonov by V. F. Mitskevich as Secretary of the Central Committee of the Communist Party of Belorussia (KPB) in charge of agriculture in 1968.

Having arranged this position/year matrix for the data set, the next step in generating a hierarchy on the basis of transition probabilities to higher strata was to select the top stratum itself. A number of considerations bear upon this choice. This stratum functions as the ultimate 'destination' of all those holding jobs in the Belorussian Republic, it defines the second stratum of jobs (on the basis of the probability of incumbents moving to positions in the top stratum), which in turn defines the third stratum and so on. Consequently, it should be limited to 'top' jobs but at the same time be large enough to accommodate the purpose of generating a second stratum which is itself sufficiently large to generate a third (etc.), such that the

Table 5.1: Sample position matrix for Belorussian Republic, 1966–86

	1966	1967	1968	...	1986
1. First Secretary of KPB	P.M. Masherov	P.M. Masherov	P.M. Masherov	...	N.N. Slyunikov
2. Second Secretary of KPB	F.A. Surganov	F.A. Surganov	F.A. Surganov	...	G.G. Bartoshevich
3. Secretary of KPB (Agriculture)	D.F. Filimonov	D.F. Filimonov	V.F. Mitskevich	...	N.I. Dementei
.					
.					
.					

hierarchy thereby derived will contain a number of strata suited to the purpose for which the model was devised.

With these considerations in mind, two sets of positions were selected for the top stratum. The first set is composed by those jobs whose incumbents regularly held positions on the Buro of the Central Committee of the KPB (i.e., Buro membership was awarded to the incumbent at at least four of the five congress of the KPB held during the time frame of the study). There is no reason to believe that these jobs are all equal in their importance. They are likely not. The point is only that regular membership on the Buro, the highest decision making organ in the Republic, defines a particular set of jobs which are set apart from all others by virtue of their incumbents' membership on a body which can be regarded the uppermost layer of the Republic's elite.

A second set of jobs selected for the top stratum is composed of national positions to which Belorussian officeholders moved during the course of their careers. The inclusion of this group follows again from the purpose for generating the positions hierarchy, namely, in order to study elite circulation and mobility in Belorussia. Here, the assumption is that moving into one of these all-union positions is equivalent to moving into one of the jobs regularly represented on the Buro of the KPB. In either case, a promotion to the top stratum has occurred. Stratum 1 jobs at the all-union level were defined as executive positions, whether in the party or state apparatuses, at the level of deputy minister of, or for the party, deputy head of a department of the Secretariat of the Central Committee or those with formal rankings above these (first deputy, minister, etc.).[11] The two sets of jobs yielded a top stratum numbering 25 positions, 13 of which were regularly represented on the Buro of the KPB, 12 of which were executive jobs at the national level.

Having assigned these two sets of positions of Stratum 1, it became clear that such a ranking would not serve the purpose of generating a sizeable second stratum for the hierarchy. That is, there is a relatively high frequency of circulation among those holding jobs in the top stratum and a rather low degree of mobility into this stratum. Moreover, if regular Buro membership and executive jobs at the national level were the criteria for inclusion into Stratum 1, might not consistency suggest that irregular Buro membership and sub-executive jobs at the all-union level constitute the criteria for membership in Stratum 2? This was the tack taken. To all those jobs which would appear in Stratum 2 by virtue of their transition probabilities to jobs in Stratum 1 were added at the onset 15 positions, 9 of which were heads of ministerial departments or sectors of the CPSU Secretariat, 6 of which were infrequently represented on the Buro of the KPB or were regularly candidate members of that body.

Once the positions comprising Stratum 1 had been specified and those comprising Stratum 2 had been partially specified, a computer program was designed to create succeeding strata for the remainder of the jobs in the data set and to assign individual jobs to individual strata on the basis of the formula:

$$S_1 = P_{i-j} + p_{i-k} \text{ (etc.)}$$

where S_1 represents the stratum to which a given job is assigned, P designates the level of probability (at this point, not yet fixed) that an incumbent in a given job will move into one of the positions in S_k (i.e., the stratum above S_1), and the subscripts, $i-j$, $i-k$, denote movement from i (initial, unstratified position) into jobs in hierarchically ordered strata (j, k) above S_1. If the computed probabilities that the holder of a given position can move to jobs in, say, the first and second strata are summed, and if this sum equals or exceeds the probability level set for inclusion into the third stratum, then the job will be ranked in that third stratum. Succeeding strata are created and composed in the same way.

Which level of probability should serve as the cut off point for the inclusion of jobs into their respective strata? Obviously, the answer to this question turns on the purpose for which this hierarchical ranking is generated. In order to employ the stratified ranking of jobs to study mobility, we should prefer a cut off point neither too high (in which case too few jobs would be grouped into too many strata) nor too low (which would produce the opposite result of too many jobs in too few strata). Consequently, some experimentation was in order. The cut off point was set first at a probability of 0.5, but this proved to be too restrictive as the computer program was able to create only 2 additional strata and rank only 40 jobs (not counting those specifically assigned to the first and second strata) under this criterion. Relaxing the cut off point by setting it at 0.4 yielded more promising results; some 168 jobs were ranked in 6 strata. This procedure is illustrated in Figure 5.1. The subscripted jobs A, B and C belong to Strata 1 through 3, respectively. The group of jobs at the bottom of the figure (X_1 X_2 etc.) are ranked by the frequency of transition of their incumbents to jobs in the 3 strata depicted here. So, job X_1, whose summed probabilities for transition to strata 1 and 2 exceeds the .4 criterion (.25 + .25) is ranked in Stratum 3; job X_2 has no transition to Stratum 1, only .25 to Stratum 2 and .5 to Stratum 3, ranking it therefore in Stratum 4; accordingly, X_3 is ranked in Stratum 3 and X_4 in Stratum 2.

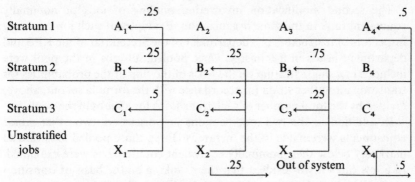

Figure 5.1: Representation of ranking procedure for jobs in sample

As the ranking progressed a snag in the procedure became evident, namely, the great majority of positions in the data set could not be assigned to strata on the basis of this (unmodified) method inasmuch as a majority of positions with nominally high rank have no transition probabilities at all. That is, if no incumbents in such jobs as, say, minister of agriculture or first secretary of an obkom ever received promotions to jobs in the top two strata, then these 'transitionless' jobs would not be ranked. Accordingly, those positions which the incumbents left in order to become minister of agriculture or an obkom first secretary would also go unranked since these transitions were also to unranked jobs. This same problem, the absence of transitions to other jobs, was also apparent in the case of many positions thought to be of middle rank (deputy ministers, gorkom secretaries, and so forth) and as such prevented the ranking of those positions which were vacated when incumbents moved to these middle-level jobs. Clearly, if the general procedure for creating and filling strata on the basis of the probability of movement to higher strata is to succeed, some modifications are required in order to deal with the positions lacking transition probabilities.

Two modifications were introduced. First, unranked positions nominally equivalent to ranked positions were assigned to the same stratum in which a decisive majority of the ranked positions were ordered. In some cases patterns were unclear and other criteria therefore became important. The first secretaries of raikoms are a case in point. Those with transition probabilities to other jobs were ranked in a number of different strata with the greatest concentrations falling in Stratum 7 and Stratum 8. By consulting the size of the party membership in their respective raions,[12] it became clear that those in Stratum 8 were also those with small party memberships (under 2000). Hence, unranked first secretaries of raikoms were assigned to Stratum 7 unless the party membership in their respective raions fell below 2000, in which case they were included in Stratum 8.

The second modification involved a pooling of jobs of nominally equivalent rank in the same organization. Examples of such job pools are inspectors or instructors in a department of the Secretariat of the KPB and department heads in a ministry. Once pooled, all jobs in the pool were included in a single stratum on the basis of the sum of the probabilities for transition into other strata (in accordance with the formula set out, above) divided by the total number of such transitions for all jobs in the pool.

In addition to the two modifications just discussed, two other minor adjustments were made in the hierarchy. First, those pooled jobs ranked markedly below their nominally equivalent counterparts were examined. In a few cases it was evident that their ranking on the basis of transition probabilities to other strata yielded misleading results. For instance the two gorkom secretaries in Soligorsk were ranked in the bottom stratum, and this because their respective pool had only one transition to another job, that of secretary of the primary party organization at the Beloruskalii mining works at Soligorsk, a position ranked in Stratum 9. Consequently, it was decided that nominally equivalent ranking would yield a more accurate result in this case and both gorkom secretaries were reassigned to Stratum 7 where the majority of gorkom secretaries had been ranked by the computer program.

A second modification was made for jobs which might be considered as sinecures. A transitionless position such as Director of the Institute of Party History seems to serve as a final destination for certain politicians whose careers had led to high ranking positions but not to jobs in the top strata. Two individuals who served as Director had previously risen to Stratum 3 jobs (Second Secretary of the Minsk Obkom, Head of the Department of Scientific and Educational Institutions of the Central Committee of the KPB). Hence, it was decided to treat positions such as Director of the Institute of Party History as sinecures rather than as promotions and accordingly to rank them one stratum *below* that from which their incumbents had arrived.

DISCUSSION

The jobs in the data set have been ordered by our procedures into 10 strata. (Details of positions are available from author on request). The shape of the hierarchy generated on the basis of transition probabilities to strata is non-pyramidal, and this aspect reflects both the nature of the data and the method used to order them. The top four strata do resemble a pyramid (especially if we subtract the all-union jobs from Strata 1 and 2), Stratum 5 enlarges the base of this pyramid considerably, the number of jobs per stratum then peaks at Stratum 6, tapers off at Strata 7 and 8 and declines in the last two strata. A major reason for the bulge in membership in the two largest strata results from the inclusion – both via the method of assigning transitionless positions to the stratum of nominally equivalent jobs and that of creating job pools which ranks all jobs in the pool according to the pool's transition probability – of sub-ministerial positions in these strata. In Stratum 5 we find 58 deputy minister positions, in Stratum 6, the heads of 135 departments of ministeries. These two sub-groups of positions form something of a special case. As the relative absence of transitions here might suggest, we are likely dealing with positions in which adjectives such as 'professional-managerial' have more salience than is true for other types of jobs in the system, and access to them is largely concentrated within the hierarchies of their respective organizations.[13] These positions are very rarely (in the data set) entered from 'outside' their organizational hierarchies and the number of cases in which their incumbents leave for positions in other organizations is equally negligible. Were we to take this aspect into account and subtract as special cases these sub-groups from the data set, the mobility-based hierarchy which we have generated would much more resemble a pyramid. Additionally, if we keep in mind the fact that a major reason for the relative paucity of membership in the bottom two strata is the method of data collection (job holders in Strata 9 and 10 appear in print far less often than do those in higher strata), then we can enlarge these strata to pyramidal proportions in our mind's eye by adding in all the other, say, raiispolkom department heads, whom we know to be in the world but whose names did not appear in the data sources.

With these qualifications in mind, the hierarchy of positions generated here seems well-suited to the purpose for which it was developed, namely, in order to analyse elite circulation in the Belorussian Republic. Although that project is beyond the scope of the present study, a number of issues associated with elite stratification in the Soviet system are engaged by the hierarchy generated here and these bear further discussion.

First, let us take up the question of central committee membership, an indicator commonly used in the field to designate the relative standing of positions (i.e., those positions whose incumbents regularly appear on the central committee are commonly regarded as having greater standing than those, perhaps nominally equivalent, positions whose members do not). If we examine the percentage figures in Table 5.2, there are strong grounds for the utility of this indicator evinced by the close correlation between regular

representation of positions on the Central Committee of the KPB and the
stratified ranking of positions on the basis of their transition probabilities.
The size of the percentages diminishes as one moves down the hierarchy,
except for a single case in Stratum 10 which we take up below. From this
perspective, regular representation of positions on the Central Committee
would appear to be a reasonably accurate indicator of the status of
positions.

*Table 5.2: Representation[a] of positions on Central Committee of KPB by Stratum
(in percentages; N = 93)*

Stratum 1	100 (n = 13)	Stratum 6	1 (n = 5)
Stratum 2	94 (n = 16)	Stratum 7	1 (n = 2)
Stratum 3	49 (n = 33)	Stratum 8	0 (n = 0)
Stratum 4	17 (n = 16)	Stratum 9	0 (n = 0)
Stratum 5	3 (n = 7)	Stratum 10	0.6 (n = 1)

[a] 'Representation' is defined as election to the Central Committee at 3 or more
of the 5 congresses of the KPB, 1966–86.

Were we to focus on the *number* of regularly represented positions
instead of their relative frequency of appearance by stratum, however,
serious questions arise regarding the utility of this indicator of status.[14]
First, if regular Central Committee representation marks a given position
for inclusion in the elite strata of the hierarchy, it is then difficult to account
for the appearance of such 'elite' positions in Stratum 5 and Stratum 6.
Second, three raikom first secretary positions are regularly represented on
the Central Committee of the KPB. These – the Molodechno, Grodno and
Orsha raikoms – are all agricultural districts which adjoin sizeable urban
centers. They might therefore be considered as particularly important
raions which provide foodstuffs to the proximate urban populations. But
this consideration would only raise the more insistent question of their
assumedly more important counterparts, say Minsk and Gomel raions,
whose raikom first secretaries are not regularly represented on the Central
Committee. It may be in fact that Central Committee membership in these
cases has more to do with the first secretaries themselves than with the
importance of the positions which they command. In the case of the First
Secretary of the Grodno Raikom this seems to be true as membership on
the Central Committee is coterminous only with the tenure of A. I.
Belyakova. In both the Molodechno and Orsha raikoms, however, Central
Committee membership was awarded to more than one first secretary. The
absence of a clear pattern makes it difficult to see how these three cases
conform to a single rule, whether it be the bestowing of Central Committee
membership on individuals or whether it accrues to them on the basis of the

positions which they hold. In short, we cannot be sure what this 'indicator' (Central Committee membership) is in fact indicating.

This confusion is compounded when we examine other cases. The Editor of the daily, *Zvyazda*, is regularly represented on the Central Committee of the KPB. Accordingly, *Zvyazda's* Editor, M. I. Delets was on the Central Committee in 1971 but, on receiving what appears to have been a promotion to Chair of the State Committee for Publications, he was demoted to candidate membership in 1976 and 1981. Then, while still chair, he was dropped from the Central Committee altogether in 1986. A similar pattern is evident in the careers of other individuals. V. V. Matveev held a spot on the Central Committee while Editor of *Sel'skaya Gazeta*, but on being promoted (?) to Chair of the State Committee on Films he was dropped to candidate membership. As First Secretary of a rural raikom, U. F. Krishtalevich was on the Central Committee, but on becoming Deputy Minister of Social Security he was dropped from the roster. The President of the Grodno Oblispolkom, N. P. Molochko, lost his Central Committee membership on becoming Belorussian Minister of Trade. First Secretary of the Zavodskii Raikom in Minsk City, V. M. Semenov, lost his membership after becoming First Secretary of the Grodno Gorkom (a position qualifying as regularly, but not always, represented on the Central Committee). This list could be extended but the point is already clear. How can this indicator denote elite standing if a sizable number of actors lose it as they advance upwardly in the hierarchy?

A second consideration brought to the fore by the method of stratification employed here returns us to the issue of bureaucracy and calls into question the analytical utility of relying on the nominal rank of positions in the Soviet system. Consider the case of the Organization-Party Work Department of the Central Committee of the KPB. Formally, the Department has in descending order of authority a head (who is ranked in Stratum 2) a first deputy head (Stratum 4), two deputy heads, three heads of sectors, four inspectors and five instructors. Interestingly, the hierarchy generated in this study ranks the deputy department heads, sector heads and instructors all in Stratum 5. Table 5.3 details the bases for these rankings by outlining the position transitions for each of these groups of jobs. Taken as a whole, these data show a tendency towards transition to other jobs in the apparatus of the KPB (17 of 27 transitions, 6 of which are intra-departmental). Also, all but one of the transitions to other organizations were to jobs in the People's Central committee of the BSSR, suggesting a close link between the Department and that organization. Most notable, however, is the similarity evinced by each set of positions with respect to the subsequent career moves made by the incumbents. We find, for instance, a deputy department head, a sector head and an instructor each making his next career move to the position of first deputy

Table 5.3: Position transitions for department heads, sector heads and instructors in the Organization-Party Work Department of KPB

Positions	Next career moves of incumbents	Stratum
Deputy department heads:	First Deputy Head, Org.-Party Work Dept., KPB	4
	First Deputy Head, General Dept., KPB	5
	First Deputy Head, Agriculture Dept., KPB	3
	Asst. to First Secretary of KPB	4
	Deputy Chair, Peoples Control Committee, BSSR out of system (two)	4
Sector heads:	Head, Dept. of Administration of Affairs, KPB	4
	Second Secretary, Minsk Obkom	3
	First Deputy Head, Org.-Party Work Dept., KPB	4
	First Deputy Head, General Dept., KPB	5
	Second Secretary, Grodno Obkom	4
	Asst. to First Secretary of KPB	4
	Deputy Chair, People's Control Committee, BSSR out of system (three)	4
Inspectors:	First Deputy President, Minsk Oblispolkom	4
	Deputy Dept. Head, Org.-Party Work Dept., KPB (two)	5
	Second Secretary, Vitebsk Obkom	4
	Second Secretary, Gomel Obkom (two)	4
	First Deputy Dept. Head, Org.-party Work Dept.	4
	Instructor, Org.-Party Work Dept., KPB	7
	First Deputy Chair, People's Control Committee, BSSR	4
	Chair, Minsk Oblast People's Control Committee out of system (three)	7

head of the department. Similarly, incumbents in each group of positions took their next jobs as deputy chairs of the People's Control Committee of the BSSR (albeit an instructor's next career move was to the assumedly more elevated position of first deputy). If rank in a hierarchy has meaning inasmuch as it denotes a series of positions over which one's career develops, then what are we to make of a case in which captains, majors and colonels, as it were, all share more or less equal chances of being next promoted to general? And when such is the case, what might relations in such a hierarchy look like? Are formal subordinates and superiors likely to behave as such in practice? At the least, this exercise alerts us to what seems a significant gulf between nominal rank and rank as determined empirically by patterns of mobility, suggesting in turn a certain lack of fit between the Soviet form of organization and bureaucracy in Weber's sense of the term.

These considerations touch on a third question connected with elite stratification in the Soviet system, that of the 'importance' associated with certain jobs and the rank which might be assigned them on that basis. One way to regard 'importance' is to locate this quality in the job itself. The director of this organization or the first secretary of that obkom might be regarded as members of an elite because the organization or the obkom is itself 'important'. It should be clear, however, that this perspective has played a very small role in developing our Belorussian elite hierarchy. Consequently, some explanation might be in order as to how, say, the First Secretary of the Frunze Raikom in Minsk City or the Director of the Minsk Tractor Factory should be ranked in Stratum 3 with ministers of the BSSR. Are these positions that important? From the standpoint of the career mobility of the actors themselves they obviously were. These were the jobs which led directly to positions in the top strata, hence their high ranking in a hierarchy based on mobility. These seem analogous to the Dnepropetrovsk and Stavropol organizations, as described in Chapter 3 by Hill and Rahr, which have fed so many politicians into the top ranks of the Soviet elite. It may well be, in fact it seems quite likely, that these jobs were used by a clique within the KPB as stepping stones to advance the careers of clique members,[15] but this conjecture would require further investigation. At any event, these cases point up the fact that the 'importance' of given positions may be radically altered when we approach it from the perspective of the relations among actors and their patterns of mobility rather than seeing it as some objective quality residing in the job.

The same is true in reverse for another position, Director of Gomsel'mash. A number of indicators would mark this job as an important one: the production of agricultural machinery figures prominently in the overall profile of Belorussian industry and, excepting the manufacture of tractors, Gomsel'mash is the Republic's leading producer of farm equipment;[16] Gomel, in which the plant is located, is the second largest city in the BSSR and Gomsel'mash is the largest firm in Gomel;[17] the Director of Gomsel'mash, as we have seen, is regularly a member of the Central Committee of the KPB, a status shared by only one other director of a firm, that of the Minsk Tractor Factory which ranked in Stratum 3 of the hierarchy. What justification, then, is there for ranking the Director of Gomsel'mash in the bottom stratum?

The answer to this question refers us back to the method of ranking and the purpose to which the hierarchy is to be put. Over the twenty-one years spanned in the data set, Gomsel'mash had only two directors, yielding one possible transition (the second director remains in the job) of which there is no record. This does not then imply that the position, lacking transitions, is unimportant; rather, it signifies that *this* position within the context of these data is of little consequence inasmuch as it is not connected to other positions or transitions among them, the investigation of which is the purpose which this hierarchy is designed to serve. Hence, however 'important' this job in its own right, (and analysis with other purposes in mind would likely rank it in another stratum) it plays no part in the study of mobility in this data set.

CONCLUSION

The analysis of elite mobility presupposes some hierarchy of positions over which mobility takes place. Yet when we inquire into the issue of hierarchy we notice that it is always something which is imposed on the data by the analyst. The rankings in the hierarchy which we impose may be validated by certain characteristics of the system under investigation, but this does not alter the fact that we are imposing an analytic scheme all the same in order to study mobility. And this 'in order to' seems the central point. The hierarchy, if it is to serve some purpose, should be designed with this purpose in mind.

Here we have generated a hierarchy of positions in the BSSR by reversing the hierarchy–mobility relationship, by taking mobility as the determinant of hierarchy in the first instance. In so doing, we have imposed some approximation of a bureaucratic hierarchy across the set of elite positions in Belorussia, a hierarchy developed out of transition probabilities to various strata in the model, one which in effect says that a job is to be ranked one rung below the stratum to which its incumbents move next. Although this procedure, due to the number of transitionless jobs in the data set, could not be carried through completely, the modifications which we introduced in order to compensate for this deficiency relied on the logic (in the case of job pools) or results (in the case of nominally equivalent positions) of the procedure itself. Beyond the utility intended for this hierarchy in subsequent research, what do the results of this exercise tell us about elite stratification in the Soviet system?

Judging from the Belorussian data presented here there is a considerable degree of similarity between hierarchy based on the formal rank of positions and hierarchy generated by transition probabilities to given strata. An examination of the detailed rankings points up this confluence. By the same token, however, there seems to be enough departure from the formal ranking in the mobility-based hierarchy to raise some important questions regarding elite stratification generally and intra-organizational career ladders in particular, as our discussion of the Organization-Party

Work Department of the Central Committee of the KPB would suggest. The implication would seem to be that a bureaucratic pattern of mobility is present to some extent, but the exceptions to such a pattern are so numerous and varied as to cast doubt on the utility of the concept 'bureaucracy' as a description of Soviet organization. At the least, the discrepancies between formal rank and the 'bureaucratic' hierarchy imposed on the data on the basis of the transition probabilities of positions likely indicate the influence of non-bureaucratic factors on mobility and, by inference, on the behaviour of actors and organizations in the system. In consonance with previous research[18] this empirical analysis of mobility suggests something of importance with respect to the structure of the Soviet system, namely, that the top authorities do not effectively command a bureaucratically ordered administrative machine which translates their policy directives into the preferred policy outcomes. Rather, this machine seems to move in many directions at once, sometimes fulfilling policy prescriptions but at least as often as not moving in directions unintended by the leadership. We have, for instance, in M. S. Gorbachev's address to the June, 1987 Plenum of the Central Committee authoritative testimony to this fact. After more than two years of the policy of *perestroika*, he laments, 'the mechanism of braking has not been dismantled and has not been replaced by the mechanism of acceleration.'[19] The machinery resists the directives, we might assume, because those in this machinery do not find themselves in relations of domination which approach that of a Weberian bureaucracy. Their incentive structures, above all for career advancement, are largely ordered by the personalized politics of patronage, cliques and elite groupings.[20] Among the advantages which might be listed for the method of ranking employed here is the fact that certain positions stand out as stepping stones or fast tracks to top elite jobs. Future research might then begin by isolating them, inquiring into the careers of those who have moved through them and use this information to aid in the delineation of these personalized (and 'antibureaucratic') elite grouping which have heretofore proven to be so effective in mounting resistance to policy changes enunciated by the top political leadership.

NOTES AND REFERENCES

1   This observation is made explicitly by: Alfred G. Meyer, *The Soviet Political System: An Interpretation*, Random House, New York, 1965, p.147; Philip D. Stewart et al., 'Political Mobility and the Soviet Political Process: A Partial Test of Two Models', *American Political Science Review*, 1972, vol. 66, December, p. 1272; John H. Miller, 'Cadres Policy in the Nationality Areas – Recruitment of CPSU First and Second Secretaries in the Non-Russian Republics of the USSR', *Soviet Studies*, 1977, vol. 29, January, p. 33.

2 Jerry F. Hough, *The Soviet Prefects*, Harvard University Press, Cambridge, Mass., 1969.

3 To illustrate, we know, for instance, that the *nomenklatura* system of appointments is the manifest vehicle for mobility in the Soviet system. One gets a position, a promotion, etc. on the basis of one's name being entered on these appointments' lists. We also know that through the *nomenklatura* mechanism one organization 'interferes' with the staffing of another organization (a party committee, for example, might hold the right of appointment or the right to veto appointments in some state organization) and that these rights are staggered such that the top official in a given organization will likely appoint some of his staff but not his immediate subordinates. Given this pattern, wherein officials often are beholden to others outside of the organization for their positions and career opportunities, it makes little sense to speak of a 'bureaucratic' mode of organization. Of course, other 'unbureaucratic' aspects of the Soviet form of organization, party intervention in policy making or implementation, the role of KGB in economic organizations, could also be cited. For discussion of the *nomenklatura* system's 'unbureaucratic' features, see: Bohdan Harasymiw, *Political Elite Recruitment in the Soviet Union*, St. Martin's Press, New York, 1984, pp. 154–73; Gerd Meyer, 'The Impact of the Political Structure on the Recruitment of the Political Elite in the USSR' in L. J. Cohen and J. P. Shapiro (eds), *Communist Systems in Comparative Perspective*, Anchor Books, Garden City, NY, 1974, pp. 202–4; Joel C. Moses, 'The Impact of *Nomenklatura* in Soviet Regional and Elite Recruitment', *Soviet Union*, 1981, part 1, vol. 8, pp. 62–102; Michael Voslensky, *Nomenklatura: The Soviet Ruling Class*, Doubleday, Garden City, NY, 1984 *passim*; Michael E. Urban, 'Technical Assistance and Political Control: A Research Note on the Organization–Instruction Department of Local Soviets', *Comparative Politics*, 1985, vol. 17, April, pp. 337–50.

4 The title of Mary McAuley's well-known and in many ways masterful article on this subject is perhaps itself an indication of the objectivist bias which has informed our approach to the problem. See her 'The Hunting of the Hierarchy: RSFSR Obkom First Secretaries and the Central Committee', *Soviet Studies*, 1974, vol. 26, October, pp. 473–501.

5 *Ibid.*; Stewart *et al.*, *op. cit.*, note 1; Peter Frank, 'Constructing a Classified Ranking of CPSU Provincial Committees', *British Journal of Political Science*, 1974, part 2, vol. 4, pp. 217–30.

Less explicit rankings of mobility can be found in Miller, *op. cit.*, note 1; Joel C. Moses, 'Regional Cohorts and Political Mobility in the USSR: The Case of Dnepropetrovsk', *Soviet Union*, 1976, part 1, vol. 3, pp. 63–89; George W. Breslauer, 'Provincial Party Leaders' Demand Articulation and the Nature of Center-Perifery Relations in the USSR', *Slavic Review*, 1986, vol 45, winter, pp. 650–72. Mark Beissinger, 'Economic Performance and Career Prospects in the CPSU Party Apparatus' (paper presented at the Eighteenth National Convention of the American Association for the Advancement of Slavic Studies, New Orleans, La., Nov. 20–23, 1986).

6 Max Weber, *Economy and Society*, University of California Press, Berkeley, 1968, p. 946.

7 Arguments against the direct application of the concept 'bureaucracy' to the Soviet form of organization can be found in: Jan Pakulski, 'Bureaucracy and the Soviet System', *Studies in Comparative Communism*, 1986, vol. 19, Spring, pp. 3–24; Don Van Atta, 'Why There Is No Taylorism in the Soviet Union',

Comparative Politics, 1986, vol. 18, April, pp. 327–37; Michael E. Urban, 'Conceptualizing Political Power in the USSR: Patterns of Binding and Bonding', *Studies in Comparative Communism*, 1985, vol. 18 Winter, pp. 207–26; Bob Arnot, 'Soviet Labour Productivity and the Failure of the Shchekino Experiment', *Critique*, 1981, no. 15, pp. 31–56.

8   The Belorussian Soviet Socialist Republic was selected for reasons of size and political orientation. My general interest in elite circulation in the Soviet Union required a unit sufficiently large to generate a data base suitable for the study of various influences on the circulation process (centralization, regionalism and patronage). This requirement would exclude single regions or small republics. On the other hand, limitations of resources precluded data gathering from all but upper-level jobs in the large republics. Given my intention of carrying out an analysis of elite circulation down to the local level (party and soviet offices in raions as well as management, party and trade union positions in large enterprises), the Belorussian Republic with a population of some ten million grouped into six oblasts seemed a logical choice. I should add that I have treated Minsk City as a 'seventh oblast', coding its party and governmental organs as equivalent to those of the other six oblasts in the BSSR.

A second consideration, that of political orientation, also entered into my selection of Belorussia. Inasmuch as a pronounced sense of nationalism in a given republic might be taken as an influence on elite circulation, an influence compounded by the reactive cadres policies of Moscow, I wanted to exclude as much as possible the national factor in order to examine Soviet elite circulation in more general terms. In this respect I have assumed that the results of a study of elite circulation in Belorussia, where nationalism is quite muted, would suggest something about, say, the Russian Republic or about other republics if nationalism were factored out. On the low level of national consciousness in Belorussia generally, see: Nicholas P. Vakar, *Belorussia: The Making of a Nation*, Harvard University Press, Cambridge, Mass., 1956; Ivan S. Lubachko, *Belorussia Under Soviet Rule, 1917–57*, University of Kentucky Press, Lexington, Ky., 1972; Brian Connelly, 'Fifty Years of Soviet Federalism in Belorussia', in R. S. Clem (ed.) *The Soviet West*, Praeger, New York, 1975, pp. 106–33; Stephen L. Guthier, 'The Belorussians: National Identification and Assimilation, 1897–1970; part 1, *Soviet Studies*, 1977, vol. 29, January, pp. 37–61, part 2, *ibid*. April, pp. 270–83; Roman Szporluk, 'West Ukraine and West Belorussia', *Soviet Studies*, 1979, vol. 31, January, pp. 76–98.

9   The main source for these data is the daily, *Sovetskaya Belorussiya* over the period January, 1966 – June, 1986. I also relied on the monthly, *Kommunist Belorussii* (1966–June, 1986), selected numbers of the daily, *Zvyazda*, and on listings which appeared (far less frequently, of course) in *Sovety narodnykh deputatov* (January, 1976–June, 1986) and *Izvestiya* (1983–86). Some data were taken from Soviet personnel directories compiled by the CIA, from Val Ogareff's *Leaders of the Soviet Republics, 1971–1980*, Dept. of Political Science, Australian National University, Canberra, 1980, and from the short biographies in relevant editions of *Deputaty Verkhovnogo Soveta SSSR*.

10   J. W. Cleary, has used a similar matrix in his analysis of the Kazakh elite. See his 'Elite Career Patterns in a Soviet Republic', *British Journal of Political Science*, 1974, vol. 4, July, pp. 323–44.

11   One particular difficulty in assigning jobs to strata involved five Belorussian officials who were named to Soviet diplomatic posts. Having no clear rule on which to base a decision, I assigned one of these positions (Ambassador to

Poland) to the top stratum because of the putative importance of this post and because of the fact that in the careers of the individuals in question (S. A. Pilotovich, A. N. Aksenov and V. I. Brovikov) this posting followed a Stratum 1 job (Secretary of the KPB or Chairman of the Belorussian Council of Ministers) and for Aksenov, led directly to another Stratum 1 appointment (Chair of the USSR State Committee for Television and Radio) while Pilotovich returned to the BSSR to enter a Stratum 2 job (Deputy Chair of the Council of Ministers) and Brovikov remains Ambassador to Poland at the time of writing. The other ambassadorial postings (to North Korea and Pakistan) were assigned to Stratum 2. These choices are admittedly a matter of judgement.

12   *Kommunisticheskaya Partiya Belorussii v tsifrakh: 1918–1978*, Belarus', Minsk, 1978, pp. 212–14.
13   Merle Fainsod was among the first to notice this feature of the Soviet system. See his, 'Bureaucracy and Modernization: The Russian and Soviet Case' in J. LaPalombara (ed.), *Bureaucracy and Political Development*, Princeton University Press, Princeton, 1963, pp. 233–67. Cleary (*op. cit.*, note 10) observes the same in his study of the Kazakh elite.
14   The empirical results of this study support the criticisms previously raised by McAuley, *op. cit.*, note 4.
15   The position of Director of the Minsk Tractor Factory was held by N. N. Slyun'kov from 1965 till 1972 at which time he became First Secretary of the Minsk Gorkom. In 1974 he moved to Moscow as Deputy Chair of Gosplan, USSR, and returned to Belorussia in 1983 as first Secretary of the KPB. In January of 1987, he became a Secretary of the CPSU.
         The Frunze Raikom in Minsk seems a rather intriguing job from the standpoint of clique politics in Belorussia. Over the period 1966–86 it has had six incumbents. Of these, three left the system (destinations unknown) after their tenures as First Secretary, one received what might be regarded as a sinecure (head of a department in the People's Control Committee of the BSSR), one remains, of course, as First Secretary of the Raikom and the other two passed through the position in Frunze to become an obkom secretary (L. M. Barabanova) and First Secretary of the Minsk Gorkom (G. G. Bertoshevich). Subsequently, Bartoshevich has become Second Secretary of the KPB.
16   *Narodnoe Khozyaistvo Belorusskoi SSR v 1981g*, Belarus' Minsk, 1982, pp. 48–53; *Belarus'*, Belarus', Minsk, 1977, pp. 86–7.
17   V. P. Borodina, *Soviet Byelorussia*, Progress, Moscow, 1972, pp. 162–3.
18   Urban, 'Conceptualising Political Power in the USSR'. (See note 7 above)
19   M. S. Gorbachev, 'O zadachakh partii po korennoi perestroike upravleniya ekonomikoi', *Izvestiya*, 26 June 1987.
20   J. H. Miller, 'Nomenklatura: A Check on Localism?' in T. H. Rigby and B. Harasymiu (eds), *Leadership Selection and Patron-Client Relations in the USSR and Yugoslavia*, George Allen & Unwin, London, 1983, pp. 64–96; J. C. Moses, 'Regionalism in Soviet Politics: Continuity as a Source of Change', *Soviet Studies*, 1985, vol. 37, April, pp. 184–221.

6. Generational Change in the Soviet Professional Elite: Procuracy Careers from Brezhnev to Gorbachev[1]

Eugene Huskey

The subject of this study is leadership change in the Procuracy,[2] an institution that has assumed an increasingly important position in the Soviet political and legal system since the accession to power of Gorbachev.[3] The immediate empirical concern of the research is the impact of the Brezhnev succession on the turnover of leading Procuracy officials at the regional, republic, and all-union levels. Put simply, how extensive has turnover been in this group and in what ways do the new leaders differ from the old? We shall offer evidence on the abandonment of Brezhnev's stability of cadres policy in the Procuracy and on the variations in personal and professional backgrounds between the Brezhnev appointees and what might be termed the replacement generation of Procuracy officials.

This case study of leadership change in a profesional group also presents an opportunity to address more general concerns relating to the circulation of elites in contemporary Soviet politics. Has the rapid turnover of elites since the death of Brezhnev respected the existing rules of career mobility, and thereby promoted the expected claimants to vacancies, or has it altered longstanding recruitment procedures in order to advance a new type of leader? The empirical evidence on this question speaks, in turn, to issues of political power and systematic change under Gorbachev. To what extent is the use of political power at this stage of Soviet development constrained by institutionalized systems of recruitment? Does continuity in the recruitment systems, if not in the cadres themselves, impede the break from evolutionary state socialism outlined by Gorbachev? It is to these issues that we return in the conclusion.

This research is based largely on biographies of the leading Procuracy officials appointed since 1978. In June of that year, the monthly Procuracy journal *Sotsialisticheskaya zakonnost'*, began publishing an extensive professional biography of each individual appointed to one of the more than 200 top positions in the Procuracy, from procurators (*prokurory*) at the regional level, to procurators and their deputies at the republican level, to the Procurator-General, his deputies, and department heads (*nachal'niki otdelov*) at the all-union level.[4] Included in the biographies are date of birth; party membership; higher educational institution attended; complete data on first, penultimate, and last postings, including date of appointment; and significant, though incomplete, information on intervening assignments. Sex and ethnicity can also be determined from the information provided. To date,[5] 232 biographies have appeared, making this one of the most extensive and systematic biographical data sets of a Soviet institutional elite.

TURNOVER IN THE PROCURACY LEADERSHIP, 1978–87

During the last four and half years of Brezhnev's tenure in office, Procuracy officials were generally secure in their positions. In the Procuracy, trust in cadres translated into an average yearly turnover from 1978 to 1982 of nine per cent (17 of 200) of the leading positions in the profession. In no single year of the late Brezhnev period did the annual turnover exceed ten per cent, and of course routine transfer due to death, retirement, and promotion accounted for much of this movement. Although these years were not without localized purges – for example, 20 per cent of the regional procurators in Kazakhstan were removed in a single month at the end of 1979 – it is clear that maintenance of continuity in personnel was a primary goal of cadres policy in the Procuracy.

The death of Brezhnev in November 1982 brought a radical change in the rate of turnover in the Procuracy leadership. During 1983, the only full year of Andropov's tenure, 52 of the 200 leading Procuracy officials were removed, an annual turnover rate over two-and-a-half times that of the late Brezhnev period. In a single year, then, one-quarter of the Procuracy leadership was replaced. This purge of procurators was tempered during Chernenko's 13 months in office, when only 29 leading Procuracy officials were removed. But the accession to power of Gorbachev in March 1985 signalled a renewed emphasis on personnel turnover (see Table 6.1). In the 12 months from October 1985 to September 1986, 41 leading Procuracy officials lost their positions. If this rate of turnover continues there will soon be few in the Procuracy elite whose current position was obtained in the Brezhnev era.

For the student of Soviet politics, this pattern of personnel change in the Procuracy is familiar. It is now the received wisdom that Chernenko's tenure was merely an interregnum, a brief and half-hearted attempt to stem the flow of new blood into the higher reaches of party and government. But in one important respect, turnover in the Procuracy does not conform to

*Table 6.1: Annual turnover rate of the procuracy elite (1978–present)**

1978[a]	13
1979	20
1980	15
1981	21
1982	13
1983	52
1984	34
1985	34
1986	37
1987[a]	42

[a] Figures from part of the year have been extrapolated over the whole year.
* Data in this and the following tables are derived from biographies published in *Sotsialisticheskaya zakonnost'*.

the general contours of recent Soviet cadres policy. While the shakeup in the party leadership began at the centre and radiated outward, changes in Procuracy personnel have been most pronounced in the periphery.[6] This is especially noteworthy because one might have expected the death in 1981 of the Procurator-General Rudenko, the premier figure in the Procuracy since 1954, to prompt a changing of the old guard in Moscow. That did not happen, however. Rudenko's replacement, the 61-year old former First Deputy Procurator A. Rekunkov, has been content with minor personnel adjustments in the USSR Procuracy. Only four persons of department head standing or higher have been replaced in the Procurator-General's office since 1981, which is a slightly lower turnover rate than that observed during the last three years of Rudenko's reign.

Quite a different picture emerges at the republic and regional levels. In the 15 Soviet republics, 10 of the current procurators and six of the current first deputy procurators have attained their posts since the death of Brezhnev. By contrast, the last four and half years of the Brezhnev era witnessed a total of only three turnovers in the post of republican procurator and four in the post of republican first deputy procurator. The effects of the post-Brezhnev succession on regional procurators have been as far reaching. Two thirds of the current regional procurators have assumed office since the end of 1982. Thus, while leadership change has been unremarkable at the centre, a purge of significant proportions has been carried out among the Procuracy elite in the periphery.

The rate of turnover in the Procuracy leadership varies between geographical areas of the country as well as between center and periphery. The appointment of a new Lithuanian procurator in early 1983 represents the only personnel change in the Baltic Procuracy elite since Brezhnev's death. Western Siberia has registered a modest turnover of five of its 14 regional procurators since the end of 1982. In the Central Asian republics, however, Procuracy cadres have departed en masse. In Uzbekistan, where problems of localism, corruption, and false reporting in the economy[7] are particularly acute, the entire leadership of the republican Procuracy was replaced after Brezhnev's death. The installation of a new deputy procurator and three new deputy procurators followed the appointment of A. Buturlin as Uzbek procurator in the summer of 1984.[8] The purge in the Procuracy leadership has therefore been nationwide in scope, but selective in its targets.

A NEW GENERATION OF PROCURATORS?

Rapid turnover of a profession's leaders serves over the short term to concentrate the minds of the elite on the commands of political superiors. But more importantly for long-term developmental processes in the Soviet Union, it presents an opportunity to recruit a new political generation, whose distinct experience and values may reshape institutional behaviour. Has the extensive remoulding of the Procuracy leadership since the death of Brezhnev brought in officials with personal and professional backgrounds that break with traditional patterns of recruitment? The analysis below addresses this question by measuring the variations in age, gender, party membership, ethnicity, education, and career mobility between the Brezhnev (1978–82) and post-Brezhnev (1983–87) appointees to leadership positions in the Procuracy.

As one would expect in any complex bureaucracy in an established and stable state, one of the major structural conditions for advancement to the elite is professional maturity, as indicated by years of service. During the nine years covered by the data, the average age at promotion to the Procuracy leadership declined significantly. After holding steady at 48 (n = 65) in the last years of Brezhnev, the average age at appointment of regional procurators began to fall after Brezhnev's death, to 47 (n = 42) under Andropov, 46 (n = 12) under Chernenko, 45 (n = 28) in the first year of Gorbachev's tenure and 44 (n = 20) in the second. Although it is still common for persons over 50 to attain the post of regional procurator, this older cohort is now being complemented by appointees in their late 30s. Since the death of Chernenko, eight of the 52 regional procurators have been under 40 at the time of appointment. The current regional procurator[7] in the Smolensk region, the fourth most populous in the country, assumed his post recently at the age of 38.

To be sure, the rapid circulation of elites occasioned by the recent succession has not led to the abandonment of the basic rules of engagement regarding age and eligibility for recruitment to the Procuracy leadership. Approximately 20 years of service remains the norm for promotion to leading positions in the Procuracy. However, those in charge of Procuracy recruitment under Gorbachev have broken with recent tradition by sanctioning the appointment to leading positions of promising Procuracy officials with little more than a decade of service in the profession. It is unclear whether this policy represents a response to immediate cadre requirements or an experiment that will give rise to a fundamental reform of career patterns of the Procuracy leadership.

The concern with age as a factor in political and bureaucratic behaviour in the USSR has been heightened in recent years by suggestions that the rising generation of Soviet leaders, who come to office without the formative influence of the Terror of the 1930s or the Second World War, may exhibit a political temperament and values distinct from their elders.[9] The rejuvenation of the Procuracy leadership since the death of Brezhnev does point to a change in the life experience as well as the stage in the life cycle of the Procuracy elite. In the Procuracy, the generation of '38, the fiercely loyal and professionally underqualified cadres promoted during the Great Purges, are finally succumbing to retirement and death. Tables 6.2 and 6.3 illustrate that only a handful of Procuracy officials appointed since 1978 experienced as young adults the darkest days of Soviet power. Indeed, the majority of appointees since 1983 were born from 1935 to 1941 and therefore came of age politically under Khrushchev.[10] It is premature, however, to assert that the Procuracy is being led by a cohort that matured politically and professionally after Stalin. Stalin-era recruits continue to figure prominently in the profession, both as unpromotable staff personnel at the base and as key members of the Procuracy elite. Of the seven persons appointed to leading posts in the Procurator-General's office since 1983, three began their legal careers under Stalin.

In general, continuity rather than change is the norm in the personal backgrounds of the Procuracy leadership. Nowhere is continuity among the elite more pronounced than in the gender of those appointed to leading positions in the Procuracy. The traditional association of men and women with particular types of careers has died hard in the Soviet Union. Until recent years, popular and official career expectations discouraged women from entering law faculties or legal institutes to train for legal careers. In 1966, when many of the rising generation of leaders in the Procuracy were receiving their legal education, the law student population of Moscow State University was overwhelmingly male (90 per cent). The law faculty had in fact the lowest proportion of women of any faculty in the university (10 per cent, the next lowest was physics with 27 per cent).[11]

Since the 1960s, however, large numbers of women have received legal training, and the Procuracy has become a respectable destination for

Table 6.2: Year of birth of procuracy officials appointed 1978 to 1987[a]

B	Year	G
B	1920	
B	1921	GG
BB	1922	G
BBB	1923	G
BBBB	1924	
BBBBBB	1925	
BB	1926	
BBBBBB	1927	GGGGG
BBBB	1928	GGGGG
BBBBBB	1929	GGG
BBBB	1930	GGGGG
BBBBBB	1931	GGGGGGGGGG
BBB	1932	GG
BBB	1933	GGG
B	1934	GGGGGG
B	1935	GGGGGGGGGGG
BBBB	1936	GGGGGGGGGGG
BBBBB	1937	GGGGGGGGGGGG
BBBBB	1938	GGGGGGGGGGGGG
BBB	1939	GGGGGGG
BBB	1940	GGGGGGGGGGGGGGG
	1941	GGGGGGGGG
B	1942	GGG
B	1943	GGGGG
	1944	GGGG
B	1945	GGGG
B	1946	GGGGGGG
	1947	GGGGG
	1948	GGGG
	1949	GGGG
	1950	GG
	1951	
	1952	G

[a] Bs represent individuals appointed under Brezhnev; Gs those appointed since his death.

female law graduates. By 1982 women occupied one-quarter of all professional positions in the Procuracy.[12] In terms of professional maturity, a significant pool of women should therefore become eligible within the next five years to assume leadership posts in the Procuracy. But an informal division of labour by gender in the Procuracy will almost certainly prevent women from competing successfully with men for the

Table 6.3: Beginning year of legal careers of procuracy officials appointed 1978 to 1987[a]

B	1939	
B	1944	
BB	1945	G
B	1946	G
B	1947	
BB	1948	
BBBB	1949	GG
BBBB	1950	GGG
BBBB	1951	GGGG
BBBB	1952	GGGGG
BBB	1953	GGGG
BBBBBB	1954	GGGGGG
BBB	1955	GG
BBB	1956	GG
BBBBB	1957	GGGGGG
B	1958	GGGG
BBB	1959	GGGGGGGGGGGG
BB	1960	GGG
BBBBBB	1961	GGGGGGGGG
BBB	1962	GGGGGGGGGGGG
BBBB	1963	GGGGGGG
B	1964	GGGGGG
BB	1965	GGGGGG
BBBB	1966	GGGGGGG
BB	1967	GGGGG
	1968	GGGGGG
BB	1969	GGGGGGGGGG
B	1970	GGGGG
	1971	GGGGGGGGGGGGG
BB	1972	GG
	1973	GGGGGGG
	1974	GGGG
	1975	GGG
	1976	
	1977	GG

[a] Bs represent individuals appointed under Brezhnev; Gs those appointed since his death.

scarce leadership positions in the profession. Women are now streamed into what are considered to be suitable jobs – work with juveniles and the general supervision of legality (*obshchii nadzor*), the latter involving primarily analysis of written documents and not work in the field.[13]

The tracking of women away from line positions and from posts in vital areas of the Procuracy's jurisdiction has thus far kept to a minimum the reserve of female cadres eligible for promotion to leading positions in the profession. Of the 232 leading Procuracy officials appointed since 1978, only one is a woman. She is N. Sokolova, appointed in the autumn of 1985 as Deputy Procurator of Kirgizia, a post she assumed in the wake of a purge of the republican Procuracy.[14] With the exception of Sokolova, women have not moved to positions higher than deputy procurators of regions or heads of departments in republican Procuracy offices.[15]

Party membership continues to be an essential qualification for recruitment to the Procuracy elite. As the occupants of posts on the *nomenklatura* lists of party committees at the regional level and above, all Procuracy officials in this study are members of the Communist Party. In fact, over 80 per cent of professional personnel in the Procuracy belong to the party, making the Procuracy one of the most 'party-saturated' groups in the Soviet Union. In Procuracy careers, this commitment to 'partiinost' begins especially early. Law students at Moscow State University had rates of party membership far higher than those of their peers in other faculties (60 per cent, the next highest in 1966 was philosophy with 32 per cent; faculties had party membership in single percentages).[16] The proportion is so great at this early career stage that party membership in the Procuracy appears to be more a prerequisite for entrance to the profession than a facilitator of career advancement, which is its common function in groups with lower levels of party membership.

It is important not to pass over the expected continuity in party membership without recognizing the impact of party saturation on professional behaviour in the Procuracy. However routinized party life has become in the post-Stalin era, it still subjects individuals to a process of political socialization and a standard of discipline not found among the general population. Moreover, the close links between party and Procuracy all too often draw procurators into local networks of party power and patronage, which compromise their role as the guardians of central interests in the periphery.

Continuity also reigns in the patterns of ethnic recruitment to the Procuracy leadership. First, the recent succession has not altered the Slavic dominance at the apex of the Procuracy hierarchy, a pattern of ethnic concentration common to all central political institutions. From 1978 to 1982, Slavs garnered 13 of the 14 leading appointments in the USSR Procuracy. Since the death of Brezhnev, Slavs have filled all eight of the vacancies at the all-union level. Thus, in the Procuracy, an institution dedicated to the maintenance of a single standard of justice throughout the country, responsible posts at the centre remain a Slavic preserve.

Whereas Slavic procurators are not limited in their geographical mobility by republican divisions, excepting the 'self-administered' republics of Georgia and Armenia, Procuracy officials of non-Slavic backgrounds remain typecast as republican or, in Soviet parlance, national cadres.[17] Slavs assumed the premier Procuracy post in Turkmenistan in 1975 and 1983, in Tadzhikistan in 1982 and 1986, and Lithuania in 1983. Slavs are also routinely appointed as deputy procurators in all non-Slavic republics. Moreover, in Central Asia Slavic procurators are present in significant numbers at the regional level, even in areas with small Slavic populations. In Turkmenistan, Slavs have filled three of the nine vacancies to posts of regional procurator since 1978 (2 of 6 since 1983), although Slavs account for only 15 per cent of the republic's population. Like their counterparts in party and KGB organizations, Slavic Procuracy officials in non-Slavic areas act as checks against 'national deviationism'.[18]

The educational levels of Procuracy leaders have also remained constant over the past decade, with all those in the sample possessing a completed higher education in law. This is a very different era, then, from the late Stalin period, when in 1947 alone the Communist Party directed 500 of its members into prominent Procuracy positions with only a one-year course in law behind them.[19] Since the late Brezhnev period, a higher legal education has been an essential qualification not only for advancement to the Procuracy elite but for initial recruitment to the profession.

As measured by the prestige of the educational establishment attended

Table 6.4: Law schools attended by procuracy leaders appointed 1978 to 1987

	1978–82 appointees N = 77	1983–87 appointees N = 161
Sverdlovsk[a]	14%	11%
Kharkov[a]	5%	7%
Saratov[a]	4%	7%
Moscow[b]	6%	4%
Leningrad[b]	8%	6%
Minsk[b]	4%	7%
Tashkent[b]	6%	2%
Alma-Ata[b]	10%	6%
Kazan[b]	4%	4%
Other universities	26%	32%
Correspondence course	6%	6%
Unknown	5%	8%

[a] Legal institutes, which are equal to university law faculties in terms of prestige and educational standards.
[b] In these cities, previously functioning legal institutes merged with, or were transformed into, law faculties of universities.

by leading Procuracy officials, the quality of the training of the Procuracy leadership has not changed. Correspondence degrees in law, a course of study that attracts large numbers of students with poor prospects for professional legal careers,[20] continue to be acceptable qualifications for promotion to leading Procuracy positions. Six per cent of the late Brezhnev and post-Brezhnev appointees to the Procuracy elite acquired their legal education by correspondence. Most leading procurators, however, graduate from the large and prestigious law faculties or legal institutions. As illustrated in Table 6.4, the distribution of law school backgrounds in the two cohorts has changed little. Only Saratov Legal Institute and Minsk University exhibited sharp increases in the representation of their alumni among the Procuracy elite, a trend apparently associated with higher turnover rates of leading procurators in areas to which graduates of these institutions traditionally migrate.

CAREER PATTERNS OF THE PROCURACY LEADERSHIP, 1978–1987

The analysis has centred thus far on the personal characteristics and qualifications of the Procuracy elite. But as Mark Beissinger reminds us in a recent study of leading Communist Party cadres, generational and other distinctions relating to personal background appear to be less influential in shaping behaviour than the specific functional and geographical contexts of professional activity.[21] An assessment of the development of a Soviet professional elite must be especially attentive, therefore, to changes over time in career patterns, which expose leaders to different sets of work roles and conditions. To determine whether the rising generation of procurators has encountered the same contexts of professional activity – and hence the same processes of professional socialization – as its predecessors, we examine below patterns of functional specialization and geographical mobility in the Procuracy elite.

New recruits to the Procuracy traditionally begin work at the district or city level as criminal investigators (*sledovateli*) or assistant procurators (*pomoshchniki prokurora*). These two staff positions give their occupants distinct perspectives on life in the Procuracy. Where the investigator's job is a profession in itself, narrowly focused on the conduct of the preliminary investigation in criminal cases, the work of the assistant procurator is more varied. The assistant procurator spends part of his time in the field, either prosecuting cases in court or conducting reviews of local enterprise behaviour. But most of his energies are concentrated on the preparation and review of documents in the local Procuracy office. And where the investigators operate with some degree of independence in the investigation of criminal cases, the assistant procurator works directly under the procurator, though the range of his responsibilities and his proximity to the procurator often grant the assistant procurator an importance belied by his title.

Since the death of Brezhnev, those with initial experience as investigators have been promoted to the Procuracy elite in ever increasing numbers. Among those elevated to leading Procuracy posts from 1978 to 1982, 48 per cent began their Procuracy careers as investigators and 34 per cent as assistant procurators. Since the beginning of 1983, the figures have been 63 per cent and 24 per cent, respectively. Whether this upsurge in the promotion of procurators with initial professional specialization in criminal affairs represents a conscious recruitment policy in the Procuracy is unknown. But one should find among the rising generation of Procuracy leaders more expertise in, and perhaps more emphasis on, problems of law and order, which represents only one of the many responsibilities assumed by procurators in their work as supervisors of legality.

A precise accounting of the patterns of functional specialization from initial position to entrance to the Procuracy elite is precluded by the incomplete data in the original Soviet biographies on mid-career changes. However, the biographical information does permit the identification of three basic career types: the staff specialist, who spends at least the first ten years or first three appointments in a staff position; the line generalist, who enters, and stays in, a 'management' track as procurator or deputy procurator after no more than two appointments; and those with mixed careers, who ratchet their way to leadership positions by accepting staff posts at higher administrative levels in order to return to lower levels as line personnel. In the wake of Brezhnev's death, the proportion of elite procurators with mixed career paths caught and then overtook that of the staff specialists and line generalists, who have continued to account for roughly equal shares of the Procuracy leadership (see Table 6.5). Besides exposing personnel to a wider range of roles in the Procuracy, the mixed career path accords higher-level procurators an opportunity to observe and socialize officials at close range before 'promoting them downward' to a leading role at a lower level of the apparatus. By ratcheting personnel through the hierarchy, this recruitment pattern may impede the efforts of local party and government authorities to integrate procurators into local networks of political power and protection.[22]

The rise of the mixed career type in the Procuracy elite appears to be part of a broader assault on localism in contemporary Soviet politics. Under Brezhnev, the Communist Party appointed most regional first secretaries from within the local elite, usually from among other secretaries as the regional party organization, the oblispolkom chairman, and the first secretaries of the major city or district party organizations in the region.[23]

Table 6.5: Career types of procuracy leaders

	1978–82 Appointees (N = 77)	1983–87 Appointees (N = 161)	1985–87 Appointees (N = 72)
Staff	33%	27%	22%
Mixed	10%	24%	28%
Line	30%	24%	21%
Other[a]	29%	26%	28%

[a] This figure includes individuals whose biographical information was insufficient to identify a career type or whose careers followed a steady progression from staff to line positions at one administrative level after another. Due to rounding of percentages, columns do not add up to 100%.

But since the accession to power of Gorbachev, the Central Committee of the Communist Party has sought to heighten its control over regional party organizations by appointing large numbers of staff personnel from the Central Committee apparatus in Moscow to head the obkoms.[24]

The practice of recruiting cadres from outside a region has spread to the Procuracy. Table 6.6 shows that the percentage of personnel 'promoted downward' from positions at republican or USSR levels to lead regional procuracies has more than doubled, from 8 per cent to 13 per cent. As a corollary, a dramatic decline has occurred in the percentage of promotees to the post of regional procurator from within the same region. If

Table 6.6: Previous post of regional procurators appointed 1983 to 1987 and 1978 to 1983[a]

	City/ District	Region Same	Region Other	Region Unknown	Republic or USSR
Procurator	11(6)		14(13)	(1)	2
Deputy Procurator	1	20(20)	24(7)	1(1)	2(1)
Department Head or Deputy			1		8(2)
Senior Investigator					(1)
Judge		2(2)			
MVD Official		(1)			
Justice Department Official		2(3)	1		
Communist Party Official	(1)	5(3)		1(1)	(1)
Soviet Official		1			
N = 96 (N = 64)	12 (7)	30 (29)	40 (20)	2 (3)	12 (5)
Percentage	13%(11%)	31%(45%)	42%(31%)	2%(5%)	13%(8%)

[a] 1978 to 1982 shown in brackets.

promotion to regional procurator from within a region occurred in 45 per cent of the cases from 1978 to 1982, the corresponding figure for the period since 1983 has dropped to 31 per cent. Institutionalized patterns of promotion within regional Procuracy offices have therefore been undermined, though not dismantled, by the attack on localism launched by Brezhnev's successors.

Although inter-regional career movement in the Procuracy has become increasingly common since 1983, the original mission of the Procuracy is still endangered by the relative geographical immobility of its leading cadres. The old tension between central and local control of the Procuracy, debated passionately at the revival of this tsarist institution in Soviet Russia in 1922, continues to haunt the profession. While in the early years of Soviet power many local party and government officials, with some supporters in the centre, favoured the subordination of the Procuracy offices around the country to local political authorities, Lenin insisted that a highly centralized Procuracy protected from local influence was essential if the young regime wished to ensure that Soviet justice was uniform 'in Kaluga as well as in Kazan'. Lenin's arguments carried the day, and the Procuracy was established as a legal organ exempt from the standard dual subordination applied to other government institutions.[25]

In the first few decades of Soviet rule the frequent movement of leading Procuracy cadres across regional and republican lines enhanced the centralized character of the institution. A case in point from our sample is N. Bazhenov, the current First Deputy Procurator-General of the USSR. Bazhenov, who began his career in 1946, rose in the Procuracy to the position of district procurator before accepting a job as secretary of the Gorky regional party organization. He was subsequently promoted to procurator of the Chuvash autonomous republic, from where he moved to the Ukraine to become deputy republican procurator. He then returned to the RSFSR to work, in succession, as regional procurator of Primorskii krai, as a department head in the RSFSR Procuracy in Moscow, and as procurator of the Kuibyshev region. After 12 years as Kuibyshev regional procurator, he was promoted to his present post in 1981 at the age of 60.

The geographical mobility evident in Bazhenov's career is now a rarity. The career data from our sample indicate that recruitment and promotion patterns have been highly localized for at least the past decade. Some movement of personnel still occurs between regions of a single republic, as the previous discussion detailed, but transfers across republican lines are uncommon. Only 20 instances of appointments across republics could be identified in this sample, and half of those were between the RSFSR and Central Asia. Even in the RSFSR, where one might expect Procuracy careers to cover rather greater distances, interregional transfers are usually confined to a single area of the republic, such as Eastern or Western Siberia or southern Russia.[26] This localization of recruitment patterns mirrors recent trends in the careers of leading Communist Party officials. Writing about regional party leaders in the RSFSR, Mark Beissinger noted that 'officials born after 1925 are significantly less likely than their elders to have worked either for the Central committee apparatus or in a region other than their own.'[27]

The absence of a truly national corps of procurators who move, like personnel in the military or the KGB, with little regard to place of origin complicates the Procuracy's highly-publicized mission of eliminating localism and corruption. Although not administratively subordinate to, or financially dependent on, local government officials, Procuracy leaders are nonetheless susceptible to local political influence. They sit on the local soviet executive committee, the party committee, and occasionally even the party bureau. Moreover, as officials on the local party organization's *nomenklatura* list, the procurators cannot afford to alienate the local party first secretary.[28] Thus, while localized recruitment patterns in the Procuracy are by no means the fundamental cause of localism and corruption in the Soviet political system, they do limit the ability of the legal organs to wage an effective compaign against them.[29]

The geographical immobility in Procuracy careers is another example, then, of the constraints on centrally-led reforms in the Soviet Union. Four of the most important policy initiatives since Brezhnev's death – the anti-alcohol campaign, the anti-corruption campaign, the campaign for labour discipline, and the campaign against report padding (*pripiski*) and eyewashing (*ochkovtiratel'stvo*) in the economy – depend heavily on the effectiveness of the Procuracy and other legal organs in carrying out central directives. Yet the political loyalties of local Procuracy officials remain divided between centre and periphery.[30] Unless the trend towards inter-regional mobility noted earlier accelerates, one cannot expect Procuracy officials to implement new policies faithfully and enthusiastically if they conflict with the local political interests.

CONCLUSION

In the two great revolutionary periods of Soviet history, 1917–21 and 1928–38, Lenin and Stalin remade the ruling class – and hence Russian society – by throwing the rascals out. Purges of the existing elites brought forth new political generations that differed fundamentally from their predecessors. Where the October Revolution replaced Provisional Government leaders with a new elite committed to revolutionary transformation, the second revolution under Stalin replaced the makers of revolution with politically immature and ill-educated *vydvizhentsy* ('promotees') who were fiercely devoted to the maintenance of the existing political order.

The maturing of Soviet society has since blunted the 'cadres weapon' by sanctifying the rules regarding the training, selection, and promotion of personnel and by eroding the distinctions between the current and replacement elite cohorts. Cadres of all ages have now undergone similar professional training and political socialization. Thus, unlike Lenin and Stalin, Brezhnev's successors confront a relatively homogenized population that advances through well-established career paths appropriate to the various professional and technical areas of Soviet life.

By the end of the Brezhnev era, the inertia engendered by long-serving elites and entrenched promotion patterns constrained central political power and discouraged a much-needed revitalization of the Soviet economy and society. In a radical departure from the cadres policy of Brezhnev, the current political leadership has swept out the sitting elite as part of its programme of *perestroika*. But more important than the scope of personnel turnover is whether Gorbachev and those around him will challenge the established recruitment systems in order to mould a new political generation committed to reform. To promote the expected claimants to vacancies would only invite a replication of the bureaucratic elite under Brezhnev, albeit in slightly younger form.

The evidence from this study of leadership change in the Procuracy indicates that the rapid circulation of elites in the profession since Brezhnev has generally respected the existing conditions for promotion to leading posts. Certain qualifications for elite recruitment in the Procuracy cannot, of course, be dropped without eroding the foundations of Soviet socialism or the professionalism essential to all advanced societies. Among these are party membership, a higher legal education, and lengthy service in the Procuracy or a related legal institution.[31] But barriers for women and non-Slavs remain as illustrations of the continuity in cultural values between the Brezhnev and post-Brezhnev eras.

One also does not encounter in the rising generation glaring anomalies in recruitment patterns that would suggest the elevation of politically favoured personnel outside of normal channels.[32] But career paths of leading procurators have exhibited a modest realignment since the death of Brezhnev. A small group of young Procuracy officials has received unusually early promotion to the elite under Gorbachev. Furthermore, the desire to combat localism in the political and legal system has apparently prompted two changes in recruitment patterns in the Procuracy. First, persons with mixed career paths – those socialized as staff officials in higher-level Procuracy offices before being promoted to lower-level line positions – now figure prominently among the Procuracy elite. Second, the deputies of departing regional procurators are increasingly being passed over as replacements for their former bosses in favour of recruits from outside the region.

These changes in the patterns of career mobility indicate that the weight of accumulated tradition in elite recruitment under Brezhnev has been at least partially lifted by the current political leadership. Indeed, as part of the cadre renewal in responsible party posts, a recent *Pravda* article proposed that the search for new leaders be extended to include persons lacking traditional qualifications.[33] It is too early, however, to reach firm conclusions about the composition or recruitment patterns of the rising generation in the political or professional elite. The evidence offered here, describing careers in the Procuracy in the years just before and after the death of Brezhnev, portrays a Soviet professional elite in transition. Whether the emerging contours of Procuracy careers outlined in this analysis acquire permanent shape, or give way to new, and perhaps strikingly different, recruitment patterns, depends on political developments that are at present unknown, even to the Soviet political leadership itself.

NOTES AND REFERENCES

1   This research forms part of a larger project on careers in the Soviet Procuracy that is funded by the National Council for Soviet and East European Research. My thanks to Todd Foglesong for research assistance and to Myron Curtis, Thomas Flory, and the staff of the Bowdoin College Computing Center for help with the biographical database. I am grateful to Janet Martin for insightful comments on an earlier draft of this chapter.

2   More than 20,000 legal professionals work in the Procuracy. The functions of the Procuracy are traditionally divided into three areas. The first is criminal investigation, where the Procuracy has responsibility for conducting investigations of most major criminal cases and for supervising all criminal investigations, whether they are carried out by the Ministry of Internal Affairs (MVD), the Committee for State Security (KGB), or the Procuracy itself. Second, Procuracy officials serve as state prosecutors in criminal trials. Third, the Procuracy enjoys power of supervision of legality (*obschchii nadzor*), ensuring that the decisions of courts and indeed all government institutions correspond to law.

3   For examples of the political leadership's recent statements on the Procuracy, see 'V Tsentral'nom komitete KPSS: O merakh po povysheniyu roli prokurorskogo nadzora v ukreplenii sotsialisticheskoi zakonnosti i pravoporyadka,' Pravda, 19 June 1987, p. 1; 'V Politbyuro TsK KPSS,' *Pravda*, 5 June 1987, p. 1; 'Soveshchanie v TsK KPSS,' *Pravda*, 11 November 1986, p. 2.

4   Procurators and their deputies are the management, or line, personnel, in Procuracy offices, which exist in each of the administrative-territorial divisions of the USSR. Beneath the line officials work staff personnel, who are either attached to the procurator (i.e. criminal investigators (*sledovateli*) and assistant procurators (*pomoshchniki prokurora*)) or work in specialized departments, which are staffed by a head, deputy head, and departmental assistants (*prokurory otdela*).

5 The latest biographies included in this study are those from the May 1987 issue of *Sotsialisticheskaya zakonnost'*. In the analysis below I assume that the actual appointment of Procuracy officials occurs three months before the public announcement appears in *Sotsialisticheskaya zakonnost'*. That is the standard delay noted when subsequent appointments of the same official provide information on the precise month of a person's previous appointment.

6 Thane Gustafson and Dawn Mann, 'Gorbachev's First Year: Building Power and Authority', *Problems of Communism*, 1986, May–June p. 4.

7 The new Uzbek procurator reported recently that every region in the republic had falsified statistics on the harvesting and production of cotton, the major crop in the republican economy. A. Buturlin, 'Po zakonu: tochka zreniya yurista', *Literaturnaya gazeta*, 10 September 1986, p. 11.

8 A similar housecleaning occurred in Kirgizia, where the replacement of the republican procurator in 1983 signalled the beginning of a thorough purge of the republican procuracy. That this was more than a routine reshuffling of personnel is indicated by the fact that all but one of the new leading cadres in Kirgizia were brought in from positions outside the republican Procuracy headquarters in Frunze. In Turkmenistan, republican and regional procuracies alike felt the effects of a purge. Ashkhabad oblast alone among the five regions of Turkmenistan did not replace its procurator in the wake of Brezhnev's death, and Krasnovod oblast has had two different procurators during the past three-and-a-half-years.

9 This study does not attempt to test empirically the impact of early life experience on professional behaviour in the Procuracy. For recent assessments of the impact of life experience on behaviour in the Soviet political elite, see Mark Beissinger, 'In Search of Generations in Soviet Politics', *World Politics*, 1986, no. 2, pp. 288–314; S. Bialer, *Stalin's Successors: Leadership, Stability, and Change in the Soviet Union*, Cambridge University Press, Cambridge, 1980, part II; S. Bialer, 'The Soviet Political Elite and Internal Political Developments in the USSR,' in W. Griffith (ed.), *The Soviet Empire: Expansion and Detente*, Lexington Books, Lexington, Mass., 1976, pp. 25–55. G. Breslauer, 'Is there a Generation Gap in the Soviet Political Establishment?: Demand Articulation by RSFSR Provincial Party First Secretaries', *Soviet Studies*, 1984, no. 1, pp. 1–25.

10 The accompanying tables also indicate that, while the careers of many procurators may have been retarded due to Brezhnev's policy of trust in cadres, whole age groups were not passed over for promotion.

11 *Moskovskii universitet za 50 let sovetskoi vlasti*, Moscow, *Izdatel'stvo Moskovskogo universiteta*, 1967, p. 722.

12 *Sovetskaya prokuratura*, Moscow, *Yuridicheskaya Literatura*, 1982, pp. 209.

13 Criminal investigative work, in partcular, is considered to be off limits to women. On this point, see a recent *Pravda* article in which one of the relatively few female criminal investigators, in this case in the MVD, describes the resistance to her career ambitions from male counterparts. N. Iashina, 'Bez prava oshibat'sya', *Pravda*, 4 July 1986, p. 3. For portraits of the professional and personal lives of three women who work as middle-level staff personnel in the Procuracy, see 'O rabote i nemnogo o sebe', Sotsialisticheskaya zakonnost', 1987, no. 3, pp. 40–42.

14 Trained in law at Frunze University, Sokolova is an ethnic Russian who was apparently raised in Kirgizia. She began her legal career in Kirgizia in 1968, when at the age of 25 she became an assistant procurator (*pomoshchnik*

prokurora) at the regional level. She then worked in staff positions in the Procuracy for 13 years before being seconded to the Communist Party apparatus for a two-year stint, presumably in the regional department of administrative and financial-trade organs. In 1983 she was appointed head of the justice department of the Osh region, and two years later transferred to her current position of Deputy Procurator of Kirgizia.

15 *Sovetskaya prokuratura*, p. 209

16 *Moskovskii universitet* ... p. 722.

17 The death of Brezhnev does not appear to have loosened the restrictions on the admission and promotion of Jews in the Procuracy. Not only are barriers erected to admission into law faculties and to recruitment by government legal institutions, advancement of Jews already in the Procuracy is rare. The biographical data indicate that no Jews were appointed to leading positions in the Procuracy in the past nine years.

18 The placement of Slavs in leading law enforcement posts in non-Slavic areas is not likely to decline over the short term, given recent outbreaks of national discontent among Crimean Tatars ('Soobshchenie TASS', *Pravda*, 24 July 1987, p. 2) and Gorbachev's willingness to appoint a Russian from the RSFSR to head the troubled party organization in Kazakhstan.

19 A. Pankratov, 'Kadry sovetskoi prokuratury za 50 let', *Sotsialisticheskaya zakonnost'*, 1967, no. 10, p. 34.

20 N. Sokolov, 'Sovetskie yuristy kak sotsial'no-professional'naya gruppa', *Sovetskoe gosudarstvo i pravo*, 1986, no. 2, pp. 53–55; 'Yuridicheskoe obrazovanie: sostoyanie i problemy', *Sotsialisticheskaya zakonnost'*, 1987, no. 3, pp. 28–9.

21 M. Beissinger, 'In Search of Generations in Soviet Politics', pp. 304–14 (note 9).

22 Unfortunately, the biographical data do not indicate, at least as regards career movements at the base of the Procuracy hierarchy, whether staff personnel in regional or republican Procuracy offices move downwards to a line position in their city or district of origin or to a different locale.

23 T. H. Rigby, 'The Soviet Regional Leadership: The Brezhnev Generation', *Slavic Review*, 1978, no. 1, p. 13. It should be noted that the recruitment of obkom first secretaries from within a region was far more common in the RSFSR than in other republics. R. Blackwell, Jr, 'Cadre Policy in the Brezhnev Era,' *Problems of Communism*, 1979, March–April, p. 41.

24 Dawn Mann, 'New trend in Party Personnel Policy', *Radio Liberty Research Bulletin*, 9 October 1986 (RL 385/86).

25 V. Kuritsyn, *Perekhod k nepu i revolyutsionnaya zakonnost' Izdatel'stvo 'Nauka'*, Moscow, 1972.

26 Transfers from Western Siberia were especially common among 'inter-area' career movements in the RSFSR. In the 23 cases where movement between areas in the RSFSR could be identified, 11 of the transfers originated in Western Siberia, which may be a testament to the prominence of the Sverdlovsk legal Institute as a feeder institution for the Procuracy.

27 M. Beissinger, 'In Search of Generations in Soviet Politics', p. 292 (note 9).

28 For an examination of relations between the Communist Party and the Procuracy, see the account of interviews with Soviet emigre jurists in E. Huskey, *Careers in the Soviet Legal Bureaucracy: Recruitment Patterns and Professional Backgrounds of Procuracy Officials at the Regional, Republican, and All-Union Levels, Final Report for the National Council for Soviet and East*

European Research, August 1986, Appendix 1, pp. 5–10.

29 Peter Solomon, 'Local Political Power and Soviet Criminal Justice, 1922–1941', *Soviet Studies*, 1985, no. 3, pp. 305–29, provides an excellent analysis of the origins of centre-periphery tensions in the Procuracy.

30 The integration of procurators into networks of local political power is now being frankly discussed on the pages of the general press in the USSR. See O. Chaikovskaya, 'Obizhaites' na menya, ne obizhaites . . .', *Literaturnaya gazeta*, 22 October 1986; S. Zamoshkin, 'Prokuror i mestnaya vlast'', *Literaturnaya gazeta*, 14 January 1987; 'Podnozhka prokuroru', *Pravda*, 15 June 1987, p. 3.

31 Although very few Procuracy leaders begin their careers outside of the Procuracy, approximately one-third spend extended periods at mid-career in legal assignments in other institutions before returning to the Procuracy. By far the largest share of these secondments are to the Communist Party's Departments of Administrative Organs, which oversee legal affairs. See F. Huskey, 'Specialists in the Soviet Communist Party Apparatus: Legal Professionals as Party Functionaries', *Soviet Studies* (forthcoming). The second most popular destination for seconded procurators is the judiciary. Patterns of inter-institutional mobility in Procuracy elite careers have not changed significantly during the past decade.

32 A noteworthy example of such a career was that of Konstantin Chernenko, who, with Brezhnev's help, rose in the party machinery despite his obvious lack of professional qualifications.

33 K. Aksyonov, 'Trebuyetsya lider', *Pravda*, 19 September 1987, p. 2.

PART III
Institutional Complexes

7. The Elite of the Defence Industry Complex

Julian Cooper

This chapter is concerned with the leading representatives of the Soviet defence industry complex, the set of organizations responsible for the development and production of weapons and their procurement by the armed forces. It seeks to establish the characteristics of this elite group of Soviet society and to assess its political role in terms of its representation on the principal organs of Party and government and its relationship with the political leadership. One of the questions of particular interest is whether there have been any significant changes over time: does this elite occupy the same position in relation to Gorbachev as it did to Brezhnev? Has the elite itself undergone changes likely to affect its political power? For obvious reasons this is not an easy topic to explore and it is not surprising that there have been few previous attempts. The secrecy surrounding the defence industrial sector presents real difficulties to the researcher, but it is the author's belief that something of substance can be established.

THE DEFENCE INDUSTRY COMPLEX

The principal institutions of the defence industry complex are here considered to include the nine specialized defence industry ministries with their production facilities and research and development (R&D) organizations, the Military–Industrial Commission, and the State Planning Committee (Gosplan) with its special departments concerned with the defence sector. In addition, representing the customer, there are the procurement agencies of the Ministry of defence and service branches of the armed forces. Military related R&D is also undertaken by scientists working at Academy of Sciences institutes and higher educational establishments. Finally, oversight of the complex is exercised by the Secretariat of the Communist Party.

The defence industry ministries

Nine industrial ministries are generally taken to represent the specialized defence sector of Soviet industry. These ministries are responsible for the development and production of almost all end-product weapons systems, although they also have a civilian side to their activities. Some military-related equipment and supplies are manufactured by enterprises of nominally civilian ministries, but this activity is not considered here. The nine ministries are as follows:

1. *Ministry of Medium Machine-building*, responsible for the development and production of nuclear warheads and devices, and also the extraction and processing of nuclear materials for both military and civilian purposes. Minister: L. D. Ryabev (b. 1933), appointed November 1986.

2. *Ministry of General Machine-building*, responsible for ballistic missiles, space launch vehicles and spacecraft. Minister: O. D. Baklanov (b. 1932), appointed April 1983.

3. *Ministry of Machine-building*, responsible for conventional munitions, fuse mechanisms and solid propellants. Minister: B. M. Belousov (b. 1934), appointed June 1987.

4. *Ministry of the Defence Industry*, responsible for the production of conventional weapons for the ground forces. Minister: P. V. Finogenov (b. 1919), appointed January 1979.

5. *Ministry of the Aviation Industry*, responsible for military and civilian fixed-wing aircraft and helicopters, and some types of missiles. Minister: A. S. Systsov (b. 1929), appointed November 1985.

6. *Ministry of the Shipbuilding Industry*, responsible for naval and civilian ships and boats, naval accoustic systems and radars. Minister: I. S. Belousov (b. 1928), appointed January 1984.

7. *Ministry of the Radio Industry*, responsible for radio and radar equipment, computers, guidance and control systems. Minister: V. I. Shimko (b. 1938), appointed November 1987.

8. *Ministry of the Communications Equipment Industry*, responsible for communications systems, including telephone, television and facsimile equipment. The main producer of consumer electronic goods. Minister: P. S. Pleshakov (b. 1922), appointed March 1974.

9. *Ministry of the Electronics Industry*, responsible for electronic components, microcomputers and a growing range of electronic end-products. Minister: V. G. Kolesnikov (b. 1925), appointed November 1985.

With the exception of the Ministry of Machine-building, created in 1968, and the Ministry of the Communications Equipment Industry, created in

1974, the ministries were organized in their present form in 1965. The elite of this group of ministries are the ministers and their deputies, the directors of major associations and enterprises, and prominent designers, engineers and scientists working at R&D organizations.

The Military–Industrial Commission of the Presidium of the USSR Council of Ministers (Voenno-Promyshlennaya Komissiya – VPK)

The VPK has responsibility for coordinating the production and R&D activities of the group of nine defence industry ministries and probably also the military related activities of other industrial ministries. Very little is known about the scale, structure and personnel of the Commission, apart from the identity of its chairman, who is always a deputy chairman of the USSR Council of Ministers. The present occupant of this important post is Yu. D. Maslyukov (b. 1937), appointed in December 1985. For many years the first deputy chairman was N. S. Stroev, but he appears no longer to occupy the post.

State Planning Committee of the USSR Council of Ministers

One of the Gosplan first deputy chairmen (currently V. I. Smyslov (b. 1928), appointed December 1985) has responsibility for the planning of the defence sector. The extent to which the Gosplan chairman is directly involved and answerable for defence sector issues is not clear. Given the wider scope of his responsibilities this post, perhaps wrongly, has been excluded from those constituting the defence industry complex elite. Within the structure of Gosplan there is a summary department, apparently responsible for overall plan coordination, and departments concerned with particular branches of industry. Between 1977 and 1985 the summary department was headed by N. P. Marakhovskii (1916–85), a Gosplan official from 1952.[3] Other state economic agencies such as the Ministry of Finance, the State Committee for Material and Technical Supply, and the State Committee for Prices will also have special departments concerned with the defence industry, but their lack of representation on national Party and government bodies indicates that their leading representatives lack the political influence enjoyed by their Gosplan colleague.

The Ministry of Defence and the Armed Forces

From the customer side, weapons procurement is the concern of a number of technical administrations of the Ministry of Defence and the service arms, under the overall leadership of a Deputy Minister for Armaments, currently V. M. Shabanov (b. 1923), appointed in 1980. Shabanov has a first deputy chief of armaments, S. F. Kolosov, for whom biographical details are lacking. Each of the services has a deputy commander-in-chief for armaments; again, the identities of some are known, but there is a lack of biographical information. From the limited evidence available it appears that the leading figures in weapons procurement (apart from Shabanov) are career military officers, graduates of military higher technical academies and institutes.

The USSR and Republican Academies of Sciences and the higher educational system

Most scientists directly involved in the development of new weapons systems appear to work at establishments of the industrial ministries. However, military-related research is also undertaken by scientists working in the Academy system and at higher educational institutes, in particular basic research having potential military application and also R&D connected with new materials and production technologies applicable in the defence sector. Since the early 1960s two Presidents of the USSR Academy of Sciences, (M. V. Keldysh and A. P. Aleksandrov) have had previous involvement in military-related research (missiles and nuclear technology respectively), and this may also apply to the present holder of the post, G. I. Marchuk. Some technical higher educational institutes play a prominent role in supplying graduates to the defence industry and also undertake research relevant to its needs.

The Secretariat of the Communist Party Central Committee

The activities of the defence industry are overseen by one of the Secretaries of the Central Committee, since July 1985 L. N. Zaikov has occupied the post. This Secretary supervises the work of the Secretariat's Defence Industry Department, which monitors the work of the defence industry ministries. The Department is currently headed by O. S. Belyakov (b. 1933, identified in the post August 1985) and has a first deputy head (not identified) and several deputies apparently responsible for the oversight of particular sectors of the industry. Deputies identified include V. Kozlov (aviation industry), N. M. Luzhin (shipbuilding) and N. A. Shakhov (ground forces equipment).

THE ELITE OF THE DEFENCE INDUSTRY COMPLEX AND ITS POLITICAL REPRESENTATION

Having established the composition of the defence industry complex, we now turn to the question of the membership of its elite and changes over time, taking as a starting point the year 1965 – the first full year of the Brezhnev period and also the year in which the branch industrial ministries were restored. An indication of who can be considered to constitute the elite can be derived from an examination of the changing pattern of defence industry complex representation on the Party Central Committee and the USSR Supreme Soviet.

Representation on the Central Committee

Certain key posts of the complex are almost invariably associated with full membership of the Central Committee. These include the industrial ministers, the chairman of the VPK, the Gosplan first deputy responsible for the defence sector, and the relevant Party Secretary. In addition there are usually a number of leading scientists and designers with defence sector connections: over the period covered the designers were generally from the missile and aviation industries. The Central Committee elected at the 27th Party Congress in 1986 was unusual in that two additional figures gained full membership status for the first time, namely the head of the Central Committee's Defence Industry Department and the Deputy Minister for Armaments. The changing pattern of representation is shown in Table 7.1. From this analysis it can be seen that there was a striking stability in the total representation of this elite during the Brezhnev years, but a modest upturn under Gorbachev in 1983.

Representation on the USSR Supreme Soviet

The Supreme Soviet provides a larger forum than the Central Committee for defence industry complex representation, although it is a forum with less effective power. Again, certain posts virtually guarantee representation; others are less certain. A feature of the Supreme Soviet is the regular election of a number of enterprise directors of the defence industry and a sizeable group of leading designers: in both cases the aviation industry has predominated. In addition to what must be considered elite representation, delegates of the Supreme Soviet also include shop-floor workers and junior management personnel of enterprises of the defence industry, but these have been excluded from the analysis presented in Table 7.2. The pattern of representation over time is similar to that found above: stability under Brezhnev, but a modest upturn since his death.

In considering the elite of the defence industry complex it is worth considering briefly its representation on the Supreme Soviets of the republics. Analysis of the composition of the RSFSR Supreme Soviet over the period in question reveals that only a very small proportion of the total

Table 7.1: Representation of the Defence Industry Complex on the Party Central Committee, 1966–86 (number of members)

	1966	1971	1976	1981	1986
A. *Full members*					
Party Secretariat officials	1	1	1	—	2
VPK/Gosplan officials	2	2	2	2	2
Industrial ministers	7	8	7	8	9
Scientists/designers[a]	3	3	6	6	5
Deputy Minister of Defence for Armaments	—	—	—	—	1
Total full members	13	14	16	16	19
As a percentage of total number of full members	6.7	5.8	5.6	5.0	6.2
B. *Candidate members*					
Party Secretariat officials	1	1	1	1	—
Industrial ministers	—	—	2	1	—
Deputy industrial ministers	—	—	—	—	1
Scientists/designers	1	2	—	—	3
Deputy minister of Defence for Armanents	—	—	—	1	—
Party secretary of defence industry enterprise	—	—	—	—	1
Total candidate members	2	3	3	3	5
As a percentage of total of candidate members	1.2	1.9	2.2	2.0	2.4
Total number of members	15	17	19	19	24
As a percentage of total membership	4.2	4.3	4.5	4.0	5.0

[a]Keldysh and Aleksandrov have been included because of their general responsibility for science as Academy Presidents. Similarly, Velikhov has been included for 1986 because of his responsibility for the informatics division of the Academy.
Source: Compiled by the author from the lists of Central Committee members elected by Party Congresses in the respective years.

delegates have been representatives of the complex. This can be illustrated by the results of the 1985 elections: only 14 of the 975 delegates were leading figures of the complex (1.4 per cent), including 5 designers, 8 enterprise directors, and the rector of the Moscow Aviation Institute. However, the list includes some figures of note: aero-engine designer N. D. Kuznetsov, the then director of the Severodvinsk shipyard (the country's principal submarine building works), G. L. Prosyankin, and the director of the Gorky mechanical works, G. S. Brevnov, who a year later became a deputy

Table 7.2: Representation of the Defence Industry Complex on the USSR Supreme Soviet, 1966–84 (number of delegates)

	1966	1970	1974	1979	1984
Party Secretariat officials	2	2	2	1	2
VPK/Gosplan officials	2	2	1	2	2
Industrial ministers	7	8	9	9	9
Deputy Minister of Defence for Armaments	—	—	—	—	1
Scientists (totals)	6	6	5	5	5
Missiles/space technology	3	3	3	3	1
Nuclear technology	1	1	1	2	2
Shipbuilding	1	1	1	—	—
Radio/electronics	1	1	—	—	—
Designers (totals)	10	9	9	10	14
Aviation	6	6	5	6	7
Missiles/space technology	2	2	3	3	5
Ground forces equipment	2	1	1	1	2
Enterprise directors (totals)	9	9	8	9	11
Aviation	5	3	3	2	4
Missiles/space technology	1	1	1	1	1
Ground forces equip./munitions	1	2	3	3	3
Shipbuilding	—	—	—	—	1
Radio/electronics	1	2	—	3	2
Other/not identified	1	1	1	—	—
Total	36	36	34	36	44
As a percentage of total delegates	2.4	2.4	2.2	2.4	2.9

Source: Compiled by the author from *Deputaty Verkhovnogo Soveta SSSR*, 1966, 1974, 1979 and 1984. 1970 from *Izvestiva*, 17 June 1970.

minister of the Ministry of the Defence Industry.[5] Examination of the elected delegates of the Ukrainian Supreme Soviet reveals a similar picture, namely a small share of the complex's elite, but the inclusion of some names of note.

Members of the complex's elite also gain representation on major city Party committees and Soviets. This can be illustrated by the example of Moscow. Full members of the city committee elected in January 1986 included a number of leading figures of the defence industry, for example, aircraft designers R. A. Belyakov, G. V. Novozhilov and A. A. Tupolev, and radio industry scientists B. V. Bunkin and V. S. Semenikhin.[6] Similarly, the Moscow city Soviet elected in June 1987 has a number of representatives of the complex (a very approximate estimate suggests they account for 2.5 per cent of the total delegates), almost all institute and enterprise directors and designers, but in this case hardly any well-known names.[7] However, representation at this level may serve as an important stepping stone for future advancement to a genuinely elite position.

The administrative elite of the defence industry complex

Biographical details have been gathered for 36 occupants of the leading administrative posts of the complex between 1965 and December 1987. Some of the relevant information is summarised in Appendix 1. Certain features stand out. Firstly, amost all are Russian; the two exceptions are Ukrainians (Slavskii and Baklanov). Secondly, all have higher education and almost all studied at engineering and other technical institutes. Four of the total were graduates of the Leningrad Mechanical Institute (formerly the Military–Mechanical Institute), a leading centre for training specialists of the ground forces equipment industry (Ustinov, Dmitriev, Finogenov and Maslyukov). Of the remainder three studied at the Leningrad Shipbuilding Institute (Romanov, Butoma and Belousov), and two each at the Moscow Bauman Institute (Afanas'ev and Shokin), Moscow University (Serbin and Bakhirev), Moscow Energy Institute (Kalmykov and Shimko), and the Urals Polytechnic Institute (Ryabov and Voronin). The prominent role of Leningrad as a source of defence sector administrators is shown by the fact that 35 per cent of the 34 for whom information on education is available graduated from institutes located there; the same proportion as for Moscow.

A striking feature of this elite group is that almost without exception its members began their careers at industrial enterprises and more than 80 per cent were at one time directors of enterprises or research institutes, chief designers or chief engineers. This even applies to V. M. Shabanov, the Deputy Minister of Defence for Armaments, who in the early 1970s served as general director of a science-production association of the radio industry. In almost all cases the industrial ministers served as deputy or first deputy ministers before taking up their ministerial posts. Not surprisingly, all 36 are Party members, the average age on joining being 26 years. All but five were full or candidate members of the Central Committee and it is a normal expectation that members of this administrative group will be elected to the Supreme Soviet. A characteristic feature of the Brezhnev period was the ageing of this administrative elite. In 1965 those in post had an average age of 55, but in 1981, the last full year of the period, it had risen to 64, and the majority were still officials with wartime experience of work in the defence sector. Since the death of Brezhnev this generation has been replaced: all but two of the fourteen leading posts in question have new occupants. At the end of the period covered those in post had an average age of under 58 years; falling to 56 if the two survivors from the Brezhnev period are excluded.

Without doubt the central figure during the entire Brezhnev period was Dmitrii Ustinov, at first as Central Committee Secretary with responsibility for the defence industry and then from 1976 as Minister of Defence. Ustinov's entire career was linked with the defence sector from the time he graduated from the Leningrad Military–Mechanical Institute in 1934. An important group of officials had close association with him during the early stages of their careers when they worked in the Commissariat (Ministry) for Armaments, headed by Ustinov between 1941 and 1953. This group includes L. V. Smirnov, who headed the VPK from 1963 to 1985, I. F. Dmitriev, first deputy head of the Central Committee Defence Industry Department from 1965 to 1981 and then its head until 1985, V. M. Ryabikov, S. A. Afanas'ev and S. A. Zverev. Dmitriev was a fellow graduate of the Leningrad institute in 1934 and his entire career was linked with that of Ustinov. The Ministry for Armaments became the Ministry of the Defence Industry and as such, possibly through Ustinov's influence, continued to supply a disproportionately large number of leading defence sector administrators. Those with a background in this ministry are L. A. Voronin (now chairman of the State Supply Committee, Gossnab), the chairman of the Military–Industrial Commission, Yu. D. Maslyukov, and the minister of the Ministry of Machine-building, B. M. Belousov. Another industry well-represented is shipbuilding. Romanov, Zaikov and V. I. Smyslov worked in the industry; Zaikov as general director of a Leningrad science-production association and Smyslov as a deputy minister.

The scientists and designers

A characteristic feature of the Soviet defence industry complex is the prominent role played by the General and Chief Designers. The post of general designer was introduced in the mid-1950s, initially in the aviation industry. Each has responsibility for leading a major field of technology within a ministry and is likely to have a major say in issues of technical policy, probably as a member of the ministry's scientific and technical council. This also applies to leading scientists, who are likely to be directors of central research institutes or science-production associations.

Biographical details have been gathered for 63 leading designers and scientists associated with the defence industry complex during the period

1965 to 1987. In view of the problems of identifying the members of this elite group and the limitations of the available biographical information, the coverage is inevitably less comprehensive and more speculative than for the administrators considered above. It is also biased heavily in the direction of older and deceased scientists and designers because of the difficulty of identifying those currently in post. Nevertheless, some interesting patterns emerge. Some details are presented in Appendix 2.

Of the total, 16 have, or had, links with the missile and space programmes and 15 with the aviation industry. In the author's view the fact that half the sample are associated with these two fields is a fair reflection of the superior status of these fields within the defence industry complex during the period covered. The third largest group (12) are those associated with what is evidently an ascendant field, namely the electronics-based technologies of radio, communications and control systems. The low representation of the shipbuilding and ground forces equipment fields reflects the fact that their representatives rarely achieve the status of public figures.

While evidence of nationality is not always available, the overwhelming predominance of Russians (at least 86 per cent) is clear; other nationalities represented are Ukrainian (3), and one each of Armenian, Georgian, Jew, Pole and Tatar. (The Georgian is A. D. Nadiradze, the late chief designer of the SS-20 and other solid-fuel missiles, the Jewish Yu. B. Khariton is believed to have been for many years a leading scientist of the nuclear weapons programme, and the Polish Zh. Ya. Kotin was a prominent tank designer.) Party membership now appears to be the general rule, but this was not the case for an older generation. Four of the latter did not join the Party: N. A. Dollezhal', designer of the first Soviet reactor for plutonium production for nuclear weapons (and also of the RBMK reactor installed at Chernobyl), P. O. Sukhoi, the aircraft designer, G. V. Novozhilov, a prominent scientist of the shipbuilding industry and Yu. B. Kobzarev, the radar specialist. Others joined at a relatively late age: Aleksandrov and Mikulin at 59, Khariton at 52, Myasishchev at 51 and Glushko at 48. The average age of joining the Party is 32, six years older than for the administrators. Of the total 9 (14 per cent) achieved full or candidate membership of the Central Committee, but a much larger number, 29 (46 per cent) gained election to the USSR Supreme Soviet. Of those reaching the Central Committee, two-thirds are associated with the missile and space technology field, and together with aviation this field also dominates in those elected to the Supreme Soviet.

Not all the scientists and designers had higher education. The two exceptions are the tank designer, A. A. Morozov, and M. T. Kalashnikov, the small arms designer. Of the 60 with higher education, 11 went to a single establishment, the Moscow Ordzhonikidze Aviation Institute, and a further 8 graduated from the Moscow Bauman Institute. The dominant position of a small number of elite institutions is shown by the fact that only six of them account for 62 per cent of all those with higher education. The other four are the Leningrad Polytechnic Institute, the Moscow Energy Institute, Moscow University and the Zhukovskii Military Aviation Engineering Academy. The association of specific defence industry specializations with particular educational establishments appears to have become more marked over time. Leading specialists have a reasonable expectation of being elected to the USSR Academy of Sciences: 80 per cent of the sample became full or corresponding members.

THE DEFENCE INDUSTRY COMPLEX ELITE AND THE POLITICAL LEADERSHIP

Leonid Brezhnev was himself a former member of the defence industry complex and it could be argued that his rise to supreme power owed much to the authority he gained as Central Committee Secretary for the defence industry and the space programme between 1957 and 1960. It was at this time that the Soviet Union acquired a strategic nuclear capability following the first successful launch of an ICBM in 1957 and also impressed the world with a series of dramatic successes in space. The contacts forged with powerful sections of the government and military probably served him well in 1964. According to one memoir account,

> During those years the office of the Secretary of the Central Committee was a kind of staff headquarters where the most important problems of missile technology were resolved, and meetings held with the participation of the most eminent scientists, designers and specialists in various fields of science, technology and production. L. I. Brezhnev was often seen in the factories where missile technology was created.[8]

As noted above, a key figure was Ustinov and the evidence suggests that his relations with Brezhnev were close. The chairman of the Military–Industrial Commission throughout the entire Brezhnev period was L. V. Smirnov, who worked for some time in Brezhnev's old territory of Dnepropetrovsk. There were other members of the Brezhnev leadership with defence industry connections, notably A. P. Kirilenko, a former aviation industry specialist, and V. N. Novikov, a senior member of the Council of Ministers with responsibility for the engineering industry. One gains the impression for most of the Brezhnev period relations between the political leadership and the defence industry complex elite were harmonious and it is likely that representatives of the latter had relatively easy and direct access to the top. The stable representation of the complex on the Party Central Committee and the Supreme Soviet provides evidence of a well-established pattern satisfactory to both sides.

Since the death of Brezhnev the situation has been transformed in a number of important respects. With the death of Ustinov the complex lost its supreme patron and spokesman. There were no significant changes in the leading personnel during the brief interval when Romanov had overall responsibility as Central Committee spokesman. Continuity with the past was probably sustained by Dmitriev, Ustinov's long-standing colleague, as head of the Defence Industry Department, and Smirnov, as chairman of the VPK. Romanov's period of office was too brief for him to be able to appoint any of his own supporters. Since Gorbachev's election as General Secretary there have been sweeping changes. By late 1987 almost all the major administrative posts of the complex have new occupants: the Ustinov regime has ended. What is more, the new General Secretary has no personal experience of the defence sector and it is unlikely that he has been able to forge relations with its leading personnel of the kind typical of the Brezhnev years. However, there is some evidence that Gorbachev has been trying to strengthen his contacts, as shown by his much publicised visits to the Baikonur space centre and the Zelenograd research centre of the electronics industry.

While Gorbachev may have had little personal experience of the defence sector this is not true of all Politburo colleagues. The Chairman of the Council of Ministers, N. I. Ryzhkov, had a technical education at the Urals Polytechnic Institute and spent many years at the vast 'Uralmash' heavy machine-building works, rising to general director. While nominally a civilian plant, the wide product range of 'Uralmash' is reported to include artillery. Two leading figures have an aviation industry background: E. K. Ligachev, who graduated from the Moscow Aviation Institute in 1943 and then worked for a period at the Novosibirsk aircraft factory, and V. I. Vorotnikov, who graduated from the Kuibyshev Aviation Institute in 1954 and then worked for several years at a local aircraft plant. By education there is yet another member of the aviation industry group: A. F. Dobrynin who graduated from the Moscow Aviation Institute one year earlier than Ligachev. Finally, it is worth noting that another rising figure, not in the Politburo at the time of writing, the Kazakhstan First Secretary, G. V. Kolbin, is another Urals Polytechnic Institute graduate; he began his career at an enterprise in Nizhnii Tagil which could well be the vast 'Uralvagon-zavod' tank and rail freight wagon works. However, in all cases apart from Ryzhkov's the defence sector experience related to a much earlier period. In general the top political leadership under Gorbachev is unusually remote from the defence sector of the economy.

With the weakening of the defence industry's informal relations with the top political leadership has come an enhancement of its formal representation on the leading Party and government bodies. In 1986 for the first time the head of the Central Committee's Defence Industry Department and the Deputy Minister of Defence for Armaments gained full member status on the Central Committee, and more designers and enterprise directors of the complex have been elected to the Supreme Soviet. However, since 1986 the continuing personnel changes have left a number of important posts without Central Committee representation. This applies to the ministers of three branches of the defence industry: medium machine-building, machine-building and the radio industry (the latter also without a minister at the time of writing). The transfer to run Moscow, of Zaikov, who had excellent credentials for the Secretaryship, has introduced a new element of uncertainty and may lead to the further weakening of the political influence of the defence industry complex.

These developments must be seen in the wider context of policy goals and priorities. During the first decade of the Brezhnev leadership the defence industry had a vital role in securing strategic nuclear parity with the United States. In so far as the complex was able to fulfil this goal the political and military leadership were indebted to it, although the latter may not always have been satisfied with the technological level of the weapons received. Hough is surely correct in his assessment that the defence industry was then extremely powerful, with a stronger political position than the military customer it served.[9] It is not surprising that during this time representatives of the missile industry gained positions in the elite, while the nuclear interest was represented by Aleksandrov as President of the USSR Academy of Sciences. One puzzle is why the shipbuilding interest did not emerge more strongly as the nuclear strategic submarine fleet expanded, but one suspects that the already entrenched aviation interest may have presented an obstacle to its rise.

As noted above, the military customer may have received weapons in adequate quantity, but not necessarily of the desired quality in terms of technological sophistication. While the defence sector may have a superior innovative performance to that of its civilian economy, there is no reason to suppose that it has been immune from the in-built drive for output expansion at the expense of quality typical of the economy as a whole. From this perspective, the political elevation of the designers and scientists which took place during the Brezhnev period could be interpreted as a deliberate attempt to strengthen the hand of those having a professional interest in novelty.

By the late Brezhnev period it is likely that the set of relations established in the past increasingly were becoming obstacles to development. As noted above, the elite of the defence industry complex, like the political leadership as a whole, had aged substantially and may well have become conservative and complacent, unable to recognize the need for change. The lack of personnel renewal and the consolidation over many years of close relations both within the defence sector and between it and the political leadership probably created substantial institutional inertia. But this was a time when new challenges were accumulating. Technology was undergoing rapid change, especially in the field of microelectronics, which in the Soviet Union appears to have suffered relative neglect, possibly in part because of the dominance of the powerful aviation, nuclear and missiles interests. In the military field, as Ogarkov warned, new technological solutions were threatening to transform radically the entire field of conventional weaponry. Finally, the economic stagnation of the late Brezhnev period became ever more serious; as the economy faltered the military burden appears to have become increasingly difficult to sustain.

This was the legacy inherited by Brezhnev's successors. For Gorbachev the revitalization and modernization of the economy is an overriding priority. Conditions conducive to rapid technological change must be created; accelerated innovation is essential for meeting the Party's economic, social and security goals. From this perspective the defence industry complex can be seen both as part of the problem and of its solution: a problem in so far as it represents a heavy burden on the economy, but a potential solution in so far as it possesses skills and experience vital to the modernization effort. In these circumstances a tenable hypothesis would be that Gorbachev is attempting to restructure the political relationship with the elite of the defence industry complex in order to restrain its influence and secure a reorientation of the complex's role in the economy.

The sweeping personnel changes under Gorbachev must have served to break up some of the long-established relationships within the defence sector and, in general, have probably weakened the internal cohesion of the complex. Without Ustinov and Smirnov it now has less authoritative spokesmen at the top levels of leadership. However competent, the fifty-year-old Maslyukov is unlikely to have the political weight of his predecessor as VPK chairman. There is also little doubt that the complex as a whole has less close relations with the top political leadership and the General Secretary in particular. The manner in which the Central Committee Secretary for the defence industry, Zaikov, was so quickly switched to other responsibilities is also indicative of a new attitude on the part of the Party leadership, suggestive of a downgrading of the sector's political standing.

There now seems little doubt that the Soviet leadership would like to divert resources from the military to civilian purposes, and to this extent Gorbachev's distance from the defence industry and the reduced authority of the complex's leadership should make this a more realistic possibility. At the same time there are efforts to improve the performance of the civilian economy by drawing on the technology, management practices and skills of the defence sector.[10] During the last five years a number of leading administrators of the defence industry have been transferred to important posts in the economy. Transferees include L. A. Voronin, previously the Gosplan planning chief for defence, now chairman of the State Supply Committee; B. L. Tolstykh, formerly a leading figure of the electronics industry, now chairman of the State Committee for Science and Technology; A. A. Reut, first deputy chairman of Gosplan for general matters, previously a deputy minister of the radio industry; and I. S. Silaev, formerly Minister of the Aviation Industry, now chairman of the newly created Bureau of Machine-Building of the Council of Ministers (a body responsible for co-ordinating the civilian engineering industry, apparently modelled on the VPK). In the recent period there have been so many cases of such transfers that there is no doubt that a deliberate policy has been pursued. If account is taken of these recent transferees, the defence industry complex's representation on the Central Committee increases to a significant extent, from the 6.2 per cent shown in Table 7.1, to 8.5 per cent (compared with an equivalent share of 5 per cent in 1981).

There are parallels to these developments at lower levels of the political hierarchy with involvement of leading representatives of the defence sector in local Party committees and Soviets, and efforts to harness their skills and authority to the tasks of economic modernization. This is apparent in Moscow, Leningrad and other industrial centres where the defence sector is strongly represented in local industry and R&D.

In yet another respect the political position of the defence industry complex has changed in the Gorbachev period. The Brezhnev-Ustinov-Smirnov almost familial relationship effectively protected the complex from public criticism of shortcomings and this probably contributed to a general perception that this was a privileged, elite sector of Soviet society. This is no longer the case. During the last two–three years members of the elite of the defence industry have been exposed to unprecedented negative publicity. This is not simply the extension of *glasnost'* into a previously closed field. Well-known figures of the Brezhnev period have been dismissed for their poor work: before, in the undemanding climate that prevailed, they were secure; now their shortcomings are no longer tolerated. The Politburo has publicly rebuked several defence industry ministers for the poor quality of the consumer goods manufactured by their ministries, in particular television sets. Several enterprise directors, including members of the Supreme Soviet, in the past often held up as model managers, have been replaced with public criticism of their inadequacies. Examples include P. V. Derunov, director of the Andropov (Rybinsk) aeroengine works, the directors of the Leningrad 'Kirov factory' and 'LOMO' associations of the Ministry of the Defence Industry, and the director of the Krasnogorsk mechanical works of the same ministry (the ministry, it should be noted, with which Ustinov had the closest past links).[11] These revelations may well have served to weaken the authority of the defence industry elite.

CONCLUSION

In this chapter we have attempted to identify the elite of the defence industry complex and to establish its changing relationship with the top political leadership. The evidence supported the view that the complex has enjoyed a position of considerable political authority and power, but it also suggests that the situation may be undergoing change under Gorbachev. Indeed, it could be argued that the success of the reform process now underway may to a crucial extent hinge on Gorbachev's ability to forge a new relationship with the defence sector of the economy, involving a reduction of its influence and some reorientation of its activities. It could also be argued that in the long run such an outcome could benefit the military. A revitalized economy would be better placed to meet its high-technology demands; a defence industry with somewhat reduced political influence could prove to be a more responsive supplier of the systems it requires.

In this chapter the defence industry complex has been treated as quite distinct from the military in the shape of the Ministry of Defence and the armed forces. In reviewing the institutions and elite personnel of the industrial sector one is struck by their separation from the military. It is true that a few leading scientists and technical specialists of the industrial sector receive military ranks[12] and officials like Shabanov occasionally switch from industry to procurement, but in general the military and industrial career structures are remarkably separate. The striking exception to this rule was Ustinov, but the very fact that he was able to 'change sides' provides evidence of the exceptional position of the defence industrial complex, and Ustinov within it, at the apogee of Brezhnev's power. The institutional framework is such that there are no upper level forums offering opportunities for the defence industry and the military to come together to present a united front to the political leadership. The military faces the defence industry in a customer–supplier relationship. On particular issues they may have a common interest, but this cannot find high level institutional expression outside the Defence Council or Politburo. Thus the leadership of the defence industry complex must be regarded as an elite group in its own right with its own interests which may, or may not, coincide with those of the military. In the author's view this analysis indicates the illegitimacy of the use of the concept of 'military-industrial complex' with reference to the Soviet Union.

This examination of the elite of the defence industry complex must be regarded as highly provisional. The available evidence is limited and casts little light on policy processes involving the complex and the political leadership. Recently it has been stated that the Soviet Union now favours the extension of *glasnost'* into the military field.[13] It is to be hoped that this will result in the provision of more solid evidence permitting illumination of a topic crucial to Western understanding of the Soviet political process as it relates to issues vital to our mutual security.

NOTES AND REFERENCES

1   The reader is referred to the pioneering article by Karl F. Spielman, 'Defense Industrialists in the USSR', *Problems of Communism*, 1976, vol. 25, no. 5, September–October.
2   See the author's 'The Civilian Production of the Soviet Defence Industry' in R. Amann and J. Cooper (eds) *Technical Progress and Soviet Economic Development*, Basil Blackwell, Oxford, 1986.
3   *Krasnaya Zvezda*, 18 October 1985 (obituary).
4   Identified from *Trud*, 15 January 1987; *Krasnaya Zvezda*, 26 July 1986; *Leningradskaya Pravda*, 6 June 1986
5   *Sovetskaya Rossiya*, 28 February 1985; *Krasnaya Zvezda*, 13 September 1986 (Brevnov).
6   *Vechernaya Moskva*, 27 January 1986.
7   *Moskovskaya Pravda*, 23 June 1987. One of the more prominent figures elected was M. P. Simonov, the head of the Sukhoi aircraft design bureau.
8   V. Tolubko, *Nedelin*, Voenizdat, Moscow, 1982, p. 183.
9   See Jerry F. Hough, 'Soviet decision-making on defense', *Bulletin of the Atomic Scientists*, August 1985, pp. 84–5.
10 See the author's 'Technology Transfer between Military and Civilian Ministries' in US Congress, Joint Economic Committee, *Gorbachev's Economic Plans*, USGPO, Washington, D.C., 1987.
11 *Sovetskaya Rossiya*, 15 June 1986; *Leningradskaya Pravda*, 17 November 1984 and 25 September 1986; *Pravda*, 23 March 1986.
12 An example of a scientist with military rank is the late Academican E. I. Zababakhin, who was a General-Lieutenant (*Pravda*, 29 December 1984). Zababakhin was a prominent specialist of the nuclear weapons industry, which because of its crucial strategic significance appears to have had especially close links with the military.
13 See the message of Gorbachev to the UN Conference on Disarmament and Development, August 1987 and the statement of Deputy Foreign Minister V. Petrovskii. According the latter: 'We are in favour of expanding glasnost and openness with regard to military activities, military doctrines and military outlays ...' (USSR. Mission to the United Nations, Press Release, no. 110, 24 August 1987, p. 6). In relation to the Gorbachev strategy it is worth noting that Petrovskii also observed that '... even today the military economy sector is closely linked to the civil sector and is doing a lot for the latter' (p. 7).

APPENDIX 1
Leading Administrators of the Defence Industry Complex, 1965–87

Name	Post	Nat.[a]	D of B	Joined Party	Higher Education[a]	Control Committee	Supreme Soviet
Ustinov, D. F.	CC Sec (65–76)	R	1908	1927	LVMI (34)	x	x
Ryabov, Ya. P.	CC Sec (76–79)	R	1928	1954	UralsPI (52)	x	x
Romanov, G. V.	CC Sec (84–85)	R	1923	1944	LKI (53)	x	x
Zaikov, L. N.	CC Sec (85–87)	R	1923	1957	LIEI (63)	x	x
Serbin, I. D.	CC DID (58–81)	R	1910	1931	MGU (35)	x	x
Dmitriev, I. F.	CC DID (81–85)	R	1909	1925	LVMI (34)	x	x
Belyakov, O. S.	CC DID (85–)	R	1933	1961	n.a.	x	—
Smirnov, L. V.	Ch.VPK (63–85)	R	1916	1943	NovIndI (39)	x	x
Maslyukov, Yu. D.	Gosplan (82–85)/ Ch. VPK (85–)	R	1937	1966	LVMI (62)	x	x
Ryabikov, V. M.	Gosplan (65–74)	R	1907	1925	LVMA (37)	x	x
Titov, G. A.	Gosplan (74–80)	R	1909	1940	LETI (n.a.)	x	x
Voronin, L. A.	Gosplan (80–82)	R	1928	1953	UralsPI (49)	x	x
Smyslov, V. I.	Gosplan (85–)	R	1928	1951	n.a.	x	—
Slavskii, E. P.	MSM (57–86)	Ukr	1898	1918	MITsMet (33)	x	x
Ryabev, L. D.	MSM (86–)	R	1933	1958	MIFI (57)	—	—
Afanas'ev, S. A.	MOM (65–83)	R	1918	1943	MVTU (41)	x	x
Baklanov, O. D.	MOM (83–)	Ukr	1932	1953	VZEI (na)	x	x
Bakhirev, V. V.	MM (68–87)	R	1916	1951	MGU (41)	x	x
Belousov, B. M.	MM (87–)	R	1934	1963	TaGRI (58)	—	x
Zverev, S. A.	MOP (63–79)	R	1912	1942	LITMO (36)	x	x
Finogenov, P. V.	MOP (79–)	R	1919	1943	LVMI (53)	x	x
Dement'ev, P. V.	MAP (53–77)	R	1907	1938	ZhVVIA (31)	x	x
Kazakov, V. A.	MAP (77–81)	R	1916	1941	VZMI (55)	—	x
Silaev, I. S.	MAP (81–85)	R	1930	1959	KazanAvI (54)	x	x
Systsov, A. S.	MAP (85–)	R	1929	1961	TashPI (na)	x	x
Butoma, B. E.	MSP (57–76)	R	1907	1928	LKI (36)	x	x
Egorov, M. V.	MSP (76–84)	R	1907	1938	VV–MIU (na)	x	x
Belousov, I. S.	MSP (84–)	R	1928	1955	LKI (52)	x	x
Kalmykov, V. D.	MRP (54–74)	R	1908	1942	MEI (34)	x	x
Pleshakov, V. D.	MRP (74–87)	R	1922	1944	MIISvyaz (45)	x	x
Shimko, V. I.	MRP (87–)	R	1938	1964	MEI (60)	—	—
Pervyshin, E. K.	MPSS (74–)	R	1932	1959	METISvy (55)	x	x
Shokin, A. I.	MEP (61–85)	R	1909	1936	MVTU (34)	x	x
Kolesnikov, V. G.	MEP (85–)	R	1925	1961	VornzhPI (na)	x	x
Alekseev, N. N.	DepMODA (70–80)	R	1914	1939	VoenETA (40)	—	—
Shabanov, V. M.	DepMODA (80–)	R	1923	1947	LV–VA (45)	x	x

Notes

[a] For abbreviations see end of Appendix 2

Other abbreviations:

Central Committee – CC x = member; — = non-member na – not available

CC DID – Head of Central Committee Defence Industry Department
Ch.VPK – Chairman of Military-Industrial Commission
Gosplan – Head of defence sector planning, Gosplan
MSM – Minister of Medium Machine-building (Minsredmash)
MOM – Minister of General Machine-building (Minobshchemash)
MM – Minister of Machine-building (Minmash)
MOP – Minister of the Defence Industry (Minoboronprom)
MAP – Minister of the Aviation Industry (Minaviaprom)
MSP – Minister of the Shipbuilding Industry (Minsudprom)
MRP – Minister of the Radio Industry (Minradprom)
MPSS – Minister of the Communications Equipment Industry (Minpromsvyaz)
MEP – Ministry of the Electronics Industry (Minelektronprom)
DepMODA – Deputy Minister of Defence for Armaments

Source Compiled by the author from biographies and obituaries published in Soviet reference works and the national press.

APPENDIX 2

Leading Scientists and Designers of the Defence Industry Complex 1965–87

Name	Nat.	D of B	Joined Party	Higher Education	Acad.	Central Committee	Supreme Soviet
Nuclear technology							
Dollezhal', N. A.	R	1899	n-P.	MVTU (23)	A	—	—
Aleksandrov, A. P.	R	1903	1962	KievUniv (1930)	A	x	x
Khariton, Yu. B.	J	1904	1956	LPI (25)	A	—	x
Muzrukov, B. G.	R	1904	1938	LTechInst (29)	—	—	x
Shchelkin, K. I.	R	1911	1940	CrimPedInst (32)	—	—	—
Zababakhin, E. I.	R	1917	1949	MGU/ZhVVIA (44)	A	—	—
Negin, E. A.	R	1921	1943	ZhVVIA (44)	A	—	—
Khlopkin, N. S.	R	1923	1945	MEI (50)	C	—	—
Missile and Space Technology							
Grushin, P. D.	R	1906	1931	MAI (32)	A	x	x
Glushko, V. P.	Ukr	1908	1956	LGU (29)	A	x	x
Pilyugin, N. A.	R	1908	1940	MVTU (35)	A	—	x
Ryazanskii, M. S.	R	1909	1940	MEI (35)	C	—	—
Keldysh, M. V.	R	1911	1949	MGU (31)	A	x	x
Yangel, M. K.	R	1911	1931	MAI (37)	A	x	x
Kuznetsov, V. I.	R	1913	1942	LPI (38)	A	—	—
Chelomei, A. N.	R	1914	1941	KievAvInst (37)	A	—	x
Nagiradze, A. D.	G	1914	1944	MAI (40)	A	—	—
Mishin, V. P.	R	1917	1943	MAI (41)	A	—	—
Avduevskii, V. S.	R	1920	1953	MAI (44)	A	—	—
Kovtunenko, V. M.	na	1921	1951	LGU (46)	C	—	—
Konopatov, A. D.	R	1922	1952	na	C	—	—
Utkin, V. F.	R	1923	1945	LVMI (52)	A	x	x
Makeev, V. P.	R	1924	1951	MAI/MVTU (50)	A	x	x
Lapygin, V. L.	R	1925	1944	MAI (52)	—	—	x
Aviation							
(a) Aircraft:							
Ilyushin, S. V.	R	1894	1918	ZhVVIA (26)	A	—	x
Sukhoi, P. O.	R	1895	n-P.	MVTU (25)	—	—	x
Myasishchev, V. M.	R	1902	1953	MVTU (26)	—	—	x
Mikoyan, A. I.	A	1905	1925	ZhVVIA (36)	A	—	x
Antonov, O. K.	R	1906	1945	LPI (30)	—	—	x
Belyakov, R. A.	R	1919	1944	MAI (41)	A	—	x
Novozhilov, G. V.	R	1925	1951	MAI (49)	A	x	x
Tupolev, A. A.	R	1925	1959	MAI (49)	A	—	x
Balabuev, P. V.	Ukr	1932	P (na)	KharkovAvI (54)	—	—	—
(b) Engines:							
Mikulin, A. A.	R	1895	1954	MVTU (22)	A	—	—
Lyul'ka, A. M.	na	1908	1947	KievPolyInst (31)	A	—	—
Kuznetsov, A. D.	R	1911	1939	ZhVVIA (38)	A	—	—
Lotarev, V. A.	R	1914	1946	KharkovAvI (39)	C	—	—
Izotov, S. P.	R	1917	P (na)	LPI (41)	—	—	—
Solov'ev, P. A.	R	1917	1943	RybinskAvI (na)	C	—	—
Shipbuilding							
Isanin, N. N.	R	1904	1926	LKI (43)	A	—	x
Novozhilov, V. V.	R	1910	n-P.	LPI (31)	A	—	—
Kovalev, S. N.	R	1919	1962	NikolaevKI (43)	A	—	—
Solomenko, N. S.	na	1923	1944	VV-MIU (46)	A	—	—
Ground forces equipment							
Petrov, F. F.	R	1902	1942	LVMI (31)	—	—	—
Morozov, A. A.	R	1904	1943	No h.edn.	—	—	x
Kotin, Zh. Ya.	P	1908	1931	KharkovPolyI (30)	—	—	x
Kalashnikov, M T.	R	1919	1953	No h.edn.	—	—	x
Shomin, N. A.	R	1923	1943	VABiMV (41)	—	—	x

(continued)

Appendix 2 (continued)

Name	Nat.	D of B	Joined Party	Higher Education	Acad.	Central Committee	Supreme Soviet
Chemical munitions and rocket fuel							
Knunyants, I. L.	na	1906	1941	MVTU (28)	A	–	–
Fokin, A. V.	R	1912	1939	VAKhZ (35)	A	–	–
Zhukov, B. P.	R	1912	1944	MKh–TI (37)	C	–	–
Electronics, radio, communications and control systems							
Shchukin, A. N.	R	1900	1944	LETI (27)	A	–	–
Kobzarev, Yu. B.	R	1905	n–P.	KharkovUniv (26)	A	–	–
Kotelnikov, V. A.	R	1908	1948	MEI (31)	A	–	x
Pospelov, G. S.	R	1914	1943	MEI (40)	C	–	–
Kisunk'o, G. V.	Ukr	1918	1944	VoroshilPedI (38)	C	–	x
Semenikhin, V. S.	R	1918	1945	MEI (41)	A	–	x
Savin, A. I.	R	1920	1944	MVTU (46)	A	–	–
Bunkin, B. V.	R	1922	1953	MAI (47)	A	–	–
Fedosov, E. A.	R	1929	1959	MVTU (52)	A	–	–
Valiev, K. A.	T	1931	1954	KazanUniv (54)	A	–	–
Balashov, E. P.	R	1935	1971	MGU (58)	A	–	–
Velikhov, E. P.	R	1935	1971	MGU (58)	A	x	x

Abbreviations:
Nationality: A – Armenian; G – Georgian; J – Jew; P – Pole; T – Tatar; n-P. – non-Party

A – Academician; C – Corresponding member of Academy
Higher educational establishments:
CrimPedInst – Crimea Pedagogical Institute
KazanAvI – Kazan Aviation Institute
KharkovAvI – Kharkov Aviation Institute
KharkovPolyI – Kharkov Polytechnic Institute
KievAvI – Kiev Aviation Institute
KievPolyInst – Kiev Polytechnic Institute
LETI – Leningrad Electro-technical Institute
LGU – Leningrad State University
LIEI – Leningrad Engineering-Economics Institute
LITMO – Leningrad Institute of Precision Mechanics and Optics
LKI – Leningrad Shipbuilding Institute
LTechInst – Leningrad Technological Institute
LVMA – Leningrad Military Naval Academy
LVMI – Leningrad Military-Mechanical Institute (now Leningrad Mechanical Institute)
LV–VA – Leningrad Military Aviation Academy
MAI – Moscow Aviation Institute
MEI – Moscow Energy Institute
METISvy – Moscow Electro-technical Institute of Communications
MGU – Moscow State University
MIFI – Moscow Engineering-Physics Institute
MIISvyaz – Moscow Institute of Communications Engineering
MITsMET – Moscow Institute of Non-ferrous Metals
MKh-TI – Moscow Chemical-Technological Institute
MVTU – Moscow Bauman Higher Technical School
NikolaevKI – Nikolaev Shipbuilding Institute
NovIndI – Novercherkassk Industrial Institute
RybinskAvI – Rybinsk Aviation Institute
TagRI – Taganrog Radio Institute
TashPI – Tashkent Polytechnic Institute
UralsPI – Urals Polytechnic Institute
VABiMU – Military Academy of Armoured and Mechanised Troops
VAKhZ – Military Academy of Chemical Defence
VoenETA – Military Electro-technical Academy
VornzhPI – Voronezh Polytechnic Institute
VoroshPedI – Voroshilovgrad Pedagogical Institute

VV-MIU – Higher Military Naval Engineering School
VZEI – All-Union Part-Time Energy Institute
VZMI – All-Union Part-time Machine-building Institute
ZhVVIA – Zhukovskii Military Aviation Engineering Academy
(28) etc. refers to date of graduation

Source
As Appendix 1

8. The Power of the Industrial Ministries

David A. Dyker

'You cannot get by without tons in our business. They figure in the plan. Resources are allocated in accordance with them. And everybody is used to them.'[1] That, in a nutshell, sums up the role and style of the industrial ministries in the Soviet economy. They are the operational focus of the cult of the gross, because plans are couched in quantitative terms, and because plan implementation is their business. They are locked into a 'game', a struggle for resources in which output performance, and indeed past input utilization, are crucial counters. The people who run them are men, mostly of engineering background who, like Mr Fedorovskii, may sometimes be too inclined to frankness for their own good. Perhaps for that reason Soviet politicians and academics, today as in the past, have found them convenient scapegoats on which to heap blame for economic shortcomings.

Most Soviet ministers and deputy ministers have been around a long time, and the impact of Gorbachev's new broom on the ministerial establishment serves only to highlight just how stable these elites have been in the past. There is, furthermore, a substantial degree of overlap between the highest level of ministerial administration and the political centre itself. The Council of Ministers is by definition dominated by ministers, though they are not, of course, all industrial ministers. In any case the Council of Ministers is perhaps the least important of the central political forces of the Soviet system. State administrators made up 28.3 per cent of the full membership of the Central Committee of the Communist Party elected at the 1986 Congress of the CPSU, much the same proportion that they recorded in the Central Committee elected at the 26th Congress in 1981.[2] Again, not all of those are industrial administrators, but a substantial proportion must be. Certainly the industrial ministerial contingent must outnumber the military, which accounts for just 7.5 per cent of the present Central Committee, and the KGB, for which the figure is as low as 1.3 per cent.

But the weight of the state administration group is placed firmly in perspective when we look at the 44.5 per cent of full Central Committee members accounted for by professional Communist Party apparatus workers. The Central Committee has, indeed, been dominated by the Party apparatus throughout the post-Stalin period. Turning from the Party 'parliament' to the Party 'cabinet', we find the picture even more sharply drawn at the level of the Politburo. Of its current full members, only Gromyko has been a minister in the past, and he not in the industrial field. Prime minister Ryzhkov has wide industrial experience, but his path to the position which has certainly in the past enjoyed something of the status of 'super-minister for industry' was through the Central Committee secretariat. Indeed most of the industrial expertise in the Politburo comes from the Central Committee secretaries who are on the higher body. Thus at the top of the Soviet political system the Communist Party apparatus is wholly dominant, with the industrial–administrative apparatus holding virtually no formal representation. At the level of the Central Committee, the state administrators are certainly there in force, but are clearly outnumbered by Party administrators. If we want, therefore, to picture the Soviet *political* system as one dominated by elite bureaucracies, we must look in the first place at the Party bureaucracy, as is done in other specialist chapters of this book, or at Party and state bureaucracies taken together, as David Lane does in his introduction. When we look specifically at the power of the industrial ministries we must come back to their key position in the *economic* system. Intermediate-level industrial administrators in the Soviet Union have played a complex, even ambivalent role – powerful *éminences grises* and whipping-boys. I will argue that this complexity is a direct reflection of the ambiguities and contradictions of the Soviet economic system itself.

THE ROOTS OF THE MINISTERIAL SYSTEM

Why are there industrial ministries in the first place? There is certainly nothing in Marx or Lenin about them, but then there is little enough in the sacred texts about *any* aspect of operational planning. Rather the ministerial structure evolved during the 1930s and 1940s, starting off, in the civilian economy, with the replacement in 1932 of the old VSNKha (Supreme Council of the National Economy) by a triad of Ministry for Heavy Industry, Ministry for Light Industry and Ministry for Timber and Forestry. That triad quickly evolved into a much more sectorally specialized system, with separate ministries for specific branches (e.g. machine-building) eventually giving way to separate ministries for sub-branches (e.g. machine-building for the chemicals industry). The military–industrial complex likewise started off with a single Ministry for the Defence Industry, but now possesses no fewer than nine specialist

ministries (see Chapter 7 by Julian Cooper). In many cases the emergence
of these more specialized ministries simply represented an upgrading of
what had been *glavki* (main administrations) of one of the original
ministries, and indeed through much of its history VSNKha had also been
organized on the basis of main administrations.[3] Thus the history of the
ministries during the 1930s was to a great extent merely the history of the
explicit institutionalization of the sectoral principle.

There seems, then, to have been a powerful organizational imperative in
the direction of sectoral specialization, and it is precisely this proclivity
which has conditioned the emergence of classic ministerial problems going
under the general heading of 'departmentalism' in the post-Stalin Soviet
economy. All the more important for us, therefore, to understand the
origins of the tendency, particularly since Mr Gorbachev is currently intent
on reversing it. It seems to me that the key here is the particular kind of
division of labour that emerged between Gosplan and the ministries in the
1930s. That division of labour was not based on the notion of multi-level
planning, the principle which underlies so much of the reform discussion of
the 1960s onwards. Under multi-level planning the centre would have
contented itself with mapping out the broad aggregates of planned
economic performance, leaving it to the intermediate ministerial level to
break those down to product level, and with the ministries in turn leaving it
to enterprises themselves to disaggregate further. Under the centrally-
planned system set up by Stalin, and still essentially in place in 1987, the
central planners (including at the present time Gossnab, the State Supply
Committee) plan right down to the product level, which involves them in a
matrix of some 16,000 variables. The ministries are formally charged with
the allocation of a couple of thousand additional product lines, plus
product lines of strictly intra-departmental significance.[4] This underlines
the limited formal role played by the ministries in the process of plan
construction. Because Gosplan is heavily dependent on the ministries as
channels of information on basic production possibilities, the *informal* role
of the ministries in plan construction is a good deal bigger. More
important, Gosplan has never had any formal powers of plan *implementation*. That is where the ministries come in to their own. It is their remit to
see that Gosplan's detailed production plans are implemented, right down
to enterprise level. In contrast to their limited formal role in plan
formulation, the ministries are almost wholly responsible for seeing that
plans are carried out, and have historically wielded an extraordinary degree
of arbitrary power in terms of setting and adjusting plan targets for
individual enterprises, allocating and reallocating capital equipment
between enterprises etc.

That explains why the principle of *vertical hierarchy* has dominated the
evolution of the formal ministerial structure. A central planning com-

mission working exclusively in terms of output priorities, mainly intermediate output priorities such as steel, fuel, energy etc., is bound to seek an executive structure that reflects that pattern of priorities. Thus the easiest way to ensure formal fulfilment of, say, targets for the production of gas and gas products is through a ministry for the gas industry with executive authority over all, or most, gas-producing installations. I emphasize the qualification 'formal', because as we know from so many 'success-indicator' anecdotes the stress on the *output* of industrial *inputs* may be very damaging to the cause of *horizontal linkages* between industrial clients and customers, and ultimately to the efficiency with which key intermediate goods are utilized. And while it may be all right for Gosplan to take a cavalier attitude to horizontal links, the ministries, which have to ensure, for example, that there are nuts and bolts with which to screw together different parts of given pieces of machinery, must take a broader view. That is why at the informal level, we find a tendency to horizontal linkage, in the main of course within departmentalist limits, just as strong as the 'official' tendency to vertical, sectorally-specialized hierarchy. The history of the evolution of the role of the industrial ministries in the Soviet economy is, to a great extent, the history of the counterpoint between these two tendencies.

THE MINISTRIES AND THE FIRST WAVE OF ECONOMIC REFORMS

It was perhaps a tribute to the impact they had had on the Soviet economy when Khrushchev, in 1957, abolished most of the industrial ministries. This was the first great act of economic reform of the post-Stalin period, and it represented an attack on an institution and on a section of the Soviet elite identified with that institution. The 'Anti-Party Group' – Malenkov, Molotov and Kaganovich, themselves with strong links to the state hierarchy – had formed an alliance with technocrats such as Gosplan chairman Saburov and Gosekonomkomissiya (State Economic Commission) boss Pervukhin, to get rid of Party First Secretary Khrushchev, whose position had been weakened by a series of political crises through 1956.

There was also mounting concern around this time about the damaging effects of ministerial departmentalism on Soviet economic performance. Capital productivity had been falling steadily since the 1930s, to an extent which could not be explained away purely in terms of capital deepening. Both politicians and economists pinpointed organizational factors as playing an increasingly large role in determining these trends. The ministries were charged with: (1) systematically overbidding for investment resources, with the result that there were always too many projects going on at any given time. This was seen as the main cause of *raspylenie sredstv* – excessive investment spread – and grossly excessive lead-times. Of course one of the reasons, pure empire-building apart, for the strength of this symptom was concern on the part of the ministries, in the context of often extreme uncertainty of supply to construction, to ensure they always had some projects they could get on and finish. (2) The ministries were charged with showing a strong inclination towards organizational autarky, building up their own networks for component and material supplies, to the detriment of considerations of economies of scale and optimal manning and transport patterns. In so doing they were, of course, merely following the logic of horizontal linkage, trying to correct the imbalances and irrationalities introduced into the economy by the principle of vertical, sectorally-specialized hierarchy. But they certainly did so in a high-cost way. Reports from the 1960s and 1970s suggest that unit costs in departmentalist ancillary complexes may be anything up to three times as high as those in plants of optimal scale.[5] More specifically, departmentalism of this nature tends to breed excessive labour-intensity in production patterns, and this was seen as particularly damaging at a time when the Soviet economy was just beginning to move from the period of labour surplus into that of labour shortage. (3) Finally the ministries were charged with neglecting environmental and infrastructural considerations. The ministries had become notorious for wanting to build all their new plants in existing large towns, whatever the external costs they imposed on the rest of Soviet society, for failing to build up adequate infrastructure when they did become involved in big projects in virgin areas such as Siberia, and for riding roughshod over any considerations of good husbandry of the Soviet ecospace.[6] Environmental damage, had, indeed, already begun to affect Soviet economic performance directly by the late 1950s, e.g. in the Virgin Lands agricultural areas, where overcropping was producing dustbowl conditions by the early 1960s. The late 1950s also witnessed the emergence of a serious demographic/labour supply problem, as a net backflow of migration from Siberia was recorded.[7] Under conditions of increasing labour shortage the young volunteers who manned the great Siberian construction projects were increasingly tempted to get back to the European USSR, confident that they would be able to find a job. By all accounts the main reason for this failure of labour supply planning was the inadequacy of material incentives, but infrastructural deficiencies in Siberia were also blamed, and ministerial departmentalism in turn blamed for that.

But it would be unfair to suggest that Khrushchev's political opponents did not recognize these economic problems. On the contrary, the Anti-Party Group sought, during its brief period of political ascendency at the end of 1956, to solve the problem through the creation of a 'super-ministry' under the rubric of Pervukhin's Gosekonomkomissiya – the State Economic Commission. Gosekonomkomissiya had originally been established in 1955 to take the load of current planning off Gosplan's shoulders and let the senior planning body concentrate on long-term planning matters. That division of labour had not worked well, and the idea now was to use Gosekonomkomissiya as a vehicle for creating an all-embracing body at central level with *directive* powers, which would be able to sort out the bad habits of the ministries, leaving Gosplan to continue to concentrate on plan construction, as before. This reflected an implicit recognition that the traditional division of labour in terms of Gosplan/plan construction – ministries/plan implementation was at the root of much of the trouble.

The regional *sovnarkhozy* which Khrushchev substituted for the ministries turned out to be at least as greedy and selfish as the latter had been. We should not be surprised at that. In an over-centralized and inflexible system in which, for example, 'spare parts are fiddly little things which do not count in the plan fulfilment report', organizational autarky in component supply is a primary condition of survival. By the same token, he who does not overbid for investment resources may end up with very little. Since everyone else overbids, Gosplan is forced to try to make an across-the-board allowance for the practice, which automatically penalizes honesty. Thus Khrushchev's reform did at least serve to underline the extent to which the typical behaviour patterns of intermediate planning bodies are in fact imposed on them by the nature of the system as a whole.

To what extent should we interpret the *sovnarkhoz* reform as a strike against the power of the industrial administrators *per se*? Abolition certainly destroyed key bureaucratic concentrations in Moscow, and forced some administrators to take jobs in the provinces with the *sovnarkhozy*. But we should certainly not equate the Anti-Party Group with an 'industrial party'. Of the three leaders of the group, Malenkov, Molotov and Kaganovich, only the last, transport commissar during the 1930s, had real industrial experience. What held them together was the fact that they had all been Stalin's henchmen – like Khrushchev himself – but had lost power and influence after the death of the dictator. Thus they were primarily politicians, and to the extent that they did deals with technocrats in their bid for power they did them with the technocrats of the *central* planning apparatus. There is no evidence that any individual industrial minister played a key role in the political events of 1956–57. At the political level, then, the industrial ministries were simply caught up in something bigger than themselves. It was surely the strictly economic dimension of the problem that focused Khrushchev's attention specifically on the industrial ministries. And because the *sovnarkhoz* reform was little more than an exercise in bureaucratic musical chairs, its impact on the *breed* of industrial administrators did not really go beyond the dimension of personal inconvenience.

By the end of the Khrushchev period the ministerial system had been to a great extent reconstituted under the alias of a complex of state committees. It was formally re-established as part of Kosygin's planning reform of 1965. Kosygin sought, through the creation of a new economy-wide network of supply offices under the aegis of Gossnab (the State Supply Committee), to limit the scope for the re-emergence of departmentalism. In practice ministerial organizational autarky reasserted itself vigorously in the years after the Kosygin reform[8] – not surprisingly, since the reform made little impact on the general problem of over-centralization in the Soviet economy, and therefore little impact on the underlying problem of supply uncertainty. By the early 1970s, furthermore, the Soviet economy found itself in the midst of a new crisis of overbidding for investment resources, and in 1970 there were 2.5–3 times as many investment projects under way as the economy could handle.[9] As Ottorino Cappelli in chapter 11 points out, the 1970s once again saw the ministries at their worst in terms of environmental abuse and departmental distortion of infrastructural development patterns. New legislation from the late 1970s sought to give local authorities much greater control over infrastructural investment, but the ministries to a great extent simply flouted it.[10]

THE REAL EXTENT OF MINISTERIAL POWER

But how did the ministries get away with it? This is, after all, a centrally-planned system, and the role of the ministries in the formulation of aggregate output plans is genuinely limited, however much they may be able to play the success-indicator game to their own advantage. (One thinks of the coal industry, which has tended systematically to overproduce lower-quality coal and underproduce anthracite etc., simply because coal with lots of rubbish in it weighs more, and is often more accessible.) The answer lies mainly in the fact that, at first sight oddly enough, the Soviet planning system has never been as centralized in relation to *investment* as it has in relation to *current production*. This paradox does, indeed, to a great extent flow from the fundamental paradox of Soviet planning, namely that the division of labour between central and intermediate planning bodies runs along the dividing line between plan construction and plan implementation. It is, *inter alia*, because Gosplan is so overburdened with current production planning that it finds it difficult to grapple with medium- and long-term dimensions, and indeed concern about this inherent weakness of the system was one of the factors lying behind the creation, by Khrushchev's opponents, of the dual Gosplan/Gosekonomkomissiya system. With that line of development fizzling out, it was inevitable that the centre would be obliged to continue to leave a very broad area of investment decision making to the intermediate-body level, whether ministry or *sovnarkhoz*.

The formal system of investment planning in the Soviet Union changed little from 1929 through to the advent of the current industrial planning experiment. Projects have been divided into two main groups – 'above-limit' and 'below-limit', depending on whether central approval was required for the so-called 'title list' (*titul'nyi spisok*), a fairly brief document of about six pages outlining the main technical characteristics of the given project. For below-limit projects the title list has been approved by the ministry itself, or by one of its subordinate bodies, with the ministry receiving finance to cover these projects on a block-vote basis. In the 1970s the 'limit' was set at 3 million rubles, though it has been as low as 1.5 million rubles in the past. In 1966, 35 per cent of total industrial investment was below limit, varying from 60 per cent for the food industry to 1 per cent for chemicals.[11]

Even with the above-limit projects, however, the ministries have enjoyed a substantial degree of decision-taking latitude. It is in the main ministries which have initially put forward proposals for projects, often, indeed, fiddling the estimates in order to get a biggish project down into the below-limit category. But the title list itself has traditionally contained little detail on the *economic* parameters of a project – it was only in 1979, for example, that it was made obligatory for title lists to include data on projected lead-times. Significantly, ministries have notoriously tended to set *planned* lead-times for projects grossly exceeding the *normed* lead-times set by the centre.[12] The detailed design documentation for a project has had to be approved by the centre only in the case of the 'the most important projects', formerly defined as those worth more than 150 million rubles.

In practice, then, the ministries, and indeed the *sovnarkhozy* in their heyday, have exercised a great deal of effective control over small-and medium-sized production investments, indeed over the bulk of upgrading investment. They have been able to change the production profile of their smaller enterprises with some freedom, sometimes to the extreme detriment of locational rationality. In particular, patterns of spatial development in outlying regions have often been distorted beyond all reason (from the point of view of region and country as a whole) by the ministerial penchant for using small enterprises, wherever located, as suppliers of components to their national networks of plants, rather than suppliers of finished output to local markets, the job they were usually intended to do in the first place.[13]

To complete the picture, we have to look at what lies behind the powerful and systematic tendency towards overbidding, a tendency which does, of course, affect aggregate above-limit investment as much as below-limit. Up until 1965 the great bulk of off-farm investment in the Soviet Union was financed on the basis of non-returnable budgetary grants. Thus investment was effectively a free good, so that there was absolutely no sanction on overbidding. The 1965 reform promised to modify this feature, by introducing the principle of financing centralized investment from retained profits and bank loans. Plough-backs did, indeed, become much more important in the 1970s, but with centrally fixed prices and comfortable profit margins there was little impact on the 'free-good' status of investment, particularly since any unused remainder or profit was automatically transferred back to the state budget. Bank credit hardly got off the ground as a form of investment finance, accounting for just 7.7 per cent of total centralized investment in Soviet industry in 1974.[14] In any case, it was at the *enterprise* level, rather than the ministerial, that this modification impinged. Only one ministry, the Ministry for Instrument-Making, was put on *khozraschet*, thus coming under the same cost-accounting procedures as enterprises. The others retained their old status as strictly administrative bodies, carrying no responsibility, for instance, for any damage caused by their acts to the interests of a particular enterprise.

THE MINISTRIES AND MR GORBACHEV'S PERESTROIKA

In April 1983, just a few months after Yuri Andropov had succeeded Brezhnev as General Secretary, a 'secret' paper was delivered to a seminar in Moscow by Tat'yana Zaslavskaya.[15] The paper argued in general terms that the centralized planned economy had had a good deal to recommend it during the period of the 'Great Leap Forward', but that it could not cope with the size and technological complexity of the contemporary Soviet economy. More specifically, and more controversially, it pinned the blame for planning difficulties primarily on an overmighty intermediate planning establishment. It was this paper, whose 'secrecy' seemed to guarantee the widest possible circulation, that set the tone for the new wave of 'ministry-bashing' of the 1980s.

Zaslavskaya's critique of the ministerial system was couched in the most comprehensive terms. Hypertrophy is the key word. The ministries are indicted for departmentalist distortion of the structure of the economy, stifling of grass-roots initiative and creativity, obstructing and distorting communication between Gosplan and actual producing units, and for being grossly overstaffed. Most important, perhaps, Zaslavskaya sees the ministerial apparatus as a clearly defined social group and a major conservative force, blocking genuine reform of the Soviet economic system.

The last point is certainly fairly taken. Even if we portray ministerial officials in the most positive possible light, as one of the key groups which keep the existing system going and ensure that plans are more or less fulfilled, we can go on to argue that *for that very reason* they are bound to have a vested interest in the existing system. What is not so clear is why this analysis should stop at the ministerial apparatus. The history of the neutralization of the Kosygin reform in the 1970s demonstrates that the most important application of the vested interest argument is to the *Party* apparatus, which Zaslavskaya does not discuss. The ultimate *positive* message of Zaslavskaya's paper, however, focuses on the need to give enterprises much more autonomy, whatever that implies for other organizations. In that respect, she set the tone for much of the reform legislation that followed.

Within a couple of months Andropov had published a decree setting up an 'industrial planning experiment', to run from 1 January 1984.[16] The decree laid down as a general principle that the role of production associations in the drafting of specific plans for specific production units should increase, while at the same time the assessment of plan fulfilment should become more rigorous. This implied a reduced role for ministries in plan drafting *and* in the process of 'adjustment' whereby traditionally intermediate planning bodies have sought to guarantee achievement of the aggregate plan. More specifically, the decree posited renewed development of the category of 'decentralized investment', i.e. investment strictly under the control of the enterprise or production association. Decentralized investment had increased greatly in importance under Kosygin's reform, but its 'decentralized' status had been much compromised during the reaction of the 1970s. There were similar clauses relating to Research and Development and welfare/infrastructural expenditures.

Mr Gorbachev was in charge of economic policy-making at Party secretariat level throughout the Andropov and Chernenko periods, but it was only after his own accession to the General Secretaryship that he was able to develop the industrial planning experiment in the way he desired. A decree of mid-1985[17] greatly strengthened the decentralized investment clauses of the original decree, predicating that retooling or upgrading investments financed from the production development fund, of estimated value up to 4 million rubles in heavy industry, and up to 2.5 million rubles elsewhere, were now to be planned independently by enterprises. What this meant effectively was that a whole category of medium-scale investment, which had previously been the preserve of the ministries under the rubric of below-limit investment, was to be handed over – experimentally – to enterprises. The implications for the traditional freedom of manoeuvre of the ministries in the investment field are obviously profound. Meanwhile the sub-intermediate level of *industrial association*, which had replaced, but hardly revolutionized the old system of *glavki* (main administrations) within ministries, was finally abolished in 1986.

While the industrial planning experiment was formally extended throughout Soviet industry on 1 January 1987, it is not clear that the provisions of the July 1985 decree have been systematically implemented. In any case, however, that experiment has now been upstaged by the Sumy/VAZ experiment, which takes the principle of self-financing to its logical conclusion, by establishing that *all* upgrading investment should be financed by the enterprise or association, through profit plough-backs or bank credit. In addition, ministries are forbidden to redistribute funds between enterprises, while norms for deductions from profits back into the state budget and into ministerial funds are fixed in advance for the whole five-year period, though they do rise steadily, year by year. At the present time, the Sumy/VAZ system is still at the experimental stage, though it is being extended throughout a number of industrial sectors in the course of 1987.[18]

Important new developments announced towards the end of 1986 spelled the end of a long era of administrative supremacy for a Soviet ministry which is not strictly an industrial ministry, but whose area of competence impinges very heavily on the industrial ministries – the Ministry for Foreign Trade. The Leninist monopoly of foreign trade which that ministry has enjoyed throughout Soviet history, giving it the sole right among Soviet organizations to operate directly on foreign markets, has now been abolished, and a select number of industrial organizations conceded the right to trade on their own account with the world economy. We should not exaggerate the importance of this measure. Fuel exports, covering some 80 per cent of total exports, are excluded, as are grain imports. It is expected that in 1987 the new system will account for just 20 per cent of total export–import activity, though for the trade in machinery the figure is expected to be as high as 40 per cent.

The measure is important for our theme in three ways. First, it obviously dilutes the power of what has been in the past one of the most powerful of Soviet ministries. Second, it consolidates many of the elements of the various planning experiments within the domestic Soviet economy, in that it introduces the principle of self-financing into the *hard-currency* dimension. Soviet organizations trading directly with the world economy will be permitted to retain a definite proportion of their hard-currency earnings, and to use these to buy foreign equipment on a decentralized basis. In addition they will in principle be allowed to agree their own prices with foreign firms, and to negotiate their own contracts with Soviet suppliers. Predictably, perhaps, middle-level administrators have found it difficult to come to terms with these new ideas,[19] partly, no doubt, because it is so clearly aimed at strengthening the general shift in decision-taking power away from the intermediate planning level towards the producing unit. But third we should note that the list of privileged organizations includes ministries as well as associations. Some industrial ministries will themselves now be permitted to come onto international markets on a semi-autonomous basis. That could mean that in the midst of the carnage of ministry-bashing some intermediate planning organs may come through with renewed power, albeit on a *khozraschet* rather than administrative basis.[20]

Of course the anti-ministerial theme has affected personnel as well as planning arrangements. Gorbachev had sacked a dozen ministers within a few months of coming to power, and while the rate of turnover has slowed the butcher's knife is still in evidence. The latest decree on the governmental apparatus again calls for staffing cuts, in addition to improved performance all round.[21] Certainly, Gorbachev has been wielding the knife throughout the Soviet bureaucratic establishment, and I have seen no evidence that the rate of renewal of middle-level cadres has been any higher in the ministerial structure than, say, in the regional Party apparatus. At the higher level there has, at the very least, been a change in style. Under Brezhnev ministers were frequently carpeted, but hardly ever actually got the sack. Under Gorbachev they are frequently carpeted and frequently are dismissed.

BUT IS MINISTRY-BASHING A BLIND ALLEY?

The implication of much of the foregoing analysis is that departmentalism and its attendant evils of distorted location patterns, production profiles etc. – in a word of many of the immediate causes of low productivity in the Soviet economy – is more a symptom than a root cause. It is in pursuance of the difficult goal of steady fulfilment of output targets in the context of overcentralization and supply uncertainty that ministers and their subordinates impose external costs on the economy as a whole. If they do so in the immediate cause of their own career advancement it is, after all, the centre which determines the success-indicator structure. Salutary, perhaps, to recall that one of the most notable casualties of Gorbachev's initial clean-out of the ministerial apparatus, oil minister N. Mal'tsev, was sacked in 1985 for failing to fulfil gross output targets. His successor, former gas minister V. Dinkov, got the job because of his proven record in terms of increasing gas production, and he will no doubt have breathed a sigh of relief as Soviet oil output grew in 1986 for the first time since 1983.

Let us try to list the pitfalls that the anti-ministerial bandwagon might lead the Soviet economy into:

1. There is an assumption that associations and enterprises will be more

'virtuous' in their attitudes to investment resources, manning patterns etc. than ministries have been. But while smaller organizations may enjoy less *scope* for the grander varieties of departmentalism, there are no a priori grounds for thinking that the pressures vary in any way from one level of the executive hierarchy to another. To the extent that associations and enterprises are now receiving more exposure to market signals, they will certainly feel more pressure for cost-effectiveness. If, however, they are still feeling the old pressures stemming from over-centralization as well, they may simply find themselves in an impossible situation. By the same token, the extension of the market principle could in principle be as easily applied at ministerial level as enterprise level. In short, it is the *economic system in its totality* that matters when we look at resource allocation patterns, not the balance of power between different levels of the executive.

2. A policy of clipping ministerial wings courts the danger of stopping the ministries doing the most important, though certainly not the most distinguished, part of their work. Soviet enterprises often complain about ministries chopping and changing plans through the plan year, and the charge is indeed undeniable. But in an over-centralized system where the centre cannot guarantee complete inter-sectoral consistency, what other approximation to 'continual adjustment' is available? And when a ministry changes an enterprise's plan on 31 December, as often happens, is it just making a nuisance of itself, or is it ensuring that one of its weaker enterprises, which it may deem has done its best with a demanding target, goes into the report as having indeed fulfilled? Finally, what are likely to be the results if industrial ministries lose their 'private' networks of, say, construction capacity? Enterprises and associations, especially those working under experimental conditions, have *enough* problems in finding organizations willing to do 'decentralized' work for them, without losing access to their most obvious channel for small and medium-scale building contracts. Once again, the conclusion must be that it is the economic *system*, not the economic *hierarchy* that has to come first as an explanation for behavioural patterns in the Soviety economy.

WHAT PRICE A NEW DIVISION OF LABOUR IN SOVIET PLANNING?

But it would be unfair to suggest that Gorbachev has only negative ideas in relation to the ministries. What he, like Zaslavskaya, really wants to see is operational control devolved much more to the enterprise/association level, and he views that, *inter alia*, as a way of releasing the time and energies of both central and ministerial planners for long-term planning, particularly in relation to technology. In pin-pointing technology as one of the key problem areas of the Soviet economy Mr Gorbachev has sought to advance on a number of fronts. The self-financing initiative at enterprise level, especially as it relates to imported equipment, tries to create grass-roots incentives for the rapid assimilation of innovations. At the intermediate level the General Secretary has been at pains to create a structure which would facilitate a broader perspective on macro-technological developments. This is one of the motives behind the creation, in 1985 and 1986, of a quintet of new intermediate planning bodies, each one entrusted with general supervision of newly defined economic 'complexes'. Within the area of manufacturing proper we now have metallurgical, machine-building and chemicals/timber/paper complexes, plus an energy complex and an agro-industrial complex, bridging over into the other main sector of the economy, under the name of Gosagroprom.

As we saw, the 'super-ministerial' idea is not a new one in Soviet administrative history. Yet it would be misleading to press the parallel with the Gosekonomkomissiya of 1956 too far. That body was programmed to bring a more powerful central voice into the process of plan implementation, in order to minimize the negative impact of ministerial departmentalism. The role of the key *Military–Industrial Commission* in the present-day Soviet economy can probably be defined in the same terms in relation to the nine ministries of the military–industrial complex. Gorbachev's new overall policy line, by contrast, is to try to solve the departmentalism problem by shifting responsibility for plan implementation down the hierarchy.

But perhaps we run the risk of over-generalization here. The remit of Gosagroprom, the State Agro-Industrial Committee, focuses heavily on supply relationships between industry and agriculture, and when we talk about industrial supplies to the farm sector we are, inevitably, talking about both technology levels *and* distributional efficiency. By the same token, however, the work of Gosagroprom, in the brief period since its creation, has been bedevilled by overlapping jurisdictions, excessive red tape, and continued supply difficulties.[22]

The other industrial complexes have not become involved in the frustrations of day-to-day management, but have, indeed, yet to come through with a clearly defined specific role on *any* dimension of Soviet economic life.[23] With a process of amalgamation of ministries, starting in August 1987, now superimposed on the industrial complex structure, the picture becomes even more complicated, and one wonders whether the complex idea may not have been upstaged. The process of *perestroika* in the Soviet economic system has still not gone far enough to permit a radical redefinition of the role of intermediate planning bodies, whether ministries,

industrial complexes or whatever. Enterprises still do not have the degree of
independence on contracts for industrial supplies which would permit them
to find their own suppliers of 'fiddly little things' *on a market basis*.
Enterprises are still not empowered to change their production profiles to
the extent, for instance, of turning themselves into specialist suppliers of
nuts and bolts or other key engineering components on the micro-
specialization pattern of Western engineering industries. Finally, enterprises are still not allowed to create *price* incentives to persuade other
organizations to study their own particular needs.

CONCLUSION

We have argued, then, that there is something a little misconceived about
Soviet policy-making on the industrial ministries over the past few years.
Like Khrushchev, Andropov and Gorbachev, not to mention Zaslavskaya,
have viewed the ministries as powerful independent actors, pursuing their
own ends to the detriment of the national interest. I have pictured them, not
quite as 'victims', but as operators constrained to break the rules and
depart from the best practice in order to keep their superiors happy on
priorities *defined by those superiors*. Alice Gorlin argues in the same vein
that:

> Western students of the second economy have pointed out that one motivation
> behind illegal activity is to accomplish economic ends which cannot be achieved
> within the official structure. Organizational reform, in creating *legal* options
> outside the ministerial structure, may be seen as an implicit acknowledgement on
> the part of the regime of the correctness of this position. The official approach is
> naive however; organizational change has been so frequent that it is now part of
> the syndrome of perpetual reform. Most of the reforms have been partial
> approaches to specific, localized problems, and as such have had unforeseen
> consequences. The approach itself has become the issue. In addition the economy
> has become so complex that it is now questionable whether any bureaucratic
> approach to identifying administrative boundaries consistent with achieving
> national goals can work.[24]

But I would not want to say that Gorbachev had got it all wrong. In his
speech to the June 1987 Plenum of the CC CPSU the General Secretary
once again stressed the need to develop the role of market forces within
industry. A formal programme for the gradual introduction of a substantial element of 'wholesale trade in the means of production' over the period
up to 1992 has been announced.[25] Now if the Soviet leaders can create a
planning system sufficiently self-regulatory to excise the success-indicator
problem once and for all, a system sufficiently decentralized to take
planning of the supply of components definitively out of the province of

central or intermediate planning bodies, then the old trouble-shooting, wheeler-dealer role of the ministries can disappear painlessly. By the same token the notion of a new, more wide-ranging role for intermediate bodies, more akin perhaps to that of the great international corporations of the West, would certainly become a practical possibility in that context. But this perspective still raises some awkward questions. Will the industrial ministries of the future be on *khozraschet*? To the extent that some ministries will be able to operate directly on foreign markets under the new regulations the answer, one presumes, must be yes. But if so, how will they relate to their *khozraschet*, perhaps fully self-financing, constituent enterprises and associations? And what about the industrial complexes? If they are not to be on *khozraschet*, what will be the incentives and the sanctions to ensure that they really do lift Soviet science policy out of the morass of paper-pushing which has dragged out lead-times in the past? But these very difficulties do, perhaps, give us some reason to end on a note of optimism. For it is clear that the logic of Gorbachev's economic policies, if taken to its ultimate conclusion, would transform beyond recognition the framework within which Soviet central planners, ministries and enterprises alike have to operate.

NOTES AND REFERENCES

1   Quoted in P. Hanson, 'Success indicators revisited: the July 1979 Soviet decree on planning and management', *Soviet Studies*, 1983, vol. 35, p. 1–13.
2   E. Teague, 'Turnover in the Soviet elite under Gorbachev: implications for Soviet politics', *Radio Liberty Research Bulletin*, 8 July 1986.
3   See A. Nove, *An Economic History of the USSR*, Allen Lane, The Penguin Press, London, 1969, pp. 212–4.
4   G. Schroeder, 'The "reform" of the supply system in Soviet industry', *Soviet Studies*, 1972, vol. 24, p. 99. Alice Gorlin ('The power of Soviet industrial ministries in the 1980s', *Soviet Studies*, 1985, vol. 37, cites a source (p. 356) which states that the ministries draw up some 50,000 material balances. This figure must include purely intra-ministerial balances.
5   D. A. Dyker, *The Process of Investment in the Soviet Union*, CUP, Cambridge, 1983, pp. 39–40 and 151.
6   Ibid., pp. 46–8 & 119–33.
7   D. A. Dyker, *The Soviet Economy*, Crosby Lockwood Staples, London, 1976, p. 108.
8   Dyker, *The Process of Investment ...*, op. cit., p. 92; *The Future of the Soviet Economic Planning System*, Croom Helm, London, 1985, p. 60.
9   Dyker, *The Process of Investment ...*, op. cit., p. 37.
10 Ibid., pp. 28–9.
11 Ibid., p. 27
12 Dyker, *The Future ...*, op. cit., p. 106.
13 see Dyker, *The Process of Investment ...*, op. cit., pp. 150–7.

14 M. Pessel', 'Kredit kak faktor intensifikatsii kapital'nogo stroitel'stva', *Planovoe Khozyaistvo*, 1977, no. 1.

15 T. Zaslavskaya, 'Doklad o Neobkhodimosti Bolee Uglublennogo Izucheniya v SSSR sotsial'nogo Mekhanizma Razvitiya Ekonomiki', *Radio Liberty, Materialy Samizdata (35/83)*, 26 August 1983, AC No. 5042.

16 'V Tsentral'nom Komitete KPSS i Sovete Ministrov SSSR', *Ekonomicheskaya Gazeta*, 1983, no. 31, p. 5.

17 'O shirokom rasprostranenii novykh metodov khozyaistvovaniya i usilenii ikh vozdeistviya na uskorenie nauchno-tekhnicheskogo progressa', *Ekonomicheskaya Gazeta*, 1985, no. 32, special supplement.

18 See D. A. Dyker, 'Industrial planning – forwards or sideways?', in D. A Dyker (ed.), *The Soviet Union under Gorbachev: Prospects for Reform*, Croom Helm, London, 1987.

19 A. Zverev, 'Valyutnye fondy predpriyatii', *Ekonomicheskaya Gazeta*, 1987, no. 15, p. 21.

20 Economist Intelligence Unit, *Country Report USSR*, no. 1, 1987, pp. 15–6.

21 'V Politbyuro TsK KPSS', *Ekonomicheskaya Gazeta*, 1987, no. 35, p. 3.

22 D. A. Dyker, 'Agriculture: the permanent crisis', in *The Soviet Union under Gorbachev ... op. cit.*

23 Speech by Gorbachev published in *Ekonomicheskaya Gazeta*, 1987, no. 27, p. 8.

24 Gorlin, op. cit. (note 4), pp. 366–7.

25 Yu. Yakutin, 'Mekhanizm optovoi torgovli', *Eknomicheskaya Gazeta*, 1987, no. 32, p. 6.

9. Foreign Affairs Specialists and Decision Makers

Neil Malcolm

The names of expert policy advisers to the Soviet leadership are on the whole now better known in the West than the names of lesser members of the Politburo. They are figures whose writings have been familiar for many years to readers of Soviet specialist journals – Aganbegyan and Zaslavskaya in economics, Shakhnazarov and Burlatsky in political science, Arbatov and Yakovlev in international relations – but who have now emerged as semi-official spokesmen. In 1987 Aleksandr Yakovlev even completed a three-year metamorphosis from director of a foreign affairs research institute to full member of the Politburo.

Questions naturally arise concerning the relationship which the specialist community enjoys with the uppermost levels of political power. Is their present enhanced prominence a temporary phenomenon or is it likely to persist? In either case, how is it to be explained? This contribution explores such questions looking at the case of the foreign policy experts.

The system of foreign affairs research institutes of the USSR Academy of Sciences has remained broadly unchanged since the beginning of the 1970s. Among the biggest are IMEMO – the Institute of the World Economy and International Relations (founded in 1956) – and the Institute for the Study of the USA and Canada (1968). Such establishments employ hundreds of researchers each, they have access to information, travel and other privileges, and they manage large-scale publishing programmes. They grew in number in the early Brezhnev years, at a time when the interest of Western observers had been stimulated by the sharp conflicts over doctrine which occurred under Khrushchev. In major pieces of research, Zimmerman and Griffiths had shown that it was no longer possible to posit a monolithic view of the world on the part of the Soviet leaders and their intellectual spokesmen and advisors. As Zimmerman pointed out in 1970, the uncertainties that this created made it a matter of urgent priority to undertake further 'empirical investigation of contemporary Soviet assessments of the international scene'.[1]

In the years that followed, much research was carried out along these lines, and many misconceptions were dispelled as a result. But many areas of uncertainty remain. Jerry Hough was able to write in 1982 that many in the West 'have come to understand the role' of the Institute of the USA and Canada and of IMEMO in Soviet policymaking.[2] But this statement was, and is, only true in the narrower sense that many writers in the West now acknowledge that the institutes do have a role in Soviet policy making, not in the sense that they have a good understanding of the extent and nature of that role.

There is a striking disproportion between the abundance of academic and journalistic writing on foreign affairs published in the USSR, and the general shortage of other information about what lies behind changes in foreign policy. We are confronted on the one hand by the virtual unanimity of leadership statements on foreign affairs, and on the other by a bewildering diversity of expert analyses (and implied policy prescriptions). In the West some react by reaffirming their belief in the unitary nature of 'Soviet doctrine'.[3] They either ignore evidence of disagreements or minimize their significance. Others seize on the published debates as an expression of homologous conflicts inside the policy-determining leadership.[4] At its best this approach can yield suggestive results, but it does entail the risk of losing sight of the distance which separates the academic world from the world of high politics in the USSR. It is also sometimes associated with an overestimation of the influence which experts can bring to bear.

What follows is intended to demonstrate (1) that academic writing on foreign affairs, far from being simple window-dressing, has been inextricably intertwined with the politics of Soviet foreign policy; (2) that it does provide clues to top-level debates, and may even influence them, but not in the obvious ways that are sometimes assumed. In the final section conclusions are drawn concerning the nature of specialist influence and its evolution.

THE FOREIGN AFFAIRS INSTITUTES AND POLITICS

Some preliminary remarks must be made about the nature of conflict over policy in the USSR. Is it even worth looking for? Odom and others have argued that it is largely a mirage engendered by 'functional specialisation' in the administration. The military press, so it is claimed, argues for vigilance, and presents a relatively hostile view of the imperialist adversary, because that is its assigned role. Likewise the foreign trade journals are expected to draw attention to the possibilities for and potential rewards of co-operation with the West.[5] But the very elaborateness of the efforts which the Soviet leadership has made to overcome the politicization and compartmentalization of its subordinate agencies, and the frequent criticism of bureaucratic parochialism, which by the mid-1980s had become quite explicit, suggest that where Soviet officials stand depends (to a considerable extent) on where they sit. Specialization, in other words, has had important *political* repercussions.[6]

Nor should we be too overawed by Soviet claims concerning the role of a coherent and all-pervading 'Marxist-Leninist ideology'. There is no longer, if there ever was, a single authority with monopoly on authoritative statements and doctrinal innovations. Of course 'ideology' *can* be used as 'a mechanism to obtain compliance',[7] but it can equally well serve as an object of manipulation by groups of officials and academics who have the job of developing and revising it.

The CPSU, the guardian of the ideology, is itself functionally differentiated. Its various components have well-defined organizational interests, which are not always properly recognized. One writer has convincingly argued against picturing the Soviet military as a group which exerts adventurist pressures on Party policy: he shows that the press organs from which hard-line statements have habitually been taken to back up this thesis are in fact controlled by the Main Political Administration of the Armed Forces (GPU), a *Party* body. But this does not imply monolithic Party control. As Payne has demonstrated, the Main Political Administration itself acted as an influence or even an organizing centre for what he calls 'militarist' tendencies inside the Party.[8]

From the very beginning the foreign affairs research institutes have been entangled in intra-Party policy debates. The original Institute of the World Economy and World Politics had to be rescued from 'Trotskyist' influence in the late 1920s and put under the practically-minded leadership of the Hungarian Communist Jeno Varga, so that it could serve among other things as a source of commercial intelligence for the industrialization drive. In 1947, after its director had misguidedly published a study suggesting that the leading capitalist states had changed their nature sufficiently to be relied on for assistance in the post-war reconstruction drive, the establishment was disgraced and closed down.[9] Discussions about reopening it began immediately after the July 1955 Central Committee Plenum which rejected Molotov's hard line in foreign policy, and it emerged again as the Institute of the World Economy and International relations (IMEMO) in 1956. It rapidly became an important source of expertise for the programme of expanding trade with the West, and of doctrinal adaptations to justify the new policies of peaceful coexistence and expanding Soviet involvement in the Third World. As the build-up to the SALT talks began in the late 1960s, a number of new institutes were set up, in particular Georgii Arbatov's USA Institute, which continued to expand as detente flourished, i.e. up to the middle of the following decade.[10]

The Party apparatus, in its turn, has exercised close supervision over the institutes. The Central Committee International Department has had general responsibility for their work, and their reports are sent regularly to it in the first instance. Department employees sit on the editorial boards of institute journals, and have in some cases themselves been past or future institute administrators. They attend academic conferences, act as supervisory editors of academic publications, and occasionally intervene directly in academic debate. Researchers are constantly reminded of their primary duty to provide the Party with the kind of information which is useful for policy making, and of their allotted task of publicising and explaining Party policies at home and abroad.[11]

Arbatov's biography is not an untypical one for a senior academic administrator in this field. He graduated in 1949 from the Moscow Institute of International Relations (which trains personnel mainly for the diplomatic and intelligence services). Among his contemporaries were Inozemtsev, a future director of IMEMO, and Zagladin, now a first deputy head of the International Department. He worked as a journalist and editor in the Party press, then as a sector head at IMEMO, and in 1964 joined the Party apparatus to act as a 'consultant' in Andropov's department for liaison with ruling communist parties. In 1967 he was appointed USA Institute director, in 1974 a full member of the Academy of Sciences and of the Supreme Soviet (where he sits on one of the Commissions on International Affairs), in 1976 a candidate member and in 1981 a full member of the Central Committee. He travelled abroad with Brezhnev and had access to his private office, and was permitted (and still is) to act as a spokesman for the regime, especially abroad. Clearly there is ample opportunity for such an individual to keep in touch with thinking in the upper reaches of the CPSU.[12]

The problem is to define what 'Party' policy is. In this sensitive process, good communications with the upper levels of the leadership are clearly essential, if catastrophes such as that of 1947 are to be avoided. Communication undoubtedly occurs as much through informal as through formal channels, and it is highly politicized. Franklyn Griffiths has described the advice tendered to policy makers by foreign policy experts as composed of 'transactional perceptions', i.e. analysis designed to reinforce particular policy options. This effort is supported, he proposes, by 'highly informal coalitions of officials and specialists', co-ordinated 'through the signalling of opinions among individuals who could not consult as a group or faction'. In all this a key part is played by senior institute administrators – the 'specialist entrepreneurs' or 'scholar bureaucrats', who may be members of the Party Central Committee and even have access to the General Secretary and his close aides. The other participants in the coalitions, or 'vertical groupings', as Jonsson calls them, may be state or

Party agencies, or even small groups of officials inside such agencies.[13]

Strenuous attempts have been made by the Soviet leadership to overcome 'subjectivism' and 'departmental dissociation'[14] and establish a 'businesslike, scientific' approach to consultation and policy making. The aim has been to institutionalize the process, by establishing co-ordinating research councils, and setting up joint committees and conferences with the task of elaborating a consensus view among academics and officials.[15] But the problem is not so easily solved. It does not require very careful examination of, say, successive CPSU Congress documents, from 1971 to 1986, to confirm the testimony of émigré scholars that they are negotiated texts, whose inconsistencies and switches of emphasis reflect the competing interests and views of the drafting agencies (bodies such as the International Department, IMEMO and the Foreign Ministry are involved).[16] It is misleading to talk of foreign policy 'ideology' in the Soviet Union, as if one were referring to a coherent system of ideas conceived in calm reflection on the evolution of human affairs. A series of doctrinal expedients have been seized on throughout Soviet history to argue for or justify successive shifts of policy. They were enshrined in concepts such as 'social fascism', 'Popular Front', 'the forces of peace', 'peaceful coexistence', 'the world division of labour', 'proletarian internationalism', 'global problems'. Occasionally lumps of pre-existing orthodoxy have been rearranged in new configurations to suit the demands of the time, but it has been more often ignored then explicitly revised. Foreign affairs specialists play an important part in providing the building blocks for this ramshackle structure and in presenting it to the world in the most favourable light. What this means in terms of their influence will be discussed below. For the time being it is sufficient to recognize that they are actively *involved* in the political game.

One of the most momentous new perceptions to gain currency was the revised image of imperialism which received official endorsement under Khrushchev. Instead of acting as a passive tool of the monopolies, unreflectingly aggressive and hostile to socialism, the capitalist state was seen to enjoy a certain amount of autonomy in selecting the best way to ensure the reproduction of the existing social order, and in particular its survival in the face of the challenge posed by socialism. IMEMO specialists argued that shifts in the world correlation of forces brought about by national liberation movements, the growth of Soviet military power, and the rise of progressive movements in the West had made the imperialists more cautious and uncertain over whether to adopt a 'hard' or a 'soft' line. The implications were clear. Coexistence and perhaps even some degree of co-operation of the two systems were possible. While Soviet strength was held to have brought this situation about, Soviet Flexibility would be needed to exploit it. Needless to point out, a large investment of resources would have to be made in research on politics in the West and on international affairs.[17]

It is possible to see this new analysis purely as theory 'catching up' with practice, in Stalin's terms, but it is more convincingly interpreted as part of a genuine and continuing policy debate, the same debate which caused Varga's downfall in 1947, which had been pursued in covert ways even in the intervening years, and which persisted long after Khruschev's change of line. New ideas about foreign policy have regularly been incubated in the specialist community for years before being adopted as official policy.[18] What is more, once they have been adopted they do not, as some assume, automatically acquire immunity from criticism.[19] Press organs sponsored by the Soviet military and by Party ideological agencies were less than eager to embrace the new attitude towards the West. The latter characteristically emphasized the threatening nature of imperialism and the need for high levels of defence expenditure, and called for discipline and vigilance in the face of ideological contamination. Between the American proposal for strategic arms limitation talks at the end of 1966 and the beginning of the talks in November 1969 there was a deluge of attacks on 'bourgeois and petty bourgeois pacificism', 'pacifist and revisionist views', excessive concern with peaceful coexistence, and so on. Warnings about increasing American aggressiveness and American plans to acquire a first-strike capability persisted until near the SALT signing date in 1972. Even after this, the military press for many years simply refrained from referring to the treaty. Party ideologists meanwhile kept up a barrage of warnings about subversive plans of the West to use detente and the accompanying widening of contacts to encourage commercial attitudes, 'property-obsessed, consumer-minded instincts', 'extreme individualism, violence, unspirituality and self-interest'.[20]

On certain policy issues, the specialist community itself has been more evenly divided. In the first half of 1957, as the struggle between the Khrushchev and Molotov factions over foreign policy came to a head, a group of experts at the Institute of Oriental Studies launched an attack on the theoretical innovations underlying Khrushchev's strategy of cultivating the ruling 'national bourgeoisie' of newly independent states such as India and Egypt. This offensive was renewed later on, when conservative elements in the Khrushchev regime began to assert themselves. The Institute of Oriental Studies Director, Gafurov, and his deputy Ulyanov-skii were closely associated with the Central Committee International Department, where Ponomarev, supported by Suslov, was fighting to preserve a more 'party-centred' approach to the developing countries.[21]

IMEMO appeared to draw support from a different part of the leadership. At the 20th Congress it was Mikoyan who had proposed its creation, and the institute's directors (Arzumanyan and Inozemtsev) and their senior colleagues tended to support Khrushchev's position fairly consistently. It was a group in IMEMO led by Georgii Mirskii which pioneered the creative development of doctrine in regard to the progressiveness of military dictatorships and other non-proletarian Third World nationalist regimes, such as the one headed in Egypt by Colonel Nasser, a man described privately by Suslov as a fascist.[22]

In the last years of Khrushchev's rule, on the other hand, both institutes (which had in any case always provided a platform for a range of views on the subject) converged towards a fairly pessimistic view of the revolutionary potential of Third World nationalism, and by the end of the 1960s IMEMO appears to have come much more firmly under the International Department's wing.[23]

Even in the apparently more consensual political atmosphere of the Brezhnev era the debates continued. Hough has described divisions among experts over the prospects for revolution and/or reform in Latin America in the 1970s, identifying three conflicting positions supported respectively by the leading IMEMO Latin Americanist, Kiva Maidanik, the Director of the Institute for the Study of Latin America, Viktor Volskii, and Boris Koval, who rose to become a deputy director of the Institute of the International Workers Movement. Leading International Department officials allowed their names to be linked with particular protagonists, Ulyanovskii taking up a characteristically 'left' stance, others generally encouraging more cautious predictions.[24]

Throughout the decade foreign affairs specialists provided enthusiastic support for the leadership's 'Peace Programme'. USA Institute publications, for example, remained on the whole remarkably optimistic about detente until well into the Carter Administration's term of office. The all too obvious difficulties which were emerging in US–Soviet relations were not ignored, but emphasis was put on the progress already made and on the benefits which could be expected to flow from persistence with existing policy. American (and, implicitly, Soviet) critics were taken to task for setting impossibly high standards and ignoring the overwhelming case for improved relations. 'Detente is not a gift from the USA to the Soviet Union (or, for that matter, a gift from the Soviet Union to the USA),' wrote one author, 'but the historically inevitable single rational path to the preservation of the human race.'[25] Soviet Americanists made scarcely disguised appeals for greater efforts to be made by both sides to achieve mutually acceptable compromises on arms control and to prevent the breakdown of negotiations 'to the benefit of militarist circles and the individual interests of particular politicians in the West'.[28]

In the 1980s, as relations worsened further, more fundamental issues re-emerged concerning the nature of American foreign policy. Aleksandr Yakovlev, the new director of IMEMO, openly challenged the predominant academic view when he wrote that 'it would be mistaken to explain the abandonment of detente by the USA simply with reference to subjective factors': the new hostility was an expression of the world-historical struggle between capitalism and socialism, and thus was likely to be durable. He painted an alarming picture of American militarism, mass anti-Soviet hysteria, and 'bourgeois state totalitarianism'. Arbatov responded with characteristic optimism: 'History did not begin with the Reagan Administration, and we shall survive the next three years.' His USA Institute colleagues, meanwhile, pointed to growing discontent in the American Establishment with current policy, and to the way the nuclear freeze movement was drawing strength from Soviet peace initiatives.[27] This does not seem to have developed as a simple pro- and anti-detente argument. Within a general position of support for relaxing tension there appear to have emerged various options, and a choice, for example, between the traditional American-oriented bilateralism and a multilateral approach which focuses more on Western Europe, Japan and the industrializing countries.[28]

Thus specialists have been caught up in complex and shifting political struggles, involving 'hard/soft' ideological splits, factional struggle and bureaucratic coalition-forming (there was support in the military press, for example, for the Foreign Ministry–IMEMO line on Third World policy under Khrushchev). The debate is also continually being affected by changes in the international environment. Unexpected developments abroad provoke leaders to solicit explanations from specialists and force the specialists to re-examine their own theories (in their role as academics) or rather to manipulate new evidence in order to back up their policy predilections (in their role as surrogate politicians). They are not simply propagandists.

RESEARCHERS AND POLICY

The working assumption so far has been that specialist publications provide an alternative forum for policy debate in conditions where more public forms of discussion are severely restricted. The evidence available about 'networks' and connections with policy changes seems to support the notion that scholarly writings represent for the Western observer 'shadows on the wall of Plato's cave', as Hough expresses it, visible intimations of the secret deliberations of the Kremlin.[29] He points out that experts are likely to try to enhance the impact of their arguments and reinforce patron–client relations by making their contributions 'fit' into the existing framework of leadership discussion. Does this mean, as one writer claims, for example, that 'the things specialists say in public about the US policy process reflect the proclivities of the leadership', that by examining patterns of use of certain concepts in academic writing we can discern analogues of 'tendencies' in Soviet policy?[30]

Terms like 'reflection' are misleading. Over-enthusiastic pursuit of scholarly/political linkages courts the danger of ignoring the specific features of academic intercourse on the one hand, and top-level policy discussions on the other. Academics resist classification into neat groupings correlated with particular policy preferences: in the USSR as elsewhere they are apt to follow their own idiosyncratic lines of analysis, and this has become more likely in the 1970s and 1980s, as they have become more numerous and their fields of study more specialized.[31] They are likely to be more consistent over time, and more extreme in the implications of what they write, than politicians. In the Soviet context officials and leaders maintain an impressive degree of consensus, which is not entirely contrived.[32]

The degree of radicalism shown by particular experts is only partly a matter of individual conviction and temperament. There are marked differences in style and content between each of three categories. The first is occupied by on the whole relatively less 'political' rank and file specialists. The second category is peopled by a group of scholar-administrators and journalists with wide-ranging official contacts, and frequently with experience as Party consultants, propagandists and even as junior officials. As one might expect, this is where the most interesting policy-relevant 'transactional perceptions' come from.[33] The third category – individuals currently occupying official positions in the Party and the state – contains some prolific authors (Shakhnazarov and Zagladin, for example, first deputy heads of the CC Liaison and International Departments respectively), but they have traditionally shunned controversy. It must be said that for this group the scope for disagreement widens noticeably at certain junctures, in the mid-1960s and the mid-1980s for example. In the Gorbachev period freedom of debate appears to have been extended both to permit a greater spectrum of opinion and to admit a wider circle of participants, including a number of fairly senior officials.[34]

Even writers in the second category are required to express themselves in ways which make interpretation difficult. It is not just a question of deciphering aesopian language (description of environmental pollution in the West as a way of raising awareness of such problems in the USSR, attacks on military expenditure as a burden on the 'American' economy, or criticism of 'Chinese' feudal socialism), 'creative debunking' (prolonged exposition of Western theories, followed by perfunctory rejection of them) and argument by implication (as in the case of the hypothesis of the 'two lines' of imperialism mentioned above) and other such techniques.[35] It is also a matter of arriving at an accurate estimate of how much of a given work genuinely represents the author's own thinking and/or leadership thinking, and how much is ritual or sugaring of the pill. Western analysts have occasionally fallen into the error of discounting too much of what they read, ignoring the distinctive features of the world view of even the most independent-minded scholars educated in a Soviet environment,[36] but the more common fault is to read Soviet writing too literally.

Specialists arguing the case for detente in the early 1970s characteristically explained the progress which was being made in Soviet–American relations as a result of changes in the world 'correlation of forces' in favour of socialism. The United States' defeat in Vietnam, its domestic problems, the arrival of rough nuclear parity were all pictured as key elements in the equation. This has been used to justify the claim that Soviet 'moderates' are really more dangerous, because they encourage adventurism by focusing on Western weakness.[37] In fact, each side in Soviet–American detente affected to perceive the other as a supplicant, although both sides had good reasons for compromising. The tendency in Soviet specialist writing in the 'moderate' tradition associated with the Academy of Sciences institutes has always been to stress the underlying strength, flexibility and likely durability of the capitalist system, which make a policy of co-operation and Fabian tactics on the part of the USSR more rewarding than one of waiting for it to collapse, and certainly less counter-productive than actively striving to hasten its collapse.[38] What the Soviet Americanists and other academics involved were doing was assisting in formulating, and subsequently in disseminating a politically-conceived *rationalization* for detente. It was designed to be palatable to conservative elements in the leadership and to the Soviet 'attentive public', the mass of *Pravda*-reading officials, hence the inflating of temporary American retrenchment in foreign policy into something of world-historical significance. The price was paid, as it was in the USA in similar circumstances, in terms of excessive expectations disappointed and embarrassing theoretical retractions later on.

Another common source of confusion is the practice whereby academics are encouraged to publicize ideas which they are genuinely committed to, as a way of providing a particularly dignified or publicly acceptable explanation of changes in policy, whether for domestic or foreign audiences. It is noticeable for example that from the 1950s onwards moves to normalize relations with the West have habitually been justified in terms of the danger and futility of nuclear war, while discussion of trade and technology issues has been relatively discreet and inconspicuous, despite the fact that they probably loom as large, if not larger, in leadership considerations.

The main conclusion that must be drawn from this brief survey of the uncertainties involved in using expert writing as a key to leadership thinking about foreign policy is that the literature in question can be an invaluable resource, but on condition that it is approached discriminatingly, in a non-*parti pris* spirit, and using the kind of guidelines that can be provided by talking to Soviet scholars.[39] Perhaps most necessary of all is to maintain a good awareness of the international and domestic environment in which Soviet policy makers operate and of the choices they have to make.[39] Broader political changes have played an important part, too, in affecting the influentiality of academics at particular times. This is the final issue to be examined.

It might be assumed, from a 'modernization' perspective, that over recent decades the increasing complexity of international relations and the corresponding deepening of the division of intellectual labour in the USSR have relentlessly been enhancing the political weight of the foreign affairs experts and turning them into a significant factor in the determination of policy. Certain Western writers have indeed proposed that already during the Brezhnev years they had emerged as an influential group, a 'lobby for detente' at the top level.[40] The picture is, however, rather less straightforward.

The kind of details already provided about Arbatov's career suggest that foreign affairs researchers are correct when they point to the personal contacts of their superiors as the best guarantee of influence. As Hough comments, opportunities to communicate orally and face-to-face with officials are the crucial thing, and they are probably fairly generously available, at the highest level, to a select group of academic administrators.[41] There are also more diffuse paths of influence – written memoranda, contributions to official drafts, restricted-circulation information bulletins, monthly journals printed in tens of thousands of copies, access to newspapers and televison, temporary and permanent migration of institute staff to Party and state agencies, especially the Foreign Ministry, and personal ties with the political elite, for whose sons and daughters foreign policy research became established under Brezhnev as a desirable career.[42]

But academics have been heavily outnumbered in the policy-deliberating process by representatives of groups which traditionally had greater authority and political muscle. Dmitri Simes, an ex-IMEMO employee, reported in 1983 that even the most senior experts were regarded as outsiders: journalists, for example, were far more likely to be regarded as '*bona fide* members of the political establishment'. Foreign Ministry figures have described the academics' role in policy making as negligible. For Dobrynin, Arbatov was 'a man of no standing and little influence'.[43] Civilian specialists suffered from particular disadvantages when they had to compete for a hearing with the military agencies which for so long enjoyed a privileged position in the Soviet decision-making structure.[44]

American observers at the SALT negotiations were taken aback to hear General Ogarkov asking US military representatives to refrain from revealing military secrets to *Soviet* civilian participants.[45] The intense degree of specialization of the soviet bureaucracy, based on the assumption that only the upper levels of the apparatus are entitled to see all the evidence necessary to form an overall view of the national interest,[46] was potently reinforced by habitual security-consciousness. Under Brezhnev the small band of Soviet civilian arms control experts were apparently obliged to work largely from Western data.[47] It is not surprising that not only émigré scholars, but those inside the USSR too found ways of complaining about the way their advice was neglected. In 1981 a leading USA Institute researcher wrote a blistering attack on 'American' officials who ignored valable analyses submitted by foreign policy brains trusts because of their 'bureaucratic inflexibility' and their attachment to 'Cold War stereotypes'.[48]

Since 1984 there have been dramatic changes. The upper layers of the Soviet defence bureaucracy have been thoroughly 'reconstructed', occasionally with a certain brusqueness. The new military spokesmen have been quick to endorse previously unpalatable notions, such as the need to avoid excessive spending on defence and the unwinnability of nuclear war. Gorbachev has declared that ensuring security is primarily a 'political problem' which can only be resolved by political means. Simultaneously an unprecedented series of arms control proposals have been made, envisaging real cuts, and a much more open attitude to verification has emerged.[49] On the civilian side, a new generation of officials has been promoted and appointed. These are men who either have been much closer than their predecessors to innovative foreign policy experts, or else have themselves worked in the institutes (in the former category are Zagladin and Brutents in the International Department, Shakhnazarov in the Liaison Department and V. F. Petrovskii in the Foreign Ministry, in the latter are Yakovlev in the Party Secretariat and I. D. Ivanov in the Foreign Ministry). The International Department is now headed by the detente-minded ex-ambassador to Washington, Dobrynin. It has also acquired, like the Foreign Ministry, its own arms control department, and resources are being channelled into academic arms-control work at IMEMO.[50] Journalists and specialists appear frequently on television and in the press as propagandisers of an officially endorsed 'new thinking' which in many instances is only what they have been advocating for years in less public forums. Their own theoretical innovations – ideas about the overriding value of survival of the human race, about the growing interdependence of security and economic interest, about the need for global co-operation to solve global problems – are now enshrined in key Party documents.[51]

All this seems to point to an enhancement of influence, but it is influence of a special kind. Specialists have always been licensed to participate at Lowi's technical, lower level of decision making. Here the day-to-day work of researchers has had small but tangible effects, making policy makers more aware of the role of personalities and religion in Middle East politics, the place of Congress in the American system, the viability of the European Community, and so on.[52] But they use sources which are open to non-specialists – the contents of speeches made by an American President are no secret, after all, and there are diplomats and intelligence personnel working in the same field. There is thus relatively less scope for self-serving or tendentious interpretation of events. In any case, their impact is likely to be so subtle as to be overshadowed by the more dramatic changes brought about by events in the external environment or in Soviet leadership politics. It would certainly be misleading to describe them as a 'lobby' in this function.

Access to the middle and upper levels of decision making has so far been sporadic, but dramatic in its effects. As we have seen, at certain junctures the 'off-the-peg' concepts and reinterpretations which specialists are continually generating and arguing over are suddenly accepted, either intact or after negotiated modification, for official use. It would be incorrect to conclude that the leadership cynically takes its pick of the new ideological material which is on offer as and when it is required, that this is purely a matter of window-dressing. The adoption of 'new thinking' is bound to affect the way decision makers conceive of their own actions, as well as how they describe them, it is bound to affect the attitudes of the attentive public, and as a result it is bound to affect the future direction of policy.

What seem to be the conditions which make such a breakthrough likely? Looking at the way specialist influence has fluctuated since the 1950s, we can distinguish five positive factors: (1) replacement of the top political leadership, (2) turnover of generations in the broader leadership, (3) a pre-existing network of personal ties between experts and relevant officials of the rising generation, (4) the availability of appropriate new ideas, (5) opportunities for policy innovation and/or a situation where existing doctrine has been discredited.

A new leadership is not essential – Arbatov and his colleagues benefitted in the early 1970s from the decision of an existing leadership team to launch out on a radical new policy – but the experience of the 1950s and the 1980s seems to show that the activism of a new General Secretary and the opportunity to make large-scale top-level personnel changes can do a great deal to neutralize the opposition of established interests.

As far as (3) and (4) are concerned, the sustained expansion of the Academy of Sciences research institutes, and of the consultation system, which took place under Brezhnev clearly played an important part.

Specialists were able to elaborate the case for policy modifications at length and in detail. Officials acquired the habit of appealing to expertise rather than to ideological authority to back up their preferences. It would not have been surprising if, during the prolonged period of interregnum which followed Brezhnev's death, Andropov made sure that his chosen successor, Gorbachev, was put in touch with sources of high-quality advice on foreign affairs. One such source would be the group who had served as consultants to him in the 1960s. In addition to Arbatov, this had included Oleg Bogomolov (director of the Institute of the World Socialist System), Fedor Burlatsky (political theorist, academic and journalist), Aleksandr Bovin (*Izvestiya* political commentator), and Georgii Shakhnazarov (President of the Soviet Political Science Association as well as First Deputy Head of the CC Liaison Department). In most cases the careers of these men did not falter under Andropov and Gorbachev, and some of them appeared to have significantly expanded their opportunities for direct communication with the leadership. Their general political orientation harmonized well with that of the other appointees named above.[53]

As for (5), by the early 1980s a number of key policy and doctrinal compromises of the Brezhnev period had thoroughly demonstrated their non-viability. In particular, large arms budgets and active support for radical regimes in Africa had proved incompatible with Soviet–American detente. Resurgent Cold War attitudes in the USA threatened trade openings, aggravated the self-inflicted entanglement in Afghanistan, and created alarming challenges in the military technology race. Illusions about the potential of the Soviet economy in its existing form, and with its existing trading and co-operation procedures, to keep up with, catch up and overtake the West were finally dispelled. New thinking was imperative.

There is a markedly cyclical pattern, then, to the rise and fall of specialist influence, as opportunities to affect the world view of successive leadership generations come and go. But there are more stable, long-lasting trends in play as well. Some apply to specialists in general – the underlying socio-economic 'developmental' imperatives for better technical advice, the secularization of ideology, and associated technocratic tendencies in elite thinking. Others are specific to the foreign affairs experts – the sheer growth in their numbers, now in four figures, their acceptance as members of policy advisory committees and as consultants, the reinforcing of informal networks.

Such long-term processes may in the end act to damp down the previous fluctuations in political influence related to leadership change and/or the requirement for new policy departures. They may also interact with them to generate a kind of 'take-off' for the experts. Certainly the early Gorbachev years have created the right circumstances for such a change. As we have seen, a number of men with professional ties and political sympathies with the leading specialists were promoted to key posts in the Party apparatus. Rival groups suffered a weakening of their position. The intelligentsia as a whole began to enjoy higher status and greater freedom of expression, as they were mobilized in support of the *perestroika*. The second half of the 1980s provides the kind of conditions in which the visibility and authoritativeness of foreign policy advisers can increase to such a level that as a community they gain acceptance as a permanent part of the Soviet establishment.

NOTES AND REFERENCES

1 W. Zimmerman, 'Elite Perspectives and the Explanation of Soviet Foreign Policy', *Journal of International Affairs*, 1970, vol. 24, no. 1, pp. 84–98. See F. Griffiths, *Images, Politics and Learning in Soviet Behaviour Towards the United States*, Doctoral dissertation, Columbia University, NY, 1972; W. Zimmerman, 'Soviet perceptions of the United States', in A. Dallin, T. Larson (eds), *Soviet Politics since Khrushchev*, Princeton UP, Princeton, NJ, 1969; W. Zimmerman, *Soviet Perspectives on International Relations*, Princeton UP, Princeton, NJ, 1969.

2 J. F. Hough, 'Soviet Policymaking toward Foreign Communists', *Studies in Comparative Communism*, 1982, vol. 15, no. 3, p. 177.

3 R. Judson Mitchell, *Ideology of a Superpower. Contemporary Soviet Doctrine of International Relations*, Hoover Institution, Stanford, 1982, pp. 81, 113; S. P. Gibert, *Soviet Images of America*, Crane Russak, New York, 1977.

4 M. Schwartz, *Soviet Perceptions of the United States*, University of California, London, 1978, pp. 102–4; S. B. Payne, *The Soviet Union and SALT*, MIT press, Boston, Mass., 1980, pp. 7–8; J. Lenczowski, *Soviet Perceptions of US Foreign Policy* Cornell UP, London, 1982, pp. 239–60; T. W. Cobb, 'National Security Perspectives of Soviet "Think Tanks"', *Problems of Communism*, 1981, Nov-Dec.

5 W. Odom, 'A Dissenting View on the Group Approach to Soviet Politics', *World Politics*, 1976, vol. 28; K. Dawisha, 'The Limitations of the Bureaucratic Politics Model: Observations on the Soviet Case', *Studies in Comparative Communism*, 1980, vol. 13; and the works by Lenczowski and Mitchell referred to in notes 3 and 4.

6 P. Cocks, 'The Policy Process and Bureaucratic Politics', in P. Cocks, R. V. Daniels, N. W. Heer (eds), *The Dynamics of Soviet Politics*, Harvard UP, Cambridge, MA, 1976; D. R. Kelley, 'Group and Specialist Influence in Soviet Politics: In Search of a Theory', in R. Remnek (ed.), *Social Scientists and Policy Making in the USSR*, Praeger, New York, 1977.

7 Dawisha, 'The Limitations of the Bureaucratic Politics . . . op. cit.

8 H. Adomeit, 'Soviet Foreign Policy Making: The Internal Mechanism of Global Commitment', in H. Adomeit, R. Boardman, *Foreign Policy Making in Communist Countries*, Praeger, New York, 1979, pp. 28–9; Payne, *The Soviet Union and SALT*, op. cit., p. 7. On differentiation in the Party see T. J. Colton, *Commissars, Commanders and Civilian Authority. The Structure of Soviet Military Politics*, Harvard UP, Cambridge, MA, 1979, ch. 9; J. Valenta, *Soviet Intervention in Czechoslovakia, 1968. Anatomy of a Decision*, John Hopkins

UP, London, 1979, *passim*; J. Hough, *The Soviet Prefects: The Local Party Organs in Industrial Decision-Making*, Harvard UP, Cambridge, MA, 1969, ch. 12.

9   E. Varga, *Izmeneniya v ekonomike kapitalizma v itoge Vtoroi mirovoi voiny*, Gospolitizdat, Moscow, 1946; 'Diskussiya po knige E. Varga', *Mirovoe khozyaistvo i mirovaya politika*, 1947, no. 11 (supplement); F. Barghoorn, 'The Varga Discussion and its Significance', *American Slavic and East European Review*, 1948, vol. 6; Griffiths, *Images, Politics and Learning* ... op. cit., pp. 35–42.

10 O. Eran, *The Mezhdunarodniki*, Turtledove Press, Tel Aviv, 1979; P. Marantz, 'Prelude to Detente: Doctrinal Change Under Khrushchev', *International Studies Quarterly*, 1975, vol. 19, no. 4, pp. 501–28; R. M. Mills, 'One Theory in Search of Reality: the Development of United States Studies in the Soviet Union', *Political Science Quarterly*, 1972, vol. 87, pp. 63–79; Griffiths, *Images, Politics and Learning* ... op. cit., pp. 273–312

11 R. R. Pope, *Soviet Foreign Affairs Specialists*, Doctoral dissertation, University of Pennsylvania, 1975, pp. 5–7, 14–15; Schwartz, *Soviet Perceptions*, pp. 170–1; S. A. Grant, *Soviet Americanists*, USICA Research Report, Washington, DC, 1980, p. 3; N. Malcolm, *Soviet Political Scientists and American Politics*, Macmillan, London, 1984, pp. 1–12; A. Brown, 'The Foreign Policy-Making Process', in C. Keeble (ed.), *The Soviet State. The Domestic Roots of Soviet Foreign Policy*, Gower for RIIA, London, 1985, p. 203; R. W. Kitrinos, 'International Department of the CPSU', *Problems of Communism*, 1984, Sept.–Oct.; Hough, 'Soviet Policymaking towards Foreign Communists', op cit., pp. 178–80; Cobb, National Security Perspectives', op cit., pp. 51–4; Ned Temko, 'Soviet Insiders: How Power flows in Moscow', in E. P. Hoffmann, R. F. Laird, (eds), *The Soviet Polity in the Modern Era*, Aldine, New York, 1984, p. 173.

12 G. Arbatov, *Cold War or Detente? The Soviet Viewpoint*, Zed Books, London, 1983, pp. vii–viii; 'Biograficheskie spravki', *Ezhegodnik Bol'shoi sovetskoi entsiklopedii 1977g*. Sovetskaya entsiklopediya, Moscow, 1977, p. 583; A. Brown, 'Andropov: Discipline and Reform?', *Problems of Communism*, 1983, Jan.–Feb., p. 21; Brown, 'The Foreign Policy-Making Process', op. cit., p. 211; Cobb, 'National Security Perspectives', op. cit., pp. 53–4; Kitrinos, 'International Department', op. cit., p. 65; A. Shevchenko, *Breaking with Moscow*, A Knopf, New York, 1985, p. 47.

13 Griffiths, *Images, Politics and Learning*, op. cit., pp. 287, 289, 297–8, 306; Zimmerman, *Soviet Perspectives*, op. cit., pp. 15–16; C. Jonsson, 'Soviet Foreign Policy and Domestic Politics: A Case Study', *Co-operation and Conflict*, 1977, vol. 12, p. 133. The phrase 'specialist entrepreneur' is Thane Gustafson's (*Reform in Soviet Politics. Lessons of Recent Policies on Land and Water*, Cambridge UP, Cambridge, 1981, p. 92), and 'scholar bureaucrat' is Eran's (*The Mezhdunarodnik*).

14 P. Cocks, 'The Policy Process', op. cit., p. 116.

15 G. Hodnett, 'The Pattern of Leadership Politics', in S. Bialer (ed.), *The Domestic Context of Soviet Foreign Policy*, Croom Helm, London, 1981, p. 102.

16 F. Griffiths, 'Ideological Development and Foreign Policy', in Bialer (ed.), *The Domestic Context*, op. cit., pp. 16, 21. See too C. Jacob in *The Guardian*, 2 March 1974; Brown, 'The Foreign Policy-Making Process', op. cit., pp. 207, 209, 213; Temko, 'Soviet Insiders', op. cit., p. 173.

17 Griffiths, *Images, Politicis and Learning*, op. cit., pp. 315 ff.; Zimmerman, 'Soviet Perceptions' op. cit.; Malcolm, *Soviet Political Scientists*, op. cit., ch. 2. Precedents for the 'two lines of imperialism' theory were found in Lenin's references to 'pacificist elements of the bourgeoisie' in 1922. Examples of Soviet work are N. N. Inozemtsev, *Contemporary Capitalism: New Developments and Contradictions*, Progress, Moscow, 1973; I. M. Lemin (ed.), *Dvizhushchie sily vneshnei politiki SShA*, Nauka, Moscow, 1965; G. A. Arbatov, *The War of Ideas in Contemporary International Relations*, Progress, Moscow, 1973.

18 Marantz, 'Prelude to Detente', op. cit., pp. 509–10. Debates *preceding* Khrushchev's new Third World policy and Brezhnev's detente with the USA are described in J. Hough, *The Struggle for the Third World. Soviet Debates and American Options*, Brookings, Washington, DC, 1986, pp. 42–4, and in Payne, *The Soviet Union and SALT*, op. cit.

19 Judson Mitchell implies this in *Ideology of a Superpower*, op. cit., pp. 80–1.

20 Griffiths, *Images, Politics and Learning*, op. cit., pp. 276–87, 434–40; R. L. Garthoff, 'SALT and the Soviet Military', *Problems of Communism*, 1975, Jan.–Feb., pp. 21–2, 25; O. Reinhold, F. Ryzhenko (eds), *Contemporary Anti-Communism; Policy and Ideology*, Progress, Moscow, 1976, p. 75; D. Ermolenko, 'Nauchno-tekhnicheskaya revolyutsiya i manevry burzhuaznoi ideologii', *Pravda*, 6 June 1973; M. B. Mitin, 'Mezhdunarodnye otnosheniya i ideologicheskaya bor'ba', *Krasnaya zvezda*, 22 November 1973 (last three titles cited in Lenczowski, *Soviet Perceptions*, op. cit., pp. 125–6); Payne, *The Soviet Union and SALT*, op. cit., pp. 30–4. See also S. B. Payne, Jr, 'The Soviet Debate on Strategic Arms Limitation: 1968 – 1972', *Soviet Studies*, 1975, vol. 27, pp. 27–45; J. Valenta, 'The Bureaucratic Politics Paradigm and the Soviet Invasion of Czechoslovakia', *Political Science Quarterly*, 1979, vol. 94, no. 1, pp. 57–8, 60–71; A. Dallin, 'The Domestic Sources of Soviet Foreign Policy', in Bialer (ed.), *The Domestic Context*, op. cit., pp. 376–8.

21 Eran, *The Mezhdunarodniki*, op. cit., p. 179. Ulyanovskii later became a deputy head of the International Department.

22 Eran, *The Mezhdunarodniki*, op. cit., pp. 222, 318. Eran relies on an Israeli CP source for Suslov's comment. See too pp. 178–208, 211–22; and Remnek, 'Soviet Scholars and Soviet Policy Towards India', in Remnek, (ed.), *Social Scientists and Policy*; K. Dawisha, *Soviet Foreign Policy Towards Egypt*, Macmillan, London, 1979, ch. 2.

23 Eran, *The Mezhdunarodniki*, op. cit., pp. 239–40.

24 J. Hough, 'The Evolving Soviet Debate on Latin America', *Latin American Research Review*, 1981, vol. 16, no. 1; Hough, 'Soviet Policymaking towards Foreign Communists', op. cit., pp. 178–9; Hough, *The Struggle for the Third World*, op. cit., pp. 169–83; Kitrinos, 'International Department', op. cit., pp. 65–7; B. Storozhevski, 'Third World Review', *Detente*, 1985, no. 3, p. 20.

25 V. V. Zhurkin, 'O knige Dzhordzha Kennana', *SShA: ekonomika, politika, ideologiya*, 1979, no. 6, p. 87.

26 V. F. Petrovskii, 'Magistrali razoruzheniya', *SShA: ekonomika, politika, ideologiya*, 1980, no. 9, p. 13.

27 A. Yakovlev, 'Istoki ugrozy i obshchestvennoe mnenie', *Mirovaya ekonomika i mezhdunarodnye otnosheniya*, 1985, no. 3, pp. 3–4, 15; Arbatov reported in *The Guardian*, 29 June 1985; A. A. Kokoshin, 'Diskussii po tsentral'nym voprosam voennoi politiki SShA', *SShA: ekonomika, politika, ideologiya*, 1985, no. 2, pp. 3–14; Yu. A. Zamoshkin, 'Yadernaya opasnost' i faktor strakha', *SShA:*

ekonomika, politika, ideologiya, 1985, no. 3, pp. 3–15. Cf. the characteristically more pessimistic view taken by G. A. Trofimenko in the same journal – 'Voennaya strategiya SShA – orudie aggressivnoi politiki', 1985, no. 1, pp. 3–15. V. V. Zagladin takes a more 'centrist' position – 'The Contemporary International Crisis and Lenin's Teachings', *Coexistence*, 1984, vol. 21, pp. 191–216 (originally published in *Mirovaya ekonomika i mezhdunarodnye otnosheniya*).

28   J. Hough, 'Soviet Perspectives on European Security', *International Journal*, 1984/5, vol. 40, pp. 39–41.

29   Hough, *Struggle for the Third World*, op. cit., pp. 267–8.

30   F. Griffiths, 'The Sources of American Conduct. Soviet Perspectives and Their Policy Implications', *International Security*, 1984, vol. 9, no. 2, p. 5 and *passim*; Griffiths, *Images, Politics and Learning* op. cit.; Payne, *The Soviet Union and SALT* op. cit.

31   Malcolm, *Soviet Political Scientists*, op. cit., pp. 150–1.

32   See D. Simes, 'The Politics of Defense in Brezhnev's Era', in J. Valenta, W. Potter, *Soviet Decision-making for National Security*, Allen and Unwin, London, 1984, p. 80; Adomeit, 'Soviet Foreign Policy Making', op. cit., pp. 34–6.

33   Striking examples are the reference to shared interests of the USA and the USSR in Lemin (ed.), *Dvizhushchie sily vneshnei politiki SShA*, p. 507; Burlatsky's article on 'planned peace', in *Literaturnaya gazeta*, 8 August 1979; and some of the works referred to in note 20.

34   See summaries provided in C. Glickham, *New Directions for Soviet Foreign Policy*, Radio Liberty Research bulletin Supplement 2/86, September, 1986; P. Litherland, *Gorbachev and Arms Control, Civilian Experts and Soviet Policy*, University of Bradford Peace Research Report 12, 1986, pp. 71–82; S. Shenfield, *The Nuclear Predicament, Explorations in Soviet Ideology*, Routledge Kegan Paul for RIIA, London, 1987.

35   Hough provides an illuminating discussion of problems of interpreting specialist writing in *Struggle for the Third World*, op. cit., pp. 13–35.

36   E. G. Schwartz, *Soviet Perceptions*, op. cit., pp. 37, 64, 154–5. See N. Malcolm, 'Soviet Interpretations of American Politics: A Case of Convergence?', *British Journal of Political Science*, 1982, vol. 12.

37   Lenczowski, *Soviet Perceptions*, op. cit., p. 272.

38   See the works by Zimmerman, Griffiths and Schwartz already mentioned; also E. P. Hoffmann, R. F. Laird, *The Scientific–Technological Revolution and Soviet Foreign Policy*, Pergamon, Oxford, 1982, ch. 3; and, as an example, V. Kobysh, G. Arbatov, 'Chto s Amerikoi?', *Novyi mir*, 1982, no. 4.

39   The author had the opportunity to talk at length to Soviet foreign affairs specialists in the USSR in 1981 and 1986, and on several occasions in the United Kingdom.

40   Cobb, 'National Security Perspectives', op. cit., pp. 51–4; Schwartz, *Soviet Perceptions*, op. cit., pp. 162–3. Schwartz cautions that the political influence of the Americanists is 'certainly less than they claim'.

41   Hough, *Struggle for the Third World*, op. cit., pp. 262–3. He cites the disenchanted comment of an institute administrator: 'Those who write don't decide. Those who decide don't read.' On the basis of interviews with 31 senior Soviet officials, Temko concluded in 1981 that men such as Arbatov and Bovin had personal contact with figures at Secretariat level and even attended Secretariat sessions. 'Soviet Insiders', op. cit., pp. 173, 179.

42   See the references given in note 11.
43   The then Soviet ambassador's opinion is cited by Z. Brzezinski, *Power and Principle*, Weidenfeld and Nicholson, London, 1983, p. 153, and by Brown, 'The Foreign Policy-Making Process,' op. cit., p. 211, who disagrees; Shevchenko, *Breaking with Moscow*, op. cit., p. 210.
44   Colton, *Commissars*, op. cit., ch. 11; E. L. Warner III, *The Military in Contemporary Soviet Politics*, Praeger, New York, 1977, pp. 268–71; Simes, 'The Politics of Defense', op. cit., pp. 82–3; D. Holloway, *The Soviet Union and the Arms Race*, Yale UP, London, 1983, ch. 8.
45   G. T. Allison, 'Conceptual Models and the Cuban Missile Crisis', *American Political Science Review*, 1969, vol. 63, no. 3, p. 700; Garthoff, 'SALT and the Soviet Military', op. cit., p. 36.
46   Gustafson, *Reform in Soviet Politics*, op. cit., pp. 93–4; Valenta, *Soviet Intervention in Czechoslovakia, 1968. Anatomy of a Decision*, Johns Hopkins UP, London, 1979, p. 34; F. D. Holzman, R. Legvold, 'The Economics and Politics of East–West Relations', in E. P. Hoffmann, F. J. Fleron (eds), *The Conduct of Soviet Foreign Policy*, Aldine, New York, 1980, p. 455.
47   I. S. Glagolev, 'The Soviet Decision Making Process in Arms Control Negotiations', *Orbis*, 1978, vol. 21, no. 4, pp. 770, 772; D. Simes, 'National Security under Andropov', *Problems of Communism*, 1983, Jan.–Feb., p. 37. Cobb and Glagolev take up extreme opposing positions on the influentiality of civilians in arms control matters under Brezhnev.
48   A. A. Kokoshin, *SShA: za fasadom global'noi politiki*, Politizdat, Moscow, 1981, p. 260. There is a more direct complaint in A. N. Smirnov, V. A. Shukov, 'O deyatel'nosti Otdeleniya filosofii i prava AN SSSR', *Voprosy filosofii*, 1978, no. 8, p. 162. One émigré researcher has claimed that Party officials 'totally disregard' academic memoranda (G. Orionova, in N. Beloff, 'Escape from Boredom: a Defector's Story', *Atlantic Monthly*, 1980, November, pp. 42–50). Temko reports a complaint by Bovin in 1981 that opportunities for him to give his opinion on policy matters had declined since the early seventies. 'Soviet Insiders', op. cit., p. 173.
49   'Kremlin high noon', *Eastern Europe Newsletter*, 1987, vol. 1, no. 1, pp. 3–5; C. Davis, '"Perestroika" in the Soviet Defense Sector, 1985–87', Paper delivered to the Annual Conference of the Centre for Russian and East European Studies, University of Birmingham, 1987; C. Schmidt-Häuer, *Gorbachev. The Path to Power*, Pan, London, 1986, p. 167; Glickham, *New Directions*; 'Political Report of the Central Committee to the 27th Congress of the CPSU', *Moscow News*, 1986, no. 9, supplement, p. 15; M. Light, 'Soviet Foreign Policy since the XXVIII Congress', Paper presented to the Annual Conference of the British National Association for Soviet and East European Studies, Cambridge, 1987.
50   F. Fukuyama, 'The Rise and Fall of the Marxist–Leninist Vanguard Party', *Survey*, 1985, vol. 29, no. 2, pp. 131–5; Glickham, *New Directions*, op. cit., pp. 12–13; Shenfield, *The Nuclear Predicament*, p. 82; D. L. Strode, R. V. Strode, 'Diplomacy and Defense in Soviet National Security Policy', *International Security*, 1983, vol. 8, no. 3; A. Brown, 'How Much Change in the USSR?', *World Policy Journal*, Winter 1986–87, pp. 68–74.
51   Glickham, *New Directions* op. cit.; Light, 'Soviet Foreign Policy op. cit.; Litherland, *Gorbachev and Arms Control* op. cit.; Shenfield, *The Nuclear Predicament* op. cit. For a confident statement of 'the new foreign policy philosophy' by Yakovlev's successor as director of IMEMO see E. Primakov,

'Novaya filosofiya vneshnei politiki', *Pravda*, 10 July 1987.

52   T. J. Lowi, 'Making Democracy Safe for the World', in J. N. Rosenau (ed.), *Domestic Sources of Foreign Policy*, Free Press, New York, 1967. See Dawisha, *Soviet Foreign Policy Towards Egypt*; Malcolm, *Soviet Political Scientists* op. cit.; H. Adomeit, 'Soviet Perceptions of Western European Integration', *Millenium*, 1979, vol. 8, no. 1.

53   Brown, 'Andropov', op. cit., p. 23; Brown, 'The Foreign Policy-making Process', op. cit., p. 211; Kitrinos, 'International Department', op. cit., pp. 65–7; J. Steele, E. Abraham, *Andropov in Power*, Martin Robertson, London, 1983, pp. 81–5.

PART IV:
Centre–Local Relations

10. Centre–Local Relations during the Rise of Stalin: The Case of Moscow, 1925–32

Catherine Merridale

How powerful were the local party organizations in the period of Stalin's rise to power? The question is of more than local interest. It is crucial for understanding the process of political transition. The system which had developed by 1932 was to dominate the Soviet Union for decades. It was consolidated after a series of rapid changes in the 1920s and early 1930s, not only within the Politburo, but also in the relationship between different branches of the political elite. Historians are still debating whether changes were entirely initiated from above, or whether some were the product of interaction between local pressure groups and elites and the central leadership. The result, too, is a matter of controversy. Stalinist government is generally associated with centralization, the complete subordination of local interests to the will of the top political elite. This idea must be questioned. We need to know how members of the new leadership sought to secure control of the local organizations, what problems they encountered and how far their results differed from those of their immediate predecessors.

Despite the fact that Moscow was the home of the Central Committee (TsK), it should not be assumed that centralization was necessarily less controversial there than elsewhere in the Soviet Union. In the national republics differences of language, culture and religion made attempts at centralization especially difficult. But individual Russian cities also had localist traditions. From an economic point of view, for example, it was hard enough to persuade people to think in terms of their province, rather than their factory or village, let alone trying to instil a sense of national co-operation. Moreover, where centralization implied the eradication of political opposition, localism often combined with broad-based resistance to the tightening Bolshevik orthodoxy. Political parties in the Moscow districts were led mainly by local figures in 1917. During the Civil War, the Moscow leadership, which included some non-Bolsheviks, was torn by heated political debates on issues such as party democracy and the rights of

227

trade unions.[1] Although a few of the city's political leaders were loyal to the
official line, in general the capital, with its loose organization of autonomous district committees and its tradition of civic independence, resisted
central attempts to impose strict discipline. However, the establishment of
a centrally controlled and loyal organization in Moscow was a priority for
the national leadership. Few governments could have been more acutely
aware of the potential effects of revolt based in a capital city than the
Bolsheviks, for whom memories of St Petersburg in 1905 and 1917 were still
fresh. Between 1921 and 1924, therefore, there was a series of purges in
Moscow.[2] This kind of intervention was not calculated to be popular with
the local *aktiv*, especially in view of the fact that almost none of the new
leadership were Muscovites.

The problem of centralization did not end with this replacement of the
local elite, however. As the capital, Moscow, was expected to stay in line
with the leadership majority, although this meant different things as the
decade wore on. Dissent, either within the elite or among the rank and file,
was more hastily suppressed there than anywhere else in the Soviet Union.
Failures were more likely to be detected. Furthermore, the strategic
importance of the city in national politics made it a target for political
groups within the Politburo. The elite in the capital was particularly
unstable between 1925 and 1930. From 1924 to 1928, the Moscow party
was headed by N. A. Uglanov, a client of Bukharin. The early years of his
office were dominated by successive struggles with the Left, first against the
Zinoviev Opposition of 1925 and then against the United Opposition of
1926–7. Shortly after Trotsky's exile in December 1927, Uglanov himself
was facing trouble, as the Stalinist group in the Politburo turned its
attention to the eradication of the Right. Despite his determined resistance,
Uglanov was removed in November 1928, and replaced by Molotov, whose
brief clearly included the establishment in Moscow of what the centre now
regarded as orthodoxy. In 1929, Molotov was succeeded by Karl Bauman,
a man noted for his vigorous support for collectivization. He, too, however,
was to exceed the limits set by the central leadership, in his case by
launching an all-out attack on the 'bourgeoisie', both rural and urban.[3] In
1930, he was removed, and Moscow was placed in the trusted hands of
Lazar Kaganovich. In all these incidents, the central leadership's strong
arm was obvious to anyone in the Moscow party. It stretched beyond the
city's political elite. Central involvement included the wooing of local
activists by Politburo members in search of support. Local affairs were
inextricably linked with national campaigns. Tensions between the Moscow organization and the centre were thus compounded of a number of
elements, including local 'Muscovite' resentment of the party leadership as
a whole and the problem of keeping abreast of the conflicting demands of
its individual members.

As well as looking at strains between the centre and the province as a whole, it is important to assess how far Moscow's political elite was affected by local pressure. Top positions went only to cadres approved by the TsK. But it does not follow that centrally-appointed officials were completely uninterested in the demands of their local membership. In their search for support, oppositionists in the Moscow leadership sometimes adopted policies calculated to appeal to sections of the local population.[4] Repression was swift, however, and by the middle of 1930 such activities were virtually impossible. Stalin's control of the party apparatus and his use of the central press and the OGPU ensured that formal opposition, never really viable after 1921, would no longer be a stumbling block for centralizers in the leadership. On the other hand, local pressures continued to influence politics in the regions. It is possible, though hard to prove, that central policy was modified in the localities in order to appease sections of the population. This is not the same as arguing that local elites were generally susceptible to 'popular pressure' (the example of the peasants in 1929–30 is enough to show that this was not invariably the case), but it may help to show that the lines of communication between the Soviet population and its leaders operated in both directions. The local leadership, indeed, was caught in the middle, charged with reconciling local needs with an increasingly narrow central policy.

Centralization in this period, as this suggests, must be viewed at two levels. Within the elite, the extent to which the TsK, or groups within it, exercised control over the local political leadership is most significant. It is argued below that Moscow's elite was closely supervized by the TsK throughout the period, and that this supervision intensified. By 1932, the Moscow Committee of the Communist Party (MK) had very little freedom of action. Its head was one of Stalin's closest colleagues and its deliberations were the subject of TsK scrutiny and frequent intervention, even in matters of detail. However, the study of centre–local relations cannot stop at the elite. It is equally important to know how far either the central or the local party elites were able to implement their decisions in the provinces. This was a much more serious problem for the party's leaders, and one which they had not solved by 1932. Various means of increasing the efficiency with which resolutions were fulfilled were tested in the period without success. The Moscow elite may have been brought under closer control by 1932, but as a whole the party was not much better equipped to ensure the fulfilment of its directives than it had been in 1925. It is at the level of implemention, where party activists modified central policies to suit local exigencies, that historians can best look for regional autonomy and elements of 'revolution from below' in Stalin's 'great turn'.

To some extent, local initiatives were encouraged by the central leadership before 1931. Rapid economic and social change created problems to which it had no solution. As a result, central guidance on some issues, such as industrial management, was deliberately hazy. It was probably not simply that senior figures had no time to frame detailed policies, but also that they shirked taking responsibility for mistakes, preferring to castigate local officials whose experiments failed.[5] Such failures were as much the fault of unrealistic national policies as of incompetence at the grass roots, but this was not acknowledged. Instead, by 1931, a new line began to emerge. Local activists were to be replaced by a disciplined, professional party network. It was hoped that this would eradicate the 'errors' caused by local inefficiency. At all levels, the local party organizations were to be brought more closely into line. The central leadership's suspicion of what it saw as recalcitrance or incompetence in the localities increased the pressure for centralization and tighter party discipline.

Even by 1932, central control was not absolute, but there had been an important shift of emphasis. However, the new policy was to prove no more successful than its predecessor. The growing importance of the political police testifies to the leadership's continuing lack of faith in the party apparatus in the localities. Even at the highest levels, local politicians were continually checked. Their performance, from the centre's point of view, would continue to be unreliable, for however willing they may have been to fulfil its demands they still had to reconcile these with local pressures. Structural problems like these continued to foil attempts at centralization. Effective central control remained elusive. The features of the Stalinist system most closely associated with 'totalitarianism' in fact arose from weakness, and there is no reason to suppose that they were carried out more faithfully, from the leadership's point of view, than any other official policy.

APPOINTMENTS IN MOSCOW – *NOMENKLATURA*

The increase in central control over the Moscow elite is nowhere better illustrated than in the case of appointment. From the early 1920s onwards, Moscow was governed by a distinct group of centrally-vetted officials. For the purposes of this study, the office-holding membership of the MK and its *buro* will be taken as defining the political elite, although other bodies, including the organs of economic administration, could equally be included.[6] Three features of the elite are immediately striking. The first is the high proportion of *podpol'shchiki*, Bolsheviks who had joined the party before the revolution of February 1917.[7] The second is the relatively low number of Muscovites, especially in the most senior positions.[8] The third, based on an analysis of the MK as a whole, is the emergence, by 1932, of a settled elite group, in contrast with the rapid turnover of officials in the 1920s.[9]

Both the high number of *podpol'shchiki* and the shortage of Muscovites can be explained by the fact that official posts in the capital were in the hands of the party appointments apparatus. By 1921, the system of *nomenklatura* was firmly established for official appointments, and was used by the central leadership to break up local cliques and staff key posts with officials of proven loyalty.[10] Like other features of central control, *nomenklatura* was initially justified by the need to keep the country united against emergencies or threatened secessions. Later, however, it also became a tool in the hands of a leadership anxious to build networks of patronage as reserves in the campaign for the political leadership. It operated through the use of two lists, one enumerating the key posts which the leadership wished to control and another containing the names of cadres eligible to fill them. A tiered network developed, with the most senior posts in the hands of the TsK and less important ones under the control of the provincial committees and the *raikoms*. Thus the MK secretary and his deputies would be appointed by the TsK, while the secretary of a *raikom* would be appointed in the first instance by the MK.[11] Appointments were handled by the cadres section of the organization–assignments department (*orgraspredotdel*) of the relevant committee.

From the leadership's point of view, *nomenklatura* was valuable because it ensured competent and politically reliable administration, but it also tended to encourage the development of a closed elite. At its higher levels, this elite was national rather than local. Officials moved from post to post around the country in accordance with central directives. Their known seniority, their privileges and their status as 'foreigners' imposed on the regional organizations from above set them apart from the party rank and file, reinforcing images of '*verkhi*' and '*nizi*'. The 'comradely' practice, which survived into the 1930s, of allowing party members to address even senior party officials in the second person singular (*ty*) rather than the formal plural (*vy*) was no more than a façade. Key posts in the capital ranked close to TsK appointments in terms of seniority. Members of the Moscow elite frequently moved on to positions in the TsK apparatus.[12] Many were also members of the TsK. In terms of experience, the TsK and MK political elites were closely integrated even in 1925, and the degree of integration would increase in the next eight years.

All this needs to be remembered when referring to the local 'Moscow' elite. At the *buro* level, there was little that was 'local' about the MK. Most of Moscow's revolutionary generation of leaders had been moved out of the capital by 1925, while the promotion of workers had yet to affect the MK's composition. Before 1932, only Khrushchev among the elite had been promoted through the ranks since the Civil War, and he was not a Muscovite. Promising recruits could expect to move upwards through the party in this period, but those from Moscow tended to be sent out into provincial organizations. Alternatively, they remained as activists at the factory or *raikom* levels. This could lead to resentment, and also made it possible for genuinely local figures to campaign against central or MK resolutions. Bukharin was not the only Muscovite to gain support in the capital by appealing to city loyalties. Factory directors, local party secretaries and *raikom* activists also did so, making the smooth implementation of central policies a difficult matter. Overt oppositionism was less common, indeed, than the grouping together of 'us' against 'them' to conceal shortcomings, avoid demands and divert criticism.[13]

If one of the purposes of *nomenklatura* was to eradicate the 'localism' of the provincial leaderships, however, its success was initially limited. Although the Moscow elite was not marked by the local chauvinism associated with some remoter areas, leadership in the capital was used in the 1920s to launch attacks on central policy. Clearly, it was one thing for the centre to appoint trusted lieutenants to Moscow positions, but quite another for it to control their activities once they were in place. During the 1920s, indeed, the very seniority of Moscow's leaders increased the likelihood that they would weigh in with their own contributions to the 'great debate' on the New Economic Policy. Despite their eminence, however, MK first secretaries were not all-powerful in Moscow, and this helps to explain their repeated failure to prevail against the party majority. Although the formal structure of *nomenklatura* provided that the majority of posts in the capital should be under the control of the MK, this did not mean that the MK secretary was an independent patron. One of the lessons of the crisis of 1928 was that the strategic Moscow *orgraspredotdel* was staffed by clients of Stalin.[14] It is probable, indeed, that *orgraspredotdel* appointments were included in the central rather than Moscow *nomenklatura*. Through this department, Stalin was able to influence other appointments in Moscow. This was a process which started well before Uglanov began to be perceived as a threat to party unity. Even in the first years of his secretaryship, the central secretariat was not prepared to allow him a free hand with patronage in the capital. Local party leaders were mistrusted by the central *orgraspredotdel* on principle. Uglanov found in October 1928 that he had no power to prevent transfers and appointments in the Moscow organization authorized by the TsK.[15] The case of Moscow thus reinforces the argument that one of Stalin's strengths was the fact that, as General Secretary, he was able to build up a network of loyal officials in strategic positions, capable of preventing the consolidation of opposition groups within the party.

The third feature of the elite, the relative stability of the 1930s, can be explained in a number of ways. The purges of the MK in 1928 and 1930 (following the defeat of Uglanov and the removal of Bauman respectively) played a part. The more independent-minded members of the MK were removed, while those who remained were warned by their example. Moreover, the appointment of Kaganovich, one of Stalin's closest allies, to the first secretaryship, provided the kind of leadership in Moscow which brooked no deviation from the official line. His deputies, including Leonov, Polonskii, Ryndin and Khrushchev, were proven supporters of Stalin. Clients and supporters of the other Bolshevik leaders, including Bukharin and Trotsky, had either formally switched their allegiance to Stalin by 1930 or been removed. At the same time, the composition of the MK changed. In the 1920s, the bulk of the delegates had been chosen on the basis of a position held in the capital, be it factory director, trust head or workers' representative. The TsK was represented by only one or two of its members, usually Molotov or Bukharin. By 1932, however, TsK representation on both the city committee[16] and the Moscow *oblast'* committee had increased to six or eight. In 1934, when the two committees were slimmed down to 95 members each, this meant that between six and nine per cent of the membership were from the TsK, including most of the Politburo. Other central organizations were also strongly represented.[17] The change was almost certainly a matter of prestige; it is hard to imagine Kirov, for example, spending much time on the local problems of Moscow. However, it also suggests that the leadership continued to mistrust local politicians, even those appointed through *nomenklatura*.

DECISION MAKING IN MOSCOW

We have seen that the increasing integration of the Soviet political elite did not result in a build-up of trust between the central leadership and the local organizations. This mistrust was crucial; it led to reductions in local initiative and a growing reliance on other organs, notably the OGPU/NKVD, to supervise local politics. It also meant that the centre would intervene frequently in local affairs. This intervention was not always controversial. Formally, the TsK was responsible for decisions affecting the country as a whole, and for the settlement of disputes between competent local authorities such as the People's Commissariats and the economic and planning institutions. However, central intervention was also used for political purposes, and in an attempt to establish the absolute subordination of local officials to the Politburo leadership. The problem here was that local officials, including the political elite, were also subject to pressure from below. Decision making in Moscow, even in the 1930s, was often the product of tensions between the centre, MK and grass roots.

Apart from the framing of general policy, there were two types of case where the central authorities, including the TsK, were routinely drawn into Moscow's affairs. The first was where the national interest was in question. Moscow was the capital, and it was also the location of a number of strategic factories, including the most important motor and aviation plants in the Soviet Union. Where these were concerned, the centre's intervention was not unexpected, although it could lead to clashes with the Moscow authorities.[18] Planning in Moscow was also seen as a matter of national importance. In 1931, a far-reaching city plan was approved by the TsK, covering virtually ever aspect of the city's development.[19] Although the plan was submitted by Kaganovich, it was clearly viewed as a matter requiring central consideration and approval.

Intervention was usually accompanied by conflict in the second type of case, however, where the TsK was called in to act as a court of appeal. There were occasions where this was a routine affair, similar to the role played by the MK in disputes between competing local organizations. On the other hand, the TsK also promoted its own interests at the expense of local elites. In 1929, for example, the TsK clashed with a Moscow organization, in this case the Moscow Economic Council (MSNKh), over the fate of the Serp i Molot steelworks. Although MSNKh argued that the obsolete factory should be superseded by a new plant on a different site, a committee composed of Kaganovich, Voroshilov, Ordzhonikidze, Mezhlauk and Gurevich resolved to save it.[20] The MK and TsK were in agreement on this occasion, but this was not always the case. For example, in 1929 an appeal to the TsK from the director of the Likhachev motor factory, calling for an MK decision to be overturned was upheld by the central authorities.[21]

The TsK could also respond to formal or informal 'appeals' from the locality. Unsolicited central intervention in local affairs was generally unpopular, but there were occasions when local activists, frustrated at the city level, sought help from the centre. It was common practice for officials anywhere in the Soviet Union to appeal to 'patrons' for assistance,[22] but for Muscovites the procedure was easier. Some members of the TsK, including Molotov and Mikoyan, regularly visited specific Moscow factories throughout the period, participating in their meetings and taking up contentious causes.[23] Others were 'adopted' by factory workers. Krzhizhanovskii, for example, was an 'honorary shock worker' at Elektrozavod.[24] The secretaries of cell *buros* in these factories thus had hotlines to the centre, enabling them to bypass local authorities or seek help in overturning local decisions. The value set on these connections by factory cell secretaries reflected the real distribution of power within the Soviet political system. Moreover, it was not only the cell secretary who benefitted at the expense of the MK. By keeping in touch with the grass roots, the TsK could oversee the work of the local Moscow organizations, be they the MK itself or the *raikoms*. It could also take prompt action to stamp out political opposition. A striking example of this was the deployment of Trilisser, a senior figure in the OGPU, to the Podol'sk machine tool factory, recently the scene of a direct attack on the policy of collectivization.[25]

In view of the TsK's supervision and the close personal and official ties between the MK and the central elite, it is not surprising that the MK seldom defied the official line. Generally speaking, it is fair to conclude that the TsK could secure ultimate compliance with its policies at this level whenever it chose to exert itself. Initiatives taken in the capital were often little more than experiments, conducted with the centre's knowledge, if not always its blessing. Bauman's 'socialist offensive' in 1929–1930, at least in the countryside, was an example.[26] Others were more successful. A number of changes in party organization first tested in Moscow were later applied nationally.[27] The capital also led the way in 1932 in providing organized party study 'days' to improve the co-ordination of propaganda work.[28]

However, it is important not to exaggerate the harmony between the Moscow elite and the central leadership. Differences persisted between the two. We have already discussed the political oppositions of the 1920s. These were well-publicized, not only because in some instances the oppositions themselves were seeking support, but also because the centre hoped to use their defeats as warnings to others. On other occasions, MK secretaries may have been unwilling to have attention drawn to their initiatives. The bias of the sources must be acknowledged. Even uncensored archives are unlikely to record cases where local officials successfully defied the party leadership. Some such tension may be inferred, however, where the removal of officials remains unexplained, as in the case of Ukhanov, the chairman of the Moscow Soviet from 1925 to 1931.

Active opposition was not the only source of disagreement. Local circumstances, including the pressure of influential interest groups, could also affect the line taken by MK officials. The gap between the elite and the grass roots was wide, but coalitions between the MK and local groups were possible in the right conditions. Again, the sources do not admit that pressure could lead to reversals in policy, especially since the Bolshevik party was already supposed to be the mouthpiece of the politically-conscious proletariat. Where local opinion found no sympathy within the political elite, it was very unlikely to make any difference, although the leadership remained wary of unnecessary confrontations.[29] But where other considerations favoured the adoption of a popular line, the MK could take unusual steps. The case of the Serp i Molot factory's reconstruction already cited showed local opinion winnning out over economic logic. The factory was in an unsuitable and cramped site, and its accident record was a scandal even by contemporary standards. On the other hand, its name was prestigious, and the opinions of its workforce were frequently cited in the press to indicate the mood of Moscow's proletariat. Moreover, it was essential not to alienate workers unnecessarily at the start of the first Five Year Plan. These considerations tipped the balance at the time in favour of the popular solution.[30]

Instances like this were not always widely publicized. In general, both central and local elites were wary of popular pressure. Official attitudes towards the self-criticism campaign of 1928 were ambivalent, for example. While self-criticism was a useful tool, facilitating the removal of troublesome specialists on the eve of rapid industrialisation and acting as a warning to others, it had the potential to go further and release a torrent of grass-roots attacks. No hint of criticism of the party leadership was permitted in the press. But there were many who doubted that the tide could be stemmed indefinitely.[31] Eventually, too, there was a victim in Moscow. Giber, the secretary of Sokol'niki *raikom*, was removed, despite the protests of the MK, because the *raikom* membership deemed him to have been compromised in one of the bureaucratic corruption scandals of 1929.[32] The target in this case had been the leadership of Gosbank. Giber was only accidentally involved. The threat of more cases like his was enough to stem the self-criticism campaign and eventually it was quietly abandoned. Popular opinion continued to be invoked by the leadership for political purposes, but in future caution about the dangers of public debate would keep spontaneity to a minimum.

IMPLEMENTATION AT THE GRASS ROOTS

Despite the elite's reservations about popular criticism, the three years after 1928 were to see greater use being made of the grass-roots *aktiv* than any other period since the revolution. Industrialization required mass mobilization, if not active support, and this could not be achieved without a committed base in the factories. The elite relied on the *aktiv* to increase productivity through 'mass work', while at the same time using it to check and even substitute for the specialized management. Like the TsK, the MK had too many responsibilities to oversee the fulfilment of every project. In all but the most sensitive cases, initiative lay with the lower levels in the hierarchy, the *raikoms* and below. It was here, rather than at the level of the elite, that policies were most often modified or evaded. There were several reasons for this. A few were inherent in the project of rapid industrialization, but most were related to the difficulties of over-centralization in a large country with poor communications and limited human resources. These, it can be argued, continued to present difficulties well after 1932.

We have already noted the tension within the party network between the nationally-appointed leadership and the local activists. Conflicts might also be occasioned by clashes of interest between representatives of different institutions. For example, the fact that a factory director and cell secretary were both members of the same party did not guarantee that they would collaborate harmoniously. As early as 1918, this problem had been identified, but there was little the leadership could do to alleviate it.[33] Since anyone seeking promotion in administrative posts needed to join the party, membership tended to have less meaning, in terms of collective identity, than did specific administrative responsibilities. For the most part, local issues were settled in accordance with prevailing circumstances, including the relative strengths of the cell secretary and the director, rather than with central guidelines, which anyway frequently failed to elaborate on details.

In addition to these institutional conflicts, problems arose when central resolutions could not be fulfilled for practical reasons. Usually, this was because of insufficient resources. Occasionally, also, it was because the resolutions themselves were more hortatory than practical. This was the case with many of the calls for proletarian recruitment, for example. As the quotas set for recruitment increased, so local secretaries were faced with the task of finding enough people to satisfy their superiors of their efficiency.[34] If the tactics used fell short of accepted standards, which they frequently did, then it was because the targets were unattainable and the penalties for failure excessive. Even the elite might turn a blind eye in some cases. After an explosion in the lamp department at the Elektrozavod, for example, no-one, even at the *raion* level, questioned the phlegmatic wording of a report which stated simply that socialist competition there had not been very successful.[35]

Subsequently, the national leadership were to blame these problems on the fact that the party had been too reliant on untrained, volunteer activists working in their spare time. This was an exaggeration; institutional and other tensions were unavoidable whoever was in charge. However, there was an element of truth in the complaint. Most activists were overworked, many had family problems or suffered poor health, and few had the time or capacity to train thoroughly for the tasks they took on. One area notably affected was party propaganda. Until the end of the 1920s, an overall shortage of qualified teachers forced the leadership to turn a blind eye to the fact that large numbers of its propagandists were former members of other parties.[36] It is true that this led to problems, especially at a time when factions within the Politburo were attempting to propagate a firm official line.[37] However, their replacement by 'proletarian' propagandists led to confusion of a different kind. Now the problem was that few propagandists, especially those hastily trained to meet the quotas set by the TsK resolution of 1930,[38] fully understood the material they were using, or the

purpose for which classes were intended. Despite strict central control of
the party press after 1930, the activities of incompetent or even disaffected
propagandists undermined the dissemination of a single political line
among the rank and file. In 1930, for example, a survey of ten worker-
propagandists in the Moscow *oblast'* found that four had received strict
reprimands for breaches of discipline, while another two had explicitly
deviated from the party line while leading study circles.[39]

As we suggested earlier, the central leadership may not have been
oblivious to the excessive responsibility laid on the shoulders of local
activists. The incalculable number of individual directives involved in
running a centralized, planned economy made gaps inevitable. The TsK
had no precedents on which to draw, no experience to help distinguish
important policy decisions from details. However, overwork, as suggested,
may not have been the only reason for the lack of central direction in some
areas. In the case of administration within factories, for example, the
leadership's position was overtly contradictory, leaving the details up to
local negotiation. While stressing the desirability of *edinonachalie*,[40] the
TsK also promoted the trials of engineers from Shakhty in 1928 and of the
specious 'Industrial Party' in 1930. These show-trials were a warning to
'bourgeois specialists' that they were particularly vulnerable, despite their
managerial status. The result was that many such specialists resisted taking
responsibility, leaving contentious decisions to party organs such as the
factory party cell and even the *raikom*. Even appointments to technical
posts, which should have been the responsibility of management, were
often discussed and criticised by party cells.[41]

Inconsistencies in central policy provided opportunities for activists to
promote interests of their own or to cover up their mistakes. They also
enabled ambitious recruits to get themselves noticed at a time when the
possibilities for promotion out of the working class were at their greatest.
In general, however, although local activists might grumble about
interference from above, they were also reluctant to accept responsibility
themselves. With penalties for failure which included loss of status and
employment and even the possibility of a severe cut in living standards,
responsibility was treated like a hot potato. Moreover, in struggles with
specialists or recalcitrant workers, party activists missed the official
backing which clear instructions would have given them.[42] Not all pressure
'from below' was for greater independence from central authority. In their
attempts to avoid responsibility, activists neglected their work, failing even
to report problems for fear that they would then be held answerable for
them.[43] In itself this was a further impediment to the fulfilment of the
centre's resolutions, and by 1931 had a name, *obezlichka*.

Before 1931, however, as we have seen, official policy relied on the
activist. The rewards, in terms of increased working class engagement with

the goals of industrialization (albeit only a section of the working class) and the curbing of 'bourgeois' influence (assumed to be on the side of moderation, if not actually in opposition to the new policies), were considerable. But so were the costs. The difficulties might have been predicted even in 1929, but it was not until early in 1931 that an economic crisis prompted the leadership to review its policies. A number of scapegoats were identified, including the local party organizations, especially the volunteer *aktiv*. Changes indicating the way the leadership was thinking appeared gradually. However, the momentum for centralization was inescapable. The number of responsible posts was reduced, and more emphasis was placed on professional *nomenklatura* administrators.[44] Recruitment was stemmed and finally stopped. In 1933, a purge would remove a number of people who had joined the party in the years of mass proletarian recruitment, now regarded as 'ballast'. In other areas of administration, the specialist came back, though now he was more likely to be a party member.[45] The influence of the lower levels in the hierarchy was reduced. The *nomenklatura* elite closed ranks, distancing itself even further from the rest of the party. Debates became more secret.[46] Links between the centre and the local elites were tightened.

CONCLUSION

What emerged from these changes? Certainly, the autonomy of local organizations was curbed. But that did not mean that the centre was fully in control. To some extent this was because its analysis of the problem of non-fulfilment was at best only partially correct. It was not entirely the fault of local activists that policies were not implemented satisfactorily. Nor was it any longer because of political opposition from regional organizations like the MK. The sources of the difficulty lay deeper. In particular central policy remained unrealistic when applied in the localities. Partly this was because the ambitions of the centre outstripped the resources available to implement them. Where raw materials or skills were unavailable, it made no difference whether the administrator in charge was a professional or an activist. Both, moreover, were likely to conceal their problems behind bland reports and doctored statistics. The centre was powerless before the problem. It could make examples of the people whose activities were most damaging, but for the most part it lacked the manpower to check on the details of fulfilment. It could turn to the secret police, but even they were not without their own interests, and thus capable of distorting information and evading central control, though in different ways.[47]

These persistent obstacles to central control should not prevent us from recognizing the important changes which had taken place by 1932. Many of the features of the Stalinist political system – intolerance of dissent, a political elite removed from ordinary party members and controlled from the centre, suppression of localism – had been apparent earlier in the 1920s. But whatever the pressures favouring centralization and the repression of political factions, it would be unreasonable to insist that the features of Stalinism were settled from 1925. Issues still open then were decided by 1932, many of them under the pressure of tensions between the centre and the localities. The retreat from 'proletarian' politics, begun in 1931, was a crucial stage. Mass mobilization was still necessary, and the needs of the workforce would continue to exert pressure on official policy, but from 1932, such pressure would no longer be mediated through a mass party. Even during the Stakhanovite experiments of the mid-1930s the working class would not again have so much influence over the formation and implementation of policy. Access to the political forum was now confined to a small elite, selected and controlled from the centre. Debate continued within that group, but it seldom spilled over into the press. The return of the specialist, too, was partly the result of centre-local difficulties. Perhaps most significantly of all, a solution had been chosen for the problem of poor communications and mutual mistrust. The methods of the political police became pervasive. The police themselves were not above corruption, or incapable of evading central directives, but at least they were willing to try to impose specific aspects of central policy on the reluctant provinces. To the leadership, the local party official was to become expendable, no longer the linchpin of centralization. Given the personality of Stalin and the general isolation of the leadership from reality in the provinces, the fact that these methods did not work, and indeed could not do so, was likely only to encourage a spiralling of repression.

NOTES AND REFERENCES

1   See R. Sakwa, 'The Party and Opposition in Moscow, 1920–Early 1921', *University of Essex Russian and East European Studies Centre Discussion Paper Series*, no. 7, January 1986. For an account of politics in the immediate post-Civil War period, see J. B. Hatch, 'Working-Class Politics in Moscow During the Early NEP: Mensheviks and Workers' Organisations, 1921–1922' in *Soviet Studies*, 1987, October.

2   In the spring of 1924, for example, 22.2% of the Moscow organization was purged, or 2072 individuals. *Rabochaya Moskva*, 17 May 1924.

3   The attack on the NEPmen was immediately suppressed by Stalin on the grounds that, unlike the kulaks, they were not an obstacle to the development of the Soviet economy. It was not until March 1930, however, that the MK was foced to review its policy on collectivization. It must be presumed, therefore, that this initiative of Bauman's was officially tolerated until its costs became apparent. Only collectivization is covered in S. Zdanovich's biography, *Karl Bauman*, Moscow, 1967.

4   Uglanov, for example, though no friend of workers, was noted for his generosity towards Moscow managers.

5   See Sheila Fitzpatrick's comments in *The Russian Review*, 1986, vol. 45, especially p. 369.

6   Their inclusion would be justified because even economic appointments had a political dimension. However, other considerations were also involved, especially before 1928, so it is simpler to confine the analysis to purely political posts. The sources used are the stenographic reports of Moscow party conferences, supplemented by biographical information from the party press, especially from *Rabochaya Moskva*.

7   By October 1927, the proportion of *podpol'shchiki* in the party as a whole was a mere 1.4% (10,758 individuals). Even two years later, three quarters of the MK *buro* and roughly 40% of the MK as a whole comprised people who had joined the party before the Revolution. Figures from *Pravda*, 9 October 1927, and *I Moskovskaya Oblastnaya Konferentsiya VKP(b), stenograficheskii otchet*, Moscow, 1929, vol. 2, pp. 217–18.

8   It is notable that no Moscow first secretary in this period was a Muscovite. By 1925, too, only one or two members of any given MK *buro* were likely to have been active in Moscow in the period between 1905 and 1917. The most eminent of these was N. N. Mandel'shtam. For others, see *Soratniki; Biografii aktivnykh uchastnikov revolyutsionnogo dvizheniya v Moskve i Moskovskoi Oblasti*, Moscow, 1985.

9   Attrition rates calculated from official figures fell from roughly 2.9 per month between November 1927 and June 1930 to 1.5 per month between February 1931 and January 1934. Between the third and fourth Moscow oblast' conferences (January 1932 and January 1934), the monthly attrition rate in the *oblast'* committee was only 0.4%, representing the turnover of only three officials.

10 For a discussion of this early phase, see the article by T. H. Rigby in *Soviet Studies*, January 1981.

11 The party press used the formula 'appointed by the TsK' for MK secretaries, although those who were subsequently disgraced would be removed ostensibly 'at their own request'. In this period, only Molotov, who was moved to other work after completing his mission in Moscow, was removed from the leadership there 'by the TsK'. These formulae suggest that the centre was anxious to avoid the justifiable accusation that it openly intervened in local politics to suppress opposition. For evidence of the MK's control of *raikom* officials, see *Partiinoe Stroitel'stvo*, 1930, no. 15.

12 Bauman, Polonskii and Leonov all moved from posts in the MK *orgraspredot del* to work in the TsK in this period. Between 1928 and 1930, Bauman held posts in the TsK's rural department and on the MK simultaneously.

13 Resentment was caused by the drafting of Moscow activists out of the city, for example. Faliks, the secretary of the party cell in the Krasnyi Proletarii metalworks, noted how it had been deprived of its 'best' cadres in the years before 1933, and in 1929, one member of the party cell there attacked the *raikom* secretary for expecting the cell to work while systematically creaming off its active members. *Tsentral'nyi Gosudarstvennyi Arkhiv Oktyabr'skoi Revolyutsii* (TsGAOR), 7952/3/96, 75, and TsGAOR, 7952/3/82, 153. This kind of problem was common, and led to the evasion of central demands that 'volunteers' be found for campaigns such as collectivization.

14 In particular, its members included Polonskii (the chairman) and Tsifrinovich,

both staunch Stalinists. Polonskii was later to be commended by Molotov for his share in the defeat of the Moscow Right. Another opponent of the Right associated with the Moscow *orgraspredotdel* was Bauman, who was Polonskii's predecessor as chairman.

15 N. S. Davydova, '*Moskovskaya partiinaya organizatsiya v bor'be za provedenie kursa kommunisticheskoi partii na sotsialisticheskuyu industrializatsiyu strany, 1926–1928 gg*', doctoral dissertation, Moscow, 1971, p. 313.

16 *Moskovskii gorodskoi komitet*, MGK, separated from the provincial organization in February 1931.

17 The *oblast'* committee of 1934, for example, included A. A. Andreev, Voroshilov, Kaganovich, Kalinin, Kaminskii, Kirov, Mekhlis, Molotov, Peters, Stalin and Yagoda. Mikoyan was a member of the MGK.

18 The TsK confirmed the appointment of directors of the AMO motorworks, among others, and took a close interest in their progress. See *Voprosy Istorii KPSS*, 1963, no. 11, pp. 122–3, *Partiinoe Stroitel'stvo* 1931, no. 8, and *TsGAOR*, 7952/3/267, 8.

19 The proposals are set out in *KPSS v rezolyutsiyakh i resheniyakh s˝ezdov, konferentsii i plenumov TsK*, vol. 2, Moscow, 1953, pp. 656–63.

20 *TsGAOR*, 7952/3/267, 8–9.

21 *Istoriya Moskovskogo Avtozavoda imeni Likhacheva*, Moscow, 1966, pp. 152–4.

22 The relationship between Victor Kravchenko and Ordzhonikidze is a vivid example of this kind of 'patronage' at work. See V. Kravchenko, *I Chose Freedom*, London, 1947, chapter 13.

23 Molotov and Mikoyan were both regular visitors at the Krasnyi Proletarii metalworks in the period before 1932. Faliks, the cell secretary at the time, recalled how Mikoyan had attended cell meetings 'regularly', contributing to the factory's reconstruction plans and 'sending us down the correct course'. Molotov, who also came to meetings, would 'go round the shops, talk to the workers, feel the pulse and mood of the workers and only then would speak'. *TsGAOR*, 7952/3/96, 84.

24 *TsGAOR*, 7952/3/490, 77.

25 Rabochaya Moskva, 21 September 1930. The context of his appointment was the sending of 'brigades' into various Moscow factories to check on the reasons for shortfalls and to help improve production practices. The other brigades, however, were headed by 'Moscow' politicians, several of them heads of trusts or trade unions.

26 His fate after 1930 suggests that the independent policy he followed in the Moscow *oblast'* was not regarded in the same light as Uglanov's 'rightism'. In other words, it is likely that Stalin knew about and at least tacitly approved of his experiment. He was removed without disgrace in 1930, and after a spell in Kazakhstan returned to Moscow to a comfortable and influential post monitoring scientific inventions. See F. G. Leonov, *Za Bol'shevistskoe ispravienie oshibok k itogam III i IV plenumov MK VKP(b)*, Moscow, 1930, p. 6, and S. Zdanovich, op. cit., p. 53.

27 Most prominently, the streamlining of the apparatus in 1931 and the attack on 'functionalism' as an organizing principle either within the party or in industry. Kaganovich's Moscow was well in advance of other local organizations, and even the TsK, in both respects.

28 In this case, a single factory, Elektrozavod, was used as a laboratory for the policy. The methods tested there were then adopted elsewhere in the city. See

Partden'na predpriyatii Moscow, 1933, which summarizes the factory's experience for others.

29 The use of the formula 'removed at their own request' for purged officials, cited above (note 11), is an example of the TsK's studied evasion of criticism. To avoid possible confrontations, even Stalin was careful to inform himself about local opinion before taking action. On the eve of his move against the Moscow Right, for example, he was rumoured to have been testing the mood of Moscow workers through contacts in the AMO factory. *Trotsky Archive*, T2534, 'On the mood of Moscow workers'.

30 It was not presented as a concession to popular demand, but as a case where the party leadership, the natural champion of the workers, successfully protected the factory's rights against a misguided, if not malevolent, 'specialist' organization. Typical was the report in the factory newspaper, *Martenovka*, headed 'We were right!' *TsGAOR*, 7952/3/253, 130.

31 The September 1928 plenum of the MK saw a number of speeches expressing concern about the implications of self-criticism for party discipline, not all of which were made by rightists anxious to save their own careers. For an example, see *Pyatyi ob"edinennyi plenum MK i MKK VKP(b)*, Moscow, 1928, p. 108. Stalin also attempted to contain the campaign, although he had earlier been one of its most vigorous advocates. *Sochineniya*, vol. 11 pp. 28, ff., 127–8.

32 To prevent his removal, Bauman took the unusual step of intervening personally at a *raikom* meeting to demand the reversal of its resolutions. See K. Ya. Bauman, *Polosa velikogo stroitel'stva*, Moscow, 1929, pp. 92–3. The move temporarily secured Giber's reinstatement, but within a few weeks he had been quietly dropped.

33 See the TsK's circular letter of May 1918, *KPSS v rezolyutsiyakh* (1970 edition), vol. 2, pp. 31–2.

34 The Serp i Molot party committee hit on the idea of adding an 'opt out' clause to ballot papers. Workers voting in the Soviet elections were invited to delete 'I join the party' or 'I join the Komsomol' as appropriate. As they later pointed out, this would have led to growth 'only on paper.' *TsGAOR*, 7952/3/267, 11–12.

35 *TsGAOR*, 7952/3/490, 42.

36 In 1925, about a third of Moscow propagandists were ex-members of either the Menshevik or Socialist Revolutionary parties. *Rabochaya Moskva*, 14 May 1925.

37 Under the guise of political 'neutrality', such propagandists might attempt to undermine the Politburo majority of the time or to propagate a specific factional line of their own. In general, their effect on party orthodoxy was problematic. On the subject of Kautsky, for example, one ex-Menshevik answered a question by musing that 'I've never agreed with Il'ich on this point.' *Sputnik Kommunista*, 1927, no. 15.

38 *KPSS v rezolyutsiyakh* (1953 edn), vol. 4, p. 485.

39 *Propagandist*, September 1930, nos. 3–4, p. 28.

40 'One-man management', by which each corner of the 'triangle' had specific duties, and should not infringe those of the other two.

41 This was clearly taking place at Krasnyi Proletarii, where the party cell discussed even the appointment of a new director in 1929. The records of its deliberations for the year are available in *TsGAOR*, 7952/3/82.

42 A speaker at the first Moscow *oblast* conference made this point. Il'ichev, a printworker, considered 'that such questions as socialist competition, the

transition to a seven-hour working day, the Five Year Plan for the development of the economy, the unbroken working week – all these issues demand from us the reconstruction of our work, both at the lower levels and at the level of leadership. I consider that the leading organs have paid insufficient attention to these questions ... Those bits of paper that they write ... are insufficient. There must be more practical work.' *I Moskovskaya Oblastnaya Konferentsiya VKP(b), stenograficheskii otchet*, Moscow, 1929, p. 60.

43 This point was made by Kaganovich. His speech attacking the excessive use of unpaid activists also paved the way for changes in party structure to minimize their responsibilities. *Pravda*, 7 June 1932.

44 Overall, the number of local cells and party groups in Moscow was reduced from 15,280 in the spring of 1932 to 3,435 in 1935. (For 1932, see V. F. Starobdubtsev, *'Deyatel'nost' Moskovskoi partiinoi organizatsii po razvitiyu obshchestvenno-politicheskoi aktivnosti rabochego klassa v gody pervoi pyatiletki, 1928–1932 gg.'*, Candidate dissertation, Moscow, 1972, p. 54. 1935 figures from *Moskovskaya gorodskaya i Moskovskaya oblastnaya organizatsiya KPSS v tsifrakh*, Moscow, 1972, p. 158.) The ratio of cells to members was reduced to about a third of its 1932 level. The activist was not the only person whose influence was thus reduced. Overall, the opportunities for individual members to get their opinions across were greatly curtailed, an effect of the reforms which cannot have been accidental.

45 See N. Lampert, *The Technical Intelligentsia and the Soviet State*, Macmillan, London, 1979, p. 56.

46 As an example, the reporting of MK plenums in the party press became more sketchy after 1929. Where previously *Rabochaya Moskva* had printed the major speeches the next day, and also extracts from the ensuing discussions, by 1929 there would be no more than an uninformative paragraph, and that usually several weeks after the event.

47 Kravchenko's account of his treatment at the hands of the Nikopol NKVD illustrates some of the tensions between the political elite and the secret police. Ordzhonikidze clearly trusted Kravchenko and attempted to protect him from personal attack. But he was only sporadically successful; Kravchenko's persecution began before his patron's death in 1936. Gershgorn, the head of the economic division of the local police instigated a succession of punitive nightly interrogations to break him. Local excesses like this were possible only because there was no detailed supervision of the police and no challenge to the philosophy behind their methods. Kravchenko, *I Chose Freedom*, expecially chapter 16.

11. Changing Leadership Perspectives on Centre–Periphery Relations[1]

Ottorino Cappelli

> We now have a vast army of employees, but we lack sufficiently educated forces to exercise real control over them. Actually, it often happens that at the top, where we exercise state power, the *apparat* functions somehow; but down below, where these officials are in control, they often function in such a way as to counteract our measures.
>
> V. I. Lenin, 1922[2]

THE STUDY OF CENTRE–PERIPHERY RELATIONS IN THE SOVIET UNION

Western discussions of Soviet politics often focus on central elites and their exercise of political power, especially in the form of their participation to the decision-making process. Centre–periphery relations are normally approached from the assumption that the centre is then able to enforce its decisions and achieve implementation of its policies. They are not treated, indeed, as a *political problem*: they are not supposed to generate any significant limits to the central exercise of political power.

Instead, this study considers centre–periphery relations in the Soviet Union as a flexible resultant of the interplay of a number of conflicting forces where the success of the centre cannot be taken for granted. It intends to highlight that localities and peripheral elites can be relatively autonomous and are able to resist central policies, especially at the implementation stage. Such an approach, it is hoped, may provide a key to some hitherto overlooked dynamics of Soviet politics and contribute to a better understanding of the political dilemmas that confront the present leadership.

The specific intention of the study is to examine in a historical perspective how different Soviet leaders have perceived and addressed the political problem of centre–periphery relations. The main sources of reference here are the political reports delivered by the General Secretaries at CPSU Congresses from 1934 to 1986 and, for the most recent period, M. S. Gorbachev's speeches at the Plenums of the Central Committee.

Following the official Soviet view of the Soviet political process, the centre is regarded here as the policy decision-maker and controller, while the periphery is the *locus* where the centre's decision must be implemented and over which control is to be exercised. The term *periphery* is used in a broad sense to indicate not only territorially defined 'localities', but the whole periphery of the administrative system, including industrial enterprises and economic institutions.

Our focus will be on the leadership's changing attitude, since the mid-1930s, towards the use of the party machine as an instrument to control and direct policy implementation. By *party machine* is meant both the primary party organizations which operate in enterprises and territorial agencies of industrial ministries, and the local party committees up to the obkom level.

The traditional Soviet view on this matter has tended to emphasize the role of subjective factors holding that, by means of a correct and centrally guided personnel policy, it is possible to allocate cadres able to control the peripheral administrative process on behalf of the centre.

Our main argument, however, is that the implementation of certain centrally devised policies and the effective exercise of political control, are constrained by *systemic* factors which are deeply rooted in the structure of the Soviet administrative system and the dynamics of bureaucratic politics. Such constraints are able to neutralize the personal, vertical loyalty of the local representatives of the central authority. The instance of industrial management and managerial power will be chosen to highlight this pattern of local bureaucratic politics. We shall see that an objective community of interests among managers and the local administrators emerges in the periphery that forces executives and controllers to merge in 'informal peripheral alliances' whose interests may clash with central directives. The party machine itself is likely to remain enmeshed in the web of mutual protection which binds together these informal alliances, and to be unable to counteract the phenomenon of 'localism'. Thus, centre–periphery relations emerge as a crucial political dilemma involving the overall governmental capacity of the system.

Two main sets of questions are addressed in what follows. The first relates to the degree of awareness publicly shown by different leaders to the systemic constraints on policy implementation and political control faced in centre–periphery relations. How have they been prepared to tackle them? To what extent have they remained convinced that a better cadre policy could 'decide everything'? The second points at the leadership's attitude towards the party machine as a means of controlling the administrative process in the periphery. In which ways have they sought to strengthen its vertical accountability? How responsive has the party machine been to central demands, and how successful in resisting the centrifugal force of localism?

THE STALIN MODEL

The relationship between the party machine, the implementation of central decisions and the exercise of political control were at the centre of attention during the Stalin era. It was indeed during the 1930s – the key dates being here the Shakhty trial of 1928 and the launching of the slogan 'cadres decide everything' in 1935 – that a peculiar answer was found to the problem of how to turn a revolutionary party into a governing party. It worked on the assumption that by reorganizing the system of selection, training and placement of party cadres, the central political authorities would have at their disposal 'the right man in the right place', thus ending their dependence on unreliable or even hostile peripheral administrators. Red directors would have to replace bourgeois specialists at the heads of the enterprises and 'true Bolshevik cadres' would direct all state and public institutions from top to bottom. Finally, new loyal cadres who were able to direct and control the whole productive and adminstrative process on behalf of the centre would be placed in command of local party committees and primary organizations. In short, by means of a correct cadre policy the central leadership should have been able to achieve the implementation of the whole range of its decisions 'down below'. It would also be continuously informed about the state of affairs on the spot, and would monitor and direct constantly the executive process. These assumptions, however, were soon to be challenged in practical life.

At the 17th Party Congress in 1934 Stalin lamented the absence of an adequate system of 'control over the implementation of central decisions', and stressed that a 'searchlight' (*prozhektor*) was needed 'to illuminate the work of the apparatus at any time'. Five years later, however, the situation in this respect was still found wanting. At the 18th Party Congress Stalin called for a less dispersed, more centralized and more 'scientific' approach to the selection and placement of cadres who were responsible for the implementation of the 'correct political line' throughout the country.[3]

The same problems came into focus again at the 19th Party Congress in 1952, a few months before Stalin's death. The political report delivered by G. Malenkov, then Chairman of the Council of Ministries, fiercely denounced the poor state of control over policy implementation in the periphery, especially in the sphere of industrial management, due to the 'connivance' of party cadres and economic executives. The party, along with the assumption of direct administrative responsibilities, had grown 'incapable of meeting all sorts of local, narrowly departmental and other antistate pressures'. According to Malenkov, the reason for this was that personnel policy had simply got out of hand. Cadres were often chosen 'not on the basis of political and work qualifications but on a basis of family relations, friendship or neighbour status':

> As a consequence of such distortion of the party line in the selection and advancement of personnel, there emerge in some organizations close coteries of people bound together by mutual protection [*krugovaya poruka*] and placing the interests of the group above the interests of the party and state.[4]

Thus, far from constituting the optimal solution to centre–periphery relations, the party machine in Stalin's years turned out to be part of the problem itself.[5] Although the leadership had come to recognize this openly, it remained convinced that cadres were *the* decisive factor. This prevented a deeper analysis of the objective, systemic constraints on implementation and control and on the responsiveness of the party machine.

However, such constraints were deeply rooted in the administrative system that had been set up in the thirties.

We know from the pioneering works of J. Berliner and D. Granick, for instance, that the managers, facing harsh pressure for gross output plan fulfilment at a high pace, not only had to overlook matters as sub-quality production and waste, but also had to engage in irregular practices (*blat, tolkach*, even corruption) in order to make the system work somehow. Furthermore, caught between over-ambitious plan indices and a persistent shortage and disorganization of supply, they had to resort to the falsification of reports and the distortion of upward information in order to maximize their resources, minimize central demands and, eventually, conceal their failure.[6]

To take another example, it is known that in order to attract and keep stable a highly mobile work-force caused the industrial managers to take over the construction of housing and the provision of consumer and social services, in order to attract and maintain workers at their plants. Although these developments were overtly favoured by central authorities, they did have some unexpected consequences: they hampered integrated regional planning and caused chaotic urban development and growing inequalities among different areas of the country. Moreover, they increased the managers' bargaining power *vis à vis* party and trade union officials, and downgraded the authority of the soviets as institutions formally entitled to co-ordinate and control territorial development.[7] However costly in social and institutional terms, this too was functional to the smooth operation of the system and the timely achievement of high-priority production targets set by the plan.

In sum, the emphasis on the achievement of few production goals in strategic areas and at all cost, worked in itself as a powerful systemic constraint on the implementation of other policy decisions related to lower priority areas. Furthermore, the stress was on achievement rather than the process of achievement, which is consistent with the target-meeting rather than rule-observing nature of the Soviet bureaucracy,[8] but provides it with great operational autonomy in choosing how to organize the executive process. The system could work effectively only to the extent that central demands focused on the attainment of few physically measurable goals, and executives on the periphery pursued those goals at the expense of any others and engaged in systematic violation of the officially prescribed rules.

In these conditions, keeping a check on public administration in the periphery was a particularly hard endeavour. Indeed, another set of objective factors specifically limited the control ability of the system.

These lay in the peculiar nature of the Soviet conception of administration and control, whereby the controllers and the controlled are all part of the same integrated system of administration, are all held jointly responsible for the achievement of common tasks, and are all subject to the same index of success which is, again, plan fulfilment. Consequently, to the extent that irregular managerial behaviour proved functional to the overall fulfilment of the plans (or its appearance) it was in the ultimate interest of all the officials to cover up, including the control personnel on the spot and their superiors in the hierarchy.

Despite the massive proliferation of control agencies in the Stalin era which, according to M. Fainsod, was intended to create an atmosphere of 'mutual suspicion' among local and departmental administrators thus producing central control, the opposite happened in the periphery. Here inter-bureaucratic tensions and conflicts were neutralized by the emergence of 'associations of mutual protection' encompassing both the controllers and the controlled.[9] As we have seen, Malenkov, who called this phenomenon *krugovaya poruka*, simply imputed it to a subjective distortion of the party line in cadre policy by individual executives and leaders. But the *krugovaya poruka* constituted, in actual fact, a 'systemic' phenomenon originating from the common imperative of plan fulfilment which presented all institutions with the same structure of goals and priorities and an analogous system of incentives and criteria for evaluation of performance. This compelled control officials at the bottom of every organization (e.g. ministerial inspectors, trade union and local soviet personnel) to enter into relations of mutual protection with the industrial managers, whatever their original personal loyalty to the centre.

These included party officials both from primary party organizations and, first and foremost, from local party committees which were dependent to a large extent on the successful performance of the enterprises within their jurisdiction. They were indeed to provide the informal horizontal integration needed to overcome the departmental fragmentation of resources and power, and without which the system could not work. But in playing this role with an eye to the common criteria for performance evaluation, the party organs could not remain independent *vis-à-vis* the vested interests of the local managers and administrators that they were supposed to supervise on behalf of the centre.[10] Their vertical loyalty was seriously challenged as the party machine found itself trapped in *mestni-chestvo* ('localism'), which is understood here as the result of flexible, informal *ad hoc* alliances among various departmental interests operating in a given territory.

Thus, the system of administration and control which developed during Stalin's time did contain some bult-in constraints on the implementation of certain kinds of central decisions and the effective exercise of control. It induced, at the same time, the emergence of peripheral inter-bureaucratic alliances cemented by 'mutual protection' and co-ordinated by the local party committees. Their decisive influence on centre–periphery relations and the measure of their power rested less in their ability to participate in decision making than in their grip on the executive process. Furthermore, they represented something more than a mere localistic, 'familistic' or patronage phenomenon to be smashed by replacing 'bad cadres' with new party men loyal to Moscow. They were rooted in a much more compelling convergence of vested interest coalescing in the periphery of the system, and constituted a functional cog in the machinery of administration. Any new 'prefect' sent to work on the spot had to come to terms with these if he was to achieve the results on the basis of which his performance, as well as that of the other members of the alliance, was ultimately evaluated.

THE POST-STALIN LEADERSHIP: KHRUSHCHEV'S ADAPTATION

With the end of the post-war reconstruction, and especially after Stalin's death, those policy areas where sub-implementation had been up till then tolerated for the sake of plan fulfilment in strategic industrial sectors, seemed to obtain deeper consideration. As a consequence, ensuring implementation of a broader range of goals and getting stable control over the whole administrative process became a more politically sensitive issue than it had been in the past. To what extent did different post-Stalin leaders become aware of the basic changes needed in this respect? In particular, how have they dealt with the primary organizational resource at their disposal, the party machine?

Khrushchev's response aimed at upgrading the role of the party and increasing its direct involvement in economic management. At the 20th Congress in 1956 he stressed that 'the success in every major matter depends to a decisive degree on its leadership and on the work of its local organizations'.[11] The increase in status and responsibility of the party machine, especially at obkom level, was particularly apparent in the Sovnarkhozy reform, which dismantled the central apparatus of several industrial ministries and transferred substantial decisional and control powers to regional economic councils. It was by far Khrushchev's most innovative initiative with a direct impact on centre–periphery relations. Moreover, it portended an alteration in former policy priorities, since more attention was to be paid by the Sovnarkhozy and the local soviets to light industry and the service sector.[12]

The new administrative arrangement, however, did not free industrial managers and Sovnarkhoz officials from pressure for plan fulfilment in key economic sectors. Neither did Khrushchev abandon the 'Stalinist' view of the party machine as an administrative tool for implementing central policies. In his first congress speech as First Secretary he even suggested that earnings of full-time party officials be made dependent upon production results in the enterprises under their jurisdiction.[13] There seemed to be little awareness of the fact that if main production achievements were to provide a common criterion for performance evaluation of both party and managerial cadres, these would continue to share the same structure of goals and priorities and this would strengthen, in turn, their vested interest in connivance and mutual protection.

In fact, in the Khrushchev period the central leadership had to confront the problem of localism to an even greater extent than before. Studying what he termed 'the alliance of community interests' between industrial managers and local administrators in those years, J. F. Hough found that the local parties had remained less 'stern enforcers of central priorities' than 'incorrigible representatives of localism'.[14]

COPING WITH THE PARTY MACHINE

If Khrushchev did not seem to be prepared to counteract the systemic constraints inherited from the past, he did seem convinced that the major flaw of the system lay in subjective factors: the personality cult, the arbitrary rule of the 'little Stalins' in the provinces and, above all, a faulty cadre policy. The way in which a heavily interventionist central manipulation of party appointments was used as one of the principal means to regain control of centre–periphery relations, shows the continuing confidence of the leadership in the old principle that (new) cadres could in fact 'decide everything'.[15] But the high rate of turnover among regional first secretaries over the years and the large use of cross-regional transfer also testify to the continuing dissatisfaction of the leadership with party personnel. Indeed, in 1961 Khrushchev sought to expand and institutionalize the 'instability of cadres' by changing the party rules so as to introduce compulsory restrictions of the term as secretary in a primary organization (two years) and a fixed turnover rate for the membership of local committees (at least half at each election). Finally, he gradually abandoned his early conciliatory attitude towards the party machine as a whole. In 1956 he had proposed to use material incentives as a means of raising the responsibility of officials for their job. In 1961, on the contrary, Khrushchev called for a widening of the non-professional, unpaid basis (*obshchestvennye nachala*), in party work and the reduction of the permanent apparatus *vis-à-vis* the ordinary activists and rank-and-file members. The job prospects for the full-time party cadre were particularly frightening: in entering the phase of 'full-scale communist construction' the party should set itself as an example of communist public self-government, where 'the people themselves will manage the affairs of society without special apparatus'.[16]

All these measures, including the ideological appeals to broad mass participation and criticism of the apparatus from below, revealed a frenetic search for better control over the performance of the party machine 'from top to bottom and from bottom to top', which was felt to be of 'paramount importance'. There was indeed growing awareness that it did not work as smoothly and reliably as expected. 'A strict procedure must be instituted – said Khrushchev at the 22nd Congress – for the rendering of accounts by local party agencies to higher party committees and to the Communist masses on the implementation of party decisions'.[17] Yet the flaw inherent in such a muddle was evident. While in themselves inadequate to restrain the centrifugal forces at work in the system, Khrushchev's measures threatened to various degrees the position of local and middle-level officials and eventually alienated consensus and support to the leader's policies and methods.

THE BREZHNEV DEAL: CHANGES IN POLICY ORIENTATION AND THE SEARCH FOR BETTER CONTROL

When we turn to consider the Brezhnev period we see that the new leadership considered a change in policy orientation along the above lines to be urgent. Moreover, it had to be of a systemic kind.

At the 22nd Congress in 1966, great confidence was placed in the economic reform, which sought to regularize managerial behaviour by economic methods and incentives where administrative pressure and controls had failed. This was coupled with the assertion that 'plans for the future' must not contain unrealistic provisions and must make effective use 'of the possibilities of the national economy'.[18] Furthermore, what in 1966 had been announced as a 'substantial convergence' of the rates of growth of group A and group B industries in the near future, at the following Congress in 1971 had become the promise for a 'certain preponderance' in the growth rates of group B.[19] (An objective Brezhnev admitted had not been achieved by 1976, and was resumed in 1981 though in a less pressing form.)

The relative shift in priorities was explained by referring both to the 'rapidly growing demands that society makes on the economy' and the 'new factors that distinguish today's economy from the economy of the late 1930s'. The stage in which it had been 'compulsory to concentrate on the highest priorities' was said to have come to an end. The new stage of development which the economy and society were entering – doctrinally defined as 'developed socialism' – was one where complexity and interdependence dominated, and demanded the 'simultaneous accomplishment of a broader range of goals'.[20]

The Brezhnev leadership showed great awareness of the fact that the new goals could not be accomplished by merely issuing *ad hoc* directives. They relied to a much greater extent on the role of the law in regulating the administrative process. New norms and regulations were issued not only in the field of industrial management and labour relations, but in all spheres of governmental administration. Under Brezhnev the legislative process revealed a systematic effort to stabilize and normalize public life, upgrade the role of formal state institutions and make the whole apparatus work by the rule. It constituted an attempt to transmit to the periphery of the system an integrated set of predictable rules of behaviour which ought to facilitate the transparency and control of administrative performance. Indeed, the stress on the rule of law can be considered the major contribution of the Brezhnev era to Soviet political development, which has been labelled by a Western analyst the 'juridicization' of the system, a move towards the creation of a 'Soviet-style Rechsstaat'.[21] The whole question of policy implementation and control came gradually to be identified, in the Brezhnev years, with the subject of law enforcement. In 1976 Brezhnev reported with pride at the 25th Congress:

> A question that we have dealt with constantly is the question of improving our legislation and strengthening socialist law and order [...] We have brought juridical norms into line with the new level our society has achieved. Statutes have been drafted covering spheres of life that in the past were outside the framework of legal regulation [...] Apparently the time has come to issue a code of laws of the Soviet state. This will help to increase the stability of our entire structure of law and order.[22]

Many of these new regulations aimed at improving control in such areas as managerial procedures and prerogatives, territorial development and planning, environmental protection, provision of social services. Moreover, they were accompanied by a reform of the institutions of local government which was crucial in the attempt to redress the balance of centre–periphery relations. It aimed at a redistribution of administrative responsibilities and authority at the local level which would strengthen the position of the local soviets *vis-à-vis* the industrial managers and departmental and localistic interests.

Despite the progress made in some of these fields over the years, however, on the whole the outcome has been poor compared to expectations. Brezhnev's programme faced the resistance of vested interests both in central and peripheral administration to such an extent that much of it got lost in the process of implemention.

It is known, for instance, that the failure of the economic reforms of the 1960s owes much to the ability of local officials and executives to resist change imposed from above.[23] Departmental interests and ministries' protection of illegal managerial practices have seriously called into question the effectiveness of the environmental legislation issues since the early 1970s.[24] In like manner, despite a long series of party directives and laws, the ability of industrial managers and ministries to encroach upon local soviets' prerogatives has been a decisive factor in hampering the reform of local government. In the field of control over housing and social services it has been so pervasive that the true state of urban and regional development bears very little resemblance to the dictate of the law. Here the question arises as to who actually governs the country – the centralized pyramid of the 'local organs of state power' or an array of industrial administration each concerned merely with its own interests.[25]

The political sensitivity of such policy failures during the Brezhnev years can hardly be underestimated, and suggests a situation in which, as has been pointed out by M. Urban, 'the actual operations of the system are largely beyond the control of the political centre'.[26]

Evidence of the political leadership's apprehensive realization of its weakness *vis-à-vis* centrifugal forces and interests is not lacking in Brezhnev's speeches at the 25th and 26th Congresses. He admitted the failure of the attempt to attain balanced development between group A and group B industries, and between branch and territorial principles. He also repeatedly stressed that the 'interests' of the enterprises and the ministries still did not 'coincide' with those of the state. Finally, in 1981 he recognized that progress in law formulation had not been followed by progress in law enforcement.[27]

It would seem that there have been attempts on the part of the Brezhnev leadership to induce at least some relevant changes in the way the system operated. These were concerned with a relaxation of plans, balance of production priorities, introduction of new material incentives, more attention to 'qualitative' policy areas and, above all, the stress on the rule of law. However, it has not been able to thwart the resistance of vested interests of both party and economic institutions which combine at the periphery of the system and act there in such a way as to alter policies in the implementation phase. Being incapable of smashing what a Western scholar has termed the 'local power elites',[28] Brezhnev offered them a 'deal' based on bargaining and consensus. This was a radical change in the Soviet leadership's treatment of centre–periphery relations.

THE PARTY MACHINE AND CENTRE–PERIPHERY RELATIONS

The content of the new deal in centre–periphery relations is exemplified in the approach to party cadre policy. It seems to have been based on a sort of pact. Job security, stable career patterns and less arbitrary central manipulation of staffing procedures were offered in exchange for more reliable upward information, executive discipline and vertical loyalty. The terms of the 'deal' can be found in Brezhnev's speeches at the 23rd and 24th Congresses; an increasingly critical assessment of how it worked was given in the two Congresses in 1976 and 1981.

Regular, foreseeable and locally-based careers were being offered for the first time to the apparatus. In return for what was termed 'complete trust in cadres', the central leadership had something to demand. First, the 'improvement of inner-party channels of information'.[29] In 1971, Brezhnev noted that 'the information that goes from the bottom to the top, up to the Central Committee' had become more efficient and that it should be continually improved and used 'as an instrument of leadership and a means of upbringing and control'. Second, discipline, though one which was not built on 'fear or methods of ruthless administrative fiat' but on a 'high level of people's consciousness and responsibility'. Third, loyalty to the centre, that is that all local organizations 'steadily implement the party's policy and serve as loyal bulwark of the CPSU Central Committee'.[30]

If the pact were respected, this was the implication of Brezhnev's reasoning, the influence of the party as a whole could be strengthened by enhancing the role and responsibility of the territorial organizations, broadening the control powers of the primary organizations in the state and economic apparatuses, and mobilizing the entire machine for the implementation of the 'correct party line'.

Western analyses of the career patterns of the obkom first secretaries under Brezhnev have confirmed that on the whole the leadership kept their promises. The pace and scope of turnover have declined, cross-regional transfers and centrally imposed appointments have decreased while a much larger proportion of officials have been recruited locally.[31] The latter point is of particular relevance. Examining the working of the *nomenklatura* system as a whole in the last two decades, J. H. Miller has suggested that its centralized nature may have grown weaker in response to systemic pressures originating from the difficulty faced by an overcentralized system to get enough detailed and undistorted information about local situations. According to this interpretation, in selecting local men to handle local problems the central leadership would not seek to prevent the identification of party officials with local interests (i.e. the formation of local elites or, as he put it, of 'regional lobbies') but would rather 'let them represent their localities in dealing with the centre'.[32] This seems confirmed by other analyses of intra-party representation of regional interests.[33] If this is so, however, the question arises as to whether these cadres have *also* worked effectively as representatives of central authority and enforcers of central priorities in their localities in any more meaningful way than in the past. To extend the question to the entire party machine, we could ask whether Brezhnev had succeeded in getting more reliable information, executive discipline and vertical loyalty in return for his new policy of trust and stability. Or, to put it another way: has the party machine respected the terms of the deal it was offered and served as a 'loyal bulwark of the Central Committee'?

If one has to judge from the sequence of policy failures recalled above, the answer is rather in the negative. On the whole the party machine seems to have been of little help in ensuring implementation of the leadership's programme, especially when this involved challenging powerful vested interests. The peripheral party cadres and the local administrators had taken advantage of the 'deal', but had withdrawn in defence of their own interests. Trust in cadres had backfired.

The report at the 25th and 26th Congress testified to the increasing awareness among the central leadership that the 'deal' had not worked as had been expected. In 1976 Brezhnev, noting the 'lax control' over local policy implementation, threatened changes in his policy of trust and stability if the situation did not improve.[34] In 1981 the toughest criticism was levelled against the primary party organizations, which followed the lead of the management when it acted 'improperly', did not struggle to overcome 'departmental and bureaucratic obstacles', and were not 'resolute and uncompromising' enough in guarding the 'interests of the state'.[33] As for the control over the implementation of decisions, it remained 'a weak point in the work of a large number of party organizations'. Here Brezhnev referred to both the quality of the leadership and the apathy of the party members and reaffirmed that, once a decision has been adopted 'control should be carried out systematically and efficiently, both from above and below'.[35]

But the weakest point of all, apparently, was the state of inner-party information, whose perfection was a basic aim of the Brezhnev deal. Brezhnev re-emphasized that upward information was essential in order to get 'a more concrete picture of the state of affairs on the local level'. But here the situation seemed to have grown worse. So ineffectively had the party machine worked as a reliable communication channel between the centre and the periphery that the Central Committee had to bypass it and resort to 'independent' channels such as the letters sent by ordinary citizens and rank-and-file members. The seriousness of the situation is revealed by the fact that a special letters department was created in the Central Committee for their systematic scrutiny which received roughly 1500 of them every day. 'Many of these letters' as Brezhnev put it 'are, unfortunately, an index of serious shortcomings at the local level.' It is perhaps indicative of the power of resistence of the local and middle-level apparatus that, although the situation had objectively worsened, at the 26th Congress Brezhnev played down the 'language of accusation' and did not threaten forced retirements. His report conveys, rather, an image of impotence when he reminds the audience, for instance, that 'democratic centralism is an immutable norm of the Communist Party's life. It presupposes, among other things, the closest possible link between the centre and the localities [. . .]. And this is a two-way link.'[36]

The Brezhnev years, whether in the realm of policy implementation or with regard to the attitude towards the party machine, point to centre–periphery relations as a crucial political dilemma with which any new 'reformist' leadership is presented. It shows that, as R. J. Hill has argued, the answer to the difficulties involved in controlling peripheral apparatuses and inducing them to act in the desired direction 'is not necessarily to send trouble-shooters from the centre'. But, on the other hand, the choice of relying on local cadres has not proved a much better alternative from the centre's point of view. 'In either case', Hill concludes, 'the reforming leadership fails.'[37]

The problem of localism has assumed such dramatic a dimension during the last decade that it can be said that Brezhnev's successors have inherited a situation in which central control over both party and governmental machines in the periphery was at its lowest point. The overall governmental capacity of the system was at stake.

SOME HYPOTHESES ABOUT CENTRE–PERIPHERY RELATIONS UNDER GORBACHEV

During his first two years in power Gorbachev has often called for the unravelling of the 'gross output tangle' [*valovy uzel*] which strangles the economy, and has stressed his commitment to the restructuring of managerial methods, the primacy of quality over quantity and the centrality of social policy. However if one is to assess the content and nature of Gorbachev's policy programme, there can be little doubt that the new leadership is presented with the problem of ensuring implementation of a set of measures which are perceived, within the country, as 'revolutionary changes.' As a consequence, it must search for adequate answers to the danger of ungovernability which confronts it. Above all, it needs to strengthen political control over the periphery of the administrative system.

THE PARTY MACHINE AND THE STRUGGLE AGAINST LOCALISM

Living examples of the centrifugal force of the local–bureaucratic alliances of interests resisting change and escaping central control have emerged with particular vigour in Soviet central press during the past two years, due to the policy of *glasnost'* and the new 'militant' attitude of the media.

Gorbachev himself has denounced more than one exemplary episode and has expressed 'serious concern'. Among the most glaring is the scandal of Rashidov's Uzbekistan, brought up in the speech at the 27th Congress. There a sort of 'impunity' was enjoyed by local officials in 'many sectors of party, governmental, and economic work' with the connivence, he suggested, of officials from all-Union bodies 'including the Central Committee' who went to Uzbekistan on many occasions and 'must have noticed what was happening'.[38] He also cited the cases of Moscow and Kirgizia and generalized by saying that 'at some stage some republics, territories, regions, and cities were placed out of bounds to criticism', 'outside the pale of control', and that this applied to party organizations, ministries, departments and enterprises.

Similarly, Gorbachev's speech at the June (1986) Plenum contained examples of 'overt resistance' in enterprises and localities where economic executives, with the backing of primary party organizations and territorial party committees, fought against people who were taking *perestroika* seriously.

The first moves of the new leadership in coping with the phenomenon of localism have shown a tendency to revive the traditional features of the pre-Brezhnevite cadre policy, though with some adaptations. A resumption of cross-regional transfers as a means of keeping a check on localism has been authoritatively advocated by E. Ligachev in his speech at the 27th Congress, and has actually taken place, especially during Gorbachev's first year.[39] On the other hand, several local cadres have been brought to Moscow to work as inspectors of the Central Committee for some time before obtaining the first secretaryship in their native regions. This unusual career pattern, apparently aimed at strengthening the vertical political ties of future local leaders, was started under Andropov and has continued under Gorbachev, although there is no evidence that it will be institutional-ized.[40] Both these arrangements are consistent with Gorbachev's state-ments against 'stagnation in the movement of personnel' made as early as at the April (1985) Plenum.[41] Indeed, on the whole the pace and scope of turnover among obkom first secretaries during the new leader's first year in power have been impressive and have not come to a halt yet, although after the 27th Congress they have declined somewhat. Nor is the new dynamism of cadre movement confined to obkom leaders. At the June (1986) Plenum, Gorbachev stated that there still were 'quite a few unresolved cadre matters' and that 'the placement of cadres should continue to be improved'.[42] A month later *Pravda* carried a leading article entitled 'The First Secretary' in which it sharply criticized not only obkom, but also raikom and gorkom leaders, referring to them by name, and implicitely announced a new wave of replacements.[43] After some time, it was revealed that 33 per cent of officials from primary party organizations had also been replaced by the end of 1986 (one third of them during that year alone).[44]

What has taken place thus far, however, might be above all a generational rotation, and it is too early to draw conclusions about cadre mobility as a long-term strategy of the leadership. The most recent evidence on this matter is not unambiguous and there already are some signs of a return to a more stable and locally based pattern of political career for party leaders.[45] Furthermore, expectations that the new party Rules would resume Khrushchev's provisions for compulsory turnover in party organs have proved unjustified, and such provisions have also been dropped from the new CPSU programme both for party organs and local soviets (a step that Brezhnev was not able to undertake in nearly twenty years).[46]

Other changes made in the Rules may be more relevant for the activity of the peripheral party machine. First, among the basic duties of the local party organs there is now the ensuring of 'improvement of output quality', while reference to 'overfulfilment' of plans has been dropped. Second, the two-fold responsibility of party cadres first to the law and then to the party is clearly stated. Third, a completely new paragraph has been inserted in Rule 28 which requires the local organs to provide 'objective and timely information about their activity and the local state of affairs'.[47]

To conclude, there are going to be new people in charge of the party machine in the periphery and trust in them cannot be taken for granted: they are held answerable for something more than mere 'plan fulfilment and overfulfilment' and are subject to stricter control from above. Relevant though they may be, these changes are nevertheless a mixture of old and new and they do not answer to the crucial political question: how to ensure that new cadres bound to new official obligations will in fact act in the desired direction and lead state and economic institutions accordingly.

It is only during the second year in power, when the new leaders came to realize publicly that resistance was stronger than expected in both the party and the government machines, that an answer to this question began to take shape. It is known in the USSR as 'political reform', and its most relevant institutional feature is the proposal to introduce multi-candidate, secret-ballot elections in party, soviet and economic organizations.

A POLITICAL REFORM FOR BETTER CONTROL?

The history of the reform has not been straightforward. A commitment, if vague, to the 'perfection of the electoral system' was inserted into the new edition of the party Programme only after public discussion of the draft.[48] In the course of the discussion it had also been proposed that the new party Rules establish multi-candidate, secret-ballot elections in party organizations, but no mention of such provision was endorsed in the final text. On the contrary, the extension of *open ballot* procedure for elections in the party was advocated by no less an authoritative leader than E. Ligachev.[47] As for elections in enterprises and economic organizations, Gorbachev dwelt on these in his congress speech, but implied that they would be confined to foremen and junior officials.[49]

Then, in the summer of 1986, dissatisfaction with the progress of implementation of *perestroika* grew more evident in the speeches made by Gorbachev in Soviet Far East. The emphasis of democratization and involving people in politics grew accordingly. But on 31 July 1986, speaking on this matter in Khabarovsk, Gorbachev cautiously affirmed: 'There may be proposals for which conditions are not ripe; then we must tell people so'.[50] It was not until January 1987, when the Plenum, expected for December and three times postponed, was finally held, that he officially submitted the proposal to the Central Committee.

Gorbachev's speech at the January Plenum aimed at considering the cadre issue in 'a broader social and political context'. He said that the people expressed 'concern' about the way the process of restructuring was being implemented in practice, and that the problems which had accumulated in society were 'deeper than we first thought'. He dwelt at length on the slackening of control over political and bureaucratic dynamics, which he presented as the essence of the 'lessons of the past'. The socialist property had often become '"no one's", free, without a real owner', and the authority of the plan had been 'subverted' by subjectivistic approaches, imbalances, and 'a host of decisions of a sectoral and regional character'. In enterprises and economic institutions the primary party organizations had allowed 'permissiveness and mutual protectionism', while 'many party members holding leading posts were outside control or criticism'.[51] The confusion of functions between party and managerial bodies, which accounted for a great part of these distortions, could be explained by subjective as well as objective factors, the latter being connected with 'a number of unresolved economic management issues'. All these negative phenomena, which had deep roots in the past, had raised 'contradictions' which were not scientifically analyzed because 'the theoretical concepts of socialism remained to a large extent at the level of the 1930s–1940s, when the society had been tackling entirely different tasks'.[52] As a consequence, the forms of organization of society which had emerged in practice become 'absolutized'.

Gorbachev's report at the Plenum of January 1987 provided a most comprehensive, systemic analysis of the problems involved in the governing of the country. It is in this context that we can interpret his electoral reform as an attempt to regain political control over the centrifugal forces which operate within the system. Here is how Gorbachev puts it:

> The democratization of society poses anew the question of control over how the party, local soviet and economic bodies and their cadres work. As far as control 'from above' is concerned, marked changes, as you know, have occurred in this respect of late.

But it is practically impossible to reach from above all the interstices of the apparatus where the informal alliances of interests flourish and, by establishing relations of mutual protection, are able to resist or distort undesired central measures. Indeed, as Gorbachev had to recognize, 'we take the necessary decisions but, as before, we do not implement them to the full and on time'. Thus,

> Even given all the importance of control 'from above', it is of fundamental importance to raise the level and effectiveness of control 'from below' so that each leader and each official constantly feels his responsibility to and his dependence on the electorate [. . .]. If we achieve such control [. . .] most matters will be solved at local level. In the conditions of broad democratism, people themselves will put things in order in their collective, town or village.[53]

The latter passage is quite explicit. The purpose of the reform is to activate a system of control over cadres which is *constant* and *effective*, much more than Stalin's 'searchlights', Khrushchev's continuing 'reshufflings', and Brezhnev's 'bargainings'. Furthermore, as Gorbachev says, referring to secret-ballot, multi-candidate election of party secretaries, this will 'make it possible to determine more accurately the degree of their authority'. That is to say, the centre could finally 'measure', through the ballot box, the power base of individual local cadres.

At this stage it is difficult to forecast the political impact the reform will have *if* implemented. It would take a number of years to see how it can affect the structure of political power and the dynamics of bureaucratic politics in the USSR. Undoubtedly, fierce resistence is to be expected from thousands of local administrators, economic managers and party cadres to whom the reform could mean a dramatic change in the rules of the game they have learned to play in their lifetime. Furthermore, there must be dozens of ways to turn elections into mere window-dressing, especially in the periphery, many of which are well known in Western societies and will be readily understood in the Soviet Union too. The pervasive power of clientelism and patronage is hardly stopped by the secret of the ballot box. On the other hand, even such a resistance would imply the development of a capacity of adaptation to rules which are new in the soviet political context and alien to the political culture of the system. For instance, however manipulated the pre-selection of candidates may be, a multi-candidate election is likely to generate a certain measure of genuine uncertainty for the career prospects of some individual cadres. As a consequence, the traditional principles of cadre policy and the *nomenklatura* system, which have up to now constituted a two-player game between the central authorities and the local officials, cannot be left completely unaltered by the presence of a third player, the electorate, with the ultimate *kratos* to choose between the alternatives with which it is presented. It is indeed the support of this third player that the central leaders are trying to activate in their attempt to regain control over the peripheral political-administrative apparatus and process. As far as we are interested here in the leadership's perspectives on centre–periphery relations, the sole decision to initiate such a change in the rules of the game is of great relevance.

CONCLUSIONS

In this chapter we have identified a pattern of political dynamics whereby 'politics' (intended here as a conflict of interests over policy) tends to 'withdraw' from the central decision-making process into the peripheral process of implementation and to act, here, in the shade. T. Zaslavskaya has recently pointed out that, until the social and motivational structure of this covert political process remains unknown, it is impossible to realize 'whose interests come into conflict with restructuring' and, as a consequence, 'measures that one would think are needed by everyone are implemented in such a distorted way as to be unrecognizable.'[54]

It is the hidden nature of their interests and their crucial position in the information flow about the executive process, that gives the peripheral politico-administrative elites the opportunity to exercise the power of deception, resistence and even opposition. The dynamics of the interaction between central and peripheral elites thus give us a centrifugal picture of the Soviet political system, with a definite amount of local autonomy and a relative weakness of the central government in crucial policy areas. While such a picture is most unusual in Western literature, it seems to be a common perception for all Soviet leaders. Furthermore, the ways they have tried to unravel the political dilemma of centre–periphery relations have differed, but they all had in common the central role assigned to the party machine as the main organizational weapon of the centre to exercise its control.

Despite apparent repeated failure to bring the party machine itself under central control, this aim has not been abandoned by Gorbachev either. But the new leadership seems now aware of the finite nature of the different alternatives tested during the first seventy years of Soviet power and seem determined to develop its analytical and governmental capacities. Gorbachev's political reform could give voice to those covert interests and compel them to express themselves openly. It could create, at the same time, a more effective and transparent channel of communication between the periphery and the centre. All this would generate conflicts, of course, both within and without the party machine, but a certain measure of *open* conflict may be now considered functional to the exercise of political control. Indeed, what the leadership needs in the localities is more trouble-makers than trouble-shooters.

NOTES AND REFERENCES

1 This study has greatly benefitted from discussion within the research group on the Soviet political system which operates at the Servizio Documentazione Paesi Socialisti of the Oriental University Institute of Naples, under the direction of Professor Rita di Leo. Theoretically, I am especially indebited to her latest 'Il partito e lo stato tra utopia e localismo', *Rivista Trimestrale*, no. 4, March, 1987.

2 V. I. Lenin, 'Pyat' let rossiskoi revolyutsii i perspektivy mirovoi revolyutsii., *Sochineniya*, Moscow: Gos. Izd. Politicheskoi Literatury, 1950, vol. 33, p. 394.

3 See I. V. Stalin, 'Otchetnyi doklad XVII s"ezdu partii o rabote TsK VKP(b), in I. Stalin, *Sochineniya*, Gos. Izd. Politicheskoi Literatury, Moscow, 1951, vol. 13, pp. 372–4, and I. V. Stalin, 'Otchetnyi doklad na XVIII s"ezde partii o rabote TsK VKP(b)', in *Vsesoyuznaya Kommunisticheskaya Partiya (bolshevikov) v rezolyutsiyakh i resheniyakh s"ezdov, knoferentsii i plenumov TsK*, Politizdat, Moscow, 1941, vol. 2, pp. 714–5.

4 See G. M. Malenkov, 'Otchetnyi doklad TsK VKP(b) XIX s"ezdu partii', in *Pravda*, 6 October 1952, pp. 7–8.

5 For an interpretation of the political dynamics of the 1930s which stresses the difficulty of the centre in ensuring implementation of its decisions and in exercising control over the local party machine, see J. A. Getty, *The Origins of the Great Purges. The Soviet Communist Party Reconsidered*, Cambridge University Press, Cambridge, 1985. In chapter 10 Catherine Merridale also touches upon similar points in relation to the Moscow party organization between 1925 and 1932.

6 See J. S. Berliner, *Factory and Manager in the USSR*, Harvard University Press, Cambridge, Mass., 1957; D. Granick, *Management of the Industrial Firm in the USSR*, Columbia University Press, New York, 1954.

7 See W. Taubman, *Governing Soviet Cities, Bureaucratic Politics and Urban Development in the USSR*, Praeger, New York, 1973; G. D. Andrusz, *Housing and Urban Development in the USSR*, Macmillan, London, 1984.

8 On this point see T. H. Rigby, 'Political Legitimacy, Weber and Communist Mono-organizational Systems', in T. H. Rigby, F. Feher (eds), *Political Legitimation in Communist States*, Macmillan, London, 1982.

9 M. Fainsod, *How Russia is Ruled*, Harvard University Press, Cambridge, 1953, pp. 328–9.

10 See J. S. Berliner, op. cit., chapter XV. As *Informant 16* in Berliner's interview project remarked referring to a district party committee, this 'was an organization where officials from different enterprises and institutions met informally and could settle things in a friendly manner'. See ibid, p. 269.

11 N. S. Khrushchev, 'Otchetnyi doklad tsentral'nogo komiteta KPSS XX s˝ezdu partii' [14 February 1956], *XX s˝ezd KPSS (stenograficheskii otchet)*, Moscow: Gos. Izd. Politicheskoi Literatury, 1956, vol. 1, p. 100.

12 On this point see H. R. Swearer, 'Administration of Local Industry after the 1957 Industrial Reorganization', *Soviet Studies*, 1961, vol. 12, no. 3, January; D. T. Catell, 'Local Government and the Sovnarkhoz in the USSR, 1957–1962', *Soviet Studies*, 1964, vol. 15, no. 4, April.

13 See N. S. Khrushchev, (20th CPSU Congress, 1956), op. cit., p. 107. On Khrushchev's view of the role of the party see E. P. Hoffmann, 'Soviet Perspectives on Leadership and Administration', in E. P. Hoffmann, R. F. Laird (eds), *The Soviet Polity in the Modern Era*, Aldine, New York, 1984, p. 112.

14 J. F. Hough, *The Soviet Prefects: the Local Party Organs in Industrial Decision-making*, Harvard University Press, Cambridge, 1969, p. 256.

15 On turnover in the party under Khrushchev see T. H. Rigby, 'The Soviet Regional Leadership: The Brezhnev Generation', *Slavic Review*, 1978, vol. 37, no. 1, March, pp. 4–5.

16 N. S. Khrushchev, 'Otchetenyi doklad tsentral'nogo komiteta KPSS XXII s˝ezdu Kommunisticheckoi Partii Sovetskogo Soyuza' [14 October 1961], *XXII s˝ezd KPSS (stenograficheskii otchet)*, Moscow: Gos. Izd. Politicheskoi Literatury, 1962, vol. 1, pp. 114–15.

17 Ibid., p. 117.

18 L. I. Brezhnev 'Otchetenyi doklad tsentral'nogo komiteta KPSS XXIII s˝ezdu Kommunisticheskoi Partii Sovetskogo Soyuza' [29 March 1966], *XXIII s˝ezd KPSS (stenograficheskii otchet)*, Moscow: Izd. Politicheskoi Literatury, 1966, vol. 1, p. 83.

19 L. I. Brezhnev 'Otchetenyi doklad tsentral'nogo komiteta KPSS XXIV s˝ezdu Kommunisticheskoi Partii Sovetskogo Soyuza' [30 March 1971], *XXIV s˝ezd KPSS (stenograficheskii otchet)*, Moscow: Izd Politicheskoi Literatury, 1971, vol. 1, p. 69.

20 Ibid., pp. 62–3.

21 R. Sharlet, 'Constitutional Implementation and the Juridicization of the Soviet System', in D. R. Kelley (ed.), *Soviet Politics in the Brezhnev Era*, Praeger, New York, 1980, p. 200.

22 L. I. Brezhnev 'Otchet tsentral'nogo komiteta KPSS i ocherednye zadachi partii v oblasti vnutrennei i vneshnei politiki' [24 February 1976], *XXV s˝ezd*

KPSS (stenografcheskii otchet), Moscow: Izd. Politicheskoi Literatury, 1976, vol. 1, pp. 108–9.

23 See, K. W. Ryavec, *Implementation of Soviet Economic Reforms. Political, Organizational and Social Processes*, Praeger, New York, 1975.

24 See, for instance, C. Ziegler, 'Soviet Environmental Policy and Soviet Central Planning', *Soviet Studies*, 1980, vol. 32, no. 1, January.

25 See the essays by H. W. Morton, 'Local Soviets and the Attempt to rationalize the Delivery of Urban Services: The Case of Housing', and D. T. Cattell, 'Local Government and the Provision of Consumer Goods and Services', both in E. M. Jacobs (ed.), *Soviet Local Politics and Government*, Allen & Unwin, London, 1983; and, in more detail, C. Ross, *Soviet Local Government. Problems of Implementation and Control*, Croom Helm, London, 1987.

26 M. E. Urban, 'Conceptualizing Political Power in the USSR: Patterns of Binding and Bonding', *Studies in Comparative Communism*, 1985, vol. 18, no. 4, Winter 1985. See also N. Lampert, *Whistleblowing in the Soviet Union. Complaints and Abuses under State Socialism*, Macmillan, London, 1985.

27 See L. I. Brezhnev, (25th CPSU congress, 1976), op. cit., pp. 22, 79, 84; and L. I. Brezhnev, 'Otchet tsentral'nogo komiteta KPSS i ocherednye zadachi partii v oblasti vnutrennei i vneshnei politiki' [23 February 1981], *XXVI s˝ezd KPSS (stenografcheskii otchet)*, Moscow: Izd. Politicheskoi Literatury, 1981, vol. 1, p. 68.

28 See V. Andrle, *Managerial Power in the Soviet Union*, Saxon House, Westmead, 1976, pp. 133–4.

29 L. I. Brezhnev, (23rd CPSU congress, 1966), op. cit., p. 89.

30 L. I. Brezhnev, (24th CPSU congress, 1971), op. cit., pp. 120, 123, 126.

31 See T. H. Rigby, op. cit., p. 121; J. F. Hough, 'Changes in Soviet Elite Composition', in S. Bialer and T. Gustafson, *Russian at the Crossroads. The 26th Congress of the CPSU*, Allen & Unwin, London, 1982, p. 59; J. H. Miller, 'Nomenklatura: Check in Localism?', in T. H. Rigby and B. Harasymiw (eds), *Leadership Selection and Patron-Client Relations in the USSR and Yugoslavia*, Allen & Unwin, London, 1983.

32 J. H. Miller, 'The Communist Party: Trends and Problems', in A. Brown and M. Kaser (eds), *Soviet Policy for the 1980s*, Macmillan, London, 1982, pp. 21–3.

33 See, for instance, H. L. Biddulph, 'Local Interests Articulation at CPSU Congresses', *World Politics*, 1983, vol. 36, no. 1, October; G. W. Breslauer, 'Is There a Generation Gap in the Soviet Political Establishment?: Demand Articulation by RSFSR Provincial Party First Secretaries', *Soviet Studies*, 1984, no. 1, January; G. Breslauer, 'Provincial Party Leaders, Demand Articulation and the Nature of Centre–Periphery Relations in the USSR', *Slavic Review*, 1986, vol. 45, no. 4, Winter.

34 L. I. Brezhnev, (25th CPSU Congress, 1976), op. cit., pp. 94, 96.

35 L. I. Brezhnev, (24th CPSU Congress, 1981), op. cit., p. 90.

36 Ibid., p. 92.

37 R. J. Hill, *Soviet Politics, Political Science and Reform*, Martin Robertson, Oxford, 1980, p. 172.

38 M. S. Gorbachev, 'Politicheskii doklad TsK KPSS XXVII s˝ezdy Kommunisticheskoi Partii Sovetskogo Soyuza' [25 February 1986], *Materialy XXVII s˝ezda KPSS*, Moscow: Izd. Politicheskoi Literatury, 1986, pp. 80–81.

39 See E. Ligachev's speech at the 27th Party Congress in *Pravda*, 28 February 1986. The appointment of the Russian-born G. Kolbin as first secretary of the

Kazakh party after the demotion of Kunaev is the most clear example of the revival of this strategy.

40   For a quantitative analysis of this new pattern of cadre policy see T. Gustafson and D. Mann, 'Gorbachev's First Year: Building Power and Authority', *Problems of Communism*, 1986, vol. 35, no. 3, May–June 1986, pp. 6–7; and Chapter 2 of this book.

41   *Pravda*, 24 April 1985, p. 2.

42   *Pravda*, 17 June 1986, p. 3.

43   *Pravda*, 22 July 1987, p. 1.

44   See *Pravda*, 14 January 1987 (previous data are given in *Pravda*, 12 February 1986).

45   This is documented in T. Gustafson and D. Mann, 'Gorbachev's Next Gamble', *Problems of Communism*, 1987.

46   See S. White, 'The New Programme and Rules of the CPSU', *The Journal of Communist Studies*, 1986, vol. 2, no. 2, June.

47   See Rules 42, 12 and 28 in 'The Communist Party Progam and Party Statutes. Final Version', in *Current Digest of the Soviet Press*, Special Supplement, December 1986, pp. 29, 31.

48   See E. Ligachev, 'Sovetuyas' s partei, s narodom', *Kommunist*, no. 16, 1986.

49   M. S. Gorbachev, (27th CPSU congress, 1986), op. cit., pp. 59–60.

50   *Pravda*, 2 August 1986, p. 2.

51   *Pravda*, 28 January 1987, pp. 1, 2.

52   Ibid., pp. 4.

53   Ibid., p. 3.

54   *Izvestiya*, 21 April 1987, p. 3.

Conclusion

12. Elites, Power, and the Exercise of Political Authority in the USSR

Stephen White

Earlier chapters in this volume have considered a number of political elites in the USSR at both a national and regional level, and have addressed some of the issues of analysis that arise in this connection. As David Lane points out in his introduction, it is essential for the further advance of Soviet elite studies that they be located within such a broader context, a context he defines as the political sociology of state socialism. A broader context of this kind suggests, in particular, that communist elites, however unitary and determined, may face considerable and perhaps increasing difficulties when it comes to imposing their priorities upon the societies over which they rule. In part, as Lane indicates, these obstacles are sociological in character: with economic development, educational levels rise, work activity becomes increasingly differentiated and professional groupings increase in number. In part also, as I shall argue in this chapter, they arise from more directly political circumstances, including the nature of the leadership itself, the existence of institutional or bureaucratic constraints upon its freedom of action, and the restraining force of public opinion. Students of Soviet-type societies, impressed by the totalitarian and other 'directed society' models, have tended to neglect constraints of these kinds; but the study of Soviet elites is seriously incomplete unless it is related to the 'conversion process' by which leadership priorities are turned into public policy by the exercise of political authority.[1]

THE SOVIET LEADERSHIP AND THE LIMITS OF POWER

The first group of constraints to be considered concerns the position of the General Secretary within the leadership as a whole. In the totalitarian conceptualization systems of the Soviet type were seen as essentially Führerist in type, dominated by a single leader who exercised ideological as well as political authority. Current, more widely accepted models generally

269

suggest that the General Secretary is typically at least *primus inter pares* within the leadership, and some have argued that the accession of a new and relatively youthful General Secretary in Mikhail Gorbachev may lead to the re-emergence of a leader-centred Soviet system of a kind that the decrepit Brezhnev and his short-lived successors did not make possible.[2] At least one reason for the gradual accumulation of power in the hands of the General Secretary is the 'circular flow of power', discussed by Gustafson and Mann, by which each successive party leader uses his influence to promote supporters who will in turn support him and promote the continued expansion of his authority.[3] Each successive General Secretary, on this basis, will feel obliged to retain his position in order to defend his 'clients', and may fear for his reputation, if not his physical security, if he should ever leave office. Each group of clients, in their turn, will feel compelled to maintain the position of their patron since their own political fortunes will largely depend upon the extent of his success.

The structural dynamics of the Soviet leadership, and the position of the General Secretary in particular, are still the subject of scholarly debate and only a limited consensus has so far emerged.[4] It is nonetheless clear that the picture so far presented is at least an incomplete one. In the first place, it neglects the structural differentiation of the Soviet leadership which has occurred since the death of Stalin, and which has placed significant constraints upon the power of the General Secretary. To some extent this has been a function of the separation of key posts. Stalin, during the latter part of his period of rule, was Prime Minister, Minister of Defence and Commander in Chief as well as party leader. Khrushchev succeeded him as party leader and (from 1958) as Prime Minister, also becoming Chairman of the Defence Council of the USSR (a post which has now become automatically attached to that of the party General Secretaryship). Brezhnev combined the state presidency (Chairmanship of the Presidium of the USSR Supreme Soviet) with the party leadership from 1977 until his death. Following Khrushchev's resignation in 1964, however, the Central Committee adopted a resolution which provided that in order to guard against the excessive concentration of power in the hands of a single person, the party leadership and prime ministership should in future be held by different people.[5] This important principle has been observed up to the present.

Both Andropov and Chernenko, following Brezhnev, combined the state presidency with the party leadership. Gorbachev, proposing Chernenko for the presidency in April 1984, observed that the Central Committee had considered it 'essential' that the General Secretary should also hold the post of Chairman of the Supreme Soviet Presidium; this reflected the leading role of the party in the wider society and had 'great significance' for the conduct of Soviet foreign policy.[6] In July 1985, however, rather against expectations, it was the veteran foreign minister, Andrei Gromyko, rather than Gorbachev himself, who was elevated to the presidency. Gorbachev, proposing Gromyko for the post, this time explained that although previous circumstances had justified the combination of the party leadership with the state presidency, the Central Committee now took the view that the tasks facing the country were such that the General Secretary should concentrate his entire attentions upon the party's own activities.[7] Gorbachev was himself elected an ordinary member of the Supreme Soviet Presidium, a position which may be felt to allow him to represent the USSR as a whole and not just the CPSU. Although this arrangement may not prove permanent (in many other communist states the party leader is also president, for diplomatic and ceremonial purposes), it does at least for the present represent a further extension of the 'separation of powers' within the leadership, removing a further (admittedly largely symbolic) set of functions from the disposition of the party leader.

A second trend which has also tended to limit the power of the General Secretary has been the increasingly 'institutionalized' composition of the Politburo and of leading party bodies. Rather than a collection of influential individuals, as one recent student of these matters has put it, the Politburo may perhaps better be seen as a collection of important posts, the holders of which are in practice entitled to full or candidate Politburo membership by virtue of office.[8] By the late 1980s the Politburo appeared to have become a combination of three distinct groupings, many members of which appeared to enjoy Politburo membership as of right: first, three or four senior members of the party Secretariat, led by the General Secretary; second, key party leaders from the country as a whole, including the Moscow city and Leningrad regional first secretaries together with the Ukrainian, Belorussian, Georgian and Uzbek republican first secretaries for most of the 1970s and 1980s; and third, key members of the state apparatus, including, for most of the same period, the President and Prime Minister together with the ministers of defence and foreign affairs, the chairman of the KGB and the Prime Minister of the RSFSR (by far the largest of the USSR's 15 union republics).

The evidence of the 1980s was that the 'institutionalization' of Politburo membership upon this basis was gaining ground, although the changes associated with the accession of Gorbachev made the trends less apparent than would otherwise have been the case. Throughout the 1970s and 1980s, for instance, the President and Prime Minister were full members of the Politburo, together with (as full or candidate members) the ministers of defence and foreign affairs (from 1973) and the RSFSR Prime Minister. Successive Ukrainian party first secretaries (Shelest and Shcherbitskii) and Belorussian party first secretaries (Masherov, Kisilev and, until his movement to the Secretariat in 1987, Slyun'kov) have been full or candidate members respectively. Yuri Solovev, who succeeded Georgii Romanov as Leningrad regional party leader in 1985, followed him into the Politburo in 1986; similarly, the new Moscow party leader Boris Eltsin took Viktor Grishin's place in the Politburo (as a candidate) in 1986, and the new Defence Minister, General Yazov, took Marshal Sokolov's Politburo seat within a month of his appointment in May 1987. A similar process of 'creeping institutionalization' has been taking place at the same time in other party bodies, such as the Central Committee.[9] The greater the extent to which leading officials owe their positions to the importance of the posts they occupy, rather than to the personal favour of the General Secretary, the greater the extent to which they can afford to diverge from the General Secretary on policy matters and the greater the extent to which he must earn this support rather than assume it.

The General Secretary, admittedly, may have helped to secure the appointment, and later the Politburo membership, of other members of the leadership in the first place. This is however no guarantee of future loyalty. T. H. Rigby has identified four separate factors underlying patronage relations:

> (1) shared loyalties and attitudes arising from common ethnic, local, religious, organizational, or professional backgrounds; (2) bonds formed through work together; (3) shared policies or ideas; [and] (4) the act of appointment itself, in the absence of any previous bonds.

The last of these, the act of appointment itself, is in Rigby's view the weakest of all such bases of support.[10] Khrushchev, for instance, was deposed by a Politburo almost all of whose members had been appointed under his own first secretaryship; and Brezhnev's position began to crumble, towards the end of his general secretaryship, although broadly the same was true. The evidence that is available suggests rather that Politburo members tend to identify themselves with the particular interest they represent at least as much as with the General Secretary responsible for their original appointment. When Molotov, for instance, was put in charge of the railway system, he 'tried to get everything he could for the railways', according to Khrushchev's memoirs.[11] Pyotr Shelest, the Ukrainian party leader who joined the Politburo under Brezhnev's dispensation, used his position similarly to advance the claims of his own republic as against others. Party membership within the Ukraine increased disproportionately under his leadership, increasing the pool of local eligibles for leading positions, and Shelest also argued quite openly for greater investment in the republic, telling delegates to the 24th Party Congress in 1971, for instance, that it was 'incorrect' to divert funds from the coalmines of the Ukraine to the production of oil and natural gas in Siberia. He is reported to have insisted privately that the Ukraine was being exploited economically by the other republics.[12]

An interpretation of this kind is certainly consistent with what we know of the Politburo and its mode of operation. In Stalin's time, according to Khrushchev, the party leader 'did everything himself, bypassing the Central Committee and using the Politburo as little more than a rubber stamp'. Stalin 'rarely bothered to ask the opinion of Politburo members about a given measure. He would just make a decision and issue a decree.'[13] By the Brezhnev period rather different practices obtained: the Politburo operated, he explained in an interview with the Western press, on a consensual basis; votes were rare, and if serious disagreements occurred they were referred to a sub-committee which would come back later with an agreed recommendation.[14] By the 1980s some of these practices had emerged publicly: the Politburo met weekly, usually on a Thursday (a brief report of its meetings began to appear from late 1982), and it had spawned quite an elaborate system of sub-committees, including, at least in the earlier part of the decade, commissions on educational reform, on consumer goods and services and on the reform of economic management.[15] The Politburo, as before, might be attended by non-members, and it might be chaired, in his absence, by someone other than the General Secretary.[16] These were all indications of an institutionalized, consensual system of decision making, very different from the personalized forms of rule of earlier decades.

Not simply, by the 1980s, was there an agreed separation of leading functions, an increasingly institutionalized pattern of membership and well-established, consensual procedures: there was also, in the early years of the Gorbachev general secretaryship, some evidence that the leadership contained differences on substantive matters of policy with which the General Secretary had no alternative but to reconcile himself. In the immediate aftermath of the Chernobyl nuclear explosion, it has been reported, Gorbachev was himself in favour of making the whole truth known at once, but found himself with only two supporters (RSFSR premier Vorotnikov and KGB chairman Chebrikov) in the Politburo. A full statement of the official position, in the event, took some time to emerge, and Gorbachev's first public comment on the event (a television address on 14 May) took place more than two weeks after the explosion had occurred.[17] The revision of the Party Rules, which took place at the 27th Party Congress in 1986, may also have represented a defeat for Gorbachev's own position. In the debate which took place before the Congress, based upon a draft version of the new Rules which had been published in November 1985, suggestions for reform were put forward in party journals (and therefore almost certainly with Gorbachev's support) which included the introduction of retirement ages and limited tenure for party officials and compulsory turnover rules for elected party bodies. In the event none of these proposed amendments was incorporated in the final version of the Rules, which the Party Congress approved on 1 March 1986.[18]

There was also evidence, albeit of a Kremlinological character, that the Gorbachev Politburo was by no means united on all the issues that it confronted. The Moscow party leader Boris Eltsin, for instance, was very clearly on the reformist wing. His speech to the Party Congress, in which he spoke openly about privileges and other shortcomings, was the most outspoken of all that were delivered to an unusually plain-speaking assembly; his speeches to party activists in Moscow itself, according to unpublished accounts, have dealt with social problems such as crime, drugs and the abuse of power in an open and forthright way.[19] Edward Shevardnadze, formerly the Georgian Party Secretary and now Minister of Foreign Affairs, was responsible for pioneering many social experiments in his own republic[20] and has since then associated himself publicly (most notably in his Lenin anniversary address of April 1986) with further 'democratization', electoral reform, the election of factory management, greater social justice and economic reform generally.[21] At the other extreme Egor Ligachev, effectively the party's second-ranking Secretary, criticized *Pravda* at the Party Congress for (in effect) allowing a discussion of the privileges and self-interest of party and state leaders, and he is on record as declaring that there would be 'no movement towards the market or private enterprise'. In a speech in June 1987 he warned that the 'class enemy' was hoping that *perestroika* would undermine the influence of Marxist–Leninist ideology in the USSR and had been making use of it to spread 'irresponsible demagogy, hostile to the interests of the toilers.'[22]

Prime Minister Nikolai Ryzhkov, who was also a Gorbachev Politburo appointee, took a similar line at the Party Congress: he told delegates there would be no retreat from centralized guidance of the economy, which was the 'fundamental advantage of socialism', and promised that the hopes of 'bourgeois apologists' to this effect would not be justified. President Andrei Gromyko, similarly, warned that 'no-one should be allowed, under the pretext of encouraging the healthy and necessary cause of criticism and self-criticism . . . to resort to fabrications alleging that there are rifts in our Party and in Soviet society.'[23] It was presumably because of differences of this kind that the January 1987 Central Committee Plenum, on Gorbachev's admission, had to be postponed three times and required a threat of his own resignation before it could take place. The Plenum itself, according to the testimony of participants, was a stormy one which gave clear expression to 'conflicts' at leading levels.[24] It would seem reasonable to assume that at least these members of the Soviet leadership of the late 1980s, together with remaining Brezhnev appointees and perhaps others, occupied a more 'conservative' position within the spectrum of leadership opinion and that the Gorbachev Politburo (like its predecessors) was a coalition of interests and opinions within which the General Secretary fell far short of unanimous and unconditional support.

INSTITUTIONAL AND BUREAUCRATIC CONSTRAINTS ON EXECUTIVE ACTION

Opposition within the leadership, however significant, is in a sense the least of the General Secretary's problems. Far more important, at least from the point of view of executive action, are the formidable obstacles to change that are located within the party and state apparatus. The checks upon executive action that exist at this level have been dubbed 'bureaucratic pluralism', 'centralized pluralism' or 'pluralism of elites' by some scholars,[25] although not all were happy to apply a pluralist label, even a qualified one, to political systems of the Soviet type.[26] There has, however, been little disagreement that phenomena such as 'narrow departmentalism', 'usurpation' (*podmena*), 'parallelism', 'localism' and others are a very real feature of Soviet institutional life, whatever the terms in which the political system as a whole might be characterized. In circumstances in which a political leadership is attempting a far-reaching strategy of 'acceleration' and 'restructuring' these bureaucratic protection mechanisms offer a good deal of scope for non-compliance with or even open opposition to centrally-determined priorities.

Gorbachev himself has certainly been in no doubt that the party and state apparatus both in Moscow and in the localities represents perhaps the most serious obstacle to his reformist intentions. In a speech to media officials just after the 27th Party Congress Gorbachev reminded them that it would be necessary to 'fight, literally fight' for every line of the Congress resolutions.[27] At the Central Committee plenum the following June he warned that restructuring was 'still proceeding slowly' and that 'inertia was still strong'.[28] Some executives, he pointed out, were 'generous in their declarations about openness, correctly speak about the role of the collective, about the development of democratic principles in life, but the trouble is that it all ends there. Thus the illusion of restructuring is created: in words all is fine, but there are no real changes.'[29] Despite the fact that the top-heavy administrative apparatus itself represented an obstacle to change, leading officials had been very reluctant to delegate any of their powers and some had even proposed new organs of government and additional staff. Several republics had made similar proposals, apparently believing that they should copy the elaborate structure of the central government in their own area.[30]

Speaking later in the year to party activists in Krasnodar, Gorbachev dealt more particularly with the Ministry of Heavy and Transport Machine-Building. Although it had been conducting its activities on an experimental basis for three years, Gorbachev noted, the forces of conservatism were still strong. Ministry officials did all they could to retain powers that should properly have been delegated to other bodies, which were the bodies that determined whether the plan was fulfilled or not. Staffing levels had apparently fallen, but the volume of correspondence remained unchanged; just as before, the ministry continued to send out huge numbers of circulars and continued to employ success indicators which were not required under the terms of the experiment. The role of cost accounting within enterprises attached to the ministry remained 'practically unchanged', and many of the responsible executives had either no knowledge at all or else a very poor knowledge of the new methods of management and economic stimulation. All of this was in a ministry which had supposedly been working for three years under experimental conditions, and which was headed by a minister who was known to be experienced and capable. Nor was this situation in any way untypical: ministries, more generally, postponed urgent tasks, effectively revising Central Committee and government directives in whose elaboration they had themselves taken part, or else proposed amendments before the ink on the original directive had had a chance to dry. Decisions were taken lightly and then disregarded, and urgent problems were left unresolved for decades. Ministries, in sum, were changing very slowly, as also were the bodies such as the State Committee on Science and Technology that were nominally responsible for monitoring them.[31]

Although, consistent with the doctrine of 'democratic centralism', there can be no direct refusal by lower levels of party and government to implement the decisions of decision makers at higher levels, central and local officials have many means at their disposal for resisting the pressures that may be placed upon them. One of the most widely practised is a form of buck-passing by which it agreed that the faults identified by the central leadership do indeed exist, but somewhere else. Alexander Yakovlev, widely agreed to share Gorbachev's own political perspectives, drew attention to evasions of this kind when he addressed Tadzhik party activists in April 1987. Some party, state and economic officials, he observed, had a kind of 'split consciousness'. On the one hand they gave a verbal welcome to the Central Committee's diagnosis of the situation in the country; but they were less than eager to apply it to their own work. They argued, he went on, roughly as follows: stagnation and inertia did indeed exist, but 'not in our collective'. Low tempos of growth and poor quality existed, but were 'not our fault'. And corruption, bribe-taking, nepotism and protectionism certainly took place somewhere or other, but 'for us was not typical'. Not surprisingly a stream of letters had indicated that *perestroika* in the localities was advancing at a 'dilatory pace'.[32]

Another widely practised stratagem is foot-dragging or passive non-compliance. Many officials, as Ligachev told a meeting in the Tatar republic in May 1986, appeared to believe that now the Party Congress had taken place 'the storm had passed' and they could sit it out quietly until the next congress.[33] A Central Committee conference which met in late September 1986 complained more generally that the policy of restructuring was being carried out 'without sufficient dynamism' and that it was encountering socio-psychological and organizational obstacles. In particular, the conference cited the 'egoistical opposition' of the apparatus as a source of delays together with 'bureaucratic distortions' and the 'inertia' of ministries and other state bodies, which abandoned old ways of working with great reluctance and refused to delegate responsibilities directly to enterprises, continuing to send out huge quantities of circulars in order to create the appearance of practical activity while at the same time failing to deal with their proper responsibilities within the appointed time.[34] Officials of this kind, as Ligachev put it at the Party Congress, confused 'acceleration' with the more rapid circulation of bureaucratic paper work.[35]

Perhaps more common than passive non-compliance is 'formalism', or purely verbal compliance with party and government directives. This was the approach adopted by those officials, as Gorbachev put it in Krasnodar, who were 'able quickly to adapt to a changing situation'. They were a 'capable people, even resourceful'. Their main concern was to:

> preserve the old, outmoded ways, to preserve their privileges, even though this is not in accordance with our principles, laws and morality or with our current policy. We see now [Gorbachev went on] how they are shouting – from every rostrum and louder than anyone else – about restructuring, although in fact they are delaying its implementation under all sorts of pretexts, including some very specious ones.[36]

The bureaucrat was particularly dangerous in current circumstances, Shevardnadze explained in his address on the Lenin anniversary, because the bureaucrat of today was 'more educated, if you wish – more qualified, better able to adapt himself, more easily capable of changing his outward appearance and therefore more seriously harmful to the [party's] cause.'[37] Bureaucrats of this kind, Gorbachev explained in his address to the Central Committee in January 1987, acknowledge criticisms to be valid, 'even thank you for them', but made no serious effort to eliminate the shortcomings that had been identified.[38]

'Formalism' overlaps in Soviet practice with 'campaignism', or in other words short-lived and perfunctory compliance with central directives. A recent example of campaignism in action, reported in *Pravda* in December

1986, concerned the anti-alcoholism campaign to which the leadership has attached much importance since its inception in May 1985. The village in question, *Pravda* reported, had been declared a 'sobriety zone', and there had indeed been a reduction in the amount of alcohol that had been sold over the past year or so. However, it emerged that no less alcohol had actually been consumed over the same period (much had evidently been home brewed). Of 65 weddings held in the locality only one had been non-alcoholic. The local library was open only between 11 a.m. and 7 p.m., which was convenient for librarians but hardly for workers looking for something to do in their free time. There were no anti-alcohol films on show in the local cinema, and the local House of Culture was empty. The struggle against alcohol abuse, it appeared, had effectively ended the year before: a few shops had been closed, a commission (*komissiya*) or two had come into existence at least on paper, and then the whole thing had been forgotten. Drunkenness, already above the regional average, had not declined, and street crime had actually increased. Not only this: an 'unbelievable incident' had occurred in which a collective drinking bout had taken place at a young people's evening in the local discotheque, with the local Komsomol secretary and his deputy both in attendance. Good results, the paper concluded, were likely to be forthcoming only when the necessary measures were undertaken 'not for the sake of form' but on a more serious basis.[39]

Official policies may also be sabotaged by local officials, who may often act in collusion with other local notables in such matters (Soviet sources refer to such alliances as 'family circles'). An 'outrageous instance' of this kind was reported by Gorbachev in his speech to the Central Committee in June 1986. The case concerned an engineer, A. I. Chabanov, who worked as director of a research institute under the Ministry of the Electrical Equipment Industry in the town of Cherkassy in the Ukraine. Chabanov's institute developed new types of machine tools and control systems for application within the industry which won international recognition and foreign and domestic orders. The factory attached to the same ministry within Cherkassy itself, however, 'stubbornly ignored the new equipment'. Chabanov was appointed temporary director of the factory as well as of the institute in July 1985, and began to organize production of the new equipment without waiting for its specification to be confirmed. Some employees complained to the ministry and to local party officials that the new director was deviating from his instructions. 'It cannot be said', Gorbachev went on, 'that they acted in an innovative way'; the director was removed from his post, and the matter was placed in the hands of the police. In the event no crimes were discovered, or even improprieties. Chabanov was nonetheless expelled from the CPSU, and when local party members sent a letter to party headquarters to let them know what had happened it was simply removed from the post by local officials.[40] The case, exceptional but hardly unique, recalls the frustrated inventor of Dudintsev's *Not by Bread Alone* published thirty years earlier.

Local officials, moreover, can engage in the 'suppression of criticism' and in the victimisation of individual critics if they judge it necessary, notwithstanding party and state regulations to the contrary. Current policies in favour of greater *glasnost'* or 'openness' have admittedly encouraged central newspapers and journals to discuss social ills such as prostitution, drug-taking and violent crime. At the local level, however, officials have been less willing to allow their actions to be critically evaluated in publications which they themselves control, and even at the centre there have been some notable violations of the new directives. In February 1986, for instance, the Central Committee severely criticized the ministries of civil aviation and the waterways for suppressing criticism in the two journals they sponsored, *Air Transport* and *Water Transport*.[41] A more remarkable case occurred when the complete print run of a local paper in the Pskov region was destroyed because it had unwisely printed criticism of the efforts of local officials to create a false impression when delegates from an all-Russian seminar on public catering visited the area. In classic Potemkin village style, shops overflowed with goods that had not been seen for a long time, the bakery was baking only high-quality bread, and buildings had been freshly painted. The whole exercise had cost thousands of rubles. Local officials, however, had decided that now the Congress was over the time for criticism had passed; the offending issue was held up and then destroyed, and a substitute edition, minus the offending article, was printed in its place. *Pravda* described the whole affair as 'unprecedented'.[42]

In this and other ways party and state officials both at the centre and in the localities have considerable resources at their disposal if they wish to frustrate the efforts of the leadership. They can provide reports to the centre which are consistent with their own preferences but not always with the whole truth; they can delay implementing central directives, or implement them in a wholly formal manner, or even (in extreme cases) attempt to undermine them, enrolling the support of other local notables and (if necessary) repressing those who bring the facts to the attention of higher bodies or the press. Strategies of this kind are of course common currency in studies of Western bureaucracies, and terms derived from this context such as 'authority leakage', 'information distortion' and 'turf battles' have an obvious application to political systems of the Soviet type. They suggest, in turn, that even a united and determined political leadership may find it difficult to achieve their objectives if those objectives fail to accord with the priorities of the central and local bureaucrats who will bear the most direct responsibility for implementing them.

POPULAR CONSTRAINTS ON EXECUTIVE ACTION

The Soviet system is obviously not one in which popular constraints upon executive action are as extensive and significant as in the liberal democracies. There is no real opportunity to challenge the regime through the ballot box (although a limited and experimental choice of candidates was introduced at the June 1987 local elections). Specialist and citizen groupings may come into legal existence only if they acknowledge the party's leading role and refrain from direct opposition to official policies (the 'informal groups' which developed in 1986 and 1987 concentrated upon environmental and other matters and generally supported the leadership's policy of *perestroika*[43]); and the press is subject to a strict and unaccountable censorship, despite modest moves under Gorbachev in the direction of greater openness or *glasnost'*. Freedom of assembly, meetings, street processions and demonstrations, again, although nominally available to all citizens under article 50 of the Constitution, are qualified by the provision that the exercise of these rights must be 'in accordance with the interests of the people and ... the socialist system'. In the Soviet view only the party may be the legitimate interpreter of matters of this kind, and in practice the exercise of the rights set out in article 50 has been restricted to approved and pro-regime groups and organisations.

It has nonetheless become apparent, particularly during the past decade or so, that public opinion is not a factor that the Soviet leadership can readily ignore. In the first place, the Soviet public have a great variety of means, from letter-writing to contacts with deputies, TV phone-ins and bodies such as the trade unions and environmental associations, to make their views known and often to insert them directly into the policy-making process through the elaborate framework of organized consultation which has come into existence under party and state auspices. If approved forms of political action prove unavailing, moreover, a second form of influence is available: 'unconventional political participation', or in other words riots, demonstrations, strikes and even (in exceptional circumstances) political violence. When official policy offends some deeply-held public sentiment such forms of action come to the fore (perhaps not coincidentally, the 27th Party Congress was the first in modern times in which three very senior speakers, including Gorbachev himself, warned that the political stability of the USSR could not necessarily be taken for granted).[44]

Many studies have already shown the ways in which public opinion may be taken into account through proper or approved channels, particularly in social or environmental questions such as the pollution of Lake Baikal.[45] More recent instances of the same kind have included the cancellation of plans to divert the Siberian rivers towards the south (the Politburo noted in August 1986 that 'broad segments of the public' had urged further study of the social and ecological consequences of such a change). At the same meeting the Politburo decided to halt the construction of a large and unlovely Second War Memorial on the immediate outskirts of Moscow, having 'taken into account the results of the extensive discussion of the project design and the observations and suggestions advanced by the public'. An open competition was to be held to decide upon a suitable replacement.[46] Less widely publicized 'victories' for public opinion in recent years have included the restoration of historic inner city areas rather than their comprehensive redevelopment, and the reversion to older and more historic place names in many urban areas.[47] The adoption of a law on 'all-national discussions of major questions of state life', promised by Gorbachev in his speech to the 27th Party Congress and duly enacted by the Supreme Soviet in June 1987, may extend such principles of consultation further.[48]

Public pressure, particularly on issues of this kind, is exercised by a variety of civic groups and associations as well as by concerned individuals, journalists and others. Civic associations are larger and more influential than is commonly assumed. The recently-formed All-Union Voluntary Society for the Struggle for Sobriety, for instance, was reported in early 1987 to have as many as 13 million members organized in 450,000 separate branches.[49] Older-established bodies such as the Soviet Peace Committee and the Soviet Women's Committee have memberships running into tens of millions and substantial publishing, international and other forms of activity.[50] More important and interesting for our present purposes are the environmental organizations that have come into existence since the 1960s, with substantial memberships, publications and demonstrated influence upon official policy within their areas of interest. One of the first such organizations was the *Rodina* (Homeland) Club, established in 1964 for the purpose of promoting the study of ancient monuments. The following year the All-Russian Society for the Preservation of Historical and Cultural Monuments (VOOPIK) came into existence; by the early 1980s it had more than 15 million members, or almost 10 per cent of population of the Russian Republic (comparable societies have come into existence in other republics of the USSR). VOOPIK appears to have been founded 'principally by initiative from below'; it has been able to canvas public support through lectures and publications, and has repeatedly come into conflict with local authorities who have taken a negligent attitude towards the churches and other historic buildings for which they are responsible. The All-Russian Society for the Preservation of Nature, with about 19 million members in the 1970s, exercised a similar influence on behalf of the environment.[51]

If public pressures through official channels are ignored, the danger from the authorities' point of view is that opposition will make itself apparent in other ways. This is by no means a hypothetical risk. One of the most substantial demonstrations in recent years, for instance, occurred in Tbilisi, the capital of the Georgian republic, in April 1978, following the publication of a draft constitution which omitted the clause stipulating that Georgian was the republic's official language. On the day the new constitution was to be adopted a demonstration of such proportions took place in central Tbilisi that the draft was altered and Georgian was reinserted as the official state language.[52] Similar disturbances took place at the end of 1986 when Dinmukhamed Kunaev, a native Kazakh, was replaced as republican party leader by Gennadii V. Kolbin, a Russian national. As *Literaturnaya gazeta* subsequently reported, the news pro- voked 'inexperienced and politically illiterate youths' to take to the streets, who were later joined by 'hooligans, drunks and other anti-social types'; nationalist slogans were chanted, and the crowd, armed with metal posts, sticks and stones, proceeded to beat up local citizens, overturned cars and set them on fire, and smashed the windows of shops and other public buildings.[53] Government sources subsequently acknowledged that up to 3000 people had been involved in the demonstrations, and that 200 had been injured; unofficial sources indicated that as many as 280 students had lost their lives, together with 29 policemen and soldiers.[54]

Popular discontent on social and economic issues has flared up in the same way on several occasions. In May 1980, for instance, it was reported that workers in the giant Togliattigrad car works in central Russia had walked out in protest against poor meat and dairy supplies. The walkout, believed to have been the largest in recent Soviet history, closed down the plant and involved more than 170,000 workers. It ended only when the authorities took steps to improve the food supply in the area.[55] Shortly afterwards, a group of paint-sprayers was reported to have held unsche- duled 'on-the-job "discussions" about working conditions' in the nearby Gorky car and truck plant.[56] In late 1986 a potentially more serious disturbance occurred at the giant KamAZ factory in the city of Brezhnev in the Tatar republic. According to the government newspaper *Izvestiya*, 'stormy protests' occurred at the plant in opposition to the introduction of new quality control procedures, which are an integral part of the new leadership's restructuring objectives. In general the introduction of new procedures of this kind, involving independent monitoring of the quality of production, could 'not be said to be proceeding smoothly', *Izvestiya* reported.[57] Soviet industrial relations, based upon relatively low levels of pay combined with job security and relatively easy-going discipline, will evidently not easily be replaced by arrangements which deliberately widen wage differentials, extend the shift system and offer bonuses and other rewards only to hard and high-quality work.

Active resistance to changes in public policy represent no more than the public face of the political leverage of public opinion, and especially of organized labour; the other side of this power is the effective veto maintained over changes in existing policies that are perceived as favourable to working-class interests. One of the most important of these is the subsidies from public funds that hold down the price of housing, transport and particularly foodstuffs. Originally, under Stalin, substantial government revenues were raised from the population through the sale of food at prices greater than those paid to producers. From Khrushchev onwards this situation began to change, and by the late 1980s it had changed to such an extent that government food subsidies accounted for about half of retail cost of such items, far exceeding the officially declared defence budget.[58] However economically irrational (bread, for instance, was being wasted or fed to animals in the late 1970s although harvests were well below target), there appeared to be considerable popular resistance to any change in these arrangements, even if (as Gorbachev insisted in his speech in Murmansk in September 1987) compensating benefits were to be introduced for the less affluent.[59] It was certainly clear, by the late 1980s, that the Gorbachev leadership was finding some difficulty in persuading Soviet working people to abandon their attachment to below-cost foodstuffs or to public subsidies of other kinds, or more generally to surrender their security of employment and relaxed pace of work, despite the fact that these were central to the leadership's programme of restructuring.

CONCLUDING OBSERVATIONS

This chapter has sought to examine some of the constraints upon the exercise of political power by Soviet elites, and constraints upon executive action in particular. It is no part of my purpose to go to the other extreme and suggest that the Soviet central decision-making system has somehow become paralysed or immobile, still less that the USSR has become 'ungovernable' or its administration 'overloaded' in the same way that (it was argued until quite recently) had become the case within the Western liberal democracies.[60] The Central Committee Plenum that took place in June 1987 showed no obvious slackening in the impetus of Gorbachev's reforms, and the General Secretary was able to strengthen his position further within the leadership by bringing three close associates (most notably Alexander Yakovlev) into membership or full membership of the Politburo.[61] Developments of this kind are in accordance with the view sometimes expressed that general secretaries, through promotions of this kind and in other ways, can usually strengthen their position within the leadership throughout their period of office, unlike western political leaders whose powers are normally greatest immediately after the election at which they have won office.[62]

A stronger position within the leadership, however, may not necessarily be translated into a greater degree of ability to influence the direction of public policy, for reasons that have been explored earlier in this paper. The June Plenum, at any rate, also provided evidence that the leadership's strategy of *perestroika* was continuing to advance slowly and to meet many obstacles of a subjective and objective character. Although *perestroika* had won an 'ideological and moral victory', Gorbachev told the Plenum, the people he had met in Baikonur had asked, 'When is *perestroika* going to reach us?' Letters to the Central Committee and other bodies had been to the same effect: 'People write that they are for *perestroika*, but see no changes in their own immediate environment'. *Perestroika* was making no advances in Armenia (where the party leadership had even had the temerity to claim it had begun before the April 1985 plenum) or in the Gorky region. Many people, Gorbachev went on, had taken the view that as *perestroika* was a long-term matter, there was no particular urgency about it. Even perfectly simple and straightforward tasks were not being undertaken, and in some respects, such as industrial discipline, earlier achievements were being lost. 'There were a lot of conversations about the advantages of *perestroika*, but little was being done in a practical sense to satisfy people's most elementary needs.'[63]

A leadership like Brezhnev's, based upon the complacent notion of 'developed socialism' and organizationally upon the 'stability of cadres', had no obvious need to confront the obstacles to change in the USSR and made little attempt to do so. A leadership like Gorbachev's, facing a serious, even (in his own words) 'pre-crisis' situation in the economy, can hardly afford the luxury of inactivity. The continuing boldness of Gorbachev's public statements, his strengthening base within the leadership, his ability (for instance) to secure agreement that a party conference will be held in 1988 which may consider changes in the party rules as well as other matters, all suggest a leadership more seriously committed to change than any we have seen in Soviet politics since the early post-revolutionary years. Any balanced assessment, however, must also take into account the obstacles to change within the leadership, within the party and state bureaucracy and within the population at large with which this chapter has been concerned. An adequate study of elites and political power in the USSR must be placed within such a broader context, one that incorporates not only the formidable and ostensibly unchallenged powers of Soviet leaderships but also the complicated 'delaying mechanism' which has repeatedly frustrated their ability to convert their formally unlimited authority into observable change in the society over which they rule.[64]

NOTES AND REFERENCES

1 Some of the issues touched upon here are taken further in the scholarly literature, for instance in Jerry F. Hough, 'The Soviet experience and the measurement of power', in his *The Soviet Union and Social Science Theory*, Harvard University Press, Cambridge Mass., 1977, ch. 10; and A. J. Groth, 'USSR: pluralist monolith?', *British Journal of Political Science*, 1979, vol. 9, no. 4, October, pp. 445–64. David Lane, *The Socialist Industrial State: Towards a Political Sociology of State Socialism*, Allen and Unwin, London, 1976; David Lane, *The End of Social Inequality? Class, Status and Power under State Socialism*, Allen and Unwin, London, 1982; The issues involved in elite research more particularly are considered in George Moyser and Margaret Wagstaffe, *Research Methods for Elite Studies*, Allen and Unwin, London, 1987.

2 See for instance Graeme Gill, 'The future of the General Secretary', *Political Studies*, 1986, vol. 34, no. 2, June, pp. 223–35. A more general account is Archie Brown, 'The power of the General Secretary of the CPSU', in T. H. Rigby et. al. (eds), *Authority, Power and Policy in the USSR*, Macmillan, London, 1980, pp. 135–57.

3 See Jerry F. Hough and Merle Fainsod, *How the Soviet Union is Governed*, Harvard University Press, Cambridge Mass., 1979, pp. 260–1.

4 See Gill, 'Future', op. cit., and Brown, 'Power', op. cit. for representative views. On political clientelism more generally, see T. H. Rigby and Bohdan Harasymiw (eds), *Leadership Selection and Patron–Client Relations in the USSR and Yugoslavia*, Allen and Unwin, London, 1983.

5 P. Rodionov, *Kollektivnost' -vysshii printsip partiinogo rukovodstva*, Moscow, 1967, p. 219, as cited in Gill, 'Future', p. 225n.

6 *Pervaya sessiya Verkhovnogo Soveta SSSR (odinnadtsatyi sozyv) 11–12 aprelya 1984g. Stenograficheskii otchet*, Izvestiya, Moscow, 1984, p. 38.

7 *Tret'ya sessiya ... 2–3 iyulya 1985g*, Izvestiya, Moscow, 1985, pp. 5–6.

8 John H. Kress, 'Representation of positions on the CPSU Politburo', *Slavic Review*, 1980, vol. 39, no. 2, June, pp. 218–38, at p. 218.

9 Robert E. Blackwell's term cited in Kress, 'Representation', p. 236n. See more generally Robert V. Daniels, 'Office holding and elite status: the Central Committee of the CPSU', in Paul Cocks et. al. (eds), *The Dynamics of Soviet Politics*, Harvard University Press, Cambridge Mass., 1976, pp. 77–95.

10 T. H. Rigby, 'The Soviet regional leadership: the Brezhnev generation', *Slavic Review*, 1978, vol. 37, no. 1, March, p. 23.

11 Cited in Hough and Fainsod, *How the Soviet Union is Governed*, op. cit. p. 476.

12 See Geoffrey Hosking, *A History of the Soviet Union*, Fontana, London, 1986, pp. 428–9; Shelest's remarks to the Party Congress are in *Pravda*, 1 April 1971, pp. 3–4.

13 *Khrushchev Remembers*, trans. Strobe Talbott, Sphere, London, 1971, p. 244.

14 *New York Times*, 15 June 1973, p. 3; Brezhnev explained Politburo procedures further to the 26th Party Congress in 1981 (*XXVI s"ezd KPSS 23 fevralya – 3 marta 1981. Stenograficheskii otchet*, 3 vols. [Politizdat, Moscow, 1981], vol. 1, p. 88). The fullest available account of the Politburo and its operation is John Lowenhardt, *The Soviet Politburo*, Canongate, Edinburgh, 1982.

15 See Stephen White, 'Soviet politics since Brezhnev', *Journal of Communist Studies*, 1985, vol. 1, no. 2, June, p. 130 n. 50.

16 Arkady N. Shevchenko, *Breaking with Moscow*, Cape, London, 1985, p. 177. Gorbachev was still on holiday while Politburo meetings were taking place in the late summer of 1986.

17 See Radio Free Europe Background Report No. 78 (USSR), 5 June 1986, p. 2.

18 See Stephen White, 'The new Programme and Rules of the CPSU', *Journal of Communist Studies*, 1986, vol. 2, no. 2, June, pp. 187–9.

19 See *Pravda*, 27 February 1986, pp. 2–3, and *Detente*, no. 7 (autumn 1986), pp. 2–5.

20 On the 'Poti experiment' particularly, see Darrell Slider, 'More power to the soviets? Reform and local government in the Soviet Union', *British Journal of Political Science*, 1986, vol. 16, no. 4, October, pp. 495–511.

21 *Pravda*, 23 April 1986, pp. 1–2.

22 *Pravda*, 28 February 1986, p. 4; *The Economist*, 7 September 1985, p. 61; *Pravda*, 4 June 1987, p. 2.

23 *Pravda*, 4 March 1986, pp. 2–5; ibid., 27 February 1986, p. 6.

24 Radio Liberty Report RL 82/87, 20 February 1987; M. Ul'yanov in *Kommunist*, 1987, no. 5, pp. 51–7, at p. 51, for the plenum.

25 The terms belong respectively to Darrell P. Hammer, Alec Nove and Gordon Skilling: see Hammer, *The USSR: The Politics of Oligarchy*, 2nd ed. Westview, Boulder, Col., 1986, p. 228.

26 See the symposium in *Studies in Comparative Communism*, 1979, vol. 12, no. 1, spring, and the discussion in Susan G. Solomon (ed.), *Pluralism in the Soviet union*, Macmillan, London, 1983.

27 *Pravda*, 15 March 1986, p. 1.

28 *Partiinaya zhizn'*, 1986, no. 13, p. 7.

29 Ibid., p. 8.

30 Ibid.

31 Ibid., no. 19, pp. 8–9.

32 Ibid., 1987, no. 10, p. 11.

33 *Pravda*, 22 May 1986, p. 2.

34 *Pravda*, 1 October 1986, p. 1.

35 *Pravda*, 28 February 1986, p. 4.

36 *Pravda*, 20 September 1986, pp. 1–2.

37 *Pravda*, 23 April 1986, p. 2.

38 *Sovetskaya Rossiya*, 28 January 1987, p. 3.

39 *Pravda*, 8 December 1986, p. 3.

40 *Pravda*, 17 June 1986, p. 3. Further developments are reported in ibid., 24 August 1986, p. 3.

41 *Pravda*, 11 February 1986, p. 1.

42 *Pravda*, 13 June 1986, pp. 1–2 (which reproduced both editions).

43 *Financial Times*, 14 October 1987, p. 2.

44 This point is noted in Peter Frank, 'Gorbachev's dilemma; social justice or political instability?', *The World Today*, June 1986, p. 94.

45 A good review of such matters is available in John Lowenhardt, *Decision Making in Soviet Politics*, Macmillan, London, 1981).

46 *Pravda*, 16 August 1986, p. 1. In the event none of the 384 proposals that were submitted and (which were inspected over a month by 140,000 members of the public) was found satisfactory. See *Pravda*, 1 March 1987, p. 3.

47 See Martin Walker, *The Waking Giant. The Soviet Union under Gorbachev*, Michael Joseph, London, 1986, ch. 10.

48 *Materialy XXVII s"ezda KPSS*, Politizdat, Moscow, 1986, p. 60. A procedure

for the conduct of such exercises, based upon East European experience, was suggested by V. O. Luchin in *Sovetskoe gosudarstvo i pravo*, 1986, no. 12, pp. 43–50.

49 *Sovetskaya Rossiya*, 10 January 1987, p. 1.
50 See *Ezhegodnik Bol'shoi Sovetskoi Entsiklopedii 1985*, Sovetskaya entsiklo-pediya, Moscow, 1985, pp. 21–30, for details.
51 See John B. Dunlop, *The Faces of Contemporary Russian Nationalism*, Princeton University Press, Princeton, NJ, 1983, ch. 3. For VOOPIK's membership, see *Voprosy istorii*, 1984, no. 10, p. 17.
52 Helene Carrere d'Encausse, *The Decline of an Empire*, Newsweek, New York, 1979, pp. 212–3.
53 *Literaturnaya gazeta*, 1987, no. 1 (January), p. 1.
54 *Guardian*, 19 February 1987, p. 6; *Independent*, 8 May 1987, p. 9.
55 Radio Liberty Research RL 461/86 p. 2.
56 Ibid., pp. 2–3.
57 *Izvestiya*, 4 December 1986, p. 1; Radio Liberty Research RL 461/86, p. 1.
58 *Pravda*, 13 June 1987, p. 1.
59 *Izvestiya*, 2 October 1987, pp. 1–3.
60 See for instance Anthony King, 'Overload: problems of governing in the 1970s', *Political Studies*, 1975, vol. 23, no. 2–3, pp. 284–96; Richard Rose (ed.), *Challenge to Governance: Studies in Overloaded Polities*, Sage, Beverly Hills, 1980.
61 *Pravda*, 27 June 1987, p. 1.
62 See Brown, 'Power', op. cit., p. 136 (which should be read in conjunction with the same author's 'Gorbachev: New Man in the Kremlin', *Problems of Communism*, 1985, vol. 34, no. 3, May–June, note 6).
63 *Pravda*, 26 June 1987, pp. 2–3.
64 The assistance of the UK Economic and Social Research Council (grant EOO23 2238) in the preparation of this paper is gratefully acknowledged.

Index

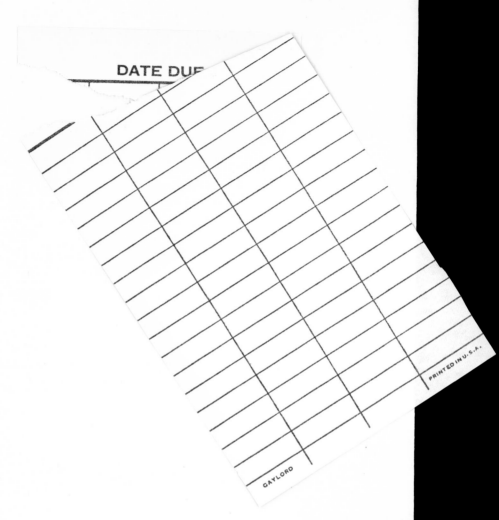